LADAKH: PAST AND PRESENT

LADAKH: PAST AND PRESENT

Dr. Prem Singh Jina

GYAN PUBLISHING HOUSE
NEW DELHI-110002

LADAKH: PAST AND PRESENT

(History, Sociology)

ISBN : 81-212-0654-5

Published in 2000 in India by
Gyan Publishing House
5, Ansari Road, Darya Ganj,
New Delhi - 110002

Laser Typeset at A.S. Printers, Delhi

Printed at Chawla Offset Printers

CONTENTS

PREFACE

Ladakh, the loftiest and remotest region of India, was an important centre of Central Asian trade, before 1947, because of its proximity to the Silk Route, traders from Kumaun, Lahul, Hoshiarpur, Kulu, Kashmir, Yarkand, Tibet and Skardu came to Ladakh and bartered or sold their commodities. The capital of Ladakh was the terminal point of the multilateral trade between India, Tibet and Central Asia. In this book an attempt has been made to analyse the extent and pattern of home and foreign trade between 1820 and 1947 AD.

Traders brought their commodities from Tibet, China, Turkistan and other adjoining territories to Ladakh and after trading with Indian merchants, returned to their respective countries before winter every year through the numerous caravan routes that converged near Leh. Knowing the importance of trade routes, the auther seeks to discuss them in detail, and also to assess the impact of trade activities upon Ladakhi society and culture.

Prem Singh Jina

ACKNOWLEDGEMENTS

I owe a deep sense of gratitude to Mr. Prahalad Singh for his encouragement. I must thank Mrs Kamala Mehra for her moral support. I am highly grateful to Lalit Mehra and Mrs Meera Bisht for rendering help.

I am obliged to Tundup Yamphel, Librarian, District Library, Lehar for providing support time and again. I would like to express deep gratefulProf. Maya Ram, Retd. Director, U.P. Higher Education, and Prof. M.C. Joshi, Member Secretary, Indira Gandhi National Centre for Arts, Delhi, whose keen interest in my study on Ladakh has always been source of inspiration.

I would fail in performing my moral duty if I forget to mention Mrs Manju Jina, who helped me in various ways to complete this work.

I am also grateful to those authors whose thoughts and works have benefited me immensely.

My thanks are due to Gyan Publishing House, Delhi, for bringing out this book in a short time.

Prem Singh Jina

INTRODUCTION

Ladakh, the northernmost region of Jammu and Kashmir state of India is the centre of old civilization. Many tribes from Central Asia and Indian plains came here, some of them settled down along the Indus river. Mons were regarded as aboriginal tribes, had their colonies in lower Ladakh, but when Dards migrated into Ladakh from Bruza near Iran or Persia via Gilgit, they could not stand before them and went to Zangskar. During 3rd century BC Ashoka sent Buddhist missionaries to Ladakh and other Central Asian countries, Mons then had established colonies in Zangskar, whereas Dards had their full control in lower Ladakh, some of them even had their establishments up to Leh areas. Mongolian tribes were of nomadic nature, they entirely depended upon flocks of sheep, goats and herds of yak. They rove throughout the year in wide but well recognized limits, living in tents. They came uplands of Ladakh round about the beginning of Christian era.

Thus, there would seem to have been a continuous movement of rival trends of settlements in Ladakh who made their way towards the more fertile valleys of Ladakh. Dards adopted a more settled and partly agricultural way of life in lower Ladakh. In the early period before the sixth century AD Mongolian tribes migrated to Ladakh and displaced those who already more or less settled in Upper Ladakh.

Introduction of Buddhism

Buddhism introduced in Ladakh probably around 3rd century BC when Ashoka sent his missionaries in Ladakh. During 2nd century AD Kanishka spread Buddhism throughout in Central Asia and had its hold in Kashmir and Gandhar. Ladakh too was influenced by this up to great extent. In fact this was the high time when Buddhism reached China across the Central Asian tracks and thereafter Chinese Buddhist monks and Indian scholars, both from China and India made long journey to and from India by way of Central Asia. Fa–Hian was the first Chinese traveller who visited India via Ladakh. During his visit on 4th century AD to India he said in his travel records that Ladakh had Buddhist population who followed Thervadi Buddhism.[1] From fourth to eighth centuries Chinese monk scholars were frequent visitors. Therefore, followed the same tradition and concept as they found during their visit in India. By the fifth century AD Mahāyāna [2] form of Buddhism took place in India, accordingly Chinese Buddhist scholars established this form in China.[3] During seventh century AD another Chinese traveller Hiuen Tsang visited India via Ladakh. He did not pay much attention about the form of Buddhism which was followed by the Ladakhis. As said earlier by the 5th century AD Mahāyāna Buddhism reached in China and Hiuen Tsang, a monk of Mahāyāna did not feel to know much about the Thervadi Buddhism which was then in Ladakh.

There is good evidence that Buddhism was first established in Tibet during the reign of Srong–brtsan-sgam–po (Srong–tsen–gam–po). He disliked Bon religion which was the old religion of Tibet because of bloody rituals. He married two Princesses, one from China and another from Nepal. Both Princesses were the follower of Mahāyāna form of Buddhism. Thus, after the marriage king Srong–brtsan–sgam–po was influenced very much by Mahāyāna. Then he not only became the follower of Mahāyāna, but also decided to spread it throughout in Tibet and its neighbouring countries. He sent many intelligent Tibetan boys to India to learn Buddhism. Thon–mi–Sam–bhota was among them a famous scholar who made Tibetan script from the Indian Gupta alphabet.[4] The other scholars were Acharya Kusara and Acharya Mahayana. Thus king of Tibet Srong–brtsan–sgam–po got whole hearted support from the Buddhist scholars and was able to introduce Buddhism of Greater cycle is Tibet. Besides, he himself received secret instructions of Buddhist Tantra and got initiations of Arya Avalokitesvara. This sect based upon tantra, and latter known rNying–ma–pa. The next successors of Srong–brtan–sgam–po did not show much interest in Buddhism. However, during 8th century AD king Ḳri–srong–lde–brtsan invited Acharya Santa Rakshita and Guru Padma Sambhava in Tibet from India for further development of Buddhism. He helped in building 6 Samyas monastery on the model of the great monastery of Odantapuri in India. They set up different Buddhist studies departments and started translation of Sanskrit Buddhist texts into Tibetan. Nevertheless in comparison of Srong–brtsan–sgam–po period, Buddhism made rapid progress, both spiritual and material.[5] But unfortunately within forty years of Khri–srong–lde–brton's death the land of Tibet broke into pieces. In 838 AD Langelarma [6] became the king of Tibet. He established Bon and persecuted Buddhism, as a result senior descendent of the old royal lineage found it impossible to remain in Central Tibet. He took refuge at the border land from Ladakh to Mustang and linked three kingdoms viz. Mar–yul, Guge and Spu–hrang. Accordingly in 9th century AD Skyi–lde–nyi–mgon became the first king of Western Tibet.[7] Later he divided the kingdom among his three sons. His eldest son, Dpal–gyi–mgon got Maryul[8], second son, Bkar–shis–mgon became the king of Guge and Sppu–hrang, and third son, lde–gtsug–mgon got Zangskar and its adjoining areas. Hence, Dpal–gyi–mgon became the first king of Ladakh, he came on throne on 10th century AD. By religion he was the follower of Mahāyāna sect, therefore, gave special patronage to Buddhism in its prapogation. At the same time Rin–chen–bzang–po, the great Tibetan figure translated many sutra and tantras with their voluminous commentaries from Sanskrit in Tibetan strengthened Mahāyāna Buddhism throughout Ladakh and its neighbouring countries. He visited India three times and spent seventeen years, presumably progressing from one Indian Buddhist master to another, seeking initiations into various traditions, as well as methods of religious practice. He is credited of the establishment of large number of monasteries and temples in Western Tibet, and since his times the present form of architecture and painting of Buddhist Art of Ladakh came into existence. In fact the painting must have been carried out under the direction of Indian artists [9], who in the manner still followed by Buddhist master–artists of Ladakh today. We may reasonably deduce that all the decorative motifs appearing on the ceiling in the old monastery of Alchi, rather to say Alchi Choskhor follows tenth century styles of north–western India, the gods and goddesses, the peacocks and the conventionalized cloud–designs. Of the frescos those depicting local people as donors and particularly interesting. Today this conventional forms continued to exist side by side with Tantra, and morecover that the texts known as tantras often formed the basis both of ceremonies and forms of meditation which could be practised quite properly within a monastic setting. The series of Mahāyāna texts, known as Sātras and Tantras.

The collection of these books still being preserved in the monasteries of Ladakh under 'Monastic Discipline' called Vinaya.[10] Later like Tibet two schools : Red and Yellow established in Ladakh. The 'Red' denotes non–reformed from the Nyingma–pas to Kargyu–pas, while 'Yellow' school was founded by Tsongkha–pa. In this way by 16th century AD almost all important Buddhist schools were established their monasteries in Ladakh.[11] And till 17th century AD Ladakh was recognised as 'Mini Tibet of India.'

Islam in Ladakh

The propagation of Islam in Ladakh region initially credited to Hazrat Amir Kabir Syed Ali Hamadani and his followers during fourteenth century AD. Though majority of Buddhist population did not pay much attention in Muslim missionaries, however, Dok–pas who were living as Dok–yul and Dras Valleys were very much influenced by them and majority of population in Dras, Kargil and its nearby villages followed Islam of Shiat sect. Even some of the villages of Dok–yul viz. Da, Hanu, Bina, Derchik etc. were influenced by Islam.

Dogra Regime in Ladakh

In 1834 Wazir Zorawar Singh conquered Ladakh and till 1840 he continuously struggled with different opposition groups. In 1841 he marched towards Tibet and fought bravely against Tibetan army in the cold high altitude region. After the death of Zorawar Singh, the Tibetan army recovered all territories which they lost during the war. But Raja Gulab Singh did not want to leave Ladakh, as it was the trade centre of Central Asia, annually hundreds of traders from Central Asian countries visited Ladakh and exchange their goods under barter trade system, thus from Ladakh, Maharaja of Jammu & Kashmir earned good revenue through taxes, levied upon traders. In 1846 a treaty was signed between British Government and Maharaja Gulab Singh of Jammu & Kashmir. Under the territory Maharaja Gulab Singh paid a sum of rupees one crore to the British Company, thereafter, Maharaja Gulab Singh became independent ruler of Jammu and Kashmir, Ladakh came under Maharaja of Jammu & Kashmir's supremacy.

British Diplomacy

During Dogra regime British Government did not stop to play political diplomacy and annually sent British Commissioners to Ladakh and asked them to send the reports on trade to the government. In those days the commerce of Ladakh was not based upon the produce or consumption of the country but its chief consideration, however, based upon its centrical situation, by which it became the great thoroughfare for an active commercial intercourse among Tibet, Turkistan, China and even Russia on one hand, and Kashmir, Punjab, and the plains of Hindustan on the other.[12] Therefore, after levying taxes upon Central Asian traders, State Government got good revenue. British

Government so wanted to see the opportunity to collect taxes directly from the traders. After the death of Maharaja Gulab Singh, British Government was able to get the opportunity to levy taxes directly upon traders and also collected the same.

Travel and Trade

Ladakh was famous for Pashmina wool trade which was imported from Rudokh and Chang–Thang later the entire wool was exported to Kashmir. Kashmiri Muslim traders had monopoly on wool business, they normally settled at Spituk and collected all wool through the Ladakhi Muslim mediators and later supplied to Kashmir. Under the treaty, Tibet and Chang–Thang had to supply all wool to Ladakh. Besides, there were some trade missions on the basis of reciprocity. These missions were to be made commercial and religious in nature. The Dalai Lama was to send a merchant mission to Leh every year with a few hundred bales of brick tea. This was known as Chaba mission. This mission while passing through Ladakh enjoyed free transport and many other facilities. Same kind of facilities was available in between Srinagar and Leh. At every halt traders got the transport and free labour facilities called 'Begari'. Like Chaba mission, there were many caravans which had hundreds horses, yaks, donkeys, sheep and goats who carried large quantities of commodities for trading purposes. In conclusion Ladakh was one of the important trading centre of Central Asia before 1947.

After Independence

As soon as India got independence and Jammu & Kashmir came under Indian Republic, Pakistan did not bear such changes and attacked on India from Kashmir, Ladakh and Jammu borders. Pakistani soldiers reached near Kashmir airport and in Ladakh near Leh. Thereore, Indian government immediately sent Indian troops to Kashmir and Ladakh by air and after severe fighting Pakistani lost the battle and returned to Pakistan. Thereafter Indian Government started developmental activities in Ladakh. Leh–Srinagar motor road was built and Leh airport also ready for airforce aeroplanes landing and taking off by the end of sixties. In the meanwhile Army started works on the Chusul airport for military purposes. In this way infrastructure changes was taking place in Ladakh slowly and streadily. After the gap of 15 years China attacked on India, we were not ready for such a surprise attack, therefore suffered with heavy casualties, China captured a large portion of Indian territory in Ladakh region. This was another setback for India. However, from Indo–China war Government of India learned a lesson that there should be strong need to strengthen the border and must have sufficient supply of arms and ammunition. Besides, Army personnel must have full training of cold–arid high altitude war tactics. In 1965 after tha gap of nearly three years Pakistan attacked India. This time our defence was very strong and our army captured a large portion of Pakistani land but India is a peace-loving country, therefore, returned the area which was captured from Pakistan. As a result Pakistan thought that India was bound to return the area to Pakistan because of international community pressure. So instead of developing harmonious relations with India, Pakistan started militant activities in India, finally in 1971 India again faced a war against Pakistan. This time Pakistan lost the battle, Bangladesh came into existence. Thereafter, some peace took place in Kashmir. Tourist business flourishing up in valley. Viewing the tourist interests, the Jammu & Kashmir State opened Ladakh for foreign tourists in summer 1974. Thus Ladakh came into the map of world tourism. Thousands of foreigners annually started visiting Ladakh. In 1999 when Kashmir valley had good number of tourists and likewise Ladakh also had higher number of tourists expectations, Pakistan again did not like such progress and sent foreign intruders with the supports of its army into the Kargil as well as Turtuk[13] sectors. Indian soldiers again fought bravely and won the proxy war. In short our Government always made different plans for the development of the Ladakh region but due to Pakistan's hostile activities such developments were hindered by one or the other reasons. However, our scientific research centres, for example, Field Research Laboratory, Astronomical Observatory, etc., are doing remarkable jobs. The Field Research Laboratory, Leh, one of the laboratories of Defence Research and Development Organisation, is the brain child of the first Prime Minister of India, Late Pandit Jawaharlal Nehru, established in 1960. Today the scientists of the Research Centre identified suitable varieties of important vegetable crops, wheat, barley, maize, mustard and alfalfa. Their scientific works are not limited up to research only, but annually local farmers get seed and seedlings from the laboratory which after cultivation they earn handsome money. Hence, FRL has very important role in order to increase the living standard of Ladakhis as well by giving moral boost for adopting modern agricultural technology in the cold desert zone it is helping Ladakhis farmers in the development of agriculture in Ladakh.

When Indian Government was fully aware for the scientific and economic development of Ladakh region it also felt that to preserve Buddhist culture, one Buddhist institute should be set up in Leh. Pandit Jawaharlal Nehru also recognised the great importance of Ladakh and accepted the request of Ven. Kushok Bakula to run institute under the financial support through Department of Culture, Government of India. Today this institute under the various objects like Intensive study of Buddhist history, culture, literature and philosophy doing remarkable job for the preservation and protection of Buddhist culture of Ladakh.

Above all Ladakh has rich heritage, Buddhist culture is still intact with traditional form. Wildlife, plants and herbs are plenty available. But because of increasing trend of tourism and population increase we have to make some measurements through which can also able to preserve Buddhist culture as well as all wild plants and animal culture of this region. I am very sorry to say that eighteen years back when I came to Ladakh for the first time, the Ladakhi culture and tradition which was then I saw is certainly no longer so today. Therefore, it is our duty to preserve the heritage of Ladakh before it may be polluted.

REFERENCES

1. According to the Therevadi Buddhism normal life of human being is around of suffering. To resolve the suffering he has to do such work which improve his rebirth, the philosophy of 'Karma' in this way helps in taking one birth to another and at last he reaches at the 'Arhat' stage where he could reduce the elements of his personal existence to such total quietude that at his death. Thus the philosophers of this Buddhist school are much concentrated with the actual nature of the basic physical and mental elements, which are only finally disperse in nirvāna.
2. The doctrine of Mahāyāna Buddhism based upon the 'Universal emptiness' empty in the sense that nothing could be predicated of anything. Thus the empty means to an end, much as we might use grammatical exercises in order to master a language, thereafter we put our grammar book away, once the language has been mastered. In fact emptiness may be called 'perfection of wisdom'. According to Mahāyāna its goal is not just to save oneself but to realize final enlightenment for the benefit of all other as well as one's self.
3. Snellgrove, David and Richardson, Hugh: 'A Cultural History of Tibet', UBS Pub., New Delhi, 1968, pp. 71-72
4. *Ibid.*, p. 75. Illustrating further Snellgrove and Richardson say, "The Tibetan alphabet consists of thirty basic letters, including vowel *a*, and

four extra vowel signs on the Indian model for *i, u, e* and *o*. As it is fundamentally a monosyllabic language. Tibetan word–syllables have been subject to considerable phonetic decay. Thus, the word for 'eight', 'brgyad', which is spelt with a whole complexity of initial consonants and was presumably once pronounced something like 'bragyad', is now pronounced in the dialect of Central Tibet as simply 'gyay'. Several sets of combined consonants, such as gr, dr and br, are pronounced nowadays in most parts of Tibet as a single sound; the three quoted now sound not very different from an English 'd'. Nevertheless the original spellings, as fixed in the time of 'Srong–brtsan–sgam–pa' and successors, have usually been preserved as the correct ones." Cf. Snellgrove and Richardon; *op. cit.* and ill, p. 75. Ladakh which was early days known Western Tibet also have Tibetan or Bhoti language but Ladakhi pronounce each letter completely.

5. Snellgrove and Richardon; *op. cit.*, p. 78.
6. Langdarma = glang–dar–ma.
7. Jina, Prem Sing, 'Tourism in Ladakh Himalaya', Indus Pub. Co., 1994.
8. Maryul = Ladakh.
9. Snellgrove and Richardon; *op. cit.*, pp. 113–14.
10. *Ibid.*
11. Tucci, Giuseppe (Tr. J.E. Stapleton Driver), 'Tibet : Land of Snows', Oxford Pub. Co., New Delhi, 1967, p. 64. The main Buddhist schools are: Nyima–pa, bkar–rgyud–pa, Sa–skya–pa and dGe–lugs–pa.
12. Moorcroft, William, 'Travels in Hindustan', Sagar Pub., New Delhi, Reprinted and Trebeck, George in India, 1971, p. 346.
13. Turtok = Now its name has been changed and called 'Hanifuddin Sector'.

PART–I

1. Land Life and Language
2. Tourism
3. Personality
4. Tradition and Society
5. Politics

LAND, LIFE AND LANGUAGE

1

BROG-YUL: THE LAND AND THE PEOPLE

D.D. Sharma

Introduction

Brog-Yul means a hilly or mountainous country (i.e. *Brog* 'hill' + *Yul* 'country'). According to Tibetan chronicles it is a land of narrow ravines and valleys situated south of the Hindukush-Karakoram ranges, forming part of Central Ladakh. Thus, Brog-Yul is a land of narrow rocky gorges of the upper Indus Valley at an elevation of 9,000 feet to 10,000 feet above sea-level. The prominent inhabited localities of this land are Garkhon, Da, Hanu and Darchiks. Garkhon is the biggest village situated at an elevation of 9,000 feet above the sea level. It may be considered the lowest and the warmest place of Ladakh region.

In Brog-Yul, gorges are high and narrow. It is said that sometimes the sun does not rise for many days because of the high gorges. Beyond Da and at a distance of 4 km. from Garkhon, towards the west, the Indus gorge gets narrower, and the mountains on both sides, steeper and higher. The approximate length and width of Brog-Yul, extending from the borders of Baltistan to nearly 50 km., beyond Leh, in Ladakh is about 150 km. However, the populated area is not more than 50 sq. kms. due to its topographical conditions.

Brog-Yul was inaccessible to the outside world for many years. Therefore, people living outside could not have contact with the Brogpas and consequently, Brog-Yul culture was not influenced to a large extent by the outsiders. Now, Borg–Yul is connected by and with both the Leh and Kargil districts of Ladakh. So, with this improvement some changes in Brog culture can easily be noticed.

Population

As there has been no regular and systematic census in the area, it is difficult to give an exact, number for the population of Brog-Yul. However, according to the 1981 census, the total population of the four prominent villages viz. Garkhon, Da, Hanu and Darchik was 2,467. If I add the other hamlets living between Hanu and Batalik, the total population of Brog-Yul would be nearly 3,000 or so.

The People

The inhabitants of Brog-Yul valley, though termed as 'Shin' or 'Shrin', are designated as 'Dokpas' (≤ Drog-pa ≤ Brog-pa) by their Tibetan speaking Balti and Ladakhi neighbours, which means "the inhabitants of mountainous region and herdsmen (Dog < Brog 'hill' + pa 'inhabitants')". Because they live in uncultivable rocky lands and one of their pastoral nomadic life they are popularly known as Drog-pas. Even now, the rearing of flocks of sheep and goats is the main occupation and forms the principal source of their subsistence. It Doka speech, the term 'nor' stands for both, 'the flocks of sheep and goats' and 'wealth'. Consequently, a wealthy person, as well as a person with large stocks of sheep and goats is identically termed as 'norchan'. In Tibetan, however, the term 'Dokpa' is generally indicative of the people who lead a nomadic life, irrespective of their habitation or class.

It is also said that before being given this appellation, these people were known as 'minaro'. The facts in this connection are available in the works of Csoma de Coros and A.H. Francke. According to the claims of Rohit Vohra when he enquired of their descents, they claimed to have inherited 'minaro' traditions. Because many of their descents while settling down in the Brog-Yul valleys married 'Minaro' women at the time when their leader Gil Singe (The lion of Gilgit) and Gapo fled from their original home Gilgit and settled down here (Vohra, 1982).

Racially, the Dokpas of Brog-Yul belong to Dardic ethnic stock who originally belonged to the regions of Hindukush, known as Daroda Country in Hindu mythology, which in later an analogy of Kohistan, Baltistan, etc., was termed Dardistan by G.W. Leitner in 1866. The Dard hymns of these Dokpas as sung by their Lapdraks (caretaker of deity) during their harvest festival days also state that their ancestors emigrated from Gilgit under the leadership of Gil Singe. According to Franke this emigration must have taken place many centuries back when the Dards of Gilgit were speaking the same ancient language of

Dards, which, to a great extent, is faithfully preserved in the speech of these Buddhist Dards of Brog-Yul. (Franke, 1977:71). But, the other Dardic language of the *Shina-Khwar* group, including Drassi, have undergone tremendous changes.

The migration of the Dokpas seems to have taken place in two groups because the Buddhist Dards (Dokpas) of Da and Garkon maintain that their ancestors migrated from Gilgit under the leadership of Gil Singe, whereas the Dokpas of Hanu say that their ancestral leader was Tho-sra-li, not Gil Singe (Jolden,1985:36). Moreover, in the vicinity of the village near Chortal pass, lies a place known as Hon-brang-Min which means, 'ripened without cultivation'. This finds a mention in the festival hymns of these people as well. The name of the place, according to them, is reminiscent of the pre-settlement phase of this land. It is said that before selecting, the Brog-Yul for permanent settlement, their ancestors came for to look at the place for the inhabitation of their tribesmen, with some barley grains. They sowed these in this place to test the fertility of the soil before going back to their ancestral land. And, next year, when they visited the place again, they found to their joy that the seeds had not only grown into fine plants, but also had fine ripened ears. This made them sure that this place was worth living in and later on, they emigrated to this land with their tribesmen, along with their Lhas (Gods and Goddesses) and settled down there.

The Dokpas have certain racial characteristics of their own. It is said that they are very proud of their race and culture. They are highly self-respecting people and will not bow or beg before any one, even in compelling circumstances. In fact, it was a matter of national policy with them to be self-sufficient in all matters, as far as possible, to save their honour and self-respect. It is said in olden days when they were the subjects of the Kings of Ladakh, Dokpas never went to him or his courts to get any justice from there. They, instead, used to settle all their disputes among themselves, which is the practice still in vogue there. It is said that they stubbornly resisted any attempt made to subdue them under their Ladakhi rulers. Hence, there is a saying in Ladakhi —'Two things are impossible viz. loading a dog and forcing labour from a Dokpa' Perhaps, it was this characteristic of these people that prompted the King of Ladakh to persuade or pressurise them to embrace Buddhism and give up their customs, language, and dresses, which the Dokpas, at least of Da and Garkon, resisted even after embracing Buddhism in the past. Commenting on their characteristics, W. Crook states, 'Inspite of rigours of the climate they are bold, cheery and an independent' race, (Crook 1977:51).

Besides their physical features, the 'Brok-skad' the language of these Dokpas also establishes, beyond doubt, that these people belong to the Indo-Aryan or Indo-Iranian speaking 'Daradas' of the N.W.F. They, due to geography, have preserved, to a great extent, the older forms of the 'Darada' language which, due to historical reasons, have undergone tremendous changes.

As noted above, after the migration of their ancestors many centuries back their contact with the speakers of their ancient language was snapped. But at that stage, the only precious heritage that they could carry with them was their language and culture, which they continued to preserve with love and reverence. In this rugged mountainous and secluded land thing were bereft of all contacts with the outside world for a long time. But, there came a time in the past when this tribe, which was proud of its language and culture, was persuaded or compelled by historical events to embrace Islam or Buddhism and imbibe their influences on their language and culture. There the 'Dards of Dras' who embraced Islam, owing to their communion with their Muslim brothers of 'Dardistan and Kohistan', were influenced by their speech and culture. Although the Dokpas of Da-Da-Do, Chulichan, and of a few more villages of the lower Indus Valley also have embraced Islam and have given up the Brog-pa dress and culture, any have not yet, given up their old Dardic tongue.

On the other hand, though the Dards of Brog-Yul too were compelled by the Tibetan rulers of Ladakh to embrace Buddhism and give up the use of their language and customs to deprive them of their separate identity, only partial impact became operative on the Dards of Hanu, who after embracing Buddhism, gave up their language, but the Dards of other localities who accepted Buddhism neither gave up their language, dress nor customs. They continued to maintain their ancestral communicative system and cultural affairs though the religious conversion had some impact upon them too.

An intensive historical analysis of Brok-skad reveals that it contains an amazingly high degree of old-Indo-Aryan elements. Most of the primary stems, nominal as well as verbal, have their sources in the O/A stems (Sharma, 1998).

This language, due to the faithful preservation of earlier forms of Dardic languages, has special significance for deachronic studies of the languages of the Dardic groups as a whole.

Socio–cultural Preservation

Although, on account of their embracing Buddhism, the Buddhist Dards (i.e. Da, Garkon, and other neighbouring hamlets), have imbibed certain cultural influences of the Buddhism practised in Ladakh, they unlike their brothers who have embraced Islam have not given up their socio–cultural traditions, inherited from their ancestors. They have preserved them to a great extent. No doubt the favourable topographical environment of their habitats which isolated them from the rest of the world for several centuries also contributed greatly. Besides, their blind faith in their Lhas, belived to be endowed with immense prowers to punish and reward their subjects, and dreadful fear of pollution from outside contact has made them stick to their traditional ways of life and confine themselves to the boundaries of the *Brog-Yul.* This has directly or indirectly contributed to the preservation of their many archaic customs and practices of socio–cultural life which are followed by them till today.

Now, due to the increasing exposure of this community to outside influences on account of an improved communication system, transportation facilities and educational awareness, the all round socio–cultural changes are bound to change themselves accordingly. Thus, such changes can be seen among the new generation. As such, it is but natural that the socio-cultural norms of traditional patterns are diluted fast and have been lost to us for ever.

Moreover, in the absence of any chronicle detailed or records of this land, depicting the lifestyle, social customs and religious practices of these people, there is an urgent need to have a detailed authentic records of their traditional past. It is, of course, heartening that in recent years some enthusiastic researchers have come forward and have undertaken the appreciable task of recording these details for posterity.

However, some of the interesting features of their socio-cultural life recorded by us and other investigators may be presented as follows:

Social Organization

Socially, the Buddhist Dard community is a casteless society. All, including the musician classes, are the members of the same racial, social and religious group. Every household is a complete unit by itself and its relations within the village community are maintained at the level of the household, which constitutes an extended family. In each generation the eldest son takes on the role of the household head and regulates the activities, duties and rights of every member of the household. For the socio–cultural activities these households are grouped into smaller units known as *Pha-spun.* Consequently, an individual within the village community or in the Buddhist Dard community as a whole is identified by his house name (*Gota-nu*). It may be interesting to note that a similar system is attested in the Buddhist community of the Gahr village of Lahul (Sharma, 1998:85). However, the affinal recruits viz. female members and the *baro* (*ghar jawa in*) have to discard their natal house name and *Pha-spun* membership and assume that of their husband or wife, as the case may be, and thus become the member of his/her descent group.

Kinship Organization

The kinship organization has a strong bearing on the social organization of a community and its forms and functions can be clearly understood from the analysis of its kinship terms and the address terms prevalent in the community concerned. The kin terms that are used for affinal and agnatic relations are not only a potential source for understanding the present state of affairs of the society, but also are potent enough to throw substantial light on its past. At the agnatic level, the basis of kinship organization is the grouping of Dokpa community in its *Pha-spun* organization which prohibits matrimonial alliances among its members and regulates their ritualistic activities as well. A female member, on marriage, is deprived of her natal house name and the *Pha-spun* membership and takes that of her husband's. Similarly, a person, if he choses his father-in-law's house as his permanent residence, becomes a *baro/magpa.* He too loses the membership of his *Pha-spun* and becomes a member of his father-in-law's *Pha-spun.* Consequently, his relation with his agnatic *Pha-spun* (kin group) is severed.

As in other communities, in this community too, the marriage system has an important bearing on the establishment of interrelationship between different Pha-spun. This can, of course, be best understood in terms of its kinship terminology. For instance, terms like *bono-bo* (elder father), *sene-bo* (younger father), *bone-aye* (elder mother), *sene-*

aye (younger mother) and identical terms for the son the nephew viz. *bio* and daughter and niece, viz. *mole*, and the absence of distinct terms for these kins indicates that both polyandry and systems of marriage were prevalent among these people.

Similarly, identical terms for the elder sister and the elder sister-in-law (H.e.br.w.) viz. *jethani/kake*, younger sister and younger sister-in-law (H.y.br.w.), viz. *Sas*, and identical terms for the husband and his brothers is an indicator of the prevalence of the practice of marrying two real sisters to one or two brothers (polygyny). In the same way, identical terms for the sister's husband and wife's brother, viz. *sajari*, may be a legacy of the prevalence of the exchange marriage system. In the same way, the currency of identical kin terms for father's sister's husband, maternal uncle and father-in-law, viz. *mumo* and for father's sister, maternal uncle's wife and mother-in-law, viz. *pepe* also indicate that their existed a cross cousin marriage system, perbaps in a limited sphere. For, contrary to the prevalence of identical kin terms for real brothers and sisters on the one hand and for sons and daughters of the father's sister's or maternal uncle's sons and daughters, may be a later development which also indicate that now this is not a universal practice and is a recent development as has been attested among the Dokpas of Hanu.

Social Custom

The Dokpas of Brog-Yul follow certain social customs which may be of interest to non-Dokpa readers. Some of these may be noted as under:

Calculation of Age

Under the influence of Ladakhi Buddhists, the Buddhist Dards of Brog-Yul follow the Tibetan calender of a twelve years cycle, which, is particularly observed in the calculation of age of a person. For this a person has to remember the name of the animal after which the year of his/her birth has been named in the calender. This period of twelve years is technically termed 'Lo-skor' in Tibetan. Thus, when a person says that he/she has completed two Lo-skors, it means he is 24 years old. Interestingly, in the denotation of age the preceding number of Lo-skor is taken into account till the succeeding year is completed. As such, the person, who has completed two Lo-skors, will continue to calculate his age as two Lo-skor till he completes the third Lo-skor (i.e. till he becomes 36 years old).

Celebration of Lo-Skor

In this community, particularly among females, the completion of the Lo-skor has a special significance. For young girls the completion of their first Lo-skor is the year of their entering puberty. All young maidens who have completed their first Lo-skor at the time of the Losar (New Year) festival are brought to the village dancing ground, clad in their best, in a procession to celebrate the festival in a festive spirits.

It is, however, interesting to note that grown up and elderly women celebrate the completion of all their Lo-skors in a big way. A grand party is arranged by them for the whole village, in which members of the village community are invited to participate in *chhang* bouts and the Lo-skor feats on this day. The lady in question is an honoured guest takes her seat near the hearth. All male guests assembled for the occasion take their seats on her left side and female guests on her right side. *Chhang* is served to all. The next item on the agenda is the dance, accompanied by music. Men start to dance, followed by women. *Chhang* is served when the first round of dancing is over. Thus continues till midnight when a second meal of *papa,* Sattu mixed with melted goat butter, is served to the guests. After this all leave for their respective homes. This celebration is so popular and is so anxiously awaited that people keenly remember the names of the persons who have to celebrate their Lo-skor in a particular year. Moreover, those who are fortunate enough to live to celebrate their sixth Lo-skor are permitted to celebrate it one year in advance (i.e. on the completion of seventy-first year).

As a matter of fact the calculation of age by Lo-skor is a normal procedure in Tibetan/Ladakhi culture as well, but its celebration of every cycle is not seen in any other Himalayan community, except this community.

Fairs and Festivals

Though the Dokpas of Brog-Yul celebrate many fairs and festivals during the year, the most important of them is the Lha festival (harvest festival) on account of its celebration (i.e. on the occasion of the harvest of the second crop in the month of October in every two years), which lasts for three days and in which a boy is made to play the role of the Lha (God). In this period during the day he has to stay in a crevice of rocks above the village and can come down to the village in the evening. He sleeps in a separate room in the house.

For this celebration *Labdrak* (the caretaker of the god) is the leading personality who sings the hymns during the festival. According to Jolden, the number of hymns is 23, but Franke said the number is limited to 18 only. However the number of hymns is not a matter of great interest. Besides on the evening of the first day of the celebration 'Labdrak', the principle dignitary of the celebration goes to the place where the inaugural ceremony is to take place. After some ritual two to three goats are sacrificed there and their meat, along with a lump of *sattu* (champa) kneaded in butter milk, is distributed among the participants. Then the *Labdrak*, the *Goba* (the village headman) and few others go dancing to the rock crevice to bring the Lha boy down from there. The Lha boy comes down with a burning incense pot in his hand at the head of the party. At the square where the main festival is to take place, this party is greeted by awaiting musicians who play festive tunes on their musical instruments. But the Lha boy, after placing the incense pot on a boulder, disappears in the crowd. With this starts the festival which lasts for three to four days.

It is during this period that hymns narrating the events of their migration from their ancestral land to this land, under the leadership of Gil Singe, are sung to the accompaniment of music to which some others, including woman, too join. It is followed by a mass dance in which all men and women take part. This goes on for three days in the evening after supper. There are two sessions, first, in the late evening and the second after dinner at night. On the first day, drinking is strictly prohibited by tradition, but on other days all the participants are free to drink, except on the dancing square. Thus, on the second and third day under the influence of heavy intoxication the dance is quite vigorous.

Mass Kissing

During these moonlit nights of the 2nd and 3rd day the custom of mass kissing takes place. All men and women, young and old, are bedecked in their best and the men are free to kiss, without restriction any lady, young or old. This lasts for nearly two hours or so. Most young men, while dancing, kiss ladies and girls of their choice and older men care to find ladies of appropriate age to kiss them. Both the sexes enjoy the custom immenscly. No one minds the advances of any participants, though this part of festival is confined to the Dokpas of Da and Garkhon only. There is a legend about the inception of this part of the festival as well (Jolden: 1985). When celebrated at Da people from Bema, Sanit, Larsong, and other nearby villages also come 'to see' this celebration.

Losar

Another important community festival, Losar is celebrated in January. The date for its celebration is decided by the village astrologer who watches the movement of the sun across the mountain peaks is the third week of December. The venue of the celebration is the village Gompa. It continues for seven days. Drinking of *chhang* and dances, with the accompaniment of music, are the main attractions. On the first day torches of cidar splinters are lit at the fall of night and are thrown at a particular place outside the village. It may be interesting that a similar function, known Halda, takes place in the Pattan Valley of Lahul as well (Sharma, 1988: 231). On the second day special food is prepared and all households are visited with it on plates and a solution *(zule)* is offered to every elderly person there. A similar custom be seen in the Pattan Valley (Sharma, 1998: 241-42).

As noted above, the festival has a special significance for young girls who are completing their first Lo-skor. They are taken to the dancing ground in a procession bedecked in their best. This gives the parents of prospective grooms a chance to choose a girl of their liking for their wards. On this occasion, walls are decorated with crescent designs and a stone is installed, before which a lamp is lit and offerings are made every day till the celebrations are over. All non-veg. items, including milk, are strictly prohibited. Any violation of this is considered to be a harbinger of misery and disease.

Myths and Pantheons of Deities

The Dokpas have their own myths about the origin of the world and creation of their race. According to their folklore mythology in the beginning there was nothing but water everywhere. It froze later on and was by gradually covered with dust. Plants and grass grew on it. Time passed and there arose three mountains of red, white and blue. On them grew three trees of sandal wood of respective shades. Then there appeared the gods and goddesses who created human beings and other animate beings. In the beginning there was perfect harmony between gods and human beings. But the lust of men for the women of the gods embittered their amicable relationship. Consequently, the Lhas cut their association with menfolk and leaving them in this, *mi-yul* (mundane world), left for their *Lha-Yul* (gods country or heaven).

Besides there are many folk narrations which are sung during the harvest festival which tell us about their race and past history.

There are many myths about their gods and goddesses. Besides the celestial gods and goddesses, there are many household and village deities which are worshipped with fear and reverence by the whole community.

Household Deities

Among the household deities 'Sa-bdag' occupies the most prominent place. It permanently occupies a place behind the hearth and is the presiding deity of fertility among human beings and prosperity of livestock and crops. It is to be protected from the pollution of birth and death. Any forbidden objects such as like eggs, cow's milk or yak's meat etc., makes it angry and is likely to in flict miseries on the members of the household. While facing the hearth inflict womenfolk sit on the left side and menfolk on the right side.

Besides, there are many village deities which exercise their influence on all matters regarding the welfare of village and its inhabitants. According to Vohra, all the three sections of the village Garkon have their own deities which are worshipped at shrines on a hill which is their abode. The chief deity 'Sring Lhamo' is worshipped universally among all the Buddhist Dard villages. Her shrine is adorned with huge ibex horns, juniper (*chilgi*) leaves and branches. Besides, there are deities with significance to a particular village or groups of villages which protect the interest of their subjects.

Social Ceremonies and Rituals

The main social ceremonies and rites among the Buddhist Dards of Brog-Yul are marriage and death. The birth of a child is no special occassion for any celebration. The delivery is conducted by elderly experienced women of the village. Birth pollution is confined to the family concerned only. The mother of the child remains impure for 10 days and is purified by the village lama through *Chhos* (a purificatory ritual).

Similarly, there is no ritual or any celebration with regard to the skizak (naming ceremony) as well. The new-born is named ten days after birth when the period of birth pollution is over.

Marriage

Among the Dokpas marriage is also not a sacrosanct rite. Rather it is a socially sanctioned contact between females and a male or male and a female (i.e. two types of marriages, viz. polygamy and polyandry), are prevalent. In the former case, two sisters together are married to a boy who is the only son of his parents, but in the latter case, a girl is married to all the brothers of a single parentage. In this case, the marriage alliance is sought for the eldest brother of the household, and the younger ones, by virtue of prevalent social custom, automatically becomes the co-sharer of this wife. However, with reference to their progeny, the eldest husband is considered as the father.

Besides, the custom of group marriage also is prevalent in community. Thus sisters may be married to two brothers, both having equal rights of access to both wives.

There being no restriction on village endogamy, most of the alliances are contracted between two households of the same village by the parents of the boy and the girl while they are still under-age. Moreover, due to restricted choice, cousin marriages and marriages between near relations often take place.

The celebration of the marriage is a simple affair. When the girl for whom the alliance has been contracted earlier, attains the age of marriage, normally when she is 15-16 years old, some relations from the boy's side visit the house of the girl's father to have his consent for the formal celebration of the marriage. On agreement, the boy's father consults the village priest for an auspicious date and intimates the same to them. Thereafter, on an appointed day, some relatives of the girl visit the house of the boy's father to collect the necessary ration, viz. grain, butter and goats, for the feast of the marriage party. In the evening, they are entertained with *chhang* and meat. The next morning, when they return to their place with the ration collected from there the relatives of the boy gather and together proceed to the girl's house without the bridegroom. On reaching there they are served with *chhang* and *papa* (a preparation of *champa* (*sattu*) mixed with butter or apricot oil). Afterwards the priest performs the *chhos* (worship). They, along with the bride, may return the same evening or the next morning. There is no dowry, except the clothes and ornaments given to the girl by her parents. However, the present of a needle by the father and the maternal uncle to the girl, is an essential item of the dowry. The bridegroom's family has nothing to present to the bride. On reaching the bridegrooms' place the priest performs the rite known as *chhyasum-phetis* and with this all the formalities of a marriage are complete.

The next day, both the boy and the girl return with a *chhapkyang* full of *chhang* to the bride's natal home and offer it to her father. On this occasion, all relatives and neighbours of the girl's father assemble there and make the boy and girl dance in their presence. The next day the couple returns to their home and a marriage feast is offered to all relatives and villagers there merrymaking.

Beliefs and Superstitions

Dokpas are very superstitious. For instance, though cleanliness is not a part of their living pattern or habitual behaviour, they are very allergic to any contact with outsiders. Consequently, when a Dokpa comes back to a village after his sojourn or a business trip outside the Brog-Yul, he must purify himself with the smoke of juniper leaves. For, according to them, the *chilgi* (Juniper) smoke has superb purificatory properties. This is why its incense is used in all religious and ritualistic performances.

They also have a blind faith in supernatural powers of ghosts, devils and fairies, and make offerings to propitiate them and to ward off their evil effects. They are terribly afraid of male violent spirits that the often possess the women and menfolk alike and harrass them. The services of exorcists are sought to drive them away. Besides the urinary bladders of goats (*munthoto*) are also hung on the right side of the room, the place where man sit around the hearth, to ward off the evil effect from these evil spirits on them.

Abhorrence to Bovine Species and Fowls

They believe that the bovine species and the fowls are abhorrent to the presiding deity of their hearth, viz. *sabdag*. Their presence or association is terribly offending to 'Him', and brings miseries to the family as a whole. Consequently, consumption of eggs, cow's milk or its products are strictly prohibited among the Dokpas of Brog-Yul. They neither keep cows or fowls, nor do they use their products in any form. The only animal of bovine species that they tolerate, out of sheer compulsion, is the Zo (a cross between cow and yak), it being indispensible for ploughing the fields. The Zo is kept in animal sheds and is driven out to high mountain pastures when the operation of ploughing and sowing the fields is over. They do not use even its dung as manure. For, they do not wish to defile their hands and crops with the dung. These species and their products are anathema to women. The men too cannot consume any milk products within the village.

They can however, consume such products while they are away from the Brog-Yul on business tours. But the womenfolk would never allow it in their homes or even within the limits of their homeland. Such is their aversion that when a cow gives birth to a calf they do not touch it with their hands, and instead push to it the udder of the cow with a long handled wooden fork.

Similarly, they are very superstitious about the pollution of birth and menstruation. A menstruating woman is prohibited from touching anything like food, water or any other household article when in her period and until purified with the smoke of *shukpa* (smoke from dried leaves of the pencileidar tree put on live charcoals) on the 4th or the 5th day. And in case of delivery, the custom it is observed for ten days when she is purified by *chhos* by the village priest.

Post-Death Rites and Rituals

Death rites and rituals are very simple among the Buddhist Dards of Brog-Yul. On the death of a person the village Lama is invited to perform a *chhos* and the *mora* (corpse) is given a bath. After this among Buddhists of Darchiks, as in Ladakh, the corpse is kept in a sitting posture, but in others in a straight lying posture, as among Hindus, and is wrapped in a white cloth. It is kept thus for seven days or at least for three days and is carried to the cremation ground in the same way. After, performing a simple ritual the body is consigned to flames an the bank of the river Indus. In this, however, offering of walnut is as essential as is a piece of sandalwood among Hindus.

After two to three days (i.e. after cremation) the ashes of the dead are collected in a pot and are brought back home to be enshrine in a miniature *chorten* which is placed on the wall of *mane* at the village outskirt. A post-death feast is given the same day. Then after two to three days another feast known as *papadis* is given. In this inclusion of meat is a must. Meat otherwise is forbidden for all these days. After this, the mourning and pollution period ends.

REFERENCES

Crook, W, (Reprint, 1973): *Races of Northern India,* Cosmo, Delhi.

Edelman, D.I., (1983): *Dardic and Nuristani Languages,* Moscow.

Francke, A.H. (Reprint, 1977): *History of Western Tibet,* Delhi.

Jolden, E. (1985): *Harvest Festival of The Buddhist Dards of Ladakh and other Essays*, Srinagar.

Leitner, G.W.V. (1877): *The Languages and Races of Dardistan,* Lahore.

Morgen Stierne, George (1926): *A Report on The Linguistic Mission to Afghanistan*, Oslo.

——————, (1932): *Report on Linguistic Mission to North-Western India,* Oslo.

Sharma, D.D., (1997): *Tribal Languages of Ladakh, Parts I–II,* Delhi.

——————, (1997): *A Comparative Grammar of Tibeto-Himalayan Languages*, Delhi.

——————, (1998): *Himalaya Ki Vismayabhumi* Lahul (Hindu), Solan.

Vohra, Rohit (1982): A Mimiograph (Article).

2

LANGUAGE PROFILE OF LADAKH

Sanyukta Koshal

This chapter focuses on how political, social and economic change influence language. It also discusses its geographical environments to serve as background, in which the Ladakhi speaking people live, its produce, and a brief sketch of the history of the region. It provides a brief description of the present day Ladakhi language, and the proposed script for writing present day Ladakhi.

Geographical Situation

Ladakh is the north-westernmost district of India and is in Jammu & Kashmir state. The geographical boundaries of Ladakh have kept on shrinking and expanding at different times, as a result of successive historical and political upheavals, mainly between the seventh century to the present. When the Dogras conquered Ladakh in 1834, its greatest extent was from the north-east to south-west. It included the valleys of Nub-ra, Central Ladakh, Chang-thang, Lower Ladakh, Kar-gyil, Su-ru, Dras, Zangs-Kar and La-hul-Spi-ti.[1] In 1839, Baltistan was conquered and made one of the *tehsil* of Ladakh. In 1846, the British Indian Government detached Spi-ti and La-hul from Ladakh and annexed it to the Kulu subdivision of the Kangra district of the Punjab. Now Spi-ti and La-hul are the two important districts of Himachal Pradesh.

In 1948, Baltistan was lost to Pakistan and it is now on the other side of the ceasefire line. In June 1979, the district was bifurcated for administrative convenience. Hence, two districts were formed–Leh district and Kargil district. Kargil is also called as Kar-gyil-lo District by locals. Kargil includes the *tehsil* of/Zangs-Kar/, /Su-ru/, /Dras/, /ba-

Ta-lik/ and Kar-gyil town. Leh district comprises the *tehsil of* valleys of Nub-ra in the north-west and north-east, Central Ladakh, Chang-thang in east and south-east and Lower Ladakh in the west.

Internally, Leh district is bound by the district Kar-gyil, and the valley of Kashmir in the west and in the south, by Zangs-kar (a *tehsil* of Kar-gyil district) and then Himachal Pradesh. It has international boundaries on the north-west with Pakistan and on the east and the south-east with China and Tibet.

The total area of district Leh is 44,000 square kilometres. It is a mountainous region. The gigantic and celebrated mountain ranges run parallel through the region and in between the ranges nestle the valleys where courageous people have established hamlets to make their homes. Ka-ra-ku-ram range bounds the region on the north-east of Nub-ra valley. The highest peak of the Ka-ra-ku-ram range in Ladakh is the Sa-ser glacier. To form a natural boundary between the Nub-ra valley and the Leh stretches the Kailash range on which is situated the famous Kha-rdzong-la pass. The road on this pass is said to be the *first* road ever built on such heights. To the south-west of Leh extend the /Zangs-Kar/ ranges, a convoluted mass of mountains separating Leh valley from the valley of /Zangs-Kar/ (Tehsil of district Kar-gyil). To the west of Leh valley and to the south-west of the Zangs-Kar valley rises the great Himalayan, the greatest range of mountains on which is situated the *Zo-ji-la* pass, which separates Ladakh from the Kashmir valley. The height of mountain peaks varies between 21,000 to 24,000 or even (according to some scientists), 26,000 feet above sea level. Inhabited villages are situated between 8,000 to 15,000 feet above sea level.

The rivers of the region lend beauty and colour as they flow through the Ladakh valley, but they do not help it much with. Snow-water streams that flow down to the valley from the mountains which provide water for irrigation and domestic use. All the tributaries merge finally into the famous Sindhu—the Indus, which enters India in the south-east of Leh valley at /Dem-chok/ and flows through the valley entering Baltistan, till recently a part of Ladakh, and now under Pakistani occupation. There are springs in almost every village or nearby. The region is also bestowed with hot-springs which have medicinal properties. Sapphire–blue salt-water lakes at various places make this region even more beautiful. Strong winds, chirping birds and wandering wild animals enliven the serene beauty of the valley.

Extreme cold and heat are the main features of the climate. In winter, the temperature falls to -25^{0} to -40^{0} celsius, depending on the altitude and in summer it rises up to $+ 25^{0}$ celsius in lower altitude areas during the day. Dryness is another feature. This region is situated at such heights that even the famous monsoon of our country bows to the great Himalayas and hence does not generously shower its water on Ladakh. Thus, it has become a high altitude cold desert. In the midst of masses of mountains and extreme heat and a cold and dry climate, the people, by dint of their hard labour, have established villages along snow water streams or wherever they can divert the water. These channels exhibit the skill, patience and hard work of the Ladakhi. The sowing to harvesting season is of four months. The heat on the lower altitudes is so severe that it takes 60 days for the barley crop to ripen. The /Tuk-cha/ (village near Leh) has derived its name from /Tuk-chu/ (sixty), because the barley crop here is ready in 60 days. The principal crop is barley, other crops are wheat, /So-a/ (another variety of barley), peas and mustard; the vegetables grown are turnip, carrot, radish and onion. Fruits are apple, apricot and a in small quantity, walnut. At higher altitudes, only barley crop is possible, that too in a small quantity. The main economic activity, in such areas, is cattle rearing. But, even in this cold desert, human hands have created green fields. The season of sowing to harvesting is of lyrical beauty.

Nature has carefully created a vista with enormous high parallel mountain ranges decorated with glaciers, valleys, rivers, streams, pastures, lakes, springs and sprawling deserts. People have inhabited and added to this landscape, fields, monasteries, palaces situated on mountains and villages with small houses. Modern life which crept into the region since the fifties, through development programmes initiated by the government, both State and Central, has further added to the landscape and to the way of life of the region. The whole landscape, particularly of some areas, is breathtakingly beautiful.

The present population of Leh district, which is predominantly Buddhist, is about a lakh or more. 15 per cent are Muslims. Christians are only a tiny minority of about 100 families. The people of / da /, / ha-nu /, / be-ma/valleys known as /Dok-pa/ in Ladakhi, follow a variant form of Buddhism, perhaps still maintaining the simplicity of earlier stages and not much influenced by Tibetan-Buddhism. Stupa and monasteries dominate the scene.

The language spoken by the people is Ladakhi. Let us now examine the historical-cum-political process which this region has experienced and its language situation at different times of its history.

Historical Background

It is always important to re-examine the past so as to clarify the base from which we advance. Unfortunately, Ladakh's past history is still shrouded in mystery because of non-availability of source material. Hence, it is rather difficult to render a comprehensive and detailed account. But, whatever material has been brought to light illustrates the following facts. For convenience, the history of this region may be divided into three periods:[2]

(i) Ancient, that is before the 10th century.
(ii) Medieval, from 10th century to 1842.
(iii) The Modern period from 1842 AD onwards.

Ancient History

Earlier, the population of Ladakh was composed of /dord/ or /dard/ and Indo-Aryan tribes. Ladakh itself formed part of the great Kushan Empire (120 AD to 162 AD). This is corroborated by the inscription found in Khal-tse. Francke also states that those ancient inscriptions in Indian Brahmi, and Kha-rosh-Thi and Sharda characters of 200. BC, which have been found at Khal-tse, more likely belong to the times of the ancient /mon/ Indian tribe. The ruins of their old castles are still called /mon/, castles. In Zangs-kar, the word /mon/ has been in use for all Indians. Francke suggests: "If the Indians of present day are called so it becomes very probable that also the ancient /mon/, who were subjugated by Tibetan Kings, were an Indian tribe." He further states, "However, in front of the ancient Dard castle at Khal-tse, there is a short inscription in a later form of Indian characters. This may be a document of civilisation of Dards."

The reign of Kanishka was also time for the spread of Buddhism. This religion had already been introduced in Ladakh during the reign of Ashoka. When Kanishka held his famous fourth Buddhist Council in Kashmir, it is believed that all his subjects, including the Ladakhi, took part in it.

During the Kushan period, Gandhara art was introduced in Ladakh, and it is believed that Ladakhi of those days spoke a Prakrit dialect. Even in Baltistan, the Kha-rosh-thi (Kharoshthi) script was in vogue.

This is proved by Kha-rosh-thi and Brahmi inscriptions which Francke discovered at Khal-tse in Ladakh.

Kashmiri scholars played a key role in spreading Buddhism in this region. It may be that the Prakrit spoken in this region was similar or closely related to the Prakrit spoken in Kashmir; because there is no evidence that the local language of that time was analysed and used for the spread of Buddhism in this region. It may be noted that though Buddhism was introduced in Tibet in the seventh century, it could not take roots till the time when the Tibetan scholar /Thon-mi -sam-bho-Ta/ came to India, studied in Nalanda and later analysed the Tibetan language and evolved a script. Buddhist literature was then translated into Tibetan. For the spread of a religion, language is an important factor. This has been proved by the success of efforts made by the Christian missionaries, who for the spread of the creed, learnt local languages and translated the Bible into them. In the case of Ladakh, the Bible was translated into classical Tibetan, which made no impact at all.

Coming back to Ladakh, from the decline of the Kushan empire at the end of the second century A.D. till the seventh century A.D., not much is known about Ladakh. Francke, summing up the post-Kushan situation in Ladakh, writes:

> As regards politics, Western Tibet or Ladakh, did not come under the Chinese, when the power of the Kushan declined. It was apparently governed by local chiefs, whose names have been occasionally preserved in inscription and tales. Thus, at Khal-tse according to a Gupta inscription, a certain Satyawati (or Shrimacharpati), and according to oral reports, fifty or sixty miles higher up the Indus Valley, a certain Suryawati, are mentioned.

In *The History of Western Tibet*, Francke writes, "With regard to the political state of Ladakh about 950 AD the chronicles of Ladakh[3] make the following remarks:

> At that time, upper Ladakh was held by the descendants of Kesar, whilst lower Ladakh was split into various independent principalities."
> He writes further, "from local tradition and inscription it is possible to gather some scanty information about the various states which were in existence before the time of the Central Tibetan dynasty. At Leh there reigned dynasty of kings who derived their origin from the mythical king Kesar; at Saspola people tell of a king

Bandel, the constructor of the ancient fort Alchi /Khar-gok/. At Khal-tse, there was a dynasty of Dard kings, whose fort was built on the bank of the Indus and whose last members were called / shirima gya-shin/. It apparently came to an end between 1150-1200 AD.

In general, this was roughly the picture of Ladakh, when /skyid-lde-nyi-ma-gon/ conquered western Tibet, Ladakh, Spiti and Lahul. He was a direct descendant of the Tibetan royal dynasty of /nye-thi-tsam-po/ the first king of Tibet, who migrated from India. When he became king of Ladakh, he did not find any trace of Tibetan rule in Ladakh. The first mention of Tibetan people in Ladakh is found in *Hudud al-Alam*, a geographical treạtise composed in about 9,82-83 AD. Petech observes that the earliest tangible tokens of the existence of Tibetan in Ladakh are the inscriptions of Alchi, dating no further back than the eleventh or twelfth century. Thus, it appears that process of Tibetanization began in Ladakh after the migration of the ruling class from Central Tibet.

The /dard/ were not easy to be subjugated. They put up a stiff resistance. Francke writes, "it is not likely that nation whom Herodotus called the most warlike of all Indians, should have given in so easily, and there are tales current which speak of the stubborn resistance of the last /dard/. The /dard/ were besieged in their castle (probably by Tibetan), and when their supplies of food and water came to an end they resolved to die together. So they all assembled in the central hall of the castle, and the oldest man pushed away the stone on which stood the central pillar supporting the roof, and falling roof buried them all." A story of /dard/ of /ha-nu/ runs as follows:

> The Tibetan kings, who considered the people of /ha-nu/ their subjects, ordered them to join the rest of the population in doing forced labour. The king was opposed by an old /dard/, who told him that the /dard/ considered it below their dignity to be the slaves of a Tibetan king. This old man was now selected to work all by himself in the presence of the Tibetan king. But all means failed to make him do any work, and at last he was condemned to be immured. When the wall reached up to his neck he was asked once more if he was ready to work, but as he still refused, the wall was closed.

Still, the old man does not seem to have sacrified his life in vain for his people; for an almost destroyed rock-inscription, a few miles above the /ha-nu/ gorge, is still shown as the edict of the king who released the /dard/ from forced labour. There is a proverb in use with regard to this incident. "You cannot force labour on a /dard/ just as you cannot put a load on a dog." It is expressed in Ladakhi as : */khyi-a khu-ru Dok-pa-las/.*

To deprive the /dard/ of /ha-nu/ of their national feeling the Tibetan king prohibited the use of /dardi/ language and posted spies to report every individual who spoke /dardi/. It is typical of a conqueror to impose his language on his subjects. But the /dard/ of /da/ and / ha-nu/valleys refused to accept it. Punished for this stubborn resistance, they were condemned to death, thrown in the river or were immured. After suffering such tyranny for a long time they arrived at a compromise with the king that they would speak /dardi/ within their inner group and the Tibetan dialect outside. This practise still continues to this day, in /da/ and /ha-nu/, of Leh district and in /Dras/ and /dar-kon/ in Kar-gyil district. The /dard/ celebrate a festival every year[4] and during these few days they want to forget that they were subjugated by a Tibetan king. During this time they want to be just /dard/. On this occasion they sing a hymn, remembering the glorious past of their forefathers and name the colonies on the Indus which were founded by the /dard/. Two tribes of /dard/ still exist in Ladakh.

The dard of Dras and /dard of da and /ha-nu/, and /gar-kon/ have preserved their original languages. The dard of Dras were converted to Islam consequently, they lost their oral traditions and customs, but preserved their language called /shina/ which they use within their group. But, the dard of /dar-kon/, /da/ and /ha-nu/ did not accept the Tibetan language, and thus preserved their original customs, and their oral traditions and identity.[5]

Francke opines: disappearance of /dard/ at Khal-tse was peaceful, as they were Tibetanised. Their customs, folk traditions, etc., were wrapped in the Tibetan language. Thus, they escaped the derogatory expressions which were used for the /dard/ who wanted to preserve their identity. The Tibetan kings were so disgusted and angry with the continuous resistance of the Dard people that they did not consider them even as human beings. These Ladakhi proverbs illustrate it precisely.[6]

Dok-pa-mi as-ku-ta shing-men

(/dard/ is not a man; /as-ku-ta/[7] is not wood. That is, /dard/ are not human beings as the /as-ku-ta/ plant is not wood).

Dok-pa tem-chik

(/dard/ has one final say: that is he is stubborn and he will never change his mind).

Dok-pa Tal-la ma-bor, sta-ri chhar-la ma-bor

(Don't let /dard/ sit in a row (where respectable people have seats); do not hang an axe on a peg, that is if an axe is hung it will fall and hurt one, and similarly if a /dard/ is given respect, he will harm the person who does so.

Nevertheless, 'Francke states: "Only in a few houses at Khal-tse a prayer in /dardi/ is still rendered to the guardian spirit of the house on New Years Day, because this deity is supposed to have not yet acquired a sufficient knowledge of Tibetan."

These were the circumstances when the Tibetan language was introduced into Ladakh. However, in present the day people of Ladakh speak the Ladakhi language which is an Indo-Tibetan dialect that developed from a variant of Tibetan introduced in the region in the tenth century A.D. The stages of development of the Ladakhi language were not known as these dialects had not been studied and analysed until Grierson took the monumental task of the Linguistic Survey of India (1908), in which he grouped the languages of the country, and wrote a grammatical sketch of each dialect and language, based on the data he collected, by sending the same story in Urdu to the local teachers to be translated into local languages. This was followed by Cunningham (1853), who gives a brief sketch of the Ladakhi language based on the Grierson's work. In early twentieth century (1907), Francke, who stayed at Khal-tse, studied the spoken language and wrote a brief account of its grammatical structure. This was followed by me in 1971, and after nine years of field work I prepared a comprehensive grammar of the present day Ladakhi that was published in 1979.

Medieval History

The history of independent Ladakh is linked with Tibetan history. By the end of ninth century, Tibet was in a state of anarchy and various chieftains were engaged in endless hostilities. Under these circumstances, in about 900 AD, Shyid-lde-nyi-ma-gon, a descendant of one branch of old ruling Tibetan dynasty, was compelled to take refuge in West Tibet. With the help of the King Purang (West Tibet), Skyid-lde-nyi-ma-gon/ conquered the whole of Western Tibet, and later also Ladakh, Zangs-Kar, Spi-ti and La-hul. Thus, was laid the foundation of the first independent Ladakhi dynasty, says a C.L. Datta,[8] /pal-gyi-gon/ or /pal-gyi-lde-rik-pa/, the eldest son of /skyi-lde-nyi -ma-gon/, inherited or conquered Ladakh for himself, after the death of his father.

Starting from 950 to 1842, Ladakh remained an independent country. The kings of the first dynasty have the prefix /lha-chhan/ attached to their names and ruled till mid-fifteenth century. The second dynasty originating from the second branch of the dynasty had the suffix /Nam -gyal/ added to their names. L. Petech points out that some of the names of the kings bear Sanskrit names, like Utpala, Naglug, Gebhe, etc. He quotes Tucchi, "there is a likelihood that Utpala belongs to the same group of Aryan-speaking clans, which in about the same period, broke into Western Tibet." Petech writes further "we don't know whether this family adopted itself to the new surroundings so as to be completely Tibetanized or the old rulers ousted the new ones." Utpala is remembered in the history as a powerful ruler and conqueror, other kings mentioned with such praises are Sing-ge-nam-gyal/ (1616-1642) and his son De-ldan-nam -gyal/ (1642-1694). Under these kings, Ladakh enjoyed the prestige of being a great empire, though each time it lasted only for a brief period.

From fifteenth century onwards, Ladakh experienced only a short lived peace during the reign of some powerful kings. Otherwise, Ladakh has been under constant attack and pressure from the Muslim rulers in Kashmir, India, and Tibet. The two treaties made in 1683 AD with the Mughals and Tibetans crushed the Ladakhi power and it never recovered from the blow.

The kings of eighteenth century are referred to as weak rulers and slaves to personal pleasures. This situation continued early nineteenth century. In 1834, Ladakh was conquered by the Dogras.

Modern History (since 1834)

Dogra attacked Ladakh in 1834, defeating Ladakhi forces, but the Ladakhi king was reinstalled as a vassal of Raja Gulab Singh. The constant revolts by the Ladakhi were crushed each time by Dogra forces. Finally, in 1842, Ladakh and Baltistan were annexed and were made districts of Jammu and Kashmir state.

Alexander Cunningham writes: "the measures which Maharaja Gulab Singh has taken for the maintenance of his power in Ladakh are judicious and effective. Many people grumble, but the dissatisfaction is principally confined to the upper classes who have lost their power. To the lower classes the change of government has in some respect been of a decided benefit; for although they may pay directly a large amount than formerly to the State, yet indirectly they pay a less sum, as there is now only one duty throughout the country in place of the numerous charges which were formerly exacted by all the districts Kahlons and petty Gyalos."

Thus, from 1846-1947, Ladakh continued to be relatively under peaceful officials appointed by the Maharaja of Jammu & Kashmir.

With the accession of Jammu & Kashmir State to India in 1947, Ladakh became an integral part of the Indian Union. Till 1959, Lhasa remained the centre for religious inspiration for the monks of Ladakh. But a new generation of Ladakhi started going to Srinagar, Jammu and later to other parts of the country for higher education. Ladakhi monks also started going to Banaras. For the last 10-15 years, young monks are being sent to monasteries established in India by the Tibetan to be ordained and thus are kept the fold.

August 1995

In August, 1995 the Ladakhi's long cherished dream of "Autonomous Hill Council status within Jammu & Kashmir State" was fulfilled. Thus Ladakhi have now the right to choose their own representatives and manage their own affairs.

The Ladakhi Language

The languages spoken in Ladakh (in two districts of Leh and Kargyil and their *tehsil*) including Bal-ti language spoken in Bal-ti-stan, now under the occupation of Pakistan, belong to the Sino-Tibetan subgroup of the Chinese family. The languages that belong to this subgroup spoken in India are known as the Indo-Burman group of languages. I divide this group further into two sub-groups: (i) languages spoken in the north-western Himalayan region; and (ii) the language spoken in the north-eastern Himalayan region. While in the former languages the tone is not a significant feature of their phonetic structure, the latter have a fullfledged tonal system.

Languages spoken in the Ladakh region are Ladakhi, /pu-rik/, /shi-na/ and /dardi/ also called Dok-skat. Shina is spoken in Dras/ valley of

Kar-gyil district, and /dardi/ or /Dok-skat/ is spoken in /da/, /ha-nu/ valleys of district Leh and in villages of /ba-Ta-lik/, and /shi-na/ spoken in dras valley of Kar-gyil district belong to /dard/ group of languages—a sub-group of the Indo-Aryan group of languages. Ladakhi spoken in Leh district and /pu-rik/ in Kar-gyil district, belong to the Sino-Tibetan sub-group. In the villages of Tur-tuk sub-valley and the village /bog-dang/ of the Nub-ra valley /bal-ti/ is spoken. The Bal-ti/ language also belongs to the Sino-Tibetan sub-group. The three villages of Chhu-shot in Leh valley are referred to as /bal-ti-yi-yul/ (village belonging to /bal-ti/ people), the language spoken here is also referred to as /bal-ti-yi skat/ (the /bal-ti/ language). But due to close connections with the Ladakhi speaking people over the centuries, the language spoken today by this community is greatly influenced by Leh Ladakhi. The same is true of the /bal-ti/ spoken in the /bog-dang/ village, which is influenced by the /nub-ra/ variant of Ladakhi language.

A majority of people of the Leh district speak the Ladakhi language. It has five regional varieties:

(i) /la-daks-si skat/ is spoken in the central valley that is Leh valley of Leh district.

(ii) /stot-skat/ is spoken in the regions situated on the higher altitudes of Chang-thang. It is referred to by various names /stot-skat/ (language of upper or higher region). /chang-pe skat/(language of /chang-pa/ people living in Chang-thang region).

(iii) /sham-skat/ is spoken in lower altitude area known as lower Ladakh, /sham-ma/ in Ladakhi. People living here are called /sham-ma/ or /sham-ma-pa/, the language spoken by them is also referred to as /sham-me skat/ (the language of /sham-ma/ (people of Lower Ladakh). Ladakhi living in /da/, /ha-nu/ and /gar-kon/ sub-valleys of Lower Ladakh, speak /dardi/ or /Dok-skat/.

(iv) /nub-ra-skat/ is spoken in the valley of /nub-ra/ and is also called /nub-re-skat/ (language of /nub-ra/).

(v) /Zangs-kar-ri skat/ is spoken in /Zangs-kar/ *tehsil* of Kar-gyil district.

The Ladakhi language is referred to in Ladakhi as /la-daks/si skat/ (the language of Ladakh) and as /la-daks-si spe-ra/ the spoken language of Ladakh. /la-dak-si-spe-ra/ is used in contrast to /choos-skat/ (the language of religion). Classical Tibetan is referred to as /chhos-skat/.

The written literature, translated or original, pertaining to relation or secular subjects like medicine, astrology, etc., is written in classical Tibetan.

Social Dialects

Besides regional dialects, Ladakhi has social dialects too which are spoken by the various social-groups that constitute the Ladakhi society. They are:

(i) /phal-skat/, /phal/ is derived from /phal-pa/ middle classes or common people, and /skat/ (language) hence /phal-skat/. This variety is used by and within the middle and low-classes, and also used for the middle and low-classes by the high class and the clergy.

(ii) /chhe-stak/ is spoken by the high classes, including royal families and the clergy. /chhe/ is derived from /chhen-mo/ (big, superior), and /stak/ (mark) hence /chhen-stak/—(the variety of the language which marks the superiority).

Both the varieties share the same grammatical structure, that is marking of numbers (singular or plural), tense (past, present, future), orientation, etc. They also share the same forms as far as adverbs and adjectives also concerned. It is the lexicon which sets a parallel system in the language, may it be nouns or verb stems. There are a large number of lexicon of /phal-skat/ which have independent counterparts in /chhe-stak/ but there are equally large number of lexicons which are formed by using various prefixes or suffixes which are added to the stems of /phal-skat/. To illustrate this phenomenon, simple examples are given below. Due to the complex system of the verbal behaviour of the Ladakhi society, people from the middle class end up using it wrongly and it is seen more in the speech of the lower classes.

Examples

Khong chips-si ka chhips	*/che-stak/*	He sat on
Kho ste ka zyons	*/phal-stak/*	The horse
sol-ja phul-la	*/chhe-stak/*	May I give
cha tang-nga	*/phal-stak/*	(you) tea
Khong-ngi zyab-lam nams	*/chhe-stak/*	He put on
Khoe pa gons	*/ phal-stak/*	Shoes.

There are definite social rules for using these varieties of the language. Within these varieties, that is, /phal-pa/ versus /chhe-stak/

and regional dialects, there are variations which are also socially determined. This variation shows the frequency of certain features used by a particular group of the society. There is another variety of Ladakhi known as /be-skat/ (language of /be -da/ the lowest caste and class in the hierarchical order of the Ladakhi society). This variety is marked by certain features, which set it apart from /phal-skat/ and /chhe-stak/. Besides, there is another language of /be-da/ community also called /be-skat/, which is used within the inner group, and they keep it a secret is annoyed. The whole community in annoyed if its member talks in this language or even teaches a few words to a member of the other community.

Classical Tibetan

In the process of the Tibetanisation of Ladakh after its conquest, the first step taken by the Tibetan rulers was the introduction of the Tibetan language for reading and writing, and at the spoken level, the language or dialect spoken by them. This variety has passed through various stages before it acquired the present form of the Ladakhi language.

In 1215 A.D., the king of Ladakh /ngos-Dub-gon/ ordered that all novices should be sent to Tibet for studies and ordination. This not only made the Ladakhi absolutely dependant on Tibet for religious studies, but it also deprived them from developing their own philosophical and literary traditions. In those days only monks were literate and a few members among the laity studied secular subjects like astrology and medicine. Later, the local /am-chi/ (doctor) and /on-po/ (astrologer) taught the next generation. But no regular schools developed in Ladakh for such studies.

The Tibetan language, in which all the Buddhist literature, religious or secular, translated or originals, is still in use for reading and writing. Perhaps this was the variety spoken in the seventh century in Central Tibet. As we have it was analysed, and then a script was evolved for writing purposes in the seventh century. The scholar, who did this pioneering work for the Tibetan language, which later became an instrument for the spread of the religious empire of Tibet was /thom-me sam-bho-Ta/, commonly pronounced by Ladakhi as /thum-mi-sam-bho -Ta/. He was sent to Nalanda University to study Sanskrit and to analyse the Tibetan language, and thus to evolve a script. Because of his profound scholarship, he was given the Sanskrit name/Sambota/

which was added to his Tibetan name/thom-mi/. During his time, he was the only scholar in Tibet who knew two languages, i.e., Tibetan and Sanskrit. He wrote a detailed grammar of the language and envolved a script based on Brahmi script which was later revised. The present script in usage resembles the Bengali script. /thom-mi sam -bho-Ta/ described the structure of the language very much in the lines of Pa-Nini. He wrote eight volumes, out of which only two are available. Perhaps, during the reign of /lang-dar-ma/, when all the literature pertaining to Buddhism was destroyed, /thom-mi sam-bho-Ta/ works might have met the same fate. Later, based on the available works /sum-chu-pa/ and /stak-juk/, jointly referred to as /sum-stak/ two volumes */rde-snying-pa/* and */rde-sar -pa/* were written. The names suggest that */rde-snying-pa/* was the earliest of the two works. They are actually a collection of lexicon. Ladakhi scholars believe that the lexicon of the present day Ladakhi resembles the lexicon given in /rde-snying-pa/. This belief is based more on assumption rather than on any authentic and scientific study.

Ladakhi Language vis-a-vis Classical Tibetan

The Ladakhi language, over a period of nine centuries, has passed through various stages before attaining its present form. After the seventh century, the interim stages of Tibetan languages or dialects spoken in Tibet or in its neighbourhood were never analysed. The Indo-Tibetan dialects spoken in India were also not studied, hence it is extremely difficult, if not impossible, to state whether the contemporary form of Ladakhi is derived directly from classical Tibetan or to come to any conclusion as regards the stage at which it branched off from the speech variety introduced in this region in tenth or eleventh century. It is also not known at what stage this speech variety branched off from the speech variety analysed by /thon-mi-sum-bho-Ta/. The speech variety introduced in Ladakh in the tenth or eleventh century had already distanced itself from the classical Tibetan by three centuries years. After the conquest, in 10th century, the region was given the name/la-daks/, and therefore, subsequently this speech variety came to be known as /la-daks-si skat/ (Language of Ladakh).

The present day Ladakhi has a lexicon which can be derived from the classical Tibetan language. As stated above, the Ladakhi scholars of the classical Tibetan language think and believe that the lexicon of the present day Ladakhi are similar to the lexicon given in */rde-snying-pa/*. An authentic statement of this nature can be made only after all such languages are studied, compared and earlier stages are systematically reconstructed.

The position of the Ladakhi language in relation to classical Tibetan is the same as it is in the case of other classical languages and the modern languages in the world. For example, the position of Indo-Aryan and Indo-Iranian languages spoken in the northern and central belt of India in relation to Sanskrit, or of modern Greek to classical Greek, or of Latin to European languages or classical Arabic to modern Arabic.

Classical Tibetan languages are known in Ladakh by various names like /pod-di skat/ (the language Tibet). It also has come to be known as /bo-di/ or /bo-dik/. In the Jammu and Kashmir Government records and in the Academy of Language and Culture of Jammu & Kashmir State, it is referred to as /bo-dhi/ or /bo-di/. Recently, this name has been changed to Ladakhi' in the government school-syllabus of the Jammu & Kashmir Government. The use of 'Ladakhi' for classical Tibetan can be confusing because classical Tibetan and Ladakhi are two distinct languages.

To conclude, even if we assume that contemporary Ladakhi is derived from classical Tibetan, we still have to accept that Ladakhi today is a distinct language, with its own complete grammatical structure.

Classical Tibetan and the Monks of Ladakh

As we have noted, the monks of Ladakh, under the rule of king/ ngos-Dup-gon/ were sent to Tibet for studies and ordination in 1215 AD. This practice continued till 1959. Some of the monks and the incarnated monks of Ladakh are reputed scholars. One such scholar, Geshes Yang-dzin Lo-bzang-zot-pa of the Thik-se monastery, had been teaching and training the incarnated and other monks in the monasteries established in India by the Dalai Lama government. By and large, the monks are trained to perform religious rituals for which they learn the text by rote till they can recite it by heart. But the same is false about comprehension. Most of them can read well, some of them can write and only a few can understand the text.

After 1959, when contact with Tibet was cut, monks from Ladakh were sent to Banaras and Sarnath for higher studies. These monks received a composite education, i.e., classical Tibetan as a major subject along with Sanskrit, English, Maths, etc. On completion of their education they got jobs in government-run schools and institutions like the Academy of Languages and Culture and also at the Central Institute of Buddhist Studies in Leh. This created complex situation in the sense that these monks, while working in temporal institutions, could not attend to their spiritual duties in the monasteries. This led to the practice of proxy, that is, getting their jobs done by other monks on payment. Gradually, their interests shifted from the religious life to the lay. A large number of monks gave up monkhood and got married. This situation was found quite alarming by the monks, especially the incarnated monks. A decision was then made according to which once again the monks of Ladakh were sent to Tibetan monasteries established in India. The results have not been very encouraging. In the last decade or so, the /sip-tuk/ monastery sent more than 100 monks, of which only two or three could complete their training.

Monks who were trained in Banaras, Sarnath and in the Central Institute of Buddhist Studies in Leh, are those who are actively trying to pursue the study of classical Tibetan and literary activities of Ladakh by writing text books for the schools and other literary works.

Diglossic Situation

The Ladakhi speaking community faces a diglossic situation[9]. All Ladakhi, irrespective of their caste and creed, speak the Ladakhi language and a small part of the community uses classical Tibetan for writing purposes. The pressure of diglossic situation is observed as follows:

Classical Tibetan vis-à-vis Ladakhi Literature

The scripts for plays, drama, etc., are written in classical Tibetan, but when they are enacted or staged, the dialogues, etc., are rendered in the Leh variety, and sometimes, when the situation warrants, in other regional dialects, as well. Earlier, plays were selected from the /nam-thar/ written in classical Tibetan and in verses. During those days, actors were expected to learn the verses and then translate and explain them in Ladakhi.

AIR Impact on Ladakhi Programmes

In 1971, the All India Radio Station was set up in Leh. Ladakhi were encouraged to participate in its activities. Programmes were planned and hence scripts were written in classical Tibetan, including the news, which was read with a Ladakhi accent. The result was a total lack of impact. Later, programmes conducted in Ladakhi were introduced. Like those pertaining to agriculture, children, discussion, interviews etc. did not require a prepared script. These programmes became popular and were thoroughly enjoyed. This prompted the authorities to replace the language of the news-broadcasts from classical Tibetan to the Ladakhi language. A few lexicon coined or borrowed from classical Tibetan language, however, were retained. The most successful programmes have been of Ladakhi music and folk songs.

Diglossic Situation in the Christian Church

The Bible was translated into the classical Tibetan in nineteenth century and churches were established in Leh and She (Shey) village. A small number of Ladakhi were converted Christianity. The text of the Bible is read in classical Tibetan by a Ladakhi priest, and is then explained in the Ladakhi language. In case the priest is non-Ladakhi, he explains the same in Hindi, Urdu or Hindustani[10] and sometimes resorts to English. For writing purposes they use Urdu and English. Young Christians studying outside Ladakh learn Hindi.

Diglossic Situation in the Muslim Community :

Muslim community faces the same situation with a slight variation. They learn the classical Arabic to read their scriptures and use Urdu and English for writing but speak the Ladakhi as their mother tongue. Muslim Mullahs are trained in the Kashmir valley with Urdu as the mediums of instruction.

Bilingualism and Multilingualism in Ladakh

It is difficult to say exactly how many languages were used in ancient times in this region. The people of those days spoke a variety of Prakrit and inscriptions found are in the Brahmi, Kharosthi and Sharda scripts. Since the medieval times (tenth to about mid-nineteenth century), Ladakhi have been speaking Tibetan dialects and Buddhists use classical Tibetan for writing purposes while Muslim Ladakhi learn Arabic.

The kings of Ladakh invited Muslims from neighbouring countries to facilitate the correspondence with neighbouring States. These Muslim families settled in Ladakh and were given land. Some of them were raised to the status of /sku-taks/ (aristrocracy). Over a period of time, they adopted Ladakhi as their mother tongue and perhaps they used Persian for writing. This was another factor which added to the diglossic and multilingual situation.

Since Leh was an important centre for traders of Central Asia and other countries, they (Ladakhis) were naturally exposed to the influence on their languages. Some of the elderly Ladakhi whom I met still speak /yar-kan-di/ (the language of Yarkand). Traders coming from the plains of India must have also added their vocabulary to this multilingual situation.

From approximately the mid-nineteenth century, a new chapter starts in the political and linguistic history of Ladakh, which became an administrative unit of Jammu & Kashmir. Urdu language was introduced here as the official language. The first school was established in Leh. Revenue records were written in Urdu. This practice continues till date. In 1885, Moravian missionaries arrived in Leh, and a church each was establised in Leh and She (Shey), where services were rendered in Hindi-Urdu, Ladakhi and sometimes even in English. Missionaries opened a school where the teaching of English was introduced. This school has now grown into a prestigious school in the whole of Ladakh.

Post Independence Language Scenario

After the accession of Jammu & Kashmir State to the Indian Union, a number of schools were opened in Ladakh and the three-language formula—mother tongue, State language and English—was introduced along with Hindi as an optional subject. Thus, it is apparent that the Ladakhi have been multilingual from at least the the tenth century onwards and perhaps since time immemorial. During the Dogra Raj (1842-1947), Ladakhi came into close contact with modern languages like Urdu, Hindi and English. Educated Ladakhi can speak and write Urdu fluently. In general, all Ladakhi, irrespective of class, caste and creed, speak Ladakhi and use Urdu for writing. It has been observed that people who learnt classical Tibetan and the Urdu prefer to use Urdu script for writing Ladakhi or Tibetan.

After 1947, and especially after 1962, when Buddhist monks went to Banaras and Sarnath to study, they learnt Hindi and some of them also learnt Sanskrit. Thus, Hindi was introduced in Ladakh by these monks. But, unfortunately, the enthusiam for learning Hindi in the region was thwarted by the State Government with its pronounced bias in favour of Urdu, the State language. The Central Government too never tried to give Hindi its due place in the region.

Today, a majority of Ladakhi can speak Hindi-Urdu which is mainly due to the Indian armed forces defending the frontier region. They not only created job opportunities for the Ladakhi, thus improving their standard of living, but also provided them with rations, medical help, transport, construction meterial, etc. They have also opened schools in far-flung villages and used their defence staff as teachers. Substantial credit goes to Hindi films and film music for popularizing Hindi in Ladakh. Now TV programmes are also doing excellent work in this field.

Thus, today's Ladakh echoes not only with some prominent languages like Ladakhi, Hindu-Urdu and English, but also with a spattering of many other Indian languages. This language scenario of Ladakh becomes more eloquent during the summer when tourists, many of them foreign, add more languages thus imparting a cosmopolitan touch. But, at the spoken level, Ladakhi, with all its regional and social varieties, is the loudest and is heard distinctly; Hindi-Urdu occupies the second place. While Urdu is used by almost all educated or semi-educated Ladakhi for writing, many Ladakhi, below 40 years use Hindi. Highly qualified Ladakhi also use English.

This multi-lingualism in Ladakh is the predominant feature not only in Ladakh, but also of India as a whole, varying from region to region and the contexts in which language is used. In the context of Ladakh this means that for rituals, classical Tibetan is used by the Buddhists and Arabic is used by the Muslims. Among themselves, Ladakhi use their mother tongue, Ladakhi, but at working places, where mixed linguistic groups work, they display a remarkable flexibility by speaking Hindi-Urdu and even English.

Thus, right from the beginning, Ladakh has faced a diglossic and multilingual situation, in which it is not an exception, because such a situation is prevalent in other parts of our country.

Language in School Curriculum

In Ladakh, the first school was established in Leh during the later period of Dogra Raj. Since then Urdu has been the medium of instruction. Moravian missionaries introduced the teaching of English in the school they established. After independence, when the three–language formula was introduced Hindi became the third language. Thus, Urdu, Hindi and English are being taught in the schools today. Moreover, two classical languages, Tibetan and Arabic are also taught in schools.

Textbooks for teaching classical Tibetan in schools are written by Ladakhi scholars. This has lid to some controversy. Some scholars, like S.S. Gergan, opinied that textbooks prepared for Tibetan children by Tibetan scholars should be used in Ladakhi schools. This was opposed by the Ladakhi scholars on the ground that those textbooks chose the topics pertaining to Tibet and Tibetans, whereas the Ladakhi wrote about Ladakh in their textbooks. This understanding prevailed and the responsibility of writing of textbooks in classical Tibetan remained with the Ladakhi scholars.

Moreover, contemporary Ladakhi scholars claim that they write simple and easy classical Tibetan. They claim "we use Ladakhi lexicon and follow the grammar of the classical Tibetan." Since Ladakhi belongs to the same family, it is possible to add a grammatical constituent to the Ladakhi word. It would be like using the Hindi lexicon and adding to it Sanskrit grammatical constituent and call it simple and easy Sanskrit. To be precise, what is taught in schools is a modified version of classical Tibetan.

In government run schools, Hindi is not taught as there is no teacher provided for teaching Hindi. While in privately run schools, missionary and others, and schools under the central school system, Hindi and classical Tibetan are taught, Islamic schools prefer to teach Urdu and classical Arabic. Private schools engage Hindi teachers on a temporary basis. The wives of defence personnel posted in Leh are hired to teach Hindi. Schools established by foreign Christian organisations teach classical Tibetan, English and the state language Urdu.

Classical Tibetan, in the school curriculum, is known as /bo-di/ and recently named as the 'Ladakhi' language /bodi/ is learnt by Buddhists, but rarely by Muslims. In short, the provision of learning modern Indian languages in the state-run schools of Ladakh is limited only to Urdu. Besides, two classical languages, namely classical Tibetan (bo-di or bodhi), vis-a-vis Arabic are also taught. The teaching of English is introduced from the 6th standard. In private schools, the teaching of English and Hindi is given priority, as they follow the NCERT or Central Board syllabus. Classical Tibetan is also taught in these schools. In Islamic private schools, Arabic is taught as the classical language. A clear picture of this profile is provided by Tables 1 and 2.

TABLE 1
LANGUAGES TAUGHT IN DIFFERENT TYPES OF SCHOOLS

Types of School	*Modern Languages*	*Classical Languages*	*Others*
(1)	(2)	(3)	(4)
Government schools	Urdu	Bo-di Arabic	English
Private schools	Hindi	Bo-di	English
Islamic Private schools	Urdu	Arabic	English

TABLE 2
PROVISION FOR TEACHING MODERN AND CLASSICAL LANGUAGES IN DIFFERENT TYPES OF SCHOOLS

English	*Hindi*	*Urdu*	*Bodi*	*Arabic*
Government schools	Private schools	Government schools	Government schools	Government schools
Private schools		Islamic Private schools	Private schools	Government schools

Standard Variety of Ladakhi Languages

The Ladakhi language, has five regional dialects. One of them, /zangs-kar/ Ladakhi is spoken in the Zangs-Kar *tehsil* of Kar-gyil district, the other four dialects are spoken in the Leh district.

Any one of these dialects could have developed into a standard variety, but the Ladakhi spoken in Leh developed as the standard language for the Ladakhi, for two major reasons:

(i) Leh has been a long standing centre of local and international trade. People from various sub-valleys of the region brought their goods to the Leh bazar for sale or exchange. This age–old practice still continues.

(ii) Moreover, Leh was the seat of power till 1842. During the Dogra Raj also, Leh was the district headquarters, and since 1947, it has been so.

Hence, the language of Leh attained prestige of communication amongst the different regions of Ladakh. The Leh station of All India Radio also adopted the Leh version of Ladakhi in its programmes. But on a political level the scanario is somewhat different. In order to influence the large number of people living in other regions of Ladakh, local leaders use the specific dialect in a particular region in their political speeches. This has, to some extent, proved a blessing in disguise for the other regional dialects of Ladakh. Nevertheless, the Leh version of the Ladakhi language enjoys the prestige of being the standard variety. Hence, it is standard for the whole of the Leh district.

Modern Literature in Ladakh

The modern literature of Ladakh is written in classical Tibetan. Ladakh scholars of classical Tibetan constitute a small group of people. Most of the Ladakhi works are published by the Leh based Academy of Art, Culture and Language. Some are published by foreign organisations established in Leh, and a few are published privately by the scholars themselves. The Academy also publishes a quarterly magazine, '*Schiraza*' in classical Tibetan, but many of the articles published in it are translation of articles originally written in Urdu and occasionally in Hindi and English. The literature produced in Ladakh in the classical Tibetan language is not understood by the majority of Ladakhi, not even by those who have learnt the language at schools.

The saddest state is that of the folk literature. Folk songs and folk tales were collected and recorded on cassettes, but while it was transcribed and prepared for printing, it was translated into classical Tibetan. Unfortunately, this recorded material was not preserved.

Shri Nawang Tshering, who is currently in–charge of the Academy of Language and Culture, made the following statement in Hindi about one of the publication, which reveals the state of the language: "We are publishing a book of Russian fairy tales, translated from English into Ladakhi, and, he added disdainfully, "we tried our best to correct the grammar, but we were so frustrated that we left it as it is, but you (*referring* to me), will like it."

Ladakhi scholars also claim that their writings are not understood by Tibetans, who use classical Tibetan language for literary purposes as they (Ladakhi) use the pure Tibetan words, meaning thereby Ladakhi use archaic forms. In their opinion, "Tibetans do not understand what we write, but when they look up these words in a dictionary, they found them there."

Most of the literature written in Ladakhi consists of articles, descriptions and poems. Poetry is very popular among these scholars. Often a 'Mushaira' (poetry-recitation session) is organised and enjoyed by the audience. In these Muslim Ladakhi also participate. These scholars write their poems and songs in colloquial Ladakhi using the Persian script. Their poems and songs are enjoyed thoroughly.

Language Scene at Present

The language scene may, at present, appear to be chaotic, but it is possible that in the due course of time, it will evolve a style of its own which one day may be known as the written variety of Ladakhi, and will be used for creative literature which is best produced in the mother tongue as it deals with the life of people, their sorrows and joys, social justice and injustice, the experiences of common people. In other words, literature will record the social history of the people. Apart from the few, the literature available is largely restricted to kings, palaces, monasteries, or incarnations.

The Ladakhi People and the Ladakhi Language

The spoken variety 'Ladakhi' is not yet used for writing, primarily because it was never analyzed and the script was not developed for writing. In the, 70's (1971-1979), this language was analyzed and a 'Ladakhi Grammar' was written (1979). A script has been evolved. But still a school prescribed grammar is essential if Ladakhi want to read and write in their mother tongue.

However, the required enthusiasm and interest for using 'Ladakhi' for reading or writing is lacking, for which there are many reasons. They are:

(i) Psychological inhibition or hesitation, firstly because for centuries Ladakhi scholars have been using classical Tibetan for reading and writing purposes, and old habits persist. Secondly, as stated above, no school grammar has been prepared yet.

(ii) The population being small in number (about one lakh) government and private agencies do not find it economical to promote such a project.

(iii) The present government (Autonomous Hill Council) thinks, perhaps rightly, that the use of Ladakhi language will add to the burden of children who are already taught three languages at school. Though this problem can be tackled by phasing the teaching of languages, for example, primary education in mother tongue using bilingual approach (as has been done in many tribal areas) and then shifting to Hindi, and later on English.

(iv) The minority of Ladakhi scholars write creative and other literature in classical Tibetan without any concern of its being read or not. This attitude towards 'Ladakhi' may lead to its extinction.

Brief Sketch of Ladakhi Script and Grammar

Ladakhi language, in all have five vowels and 33 consonants. The script suggested and being given below is based on my works: Ladakhi Phonetic Reader, Ladakhi Grammar and Socio-linguistic study of language variation in Ladakhi. The script suggested is a modified version of the Tibetan script used for writing classical Tibetan. The language, through centuries, has undergone changes and thus new sounds have emerged. Consonant clusters have been simplified and some of them have developed into independent sounds. Taking all these aspects into consideration, the script for writing the Ladakhi is proposed as follows:

Vowels:

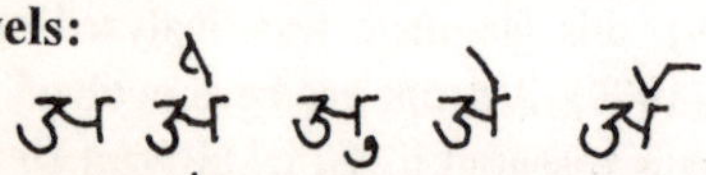

a i u e o

Consonants:

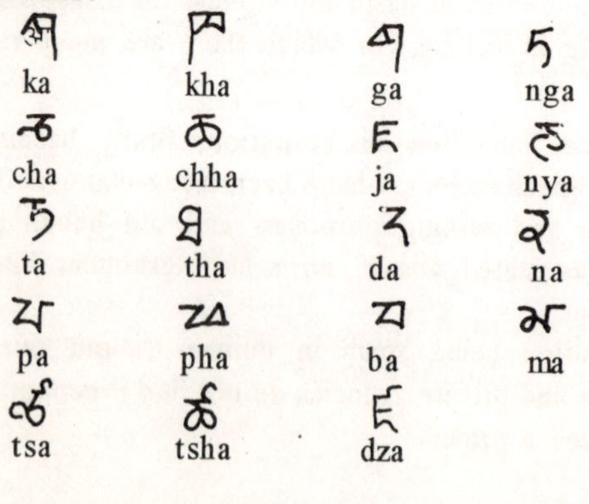

Ta (or ṭa)	Tha (or tha)	Da (or da)			

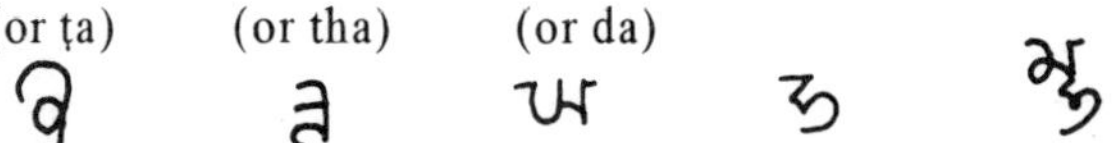

zya (or ž)	za	ya	ha	lha	

ṛa	ḷa	wa	sha (or ṣ)	sa	s

Besides, there is a retroflex flapped consonant /r̥/, which occurs in onomatopoeic words and in few other words, for example:

bu-r̥um	Sound produced when something is thrown into water (river, stream, etc.)
ba-r̥ak	Sound produced by boiling liquid, like milk, water, etc.
pi-r̥ak	Sound produced in water by fish leaping about in the water. /pi -r̥ak/ is also used when a person is speechless due to fear, astonishment, etc.

Thus, Ladakhi has five vowels, that is a, i, u, e and o. All consonants have inherited vowel sound /a/. All vowels occur initially and finally. Initially the vowels are written in their full form as given above, and with consonant medially and finally. The 'Matra' are used as in Hindi, e.g.

Ka Ki Ku Ke Ko

The length is not a meaningful phenomenon in Ladakhi and thus not marked, but the inherited vowel /a/ is the final position of a syllable is lengthened, for example :

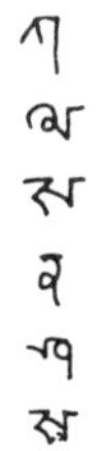

Kā	-	pillar
lā	-	pass
Sā	-	earth
nā	-	nose
shā	-	meat
Sā (or ṣa)	-	hair and so on.

/i/ and /u/ are relatively long in the final position. Vowels get slightly nasalized in the vicinity of a nasal sound.

In all, there are 33 consonants, out of which only nine occur in the final position, and a word can also end with a vowel. They respectively are:

ག	ད	བ	ར	ལ	ས	ན	མ	ང
g	d	b	r	l	s	n	m	ng

ཨ	ཨི	ཨེ	ཨུ	ཨོ
a	i	e	u	o

(i) Ladakhi is a monosyllabic language, each syllable marked in writing. Therefore, the distributional terms like initial, medial and final refer to: syllable initial, syllable medial and syllable final. A word can be a combination of various syllables.

(ii) The voiced consonants /ga, da, ba/, are pronounced as vioceless /ka, ta, pa/ respectively in the final position before a pause and also if the following syllable has a voiceless sound, but followed by voiced consonant they retain their original voicing quality, i.e., they remain /ga, da, ba/. The inherited vowel /a/ in the final consonant of a syllable is not pronounced.

Examples

mig → mik eye
lag-pa → lak-pa hand
but pag-ma → pag-ma bride, because nasal /m/ in the following syllable is voiced.

Structure of a Noun Phrase

A Ladakhi sentence consists of one or more noun phrases; a noun-phrase has various constituents in a phrase. To illustrate it in detail is not possible here; some examples, however, are given below:

a-	po-mo	ring-mo	ma-	rde-mo
|	|	|	|	|
that	girl	tall	very	beautiful

that tall very beautiful girl ....

The number indicating constituent is added at the end of noun phrase, which is followed by a case suffix.

a	po-mo	ring-mo	ma	rde-mo	gun	-ni
↓	↓	↓	↓	↓	↓	→
that	girl	tall	me	beautiful	plural, marker	Ergated Suffix

The adjective forms the part of the noun phrase. Plural is marked by adding /-gun or kun, or sak/; numbers and words like/tshang -ma/ (all), /mang-po/ (many) etc. Then there are pronouns which are used in place of nouns.

They are:

nga	nga-zya	nya-tang
I	We	We

First person plural pronoun shows inclusive-exclusive distinction.

(i) nga-zya (we) is exclusive
nga-tang (we) is exclusive

(ii) khyot khyo-rang nye-rang
you you you
/khyot/ is used in intimate context, for God, and also to convey derogatory meaning.

(iii) /khyo-rang/ is used for people of equal status, in informal situations.

(iv) /nye-rang/ is used to address the people higher in status and in formal situations. Its plural is /nye-zya/.
/khyo-zya/ (you) is used as the plural of /khyo-rang/, but is less frequent. Generally plural marker -/gun/ is added to /khyo-rang/ and sometimes even to /kho-zya/. Other pronouns take plural marker /gun, kun, or sak/. Only /rang/ is used as a singular in the most intimate situation, and also for respect with kinship terms.

(v) /kho/ (he) is used in informal situations; and for younger persons.

(vi) /khong/ (he) is used for a person to whom respect is to be given.

Third person pronouns of Ladakhi are comparable with Hindi /tu, tum, āp/.

Demonstrative pronouns are /i-bo/ (this), and /a-bo/ (that); /o-te-bo/ (that); /te-bo/ that. This distinction is made when an object or a person in question is away from the speaker in terms of space/ distance.

te-bo	Away but in a close distance
a-bo	Away in a far distance
o-te-bo	Further away in distance but within sight

Interrogative Pronouns

su	who
ka-bo	which
chi	what

Indefinite Pronouns

tshang-ma	All
kha-chik	Some
mang-po	Many

Reflexive Pronouns

-rang is added to the pronominal stem. For example:

nga-rang	Myself
Khyo-rang-rang	Yourself

Then there are adjectives like /ghyl-la/ (good), /rde-mo/ (beautiful), and a large number of adjectives which are derived, e.g. /shet-chan/ (brave) /Dis-Kan/ (written), etc., and the Indicative adjectives. Then there are numerals which Ladakhi can count from /chik/ (one), to /bum/ (one lakh), and some can count up to /tung-chur/ (ten crores).

The grammatical category, which expresses the relationship of a noun with the other nouns and the verb, is called case. Ladakhi language has seven cases. They are:

(i) *Direct Case:* It is used for expressing the subject of the intransitive verb. In some cases, the subject of the transitive verb is also expressed by direct case, like /za/ (eat), /thung/ (drink) which can optionally take eragative case, and /jal/ (visit), and the direct object, except of /lta/ (see), /nyan/ (hear), etc. This case is left unmarked.

(ii) *Ergative Case:* It is used for expressing the subject of transitive verbs, except a few verbs. This case realised in various forms. If a stem ends in a consonant, the ergative case is composed of the final consonant + /i/ if the stem ends in /i, u, e/ suffix /yi/ is added, if the stem ends in /a/ it changes into /e/ and if stem ends in /o/, /e/ suffix is added.

In continuous speech often the 'Sandhi' rule operates and /o/ changes to /e/.

(iii) *Dative Case:* This case expresses various relations:

(a) for indirect object,

(b) for expressing possession,

(c) for expressing allocative relationship,

(d) for expressing direction, and

(e) for the direct object of verbs like /lta/ (see), /nyan/ (hear), etc.

If a noun stem ends in a vowel, the /-a/ suffix is added; in consonant like /-b, -g, -m, -n and -ng/ the suffix is formed with the final consonant of the stem + /a/, and if the stem ends in /-d, -s, -r, -l/ the suffix /-la/ is added.

(iv) *Instrumental Case:* It is marked by the suffix -nang. It is used for expressing the instrumentality.

(v) *Associative Case:* It is expressed either an inherent, or a casual association of thing or a person with some other thing or person. It is marked by the suffix /nang-nyam-po/.

(vi) *Ablative Case:* It expresses the separation of a thing or person from another thing or person. It is marked by adding the suffix /-ne/.

(vii) *Genetive Case:* It is used to express the relationship of something or someone with something or someone. The genetive suffixes are formed as : if a stem ends in a consonant, the genetive case is composed of the final consonant of the stem plus /i/, if stem ends in vowels /i, e, u/, then /-yi/ suffix is added; if it ends in /a/ it changes to /e/; and if it ends in /o/, /e/ is added to the stem, but 'Sandhi' rule operates and /o + e/ changes to /e/.

Table 3 illustrates this process:

TABLE 3

Direct case	*Ergative case*	*Dative case*	*Instrumental case*	*Associative case*	*Albative case*	*Genetive case*
nga (I)	nge (II)	nga-a (to me)	nga-nang (by through me)	nga-nang nyan-po (with me)	nga-ne (from me)	nge (my)
So-nam (proper name)	So-nam mi	So-nam la so-nam (to so-nam)	So-nam-nang (by through so-nam)	So-nam nang-nyam -po (with so-nam)	So-nam ne (from so -nam)	So-nam mi (of so -nam)

Instrumental case is used preferably with inanimate objects. For example:

nge	snyu-qu	-nang	yi-ge	Dis-pin
↓	↓	↓	↓	↓
Ist Person Ergative Case	Pen Noun	With Instru-mental Case	Letter Direct Object	Wrote Verb

The Ladakhi verbal system is complex and elaborate and is different from that of other Indian languages.[12] The Ladakhi verb stem expresses several features of orientation towards an action.

Besides, the action is located in the present time, or prior to it, or is going to take place in future with element of probability, degree of probability, likelihood, etc., of its occurence, the aspectual characteristics of an action like its continuous nature, its completion, etc. The verb phrase also expresses the important semantic components, that is speaker's involvement or commitment, speaker's witnessing the action or not, his knowledge of the same or otherwise (direct or indirect), his uncertainty or otherwise the varacity of the action; the fact that speaker himself feels or experiences something or reports on someone else's action, the fact that something appears to be 'X' based on the outward appearance of reality (whether actually true or not) all these semantic distinctions are marked explicity in the verb phrase. These semantic distinctions are termed as orientation in the Ladakhi grammar. The minute details expressed by the phrase of Ladakhi is amazingly interesting.

Ladakhi speaking persons feel that their involvement with the environment, and interactions with universe are the factors which influence or affect their life and thinking. They also, believe that their actions, thinking and evolution of the environment also shape the universe and its continuous non-static situation. This is why they find that their reaction to the environment and universe is fundamentally different from those who speak other Indian languages.

Ladakhi verb forms can be classified into finite and non-finite forms. The Ladakhi verb form is composed of a verb stem followed by one or more suffixes. The verb stems fall into two basic categories: (a) transitive and (b) intransitive. Ladakhi has several pairs of sub-systems in the verbal composition resulting in an elaborate pattern.

This is a very brief account, rather a gist, of the verb stem or verb phrase. To illustrate, below a verb phrase is formed, an example is given below:

so - nam	- la	chu	bring -	tshar -	thub -	gos -	sat -	pin
proper name	Dative case	Noun direct case	Transtive verb stem	compe- tive	Abili- tative	Desi derative	Repor- tive	Past suffix
Sonam		Water	Cross					

Sonam had the ability to desire to have finished crossing the water (river) so has been heard or known through some other sources.

This translation is quite literal hence inadequate and may be even clumsy. It means that (It) has been heard (that) Sonam wanted it, and could cross the river.

In Ladakhi language the following punctuation marks are commonly used:

Full stop (.) marks completion of a sentence.
Comma (,) marks a slight or break between parts of a sentence.
Semi-colon (;) marks a division greater than a comma in a sentence.
Dot (.) marks the syllabic boundary.
Space ( ) marks the word boundary.

Ladakhi and Other Languages

Ladakhi speakers have always been in contact with other language speakers. From ancient times and more since the nineteenth and twentieth centuries, the Ladakhi have been in constant contact with Hindi-Urdu Kashmiri speaking people and, to some extent, with English speaking people as well.

Ladakhi, in earlier times, as a trade centre, had all the favourable circumstance to have developed a pidgin a language as the Ladakhi came in contact with traders speaking various languages. But, in spite of this situation, no pidgin language developed in this region, perhaps because only a small section of the population communicated with the traders, and also because the range of communication was limited.

From the tenth century onwards, in the process of Tibetanisation of the region, which started in the eleventh century, the conqueror king successfully managed the people to give up their language, and to accept the Tibetan dialect.

Simultaneously, the monks were sent to Tibet to learn classical Tibetan. Till the late nineteenth century, perhaps they were the only educated people. Monks preached the Buddhism and they attained this knowledge through Tibetan. Both monks and classical Tibetan claimed and continue to claim the respect of the Ladakhi. Literature connected with religion and other secular subjects like medicine, astrology, etc., were being translated from Sanskrit, Prakrit and Pali into Tibetan since seventh century. Tibetans have been great translators. They even translated the proper names with such perfection that it is easy to reconstruct them in Sanskrit. For example:

/buddha/ :	/sang-gyas/, /sang/ (Prakashs), /gyas/ (Vistara),
/shweta ta-ra/ :	/dol -kar/, /dol/ is derived from /dol-ma/ (ta -ra), and /kar/ (white).
/manjushree/ :	/jam -pal/, (commonly pronunced as janspal) /jam/ is from /jam -po/ (soft, beautiful), and /pal/ is from /pal -dan/ with splen-dour).

But they did not translate Mantra, e.g. /om-ma-ni pad -me hum/ and other Mantra; and some lexicon were also retained, e.g. /shri/ /tsan -dan/ (chan-dan), /ganga/, /panDita/, etc. These words are used in Ladakhi as well. The proper names of Ladakhi and Tibetan have the same origin, but Ladakhi proper names are different in shape. Here is an example:

Ladakhi Dol-Kar → Do-Ka in Tibetan

Ladakhi Kun-dzes → Ku-dze in Tibetan (u in Ku- is nasalized).

The language which have smoothly penetrated into Ladakhi society are Hindi-Urdu and Kashmiri. Kashmiri could not compete in the medieval period of history. The Tibetan language became the vehicle for learning all about religion. All efforts made before that by Kashmiri Pandits to preach religion were pushed to the background and yet some Kashmiri words have become a part of the Ladakhi language. Later on, during Dogra rule, Urdu gained acceptance and this language became the means of getting jobs. After 1947, Hindi came to Ladakh with defence personnel, and Hindi films and music. Tourism enhanced the importance of English. Being in frequent use, and sharing of India's cultural ethos, Hindi Urdu vocabulary has been absorbed in Ladakhi. To illustrate this phenomenon, some words are given below:

(i) *Kashmiri Words or Hindi-Urdu Words vie Kashmiri:*

Thul	Egg
bok-cha	A bundle to be carried on the back
tak-bak	A broad shallow dish
dik	A cauldron

(ii) *Hindi-Urdu*

tha-li	A round shallow dish
Kang-Top	Cap, from Hindi Kantop
Sur-na	An instrument similar to shahwai
gan-Ti	Bell, from Hindi-Urdu ghanti
galat	Wrong
Thik	correct
hoshiyar	clever
ma -ja	enjoyment from Hindi-Urdu maza
Sha-bash	bravo (used in folk dances)
Jam-mat	companion (found in folk songs) etc.

Some names of the vegetables :

a -lu (potato)	from ālu
go -bi (cauliflower)	from go-bhi
pa-lak (spinach)	from pālak.

The interesting feature is the use of /ki/ (that), this conjunction has embedded itself in the Ladakhi language so well that it is not easily noticed.

According to Emeneau, India is a "Linguistic area", and languages spoken in India keep continuously influencing each other. Ladakhi is no exception. The nasal system of Ladakhi, to a great extent, has directly come under the spell of Indo-Aryan nasal system. It may not be long before the verbal system of Ladakhi has its powerful influence on Hindi-Urdu through the "Ladakhi-Hindi-Urdu" speech variety.

REFERENCES

1. Ladakhi words, including the names of languages spoken in the region, and the names of various *Tehsil* and districts, are phonetically hyphenated after each syllable, in order to achieve clarity in pronouncing them. Ladakhi is a syllabic language and each syllable is a meaningful unit. Ladakhi, Hindi,

Urdu and Sanskrit words are not marked for plurality by adding /-s/ instead following verb indicates it. Some of known village and river names starts with capital letters, otherwise all Ladakhi words and personal names start with small letters and given in slash, for example /la-daks-si skat/ (Ladakhi language), because capital letters are used for retroflex sounds.

2. The historical statements are based mainly on and quoted from the following works; for futher details these may be consulted:
   (a) Alexander Cunningham, *Ladak, Physical, Statistical and Historical, with Notes of the Surrounding Countries,* London, 1854.
   (b) A.H. Francke, *History of Western Tibet* (1853); *Ladakh* (1905), and other works.
   (c) C.L. Datta, *Ladakh and Western Himalayan Politics* (1819-1848), 1973.
   (d) L. Petech, *The Kingdom of Ladakh, C.* 950-1848 AD., 1977 and other works.
3. *Chronicles of Ladakh* is a documented history of Ladakh written in Tibetan. There are five manuscripts which were utilised by A.H. Francke in preparing his edition. This was revised by F.W. Thomas.
4. In one year it is celebrated in /da/ and next year in /gar-kon/, in third in the village, which is now in Pakistan occupied area, thus there i- a gap of one year.
5. If this oral tradition is not recorded and preserved now, it will become extinct and will be a great loss to posterity, as this is the only important source to unravel the past history of this area until now.
6. With a development programme in the region, /dard/ are being educated. One of the /dard/ of /ha-nu/, who is an engineer has been married to the daughter of a respectable family of Leh.
7. /as-Ku-ta/ is a short plant with thick trunk found on the mountains. Its length is so short that it is of no use.
8. C.L. Datta is perhaps the only historian who refers to the dynasty as the Ladakhi dynasty. Otherwise, the dynasty is often referred to as the Tibetan dynasty. It may be interesting to note that, according to historians, Tibetan and others, the first king of Tibet migrated to Tibet from India, but is never referred to as Indian dynasty, though his dynastic name / Ikshawaku Vansh/ has been preserved in the Tibetan translation /ku-ram-shing-pe dung-gyut/.
9. The diglossic situation of a language means a situation in which a community speaks their mother tongue, but uses another language for reading and writing.
10. I call it Hindi-Urdu because, first, at the spoken level, both these languages are the same, and secondly, the difference created at the written level is artificial. This is because the language called Hindi is loaded with Sanskrit

vocabulary and Urdu with Arabic and Persian vocabulary. But, for a writer of Hindi or Urdu, no vocabulary is restricted or prohibited. Therefore, 'I am convinced that these are two facets or two styles of the same language'. Ashok Kelkar's book *Hindu.*

11. Any script can be utilized to write a language. Many Ladakhi use Persian script for writing Ladakhi.

12. I always feel that Ladakhi speakers, while speaking Hindi, must find Hindi quite inadequate to express themselves properly, Prof. William Labove, Faculty of Arts and Sciences, University of Penylvania, Philadelphia, wrote to me after having read through Ladakhi grammar:

    "I used the evidential system as a way of illustrating Whorf's ideas about how language influences the way we think about the world, through determining what we have to say. The point has been made about other evidential systems that speakers find it difficult to use a language that ignores the fine distinction they make about how certainly a thing is known. Is that true for Ladakhis? What happens when they talk in Hindi ? Are they embarassed about the use of bold statements that don't specify the kinds of inferences they are making? or Do they find other ways of compensating for the lack of suffixes?"

3
DEVELOPMENT OF THE LADAKHI LANGUAGE

Fr. C.D. Sebastian

Introduction

Man's ability to learn the language of his group and pass it on to others, and thus transmit experience, is the basis for the development of culture. Man has various ways of developing culture through language. By means of language, a human being can hear and learn about the past experiences of others. Thus language becomes the string that unites the past with the present and the future of a people. And the development of a language of a people is necessary for the existence of that particular people with all its distinctive traits of culture. Ladakhi is a language which gathers momentum in pursuit of progress and growth.

Being a student who is very interested in linguistic studies and in the light of my study and research in the north-eastern part of India, for four years, and the last three years of learning and growth of Ladakhi, I do appreciate the progress and growth of Ladakhi. This article is an outcome of that great appreciation.

Taxonomy

The Ladakhi language belongs to the Sino-Tibetan family. There are more than four hundred Sino-Tibetan languages and dialects. 'A third of the population of the globe speaks one or more of these languages'.[1] Sino-Tibetan languages are divided into six groups: Sinitic (Chinese); Daic (Thai); Bodic (Tibetan, etc.); Burmic (Burmese, etc.); Baric (Bodo, Garo, etc.) and Karenic (Karen).[2] Bodic division can be divided into: West Bodish Unit, Central Bodish Unit, South

Bodish Unit, etc. And in the West Bodish Unit comes Balti (Purik), Ladakhi and Lahuli[3]. Paul K. Benedict divided it in the following way[4]:

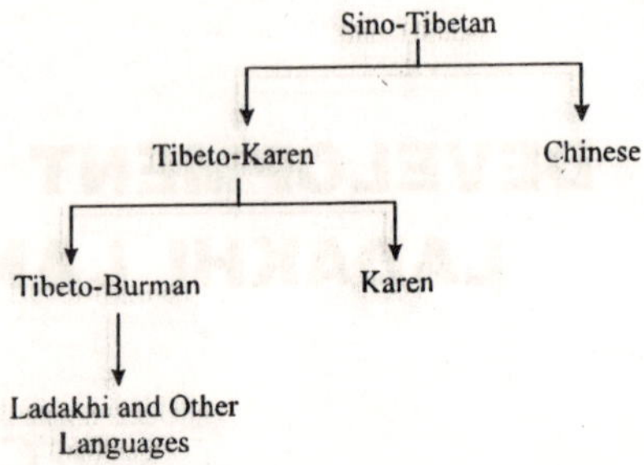

Formation of Ladakhi Alphabet

According to scholars, before the seventh century, Ladakhi had no script. It was, with Thon-mi-Sambhota, the script was formulated for Tibetan as a whole. As the opinion of contemporary scholar Jamyang Gyaltson, Thon-mi-Sambhota must have made the grammar according to the language of Ladakhi.[5] The script had thirty consonants and four vowels. And the script invented by Thon-mi-Sambhota is used in both Tibetan and Ladakhi.

Diverse Opinions in Naming the Language

Scholars vary about the name of the language. Some are of the opinion that the original name, Tibetan, must be preserved, because basically it is the same root language, whether it is spoken in Baltistan or in Sikkim, in Bhutan or in Ladakh. They argue that the Tibetan language can be the common property of different communities belonging to different countries, as English is in the USA. and the UK.[6] While others hold the view that the name should be 'Boti'. Still others want the name to be 'Ladakhi'. As far as the author is concerned, he deals with the language of Ladakh, so in the paper, it as Ladakhi. It is true that we cannot separate Ladakhi and Tibetan into two water-tight compartments, because the language is the same in both with only a slight difference in accent, pronunciation and colloquial formulations.

Development and Growth of Ladakhi

Though Ladakhi as such is derived from Tibetan, it developed in its own way down the ages as a language. Some refer to it as a dialect, but it is far more than a dialect. In a real sense it is a language. The following points prove this claim:

Ladakhi Grammar and Dictionary

The grammar as such, is the same in Tibetan and Ladakhi. But grammar books have been written and published in Ladakhi. Jamyang Gyaltson published a grammar book named '*Norboo-Gyan*'. The Ladakhi dictionary was published by the Ladakh Ecological Development Group in 1991.

Ladakhi Literature

There is a lot of distinct Ladakhi literature. Many genres, brought out by various authors, in Ladakhi, they include story, drama, essay, history, poetry such as like, *Chimet Ster* by S.S. Gergan, *Kun-Gsal Melong* by Tashi Rabgias (both history books), *Zun Pang pe Dasbun* by Jamyang Gyaltson and *Tis Sal Ke Bad* by Thupstan Paldan (both stories), *Singye Namgyal* (drama) by Nanyang Gyaltson and poems by Tashi Rabgias, Akbar Ladakhi and Phande Lekshad. These poems have social and secular themes. Folk songs of Ladakh have been collected and published by Tashi Rabgias. The themes of the folk songs are romantic and pastoral. Among the prose works, Gyaltson's 'Rchon sdig skyranga' is prominent. It is important to note here that the many translations of Kangyur and Stangyur from Sanskrit to Tibetan were made by Ladakhis, like Phagpa Sherap and Tsultim Gyalwa.

Newspapers, Magazines and Other Publications

There are number of publications which gave a marvellous thrust to the progress and development of Ladakhi. I list some of them here: *Phonya*, *Stendel*, *Ladags Melong*, *Sherabzom*, *Shesring Melong* and *Lo-Khor gi deb* (containing an anthology of Ladakhi writings). It is praiseworthy that when the Radio Station and other information centres were not established in Leh-Ladakh, a newsletter *Yargyal Kongphel* was brought out periodically by Tashi Rabgias, to give general awareness to the public on development in various fields. At present there is no Ladakhi daily. But the day is not very far when a daily newspaper in Ladakhi will reach the people of Ladakh.

Ladakhi Textbooks in Schools

Textbooks like the Ladakhi Reader have been prepared by a select committee for the schools in Ladakhi. Now such readers are available for classes from I to X. And Ladakhi is being taught in every school. There is a generation in Ladakh who cannot read and write Ladakhi, by no fault of their own. It happened because in the educational system of the past they were not taught Ladakhi. Now students are taught Ladakhi in the schools and in the times to come all will be literate in the Ladakhi language.

Cultural Programmes

Various cultural programmes like songs, folk dances and drama are presented and enacted in Ladakhi. One can witness all these in their pomp and show and in regal splendour during the Ladakhi festival which takes place every year from the first to fifteenth of September.

There are drama clubs like 'Lamdon" and "Nyamso". The Ladakh Cultural Academy is an important agent which propagates and encourages cultural programmes in Ladakhi.

Radio Programmes

A commendable job is being done by AIR, Leh, with regard to Ladakhi programmes. The AIR station in Leh has made a remarkable progress down through the years since its inception. There are regular broadcasts of news bulletin, dramas, folk songs, language classes, and other programmes in Ladakhi. And the language which is being made use of must be considered as the standard Ladakhi form. It clearly proves that Ladakhi has got developed to stand as an independent language.

Other Features in the Progress and Development

Assimilation of other Languages :

When a language assimilates words and expressions from other languages for better communication, the language grows.

In daily usage, many words from other languages can be heard in Ladakhi, particularly in the Leh town and suburbs. Though some may say that such elements from foreign languages should be eliminated, the language actually gets enriched by the interaction of many tongues. Some words can be shown as an example:

Gādi	—	Vehicle
Thīk	—	all right
Ālu	—	Potato
Tul	—	egg

Jahāz	—	aeroplane
Phulgobhi	—	cauliflower
Thāli	—	plate (for eating)
Bilkul	—	definitely
Dāk	—	post (mail)

These words are taken in Ladakhi either from Hindi, Urdu or Kashmiri.

Use of Honorific Forms

The beauty and sweetness of Ladakhi lie in the use of honorific forms. This is an integral part of Ladakhi. Honour is generally given to strangers, elders and respectable people. 'LE' is used at the end of a sentence for expressing politeness and respect. 'LE' is added to proper names also to express the same. As for example:

Sol-ja—honorific term for tea, that is, the tea offered to someone else, or of someone other than that of the speaker, it is simply 'Cha'.

Nomo-le— O! girl (or young girl)

Khamznag-in-a-le— Are you well.

Conclusion

Some may say that there are many dialects in Ladakhi itself, and wonder which should be considered as standard Ladakhi. And the language spoken in Ladakh is variable with probably every village, or rather every valley, has its own dialect. To this question I answer that Leh is the capital of Ladakh, and the language spoken in Leh should be considered standard Ladakhi. Again the language on radio and in other publications shall be the standard Ladakhi. Whatever may be the various claims and views of those in the sphere of linguistics, let us appreciate and acknowledge the progress and growth of Ladakhi as a language.

REFERENCES

1. Robert Shafer: *Introduction of Sino-Tibetan* (Wiesbadan : Otto Harrasowitz), 1974, p. 1.
2. *Ibid.*
3. *Ibid.*, p. 2.
4. Paul K. Benedic : *Sino-Tibetan: A Conspectus*, Cambridge University Press; 1972, p. 6.

5. Jamyang Gyaltsan : 'Sabda Vidhya', In : Ladakh Prabha (3), Tashi Paljor (ed.), C.I.B.S., Leh, 1985, p. 58.
6. Tsewang, Lobzang: 'Problem of Ladakhi language and its solution', In : *Ladakhi Prabha* (3); *Tashi Paljor* (ed.), C.I.B.S., Leh, 1985, p. XXXVIII.

TOURISM

4

BODI SPEECH AND THE BUDDHIST MONASTIC LINEAGES IN LADAKH

Anandamayee Ghosh

Bodi is a phonetic simplification of the Bodyig. *Bod* means Tibet and *yig* means letters or writings. Again to non-Buddhist inhabitants of Ladakh prefers to use Bodi for the language spoken by the Buddhists.

In Ladakh the majority of population are Buddhists. Among others Muslims and Christians happen to be the local inhabitants. For the last few decades a sizeable number of non-Buddhist military personal belonging to the other parts of India as well as government officials of J & K State and those officials of government of India have reached there for the sake of service. As a result of that the Bodi speech has now been cornered and become limited among the Ladwags pa or Maryul pa, Purig pa, and a few Balti speakers. The Dokpa or Dokmi have their indigenous tongue. Despite that Bodi holds a potential in preservation of the Buddhist scriptures Kanjur & Tanjur (bka' 'gyur, bstan gyur) in the classical Tibetan. The phonetic characteristics of Tibetan are: (i) Monosyllabic, the initial consonants with a latent vowel and the finals, (ii) Isolating, the particles tend to cohesion (cig, zhcs, sing, ky, etc.), (iii) Alphabetic, innovated in the model of angular and circular drawing, (iv) Non- inflection (rare instances of inflections with vowels like mis, mir), (v) Frequest tendency of agglutination distinct from the compounds and (vi) Four tones are used by morphological structure (fo, mo, ma ning, shin tu mo).

Moreover the contemporary literature in Ladakh holds a close affinity with Bodi speech and therefore has a great influence as a mode of communication in the Buddhist community.

The Buddhist in Ladakh are heterogeneous ethically. Also they adhere to different lineages of the Buddhist teachers like Padamasambhava, Naropa, Virupa, Atisa and Dipankara, who had been the Indian pirots to develop separate lineages during Buddhism in Tibet from eighth to eleventh century A.D. These lineages were named on four schools among the Tibetans such as Nyingma (r ñuṅ ma, old Tantra school, Ka (r) Gyu ('bkah 'brgyud, commandment lineage), sa skya (according to the place name, gray brown soil) and Kadam (bka 'gdams, commandment with prescribed teachings). The last one subsequently was reformed as Gelu (dge lugs, principle of the pure precepts).

Ladakh is the western gateway of entrance from Nyari Khor Sum (mna ris khor gsum) and of Central Tibet (Yar lung valley). Today Ladakh is, therefore, rightly named Mang yul land of many people.

It is to mention that Kashmir was a seat of Sarvastivāda and mūlasārvāstivada Buddhists since the pre-Christian period. Moreover the eminent Buddhist teachers in Kashmir were invited to the royal court of btsan rulers since the eighth century A.D. among them Jina Mitra, Dana Sila, Silendra Bodhi, etc., deserve mention (Francke, 1926). Subsequently a faction of the royal family shifted to the western Tibet and came down to Ladakh by the eleventh century A.D. as the Ladakhi royal records mention.

Among the four important Buddhist lineages Nyingma pa, Ka (r) gyu pa and Gelupa are predominant in Ladakh. The distribution of the monasteries belonging to the above schools are shown below.

(i) Alchi choskor
(ii) Wanla monastery
(iii) Rizong monastery
(iv) Pheyang monastery
(v) Spituk monastery
(vi) Thiksey monastery
(vii) Hemis monastery
(viii) Karsha monastery, etc.

In general it is to mention that the Bodi speech played an important role in the growth of Buddhist culture in Ladakh. As a result of this, many Tibetan vocabularies and expressions, which have not been always available in Sanskrit texts (upto twelfth-thirteenth century A.D.) were innovated and made use of by them in Bodi, by the eminent teachers of above mentioned Buddhist schools of Tibet. For instance:

Ladakhi	*English*	*Sanskrit*	*Tibetan*
gci po tse	solitary	ekāntam	gcig pur
rkṅa ra	sound of foot step (an instance of sound simplification)	caranarāva	rkais sgra (da)
sems skr bcoscas	winning the mind	manohara	yid 'phrog pa
men ze	clean	suddha	sbyans (ma)
bol bo	soft	man̄ju	'Jam pa
ban ba	to be wet	adrāyate	rlon pa
sol cas	disperse	niryata	son̄
dpun gtad	helper	sahāya	rogs pa
'byi dgos	article to offer	naivedya (may correspondence to tor ma)	'byin dgos
hi lin	astonished	ascarya	no tshar ba
fan cas	to heal	niroga	gso ba
cub cad	silent	maunam	sdra med par

Rin chen bzan po preferred to translate the Sanskrit terms with vacyartha, i.e., the significant contention as laid out in a word instead of abhidha that is derivative connotations. For instance:

	Sanskrit	*Tibetan*
1.	Manorama	yid (du)' ori
2.	Manohara	yid 'phrog pa thog
3.	Manasikāra	yid byed pa

The above three instances are cited here to speak about a tendency of standardisation of Sanskrit terms into Tibetan. In Sanskrit No. 1 suggests that which enjoys the mind (vacyartha); while No. 2 suggests that which steals the mind (Lakshnartha) and No. 3 manosikara that functions in the mind (abhidha in aluk compound). The Tibetan translation in course of its standardisation such mannerism developed. In this connection attention may be also invited to the requirement of translating the snon nag me lon. Kavayadasa of Acharya Dandi.

Subsequently the phyi dar brought renaissance in the Tibetan literary composition. Also see more examples:

Sanskrit	*Tibetan*
1. mounam	syra med par
2. mounam	kha rog par
3. mounam	cuń mi smra ba

Here the Sanskrit mounam (to be silent) has been translated in three different expressions. Semantically three different expressions connote three contexts. No. 1 implies 'to be in no sound' or soundless, which may correspond to Sanskrit 'nihsabda'; No. 2 suggests 'to keep silent' corresponding to Sanskrit 'tusnimbhava'. The third one corresponds 'not to speak a little', Sanskrit 'na kincid uktam' (that is anutam).

Sanskrit	*Tibetan*
1. Vistāra	rgyas pa
2. Vistara	rgyas pa
3. Caya	rgyas pa
4. Vaddhi	rgyas pa
5. Vīpula	rgyas pa

It is to note that rgyas pa as the verb root gya pa corresponds to Sanskrit tanoti (to spread). In course of Sanskrit rendering 'rgyas pa' has been used in different Sanskrit words as shown above.

The Mahāvyutpatti mentions Latitavistara in Tibetan rgyas cher rol pa (1331), rgya che rol pa las -- -- -- (7954)

It is evident that Mahāvyutpatti translates vistara as rgya che, rgya cher (1.31) while subsequent translation in the snon nag me lon (kavaya dasa) vistara is rendered as rgyas po

a	b	c d	e	f	
misrāni	*nālakādīni*	*tesam*	*anyatra*	*vistara*	
a	b	c	d	e	f
Spel ma	*zlos gar*	*ta sogas te*	*/ de dag*	*rnams nigzhan na*	*rgyas.*

The above instance goes in support for the tendency in standardisation in Sanskrit rendering.

It is evident from above that the inhabitants of Ladakh, particularly the Bodi people accepted the classical Tibetan for their religious literature. They are mostly Buddhists, having a few Muslims and

Christians as exception. But, the Ladakhi families due to economic reasons hold an integration as regards their religious Catholicity. In course of my field work I came across some families with religious freedom. An instance may be cited when husband is Buddhist while 'mrs' is Muslim lady. Similarly the Buddhist husband goes to the church with his Christian wife and same lady joins her husband in a Buddhist festivals. As a result of that classical Tibetan words have inadvetantly entered in Ladakhi polite speech. In villages, however, some dialects are used amount themselves with specific intonation prone to localization. For instance in the Nubra Valley Muslim families speak Bodi with a tendency of Persian/ Urdu intonation, whereas the Dokmi speaks in his own way close to the Bodi of the Leh district.

In this respect a case of language integration in Ladakh is a healthy instance when the rest of the country justifies the speech identity by variants like Bengali, Assamese, Telegu, Kannuri, etc.

REFERENCE

Francke, A.H. : *Antiquities of Indian Tibet,* 1926, p. 82.

5

TOURIST ATTRACTIONS OF LADAKH

Prem Singh Jina

Introduction

Ladakh is the northern-most region of the state of Jammu and Kashmir and one of the loftiest regions inhabited by tribal people. Four major mountain ranges the Great Himalayan, Zangskar, Ladakh and the Karakoram—pass through it. A maze of enormously high snowcapped peaks and the largest glacier outside the polar region dominate the terrain. Valley heights can range from 8,000 to 15,000 feet while passes of up to 20,000 feet and peaks reaching above 25,000 feet determine the land's temperature, which during summer exceed about 36°C, while in winter it reaches –30°C at Leh and –50°C at Dras. Thus, for three months, the whole region faces sub-zero temperature. The months from December to February are very hard. Waterways, waterfalls and even lakes freeze. But on a clear sunny days the temperature goes over 20°C. Rainfall is very low with only 4 to 5 inches and it is the melting snow in summer which sustains Ladakhi life in this arctic zone. High aridity and low temperatures lead to sparse vegetation and, as a result, the entire Ladakh landscape looks like a desert[1].

Tourism

Many foreign travellers visited Ladakh before 1947, among them were Azevedo, Clivera, Desideri, Adolf, Robert Shragintweit, William Moorcroft, George Trebeck, Dr. Henderson, Alexander Cunningham, Shaw, Hayward, Forsyth, Golden Trotter, Mr. & Mrs. Ujifarvy, Welbie, Malcolm, Deasy, Seven Hedin, Younghusband, etc. In 1947 Ladakh was closed to visitors because of the Indo-Pak war. However, in the summer of 1974, after a long ban of 27 years, it was thrown open to foreigners. Since then thousands of foreign tourists annually visit Ladakh.

Places of Tourist Interest in the Leh District of Ladakh

Buddhist Monasteries

Buddhist monasteries in Ladakh are known as Gompas. They are the most attractive feature of the landscape. Every major village in Leh district has Gompas. Normally Gompas are situated on the highest point of a mountain peak or majestically sprawl over cliff-sides and located in the vicinity of villages, these aesthetically pleasing architecturally interesting Gompas provide the focus for the faith of the highly religious Buddhists. They are the places of worship, isolated meditation and religious instruction for the young. Foreign tourists come here annually not only witness the beautiful statues and paintings but also participate in their annual festivals.[2]

Following are some monasteries of tourist interest:

Alchi Choskor: About 70 km. from Leh, on the bank of the Indus river, it was built by Lochava Rinchen Zanpo in the tenth century A.D. One can see beautiful wall paintings and three large images made of clay and painted brightly. It is looked after by monks of Likir monastery[3].

Namgyal Tsemo: It was built by the King Tashi Namgyal in the sixteenth century A.D. It forms a part of the Leh palace complex and is looked after by the monks of Sankar Gompa who regularly come to the monastery and lights the butter-lamps in front of the images.[4]

Sankar Gompa: It is situated about half a kilometre from Leh market, and is a relatively modern monastery. This is a yellow sect monastery closely associated with the Spituk monastery, and serves as the residence of the head lama or rinpoche Kushok Bakula. There are many Buddhist deities and paintings in the Gompa.[6]

Spituk Monastery: This monastery is situated about 8 km. away from the Leh down towards Leh-Srinagar Highway. It stands prominently on the top of hillock commanding a panoramic view of the Indus Valley for miles. It is also a landing mark for aeroplanes. On the left side of it is the Leh Airport. This monastery was constructed in fifteenth century A.D. and has many icons of Buddha and fine *thankas*.[7]

Phyang Monastery: It is about 23 km. away from Leh on the Leh-Kargil road and looks like a huge palace from afar, built by King Jamyang Namgyal who called Denma Kunga Trakpa from the lake Mansarovar and later became the head of the monastery. This monastery belongs to Drigung Kargyudpa order. In simple way it can be identified by Red Cap. There are many statues and various forms of paintings in the monastery.

***Shey Monastery*:** This monastery is about 15 km. from Leh and a tourist attraction. There is a famous Buddha statue which is about 40 feet high and occupies two stories of the building. Besides it has many beautiful paintings and statues.[8]

Thiksay Gompa: This monastery is about 4 km. ahead of Shey. It is one of the largest and architecturally most impressive monasteries of Ladakh.

Hemis Gompa: It is the richest monastery of Ladakh, situated about 40 km. towards the Leh-Manali highway. The Hemis festival of the monastery is very popular among Indian as well as foreign tourists. It has a thanka of the Padamasambhava which is the largest in Ladakh and unfurled once in 12 years.

It belongs to the Drugpa sect which flourished under the Namgyal dynasty, and particularly under King Senghe Namgyal. This monastery has many thank, statues, chortens and beautiful wall paintings.

Chemvey: This monastery was constructed as a funeral act of merit on Senghe Namgyal's death in 1645. It is situated about 45 km. from Leh in a picturesque valley leading to Changla. There is a cave close to the monastery and it is said that Padmasambhava, during his visit to Ladakh, meditated here.[9]

Stakna: A few kilometres away from the Thikse monastery on the right side of the Leh-Manali Highway the Stakana monastery is built on a 60 metre high isolated rock.[10]

Matho: Situated on the opposite bank of the Indus river, across Stakna, the Matho monastery is situated on the hillock. It is famous for oracles during its annual festival. Here two lamas selected as oracles undergo long periods of meditation and after gaining spiritual strength come out in public with swords and knives, cavorting blindfold along narrow parapets.[11]

***Stok*:** Just across the river from Leh is the palace of the banished royal family called the Stok palace, which has a museum of artefacts associated with the dynasty on the upper side of the village there is a small monastery controlled by the Thicksey monastery.

Basgo: 40 km. from Leh there is a monastery with beautiful statues and paintings of the sixteenth century A.D. In 1680, Mongolian troops were held up for about three years here by the Ladakhi army.

Likir: This is one of the oldest monastery in Ladakh founded in the eleventh century A.D. It has many old thankas besides many Buddhist images, stupas and wall paintings.

Lamayuru: Also known as Ying Drung. It is a Drigungpa order monastery which was taken under Phyang monastery during King Jamyang Namgyal period.

Mulbek: Here lies one huge rock carving image of Chamba, the future Buddha, and also a small gonpa.

***Phokar-rangzung*:** There are many Buddhist images which are natural and can be seen in the high mountain rocks.

Tak-Thog monastery: It is the only Nying-ma-pa (Nyingmapa) order monastery in Ladakh, situated 50 km. east of Leh.

Wanla: Near to Khalache (Khalatse) there is a small Gompa of the eleventh century A.D. with ancient Buddhist statues.

Atiche: On the opposite side mountain of Lamayuru monastery about 10 km. from Lamayuru is an old monastery with Buddhist statues.

Tingmosgang: Situated here are two monasteries on the top of hillock. It was once the residence of royal family.

Tia: There is one small monastery which follows monastic rules strictly.

Sabu: It is a sister concern of the Spituk monastery near Leh.

Jo-Khang: A modern ecumenical Buddhist temple in the main bazar of Leh.

Deskit: It is a subgompa of the Thiksey, and has Gonkhang Dukhang and Stangur Khang in which statues and portraits of Buddhist deities are beautifully placed.

Skamphuk: A small gompa and branch of the Hemis monastery has statues such as Padmasambhava, Padma Lhamo, Lama Stagchen Raspa (Stag Tsang Raspa), Sakya Tub & Kunken Padma Karpo.

Hunder: This is a small Gonpa in Nubra valley just beside the bridge and has Sakya Thuba statue.

Samstanling: It is a subgonpa of Rizong monastery in Nubra valley opposite of Diskit. One big chorten of Lama Tsultim Nima and Paintings of Buddhist deities are attractive pieces.

Inca: Just opposite of Panamik hot spring in Nubra valley is a branch of Diskit Gompa. Here on a wall 'Da Chumba Nima's' footprint is preserved.

(B) Other Places of Tourist Interest

Mani Wall

Near every village there Mani walls have been constructed. Each Mani wall consists of numerous stones and slabs, inscribed in Tibetan alphabets (Buddhist Mantras) and artistic carvings of various Buddhist deities. There are maximum, inscriptions of the 'Om Mani Padme Hum' mantra, engraved on stone plates.

***Mani Wall of Choglamsar*:** Starting from a small bridge near State Bank of India, Choglamsar and up to Indo-Tibetan Border Police camp boundary, a long mani wall about 6 feet wide and 5 to 6 feet high is one of the important cultural monuments of Ladakh.

***Housing Colony Mani Wall*:** It is a long mani wall starting from one corner to another of the Housing Colony.

***Mani Wall back to AIR*:** This mani wall is almost of the same height, width and as of Housing Colony Mani Wall.

***Basgo Mani Wall*:** It is a long mani wall between Nemo and Basgo village.

Besides, there are many small mani walls throughout the Leh district of Ladakh region.

***Lakes*:** There are many salt water lakes in Leh district like Starsapuk Tso (fresh water), Tso–kar (salt water), over the Polokangka–Pultang Tso (near Panamik) in Nubra Valley, etc. But Tsomoriri and Pangong-Tso are very popular among tourists.

***Pangong Tso*:** Situated at 13,930 feet, a long narrow basin of island drainage, it occupies a length of 40 miles and 2-4 miles in width.[12]

***Tsomoriri*:** It extends 15 miles in length and 3-4 miles in breadth, situated at a height of 14,900 feet above sea level. It is a breeding centre for rare birds migrating from Central Asia.[13]

Palaces

Though many palaces in Ladakh are now ruined, they are important for tourists. Some of them are as follows:

***Leh Khar*:** It is nine-storey palace built by King Senghe Namgyal and situated just above the Leh town.

***Stok Palace*:** The royal palace is situated opposite the Choglamsar across the Indus river.

***Shey Palace*:** It is in ruined condition and situated on a hillock of Shey village.

***Tingmosgang*:** The palace and fort of Tingmosgang are in ruined condition.

***Basgo*:** It was once the residence of the royal family but is now in ruined shape.

Besides, the royal fortresses of Tangche, Wanla and Skrubuchan, are equally interest for tourists.

Institutions

In Ladakh Buddhist institutions are important for tourists. They can learn Buddhism in a better way with the help of these institutions.

***Central Institute of Buddhist Studies*:** It is a centre of Buddhist studies and has a rich library on Buddhism.

***Mahabodhi Meditation Centre*:** Near the Central Institute of Buddhist Studies, Mahabodhi Meditation gives the training of Buddhist Meditation.

Besides, the Tibetan refugee school at Choglamsar, the Moravian Church, the Ladakh Ecological Centre, the Zorawar fort near Leh, the Ladakh Santi Stupa near Changspa, the Leh mosque, the Shey mosque, the Chusot (Chhushot, Imambara, etc.,) are some of the places of tourist interest.

Tourist Places in Kargil District

Monasteries

There are a few monasteries in Kargil circuit. However the highest number of monasteries are situated in Zangskar Tehsil which is a Buddhist dominated area. Here follows a brief description:

***Shergol*:** Situated across the Wakha river, right of the Leh-Kargil road.

***Urgyan Dzong*:** It is a meditation retreat and has a small monastic establishment.[14]

***Wakha Rgyal*:** A small monastery on the top of the Buddhist village constructed by the Buddhists.

***Rangdum*:** Situated 130 km. south-east of Kargil and has eighteenth century A.D. Buddhist monastery with about 40 lamas.[15]

***Stagrimo*:** The Stagrimo monastery with about 30 resident lamas clings to a tree-covered ridge above the old Padum town, about an hour walking distance.[16]

***Sani*:** It is situated at 6 km. west of Padum in Zangskar, in Kargil district. The chief attraction here is the castle like monastery Sani. By legend it was initially founded by Kanishka during second century A.D. on account of the Kanika Stupa which stands at the backyard of the walled complex.[17]

***Karsha*:** The largest monastery in Zangskar of about 150 resident monks. Built on the mountainside above the Stod river.[18]

***Stongdey*:** It is situated about 18 km at the north of Padum, on the road leading to Zangla.[19]

***Zangla*:** This monastery is lying deep in the northern arm of Zangskar at the end of a 35 km. long rough road from Padum.[20]

***Bardan*:** The Drugpa school (Drug-pa) monastery is situated about 12 km. from the Padum in south.[21]

***Phugthal*:** It is one of the most isolated monastery in Zangskar, founded in the early twelfth century A.D. It has frescos almost contemporary to those at Tabo and Alchi monasteries.[22]

***Zongkhul*:** It is a cave monastery of Zangskar falls on the Padum-Kishtwar trekking route. The famous Yogi Naropa meditated here.[23]

Other Tourist Spots

***Kargil*:** The second largest town of Ladakh and headquarter of the district of same name, once served as an important trade and transit centre in the Pan-Asian trade network. Today serves as an important base foı adventure tours in the heart of the Himalayas. It is a take off station for visiters to the exotic zangskar valley and those who are coming from Srinagar and Leh have to make a night halt here before starting the second leg of their journey.[24]

***Dras*:** Situated 60 km. west of Kargil on the road to Srinagar, famous for the second coldest inhabited place of the world. During winter season temperature falls –50°C.[25]

***Kartse-Khar*:** An ancient village in Kartse valley. It has a 7-metre tall rock sculpture of the Future Buddha of the seventh or eighth century A.D.[26]

***Panikhar*:** Situated 67 km. south of Kargil. From here one can see a complete view of Mt. Nun-Kun.

***Nun-Kun Massif*:** For mountaineers, the Suru and Zangskar valleys are very important. There are a number of spectacular mountain peaks that attract climbers from all over the world. In Zangskar, the Drag-Drung Glacier, adjoining Penzi-la, is a challenging one, but the Nun-Kun massif is more popular. It comprises several peaks, chief among which are Nun (7,135 m) and Kun (7,087 m). Kun was first conquered in 1913, by the Italian mountaineer Piacenza, while Nun, the highest summit of the massif, was first scaled by the Swiss climber, Madame Claude Kogan in 1953.[27]

The massif can be approached from Tangol (70 km. from Kargil) and Gulmatango (110 km. from Kargil). Some approaches are also made from Parkachik (90 km. south of Kargil) along the Parkachik glacier. The other known peaks in the massif are Pinnacle (6.930 m); White-Needle (6,500 m); Z-1 (6,400 m) and D-41 (5,600 m). In addition there are many unnamed peaks in the altitude range of 5,500 m to 6,509 m in the same area. One more peak 'Bobank' is also important for mountaineers. It is situated beside the Nun-Kun massif.[28]

In Zangskar, among the mountain peak group, the best known peaks are Z-2 (6,175m), Z-3 (6,270 m) and Z-8 (6,050 m). In addition there are many unnamed peaks in the area in the altitude range of 5,000 m to 6,000 m.[29]

And so, Ladakh is not only culturally rich but also famous for trekking and mountaineering.

REFERENCES

1. *Ladakh*; A booklet published by the Ministry of Tourism, Govt. of India, 1990, pp. 1-2.
2. *Ibid.*, p. 7.

3. *Ibid.*, p. 10.
4. *Ibid.*
5. *Ibid* and Sumi, D. Tokan; Oki Masato and Hassnain, M. Fida; *Ladakh, The Moonland,* Light and Life Publishers, New Delhi : 1975, p. 33.
6. *Ladakh*; A booklet published by the Ministry of Tourism, *op. cit.*; p. 10.
7. *Ibid.*
8. Sumi, D. Tokan; Oki, Masato and Hassnain, M. Fida : *op. cit.*, p. 34.
9. *Ladakh*; A booklet published by the Ministry of Tourism, *op. cit.*, p. 11.
10. *Ibid.*
11. *Ibid.*
12. Drew, Frederic; *Jammu and Kashmir Territories*, Cosmo Pub., New Delhi; Indian Print 1976, p. 318.
13. *Ibid.*
14. *Ladakh : Kargil & Zanskar*; Booklet published by J & K Tourism; p. 11.
15. *Ibid.*, p. 22.
16. *Ibid.*, p. 27.
17. *Ibid.*
18. *Ibid.*, p. 28.
19. *Ibid.*
20. *Ibid.*, p. 29.
21. *Ibid.*
22. *Ibid.*, p. 30.
23. *Ibid.*, pp. 31-32.
24. *Ibid.*, pp. 5-6.
25. *Ibid.*, p. 14.
26. *Ibid.*, p. 18.
27. *Ibid.*, p. 43.
28. *Ibid.*, p. 44.
29. *Ibid.*

6

THE ROLE OF GREEN TOURISM IN LADAKH

Prem Singh Jina

Green tourism means encouraging local culture while protecting natural resources. It encourages tourists to stay with local inhabitants as a paying guest, sharing their life and food. This brings income to the people without disrupting their traditional occupations. Sustainable developmental activities can take place without disturbing its ecology.

In Ladakh, during recent years, say after the summer of 1974 foreigners come in large numbers. Today, about fifteen thousand foreign tourists visit Ladakh annually. Ladakh attracts tourists by its natural beauty and dominant Mahayani Buddhist culture. Tourism helps the economy of this region. But when tourists destroy the culture and its beautiful environment, it cannot be tolerated.

To increase tourism, the J & K Government has allowed tourists to visit the inner parts of Ladakh. They can now visit Pangong lake, Tsomo-Riri, Da-Hanu and Nubra Valley. Tour operators conduct tours for these areas.

During summers they occupy some areas around the village and make their tent houses for tourists. As a result, the local inhabitants of these areas as not benefit and instead, the flux of tourists disturb the natural beauty of these places.

Before the opening likes of the Bar-Headed Goose, Black-Necked Crane and Brahminy a number of the migratory birds would frequently visit Tsomo-Riri and its neighbouring areas. They are now going down day by day. Earlier, they did not fear from local people, and choose Tsomo-Riri lake for their breeding. Today tourists pitch their tents all around villages near the Tsomo-Riri, and the hustle and bustle of their vehicles and strange crowds, zooming their cameras on breeding birds from the nearest possible distance, disturb the peace of the natural environment and affect the behaviour of migratory birds.

Sociological Damage

In the Da-Hanu area of Ladakh, people had preserved their old traditional Aryan culture. Now, the influx of foreigners, disturb their social and culture identity. They dump garbage, or other wastes their tents. Such activities of foreigners not only disturb the social and cultural activities of the 'Dokpas', but pollute the environment.

In Nubra Valley, tourists cut bushes from the nearby forest for fuel. This activity encourages deforestation and in long run, has very serious consequences.

In the Chang-Thang region tourists have disturb the nomadic system of Changpas. Photographic focus upon them is bound to change their sociological and traditional style of living.

Cultural and Environment Threat

Foreigners who visit Ladakh generally use packed food products and mineral water. It has been noticed that while they go for trekking along the countryside of Ladakh, they throw waste material along the trekking routes. These materials are not decomposable and, therefore, damage the ecosystems and degrade the environment.

Moreover, foreign trekkers, while going for trekking, do not have sufficient fuel materials, therefore, along the trekking routes they use plants and bushes as fuel. This tendency causes ecological imbalances.

Today, the increasing number of foreign trekkers is decreasing the number of wild animals along the trekking routes, as they do not graze along the routes and go up to the higher mountains because of fear. Thus, wild animals are now changing their grazing habits and places because of foreign trekkers.

The half-naked foreigners, with their open hugging, kissing and smoking insult and pollute the traditional culture of Ladakh. As a result, the young generation in Ladakh is copying such patterns of behaviour and have even started smoking at an early age, some of them even with drugs.

Thus, experimenting due to the danger caused by foreign tourist based activities in Ladakh, the role of 'Green Tourism' becomes very important. Green tourism, if encouraged, may bring income to the people without disturbing their traditional occupations.[1]

To protect the cultural and environmental conditions of the newly opened Ladakhi's countryside areas from tourists, the inhabitants of these areas should organise themselves and charge entrance fees for their areas with the help of State Government Agencies. Thus, from the amount so collected the government should release 50 per cent to the villagers of Da-Hanu, Nubra and Chang-Thang. The name of villagers should be sent by the 'Gobas' of the respective villages to the government annually. Government authorities should then sanction an amount on a priority basis to those villagers who are really needy and will invest the money in construction. If this practice is adopted, Ladakhis can accommodate foreigners in their traditional style.

Therefore, the above conservation Area Project may help in removing the price competition and hamper the tent rush at the sights of Tsomo-Riri lake, Da-Hanu and Nubra Valley.

In fact Green Tourism will encourage an understanding between guests and hosts, and both together preserve the environment by planting trees and following the environmental norms such as:[2]

1. Foreigners should go to the newly opened tourist places through the registered trekking agencies.
2. They should cover their body and not smoke while trekking along villages.
3. They should follow only prescribed trekking routes.
4. While trekking, trekkers should not allowed to split into sub-groups.
5. Trekkers should not be allowed to destroy the environment and carry such things as: non-combustible and non-biodegrable items with them which can pollute the atmosphere.

Recommendation for Tourists

In addition to the above environment protection norms, tourists should follow the following code of conduct in order to encourage Green Tourism in Ladakh:[3]

1. Be self-sufficient in fuel supplies, except in areas of abundant wood. Even then, use only dead wood.
2. At camp sites, bury all bio degradable rubbish and excreta. Cover it totally with earth or leaves.

3. Avoid disturbing and startling birds and animals.
4. Follow monastic rules while entering the monasteries.
5. Respect Ladakhi social customs and cultural values.

REFERENCES

1. Ali, Aamir: *An Introduction, In Environmental Protection of Himalaya—A Mountaineers View:* Aamir Ali (ed.); Indus Pub. Co., New Delhi, p. 16.
2. Khoo, Mick: *Himalayan Ecotourism*, Ladags Melong, 1995, p. 31.
3. Band, George: 'The Green Expedition to Bhutan; In: *Environmental Protection of Himalaya—A Mountaineers View, op. cit.*, p. 31.

7

SHEY—ONE OF THE OLDEST PALACE OF LADAKH

Rev. Tsewang Rigzin

The Shey village of Ladakh is about 12 kms from Leh, the district headquarter of Leh. During olden times, it was the capital of Ladakh, and the first village in Ladakh dating to the tenth century A.D. It is situated at the bank of the Indus river. On the other side, at the north, one can witness a rocky mountain chain. It is Buddhist dominated, and about 90 per cent of the total village population are Buddhists, 8 per cent are Muslim and the rest, 2 per cent are Christians.

The Royal Shey palace is situated in the Shey village. It can be seen on the top of the rock hill with the monastery above the main highway. This rock, from a distance looks like an elephant, but today its ruins can be seen.

The Shey palace was constructed by the king of Ladakh, Lha-Chen-dpal-gyi-gon, in tenth century A.D. Later, this remained Ladakh's capital until the seventeenth century, when King Senghe Namgyal shifted his palace to Leh.

One big monastery is attached to the palace. It has two storeys, enshrining a colossal bronze image of Buddha. This Buddha image is the biggest in bronze and gold in Ladakh, and was constructed by King Rde-ldan Namgyal in memory of the kindness of his deceased father Senghe Namgyal.

The monastery has beautiful wall paintings. The wall on the upper story shrine depicts the life of Lama Stag Tsang Raspa, who was the Royal Guru of King Senghe Namgyal. Besides, the paintings on the wall of the big hall at the ground floor have the figures of Buddha of the Bhadra Kalpa and on the northern wall the paintings of Cakarasamvara and Aksobya are beautifully depicted. All these paintings are shaded with pure gold.

On the backside of the monastery, there is one big stupa. This stupa is 35 feet high and 71 feet at base. The upper part of the stupa (i.e. wheels, sun, moon and umbrella parts) is made of copper and gold. This stupa was constructed by the famous Ladakhi King Senghe Namgyal in the memory of his deceased mother.

The monastery belongs to the Dugpa Kargynd-pa school and is controlled by Hemis monastery. Hemis sends one monk as in-charge to the Shey monastery, for a certain period, according to Hemis monastic rules and regulation.

The big stupa near the monastery of the Shey palace has historical importance. Here are some views of historians about the stupa:

1. According to A.H. Francke, King Senghe Namgyal constructed Leh palace, Mane Wall (i.e. Leh Manthang) and the great Buddha image. But he does not mention the stupa. Therefore, the stupa may have been constructed either before or after the Leh palace.
2. Yoseph Gergan opinied that the big stupa was constructed by Senghe Namgyal in 1595 for his deceased mother.
3. Some historical books say that both the stupa and the ground floor Buddha image were constructed at the same time.

The historical facts which are available or mentioned above about the big stupa may be right, but I disagree with them on the following grounds:

1. A.H. Francke says that King Senghe Namgyal constructed the Leh Palace, the Mane Wall and The Great Buddha image in the same period. I feel A.H. Francke was confused while explaining the historical facts, as he was unable to explain about Buddha, rather, we had not been identified, "The Great Buddha". In my opinion, if A.H. Francke meant "The great Buddha" was nothing else but the Buddha image of Shey made of clay, he could be wrong or mistaken because, according to the Shey village tradition, 'The Great Buddha', means the "Great Bronze gold plated Buddha'.
2. Yoseph Gergan fully agreed with A.H. Francke and said that the stupa of Shey was constructed in 1595.

Therefore, if we consider Yoseph Gergan's view, then the Stupa becomes 402 years old at the end of 1997. He also said elsewhere that the 'Bronze-Gold Buddha image' on the ground floor of Shey monastery was built in 1440 A.D.

Now comparing both statements about the stupa and the Buddha image of Shey monastery, we find he was totally confused as both have more than a 100 year difference which is not correct.

I also disagree with the third statement that the Shey stupa and the Buddha image was made at the same time. In my opinion, both were constructed by Senghe Namgyal but not at the same date or time. The following Tibetan inscription shows the fact:

"blama Stag Gyi mtsan Chan yin,

rgyalpo Senghe Mtsan chan yin,

rgyalmoi skalpai mtan chan yin,

chosblon Abhir mgarmo yin,

mchod-yon de dus bzhenga Ra yin."

(The great stupa was constructed by King Senghe Namgyal in the presence of lama Stag Stang Raspa, together with his minister Akhil Garmo and the Queen Skal Zang Dolma.)

The inscription further enlists those artists who were involved in the construction of the stupa. They were:

1. Manager—He was from Sakti village of Leh district, and was popularly called Sheldong.
2. Goldsmith-Palden Tsering belonged to Chiling village.

In conclusion, the grand stupa and 'the Bronze-Gold Buddha' image were constructed during the reign of King Senghe Namgyal. However, further research work is needed to give the factual position for the construction of stupa, Buddha image, Shey monastery, Shey palace and so on.

REFERENCES

1. Jina, Prem Singh: *Ladakh: The Land and the People*, Indus Pub. Co., 1996.
2. Rigzin, Tsewang: 'Shey palace,' In: *Rigpe Dudachi*, CIBS, Leh., 1979.

8

SOME MUSLIM MONUMENTS IN LADAKH: A CASE STUDY OF LEH DISTRICT

Mohammad Asgar Nangso & Prem Singh Jina

Islam put roots in Ladakh in the fourteenth century AD when Lhachen Sherab was king of this region. Shey was then the capital of Ladakh. Unfortunately, 'in 1384 AD, Ladakh's capital saw heavy floods which caused large–scale destruction. To recover from the flood the king requested Mir Syed Ali Hamdani, "to come to Ladakh immediately and help them overcome the crisis."

And so, Mir Hamdani came to Ladakh and later went to Shey and sat in prayer near the Indus. Because of his prayer people reached safer places and escaped from the flood. Pilgrims from the different parts of Ladakh came to Shey to see Hamdani, and were influenced by his preaching. Later, they constructed a mosque at Shey, popularly known as the "Shey mosque". It is said that whoever goes to the Shey Mosque and offers prayers there God will, fulfil his or her wishes. During the Dogra war, the Ladakhi king and his Muslim queen also offered prayers in this mosque until Ladakh was occupied by Dogra invaders.[1]

The second historical mosque was built during seventeenth century AD in Leh. This mosque is known as Jama Masjid. According to the chronicle of Ladakh, the Jama Masjid was built under an agreement between the Mughal Emperor Aurangzeb and King Deldan Namgyal of Ladakh. The chronicle says:

"Hadam Khan of Skardu wanted to occupy Khapulu and Sarlang from Babar Yakub with the help of King Deldan Namgyal of Ladakh.

Therefore Hadam Khan with the support of King Deldan Namgyal attacked Thorche Khar, Babar Yakub could not defund Thorche Khar and became the prisoner of Deldan Namgyal's army who later sent him to Bodhkharbu in the prison. Then the Chorbar region came under Ladakh. However, Deldan Namgyal gave some portion of Thorche Khar to Hadam Khan. When this news came to Skardu, the Skardu king became very angry upon Ladakhi King and decided to take revenge. He attacked Bodhkharbu, King Deldan Namgyal sent his army to Bodhkharbu, but he was defeated. Thus, Shahmurad of Skardu occupied Bodhkharbu from Ladakh army. During this period fifty Ladakhi soldiers ran away from the war and came to the Ladakh's capital. He met King Deldan Namgyal and told him about the details of the war. To stop the war and to reoccupy Bodhkharbu from King Shahmurad, Ladakh's king sent the following proposal to Skardu through his messenger:

"If you return the Bodhkharbu to Ladakh your two brothers will be returned to you."

King Skardu accepted the proposal and returned Bodhkarbu along with Ladakhi prisoners to Ladakh. Thus King Deldan Namgyal reoccupied Thorche Khar. But in Kashmir the Mughal emperor was not happy with this. He therefore sent an agreement proposal to king Deldan Namgyal. Under the agreement he asked Deldan Namgyal to build a mosque in Leh soon, otherwise he would attack upon Ladakh and kill him. King Deldan Namgyal called a meeting after receiving the same from the Mughal Emperor Aurangzeb's messenger. In this meeting all Muslim leaders were called. Finally it was decided that King Deldan Namgyal would give land for the construction of mosque in Leh and follow the agreement."[2]

Leh Jama Masjid

King Deldan Namgyal finally donated the site for the construction of the Jama Masjid mosque in Leh. In 1661-62 AD, he made an agreement with Safi Khan, the Mughal Governor of Kashmir, on behalf of the Mughal Emperor, and donated a portion of a large field near Leh to the concerned authority for construction of the mosque.[3]

Later, the Governor of Kashmir deputed his representative, Sheikh Mohi-ud-din to Leh, to build and supervise the construction work, of the mosque in Leh. When construction work was completed and the mosque erected, Safi Khan sent this information immediately to

Emperor Aurangzeb. The Mughal Emperor, happy to know this, gave a prestigious honour to King Deldan Namgyal.[4]

According to local historians, Mir Syed Ali Shah Hamdani came to Leh and offered prayer at the site of present Jama Masjid. Therefore, the spot is dedicated to him. It is said that earlier this spot was coverd with satin and brocade snow. Now this portion is covered with wooden boards and inscribed with Holy names. Hence, this place has been preserved by the local Muslims down the ages.

The Muslims of Ladakh have been taken care of this mosque. The Jama Masjid has been renovated and extended according to the requirements several times. The last such renovation and extension took place in 1986 and 1994 respectively. In 1994, two minarets each of 90 feet height, were built.

During King Senghe Namgyal, one great Saint stag-Tsan-Raspa visited Ladakh. He was the head lama of the Hemis monastery of Ladakh. To strengthen the friendship he presented a staff to the Imam and Imam presented a manuscript of the Holy Quran to Stag-Tsan-Raspa, which is still preserved in the Hemis monastery. Nowadays, every Friday, this staff is used by the Imam while giving sermons from the pulpit.

Leh Jama Masjid has two parts the summer prayer part and the winter prayer part. During summer, Muslims offer prayer five times in a day, and therefore a large part of the mosque is used. This part is known as 'Khanka'. During winters, the smaller part of the mosque is used and this part is called 'Hamam'. Here hot water facility is available and the place remains hot throughout the day.

The Leh Jama Masjid is a mosque of Sunni Muslims. Here, all Muslims of Leh and its surrounding villages, gather on Friday and offer prayers together. The mosque can accommodate 350 people who can offer prayer together at a time. The floor of the mosque is covered with prayer mats (carpets). There are two long carpets (38 ft 6 inches X 7 ft + $7^1/_2$inches) each. They were offered by Khauja Hyder Shah and Nassir-ud-din Shah who brought these carpets from Yarkand in 1861 AD.

Besides there are about twenty mosques in Leh. Some of them are as follows:

1. Imambara Chhushot Yogma (old) 17th century AD Shia Muslim.

2. Imambara Chhushot Gungma 17th century AD Shia Muslim.
3. Hunder mosque—build by Gyal Khatun during 17th century AD.
4. Thiksey mosque—built in 1827 AD (Approx.)—Shia Muslim.
5. Imambara Thiksey—About 18th Century AD—Shia Muslim.
6. Thiksey mosque—Sunni Muslim, about 18th century AD.
7. Mosque in Housing Colony—
   This mosque was inaugurated by the Minister of State for P.W.D. in 1984.
8. Shenam Mosque—Built in 1994.
9. Harzay Mosque—Built in 1993.
10. Yourtung Mosque—Built in 1991-92.

REFERENCES

1. Sheikh, Abdul Gani : *Muslim Monuments in Ladakh*, Ladags Melong, Spring 1997, p. 25.
2. Tullah, Hashmat : *Tarik Jammu*, 1937, pp. 306-7.
3. *Ibid.*, p. 308
4. Sheikh, Abdul Gani, *op. cit*, p. 24.

9

CULTURAL HISTORY OF MANGTRO MONASTERY OF LADAKH

Prem Singh Jina

Importance of Mangtro Monastery

Matho or Mangtro monastery was built during fifteenth century AD by a Sakya scholar Dorje Palsang.[1] During olden days this monastery was popularly known as Thubten Shaling Chokhor. Thereafter many Buddhist scholars visited the monastery and contributed to the development of the monastery. Among the scholars, Sonam Lodo and Jamgon Lhungrub Chophel are very popular, who placed the monastery on a firm basis by contributing towards making many images, publishing religious scriptures, erecting many reliquaries, and other monastic activities.

Higher Monastic Education

During olden days Ladakhi lamas from all monasteries visited Tibet to seek admission to their respective head monastery for higher education in Buddhist philosophy. This tradition was also adopted by the Mangtro monastery, under which annually some monks were selected through monastic examination by the senior lamas of the monastery who were later sent to Sakya and Ngor in Tibet for further studies. After completing their education they had to return to Mangtro monastery and perform ceremonies and practise meditation in the monastery according to the tradition which they had been taught at the religious centers in Tibet. In 1959 after the occupation of Tibet by China this tradition for sending lamas to Tibet for higher education came to an end. But the rituals and prayers which were conducted by the lamas of the monastery thus preserved an unbroken link with the old religious tradition as practised in Tibet.[2]

Buddha's Miracle Day

Every year Mangtro monastery celebrates Lord Buddha's Miracle day in the monastery from the seventh to the fifteenth day of the first month according to the Tibetan calendar. During the course of this celebration, Hevajra rituals are performed for one week then special pujas to Mahakalas and other Dharma protectors are performed.

1. Hevajra rituals	First for seven days
2. Special pujas to Mahakala and other Dharma protectors	On the fourteenth and fifteenth day of the first month of the Tibetan calendar. These include the performance of religious dances.

Matho Nagrang

Also known as 'The festival of the blindfolded acrobatic oracle monks'. This is two days festival held at the Mangtro monastery on the 15th day of the 1st Tibetan month. It is the only Saskyapa monastery in Ladakh. During the festival, the two oracles the of monastery make a public appearance in their full spiritual form. There oracles, actually monks of the monastery meditate in complete isolation for a full month in preparation of entering in a state of trance and invoking the spirit of the deities.[3]

On the day of the festival, they invoke and receive the deities and come into their full spiritual trance. They run over the high rise ramparts of the monastery, jump from one balcony to another and execute a number of acrobatic feats, all done blindfolded ![4]

The festival is celebrated by the monastery for the welfare of all living beings. According to the tradition the annual celebration of the monastery means : "It fulfils the purpose to render the prosperity and health of the living and to help along to a good rebirth those who have recently passed away."[5]

During the festival the occurrence of the annual oracle is an important scene. They are the special protectors known as 'Rongtsen Karmar' of the monastery. The appearance of oracles activities during the festival is not new. This tradition continually brings special attention to the monastery since its foundation.

Origin and Growth of Oracles in Monastery

The oracles of the monastery are originated from the eastern part of Tibet. Originally as said earlier, the two protectors were brothers and lived at a place called Kawa Karpo. Later they attached to the Sakya scholar Dorje Palsang. When Palsang came to Ladakh they also followed him. Because both protectors were very strong and violent, therefore to propitiate them Dorje Palsang made sacrificial cakes, later he settled down in the upper part of the valley.[6]

Selection of Oracles

The oracles are chosen from the monks of the Mangtro monastery according to the basis of seniority. They are chosen about every five years. Thus while selecting the names of two lamas, some senior lamas name are put into a bowl which is then slowly whirled around until two names fall out. In case after three attempts one man's name has never fallen out, then that man will never be chosen as the oracle. This selection is done during the fifteenth day of the tenth month in every five years interval. This time all monks of the Mangtro monastery gather at the main hall of the monastery and perform Mahakala puja before starting the selection process of the orcles.[7]

Training of Oracles

The selected lamas for oracles have to go through a religious training according to the monastic tradition. The details of which are as follows:

"First they must stay in a one-year meditation retreat and propitiate 'Shi Hevajra', perform sacrificial cake offerings to the Dharma protectors and other activities. Then beginning from Sakya Pandita's Mahaparinirvana day which falls on the fourteenth day of the eleventh month until the sixth day of the first month they must remain in very strict retreat. During this retreat they mostly meditate on 'Hevajra', offer 'tormas' (sacrificial cakes) to the Dharma protectors especially to 'Rongtsen, Karmar'. During the retreat they must keep very clean, bathe once every week, and receive baths of scented water from the Vajra Master of the monastery. Each year they actually end their retreat on the tenth day of the first month. As they end their retreat each, in their own room, they immediately enter into a trance as the protectors, 'Rongtsen Karmar', enter into their bodies. Having first visited the monastery's temple in this trance state, they then visited the Mahakala shrine rooms. Then they allow people to meet them and if they are asked questions, oracles answer them. Next they go to another Mahakala shrine room named Chisa and, having taken a seat on the vernadah in front of this shrine room, they meet the general public and predict all the events that will occur during the following year in Ladakh. Next, from among the crowd, they choose four men to bring huge piles of Juniper shrubs from the lower part of the valley at a place called Hemi Shukpachen which will be used for the purpose of remaking their own shrine. Blessings are given to these four men, further protection cords are bestowed and then they are sent off. The selection of the four men having been completed, their trance fades out for that day. Then on the next day, the eleventh, they again enter into a trance while in their rooms. Again in this trance state they leave their rooms, go to the temple and Mahakala shrine rooms and then receive high lamas and high officials for audience. To these high officials the oracles give presents of their old clothes and other articles which the officials accept as talismans and in exchange offer new articles of clothing and other objects. On the twelfth and thirteenth they again enter into a trance and perform no particular activities except to meet visitors and give predictions to individual questions. On the fourteenth day they enter into a trance as before and in the courtyard of the monastery perform religious dance together with other men who are dressed as Mahakala and surrounding deities as well as two deers. The man dressed as Mahakala then performs a ritualistic ceremony in which the two oracles assist and watch over. On these four days (i.e. 11th to 14th), the oracles come out of their trance in the courtyard where they had just performed some religious dances.

On the following day, the fifteenth, first the oracles bathe and then a wrathful face is drawn on their chests and backs. They are clothed only with a pair of underwears over which a tiger skin skirt is placed. They are also adorned with ornaments of bone and many small relic boxes worn as bracelets which were given many years ago by a Ladakhi queen. They have to place a cloth mask over their faces which only has one small opening at the nose and much, hair at the top. Furthermore, a small drum and a *gende* (a wooden rod which is struck in order to call monks together) are held in their hands. It is said that on this day 'Rongtsen Karmar' enters into the men in the form of the transcendental knowledge of 'Mahakala'. Next the Vajra Master and monks perform a special ceremony. Having completed this, the two oracles enter the temple holding above their heads the upper robe of Dorje Palsang. Actually, in ancient times, it was said that the oracles would fly into the temple by holding aloft this robe. In the temple they receive blessings from the Vajra Master and then visit many places, such as the inner part of the temple, upper 'Mahakala' shrine, the ancient king's palace ruins and the 'Mahakala' shrine in the lower part of the temple which is known as Kalon Gonkhang. While visiting these various places they meet people and give predictions to any queries asked. Having returned to the temple's courtyard, they take up roasted barley flour and throw it in every direction. This signifies in which part of the country crops will be good, in which part bad, etc., depending upon the amount of flour falling in any particular direction. Finally they pray for the preservation and increase of Lord Buddha's Dharma and for the prosperity of the country. Having done this their trance ends.

Everyday from the 10th onwards the oracles do their normal daily prayers, make offerings at the various shrines, receive scented water baths from the Vajra Master, and other activities. Also when the oracles are in trance they sometimes run along the top of the outer walls of the courtyard and on the edges of the roof at a very fast pace, yet they never fall. Also they sometimes cut their mouths and hands with very sharp knives and bleed very much. However, on the following day no traces of wounds or scars can be found on their bodies. One other event which makes people marvel and produce faith in them is on the fifteenth when the oracles go about with a mask which has no openings at the eyes for them to see. It is said that they are able to see through the eyes of the wrathful deities which are drawn on their chests and backs. The tradition of wearing this mask was begun by an ancient Ladakhi queen who wanted to test the superhuman powers of the oracles.

The seventh, and final day on which the oracles must enter into trance is not until the eighth day of the second month. Early in the morning servants and horses arrive from the Hemis monastery and from the king of Tokpa. Having bathe performed their morning prayers, etc., they then leave the monastery. At a certain place along the way to the upper part of the valley they enter into a trance. In this trance state they ride on horses until they reach the original shrine of 'Rongtsen Karmar' which is made of juniper shrubs. Upon reaching the shrine they examine the gains which are contained in a vase that is in the shrine itself. This again foretells whether or not the crops will be good for the coming year. Finally the protectors leave the bodies of the oracles and absorb into the recently exchanged juniper shrubs. Thus the oracle for the year comes to an end."[8]

Mangtro Monastery Buildings

The monastery has as many as eight Lhakhangs/ Dukhkangs. The details of which are as follows:

1. Dolma Lhakhang
2. Kangyur Lhakhang
3. Landas Lhakhang
4. Changchub Chorten Lhakhang
5. Gonkhang
6. Dukhang
7. Soma Dukhang
8. Sangyas Khang.

Dolma Lhakhang

In this lhakhang twenty-one Dolma statues are placed. Besides twenty-one thankas of Green Dolmas are also hung through the walls. There is no wall painting. Because in this lhakhang only Dolma statues and thankas are placed therefore this lhakhang named after them as Dolma lhakhang Fig. 8.1.

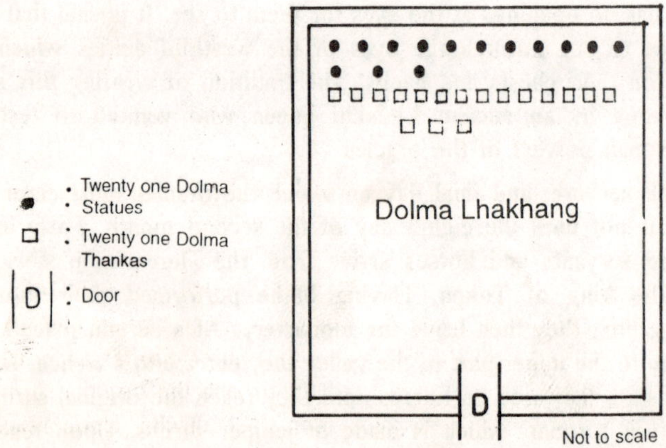

Fig. 8.1: Status and thankas in Dolma Lhakhang.

Kangyur Lhakhang

Here religious pothis called Kangyur are placed. It is like a library where all pothis related with monastery are well preserved Fig 8.2.

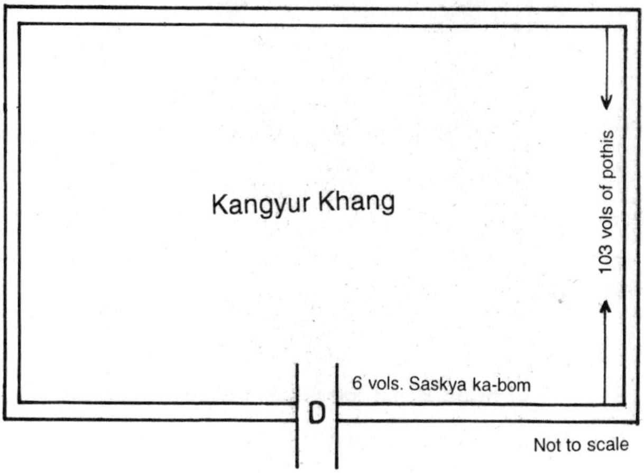

Fig. 8.2: Religious pothis in Kangyur Khang.

Landas Lhakhang

This Lhakhang is about five hundred years old. It has the following main statues Fig. 8.3.

1. Dung Va Dorje Palsang
2. Chamba
3. Jamyang
4. Chepakmet

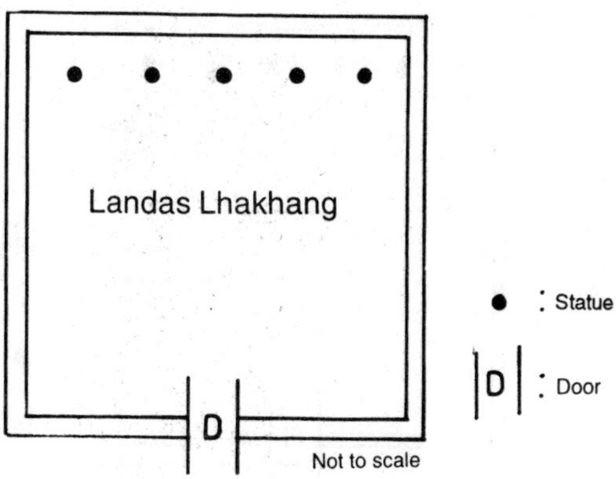

Fig. 8.3: Statues in Landas Lhakhang.

Changchub Chorten Lhakhang

In this Lhakhang two Buddha images are placed Fig.8.4.

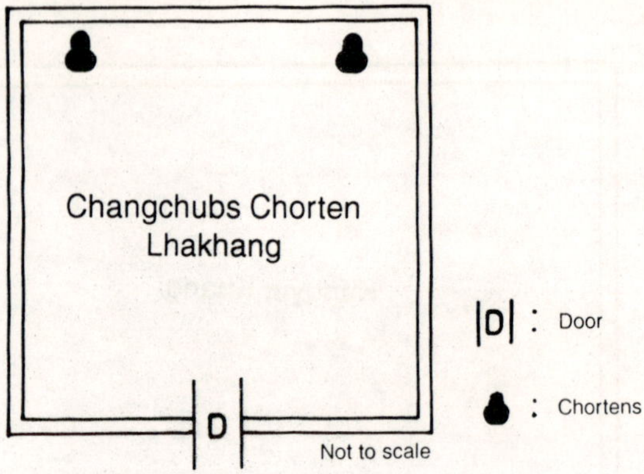

Fig. 8.4: Statues in Changchub Chorten Lhakhang.

Next to the Changchub Chorten Lhakhang head lama'a room, this is known as 'Zimskhang'.

Gonkhang

This room is very dark, children, girls and ladies are not allowed to enter in this. It has various forms of Gonpo and deities in Yab-yum forms. Probably Gonkhang is the oldest one in the monastery.

Dukhang

It is about three hundred years old consisting of wall paintings and statues Fig. 8.5.

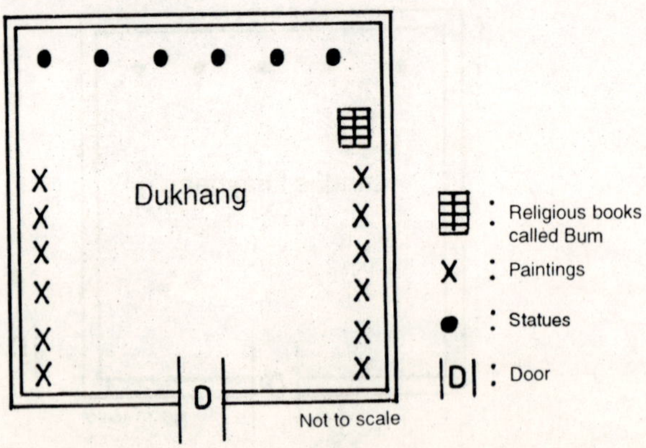

Fig. 8.5: Statues and Paintings in Dukhkang.

Paintings on walls :

(a) Side wall :

(i) Mahakala
(ii) Chepakmet
(iii) Nambar Namjat
(iv) Sakya Pandit
(v) Sakya Chen

(b) Opposite wall

(i) Chongkhapa
(ii) Sakya Pandit
(iii) Sangyas Smanla Buddha (Sangyas chen sman-bla)
(iv) Chandazik
(v) Namsas
(vi) Chosgyal

Statues:

(i) Buddha
(ii) Avalokitesvara (Chukrikzal) : Central statue
(iii) Chepakmet
(iv) Chamba
(v) Sakya Chen

Soma Lhakhang (Dukhang)

It is a new Dukhang about 20 years old and has beautiful statues and paintings Fig. 8.6:

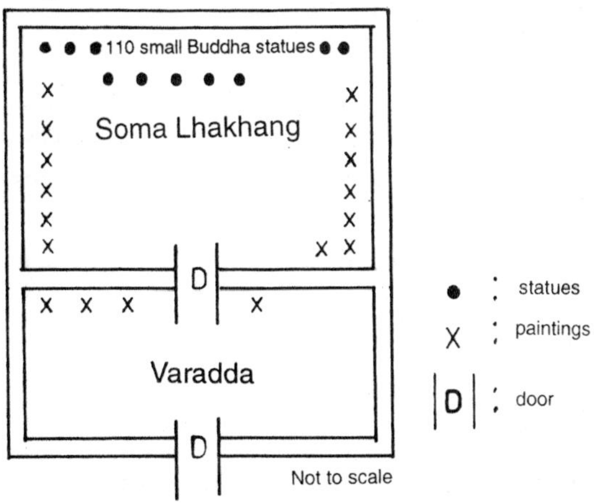

Fig. 8.6: Statues and paintings in Soma Lhakhang.

Paintings on the Walls of Soma Lhakhang :

(a) Paintings on Varanda walls

(i) Salu Phapo (*shar bgand spyod*)
(ii) Jambuling (*lho Jambuling*)
(iii) Nub Palan Cot
(iv) Can thamiyan (*byang dgra mi s*)

(b) Paintings on one side wall in some Lhakhang :

(i) Rongchen Karmar
(ii) Tumba Dorje (blma-tumba Dorje)
(iii) Sakya Lama
(iv) Sakya Kunga Niva (Sakya Kunga)
(v) Padam Subhava
(vi) Buddha

(c) Paintings on Other Side Wall in Soma Lhakhang :

(i) Nastan chostuk (16 Arhad)
(ii) Lama Birvapa
(iii) Milarepa
(iv) 16 Arhad
(v) Nambar Nagzat
(vi) Gonkhar
(vii) Riksumgonbo (Rik-sum-gon-bo)

Statues in Soma Lhakhang

(i) 110 Small Buddha Statues
(ii) One main Buddha statue at the centre
(iii) One side 4 Buddha statue.

Sangyas Khang

One three storey (i.e. about 30 feet) in height Buddha statue is placed in this Lhakhang. Besides it has one changchub chorten 300 years old and 110 vols. Kangyur and Stangyur religious pothis, here Namgyal stontok mandala is also made.

In this Lhakhang the following paintings are depicted on the walls.

1. Chepakmet
2. Naropa, Tilopa, Melarepa, etc.
3. Senge Da
4. Tsering ma
5. Guru chengyangt (Guru mchari brgyat)

6. Padmasambhava
7. Lhacam Mandarava.
8. Khando Eshe Chosgyal
9. Padmasambhava mandala
10. Gonpo Lhundup
11. 16 Arhads
12. Sari and Modgali Puttra with Buddha
13. Stag-Tsan-Raspa (Stag. Changas rin po che/wearing Kashmiri cap, it is said that he went for Haj also)
14. Kunga-Choskyi Nima (Kun-dga-chos kyi-nyi-ma) 12th reincarnation of Dukchen Rinpoche skutang
15. Melaraspa
16. Dorje chang
17. Kargyut chechang (mandala)

Sangyas Khang is about 317 years old and has very old and beautiful paintings. Besides the monastery has a valuable collection of very old and beautiful thankas, some of them have mandala paintings.

Though monastic activities in Mangtro earlier to 1968 were conducted by the lamas smoothly, the monastery authority sometimes felt that Mangtro should have strong leadership who could take decision firmly and broadly. Therefore, His Holiness Sakya Trizin, head of the Sakya Sect requested Luding Khen Rinpoche to look after the Mangtro monastery. He arrived at Mangtro monastery in 1968 took charge of the headship in the monastery. Today under the leadership of Luding Khen Rinpoche, the religious affairs of the monastery have been stable and are steadily increasing.[9]

Luding Khen Rinpoche started to make a new programme underwhich some old traditions have been revived and through his teachings, monks of the monastery started practising many meditation retreats. He is now giving more time to the monastery so that discipline should be maintained in the monastery as well as religious affairs may go smoothly. Through his efforts some money has been collected and is being used for the renovation of the assembly and decorated with religious objects and paintings. Besides, he has offered three large images of Lord Buddha, and one hundred smaller ones. These images have gold overleaf. He also offered fifteen large paintings and many small ones to the monastery.[10]

In conclusion the Mangtro monastery has unique annual festival. Two oracles during the festival come and run here and there among the people. They run and jump over walls and roof, blind-folded, but never fall. This is miracle incident and fun for the tourists. When the festival in over, they become normal and the cloth over their eyes are removed.[10]

REFERENCES

1. Jamyang Gyaltsen: Buddhism and Mangtro Monastery of Ladakh; In: *Recent Researchers on the Himalaya,* Prem Singh Jina (ed.); Indus Pub. Co.; 1997, pp. 78-81.
2. *Mangtro Monastery*; A booklet published by the Mangtro Monastery in Ladakh.
3. *Ladakh : Monastic Festivals,* 1996-99; J & K Tourism Pub., 1996.
4. *Ibid.*
5. *Mangtro Monastery :* A booklet; *op. cit.*
6. *Ibid.*
7. *Ibid.*
8. *Ibid.* & This brief account of the oracles at the Mangtro monastery has been written by Luding Khen Rinpoche, Jamyang Tenpa'i Nyima, an abbot of the Ngor Evam monastery in Tibet and at present head of Mangtro Monastery in Ladakh.
9. *Ibid.*
10. Sumi D. Tokan; Oki, Masato and Hassnain, M. Fida : '*Ladakh: The Moonland'*, Light & Life Pub., New Delhi, 1975, p. 32.

10

ORIGIN AND GROWTH OF NYINGMAPA SCHOOL

Dr. (Rev) Konchok Rigzin

Introduction

There are many Buddhist schools or lineages in Tibet, but four among them are major traditions, in Tibetan language, we call them 'cho-lug'. They are:

1. Nyingmapa
2. Kagyudpa
3. Sakya
4. Gelugpa

Nyingmapa is the ancient Buddhist tradition and was founded by Padmasambhava[1] in ninth century AD Kagyudpa is the other sect of Buddhism. This sect was founded by the great translator Marpa (1012-1099 A.D.) during the middle of tenth century AD: Next important Buddhist tradition was Sakya. It was founded by Khon-Konchok Gyalpo (1034-1162). The Gugpa sect of Buddhism was founded by Je-Tsong Khapa (1357-1410) during fourteen century A.D.

Buddhism in Tibet

During King Srong-tsen-Gampo[2] and Thri Srong Deutsen[3] (i.e. from seventh century to eight century) Buddhism flourished without any difficulty. The development process of Buddhism was widely recognised throughout in Tibet without much improvement in its traditional practise. However, after eleventh century AD when Indian Buddhist scholars came in Tibet, some reformation of Buddhism took place, it was nothing else but Tantric form of Buddhism.

Buddhism during King Thri Srong Deutsen

In ninth century AD King Thri Srong Deutsen became the powerful ruler of Tibet. He was a Buddhist scholar and fully devoted himself for the protection and development of Buddhism. He invited Acharya Santaraksita[4] from India and asked him to build Sam ye monastery[5] in Tibet. Unfortunately some jealous minister and local evil spirit orators jeopardized this religious deed. Therefore, king invited Guru Padamasambhave[6] in Tibet on the advise of Acharya Santaraksita. Thereafter Padmasambhava came in Tibet and through his enlightened power he easily pacified the evil forces and constructed the Sam ye monastery.

As said earlier Nyingmapa is the oldest Buddhist tradition and follows the Ancient Tantra. This tantra includes all teaching which are given directly by various Buddhas to different sages through their pure visions.

The Ancient Tantra is broadly classified into six levels—Kriyayoga, Cāryayoga, Yogatantra, Mahayoga, Anayoga and Atiyoga. The first three all together known as 'Outer Tantra' and rest are put into 'Inner Tantra'.

Nyingmapa's Scriptures

Nyingmapa scriptures consist the canon of Sutnic and Terma. The Terma has tantric teachings and commentaries. In other words, Terma consists of thousand tantric scriptures related with the sacred objects hidden in earth, water, sky, mountains, lakes, rocks, mind, etc.

Terma represents a profound, authentic and powerful tantric form of Buddhist training. The scriptures may be discovered by miraculous power of spirit. No man unless he has enlightened power can realize these.

Nine Heart Sons of Nyingmapa

Though Padmasambhava established Nyingmapa sect in Tibet, his nine disciples helped him for its propagation in Tibet and its neighbouring countries. They are as follows:

1. King Thri Srong Deutsen
2. Nub Chen Song gye ye shey
3. Ngen lam Gyal wa chog yong
4. Nub Nam Khai Nying po
5. Nyag ye shey zhon nu

6. Ye shey Tso gyal
7. Drog mi pal gyi ye shey
8. Long pal gyi song, and
9. Vairocana

Vairocana among the Padmasambhava disciples became famous for the translation works of Nyingmapa doctrine texts. Ngog-lo-lo-den-shey-rab has written his views about him:

> Vairocana's knowledge of translation is limitless like sky. Ka Wa Pal tseg and Chog ro Lui Gyal tshan translation works like the sun and moon (i.e. Varirocana is the founder of translation work whereas Ka Wa Pal tseg and Chog so lui Gyal tshan had enlightened this work throughout in Tibet). Thereafter, Rinchen Zangpo became the great, translator, his works recognised as the 'down star' which twinkle brightly at the morning. Then comes others like me who are like fireflies.

Ladakh during ninth century AD was a part of Western Tibet. Therefore, while propagating Nyingmapa school of Buddhism, Padmasambhava visited Ladakh, later he founded a monastery near Leh about 50 km in east direction. This monastery commonly known as now 'Tak-Thog'. Earlier it was on rock now the new building is constructed on ground level and contains the images of Guru Nang Srith Zilon in a central position; to its right lies an image of Guru Padma Gyalpo. Thus Tak-Thog is the only monastery belonging to Nyingmapa sect.[7]

REFERENCES

1. Padmasambhava (Lotus Born Master) : Guru Rinpoche (The precious master).
2. Srong-tsen-Gampo: He was the king of Tibet born in the Fire Ox year (i.e. 617 AD) and died in the Earth Dog year (i.e. 698 AD).
3. King Thri Srong Deutsen: He was born in the Iron Horse year (i.e. 790 AD) and died in the Earth Tiger year (i.e. 858 AD).
4. Santaraksita : Acharya Santaraksit was a great Indian Buddhist scholar. During ninth century AD he was the abbot of Nalanda University, Bihar; India.
5. Sam ye monastery : It is the oldest monastery in Tibet and was built in the ninth century AD by king Thri Srong Deutsen under the guidance of Guru Padmasambhava and Santaraksita. It has one big, three-storey temple at the centre and other temples are at the four sides of the main

temple. Besides eight small temples along with stupas at the four corners are also built. This structure is surrounded by high wall topped by 108 small stupas. During olden days this monastery was the main centre of Buddhism and worship. Learned lamas along with Indian Buddhist scholars translated many Buddhist texts from Sanskrit into Bodhi. Besides it was one of the famous meditation centres in Tibet. The monastery has a rich library in which Buddhist texts were brought from India, Nepal and other Central Asian countries. In fact Samye monastery is rich in all aspects of Buddhism including the good collection of religious statues and other related objects.

6. Padmasambhava : He was born in Oddiyana (Tib., Ogyen) in India. Today it is in Swat Valley of Pakistan.

   As Padmasambhava was born from a lotus of milky ocean therefore his name is derived from the lotus (Padma). Later King Indrabodhi of Oddiyana brought him in his palace. He had no son, so, he wanted to marry him with Kha-dro-Od Changma and relinguish his throne to him. Padmasambhava did not agree with the king and decided to lead an ascetics life. Then he went to Sahora (near Mandi, Himachal Pradesh of India). Here Princess Mandarava became his disciple. Padmasambhava gave her many esoteric teachings. Princess Mandarava thus got very much influenced by Padmasambhava, she was then without delay, attentively taking the teaching of Padmasambhava. On the other side her father did not like such relations with Padmasambhava. He, therefore, ordered his minister to give punishment to Padmasambhava. Accordingly Padmasambhava was burnt to death, suddenly a miracle took place, Padmasambhava instead of burning immediately transformed himself into a lotus. King and his public was witnessing this scene. Later, the king realized his mistake and became his devotee.

7. *Ladakh :* A booklet published by Ministry of Tourism, Govt. of India, 1990, p. 15.

11

MURALS OF 'MGON-PO' IN GON-KHANG OF PHYANG MONASTERY OF LADAKH

Prem Singh Jina

Gon-Khang derives its name from 'm Gon-po'. It is the oldest temple in the Phyang monastery having various forms of 'm Gon- po'. They are depicted on walls and installed in front of the door in Gon-Khang.

mGon-po is called Mahakala in Sanskrit. In fact a dharmapala who has two sides to his character—death and to give richness, is mGon-po.

According to the Buddhist tradition the wrathful form of mGon-po destroys the enemies of Buddhist teachings. The Vajrayana Buddhism also accepts a number of Hindu deities into their pantheon, one of whom is mGon-po or Mahakala.[1]

mGon-po has as many as seventy-five forms : Aghora-mGon-po, Ajita-mGon-po, Anghora-mGon-po, Arya-(Attis)-Krama-Mahadeva-Srigvala-Mahakala, Arya-(Atisa)-Krama-Simha-Vahana-Traksad-Mahakala, Astat Maka-Panjara-Mahakala, Ayuganmetu Mahakala, Ayur-Vardhana-Sita-Caturmukha-C.Cri-Mahakala), Ayuspati Mahakala, Ayuspati-Syama-Mahakala, Begca Mahakala, Beg-tse Mahakala, Begtse-Mahakala, Byhagavan-Mahakala, Beg-tse-mGon-po, Beng-ma-ha-kala, Bhagavad Mahakala, Bhagavat-Mahakala, Bhaavat-Mahakabhratr-traya, Bhayada (?)-Mahakala, bka'-rgyud-pa ' i-mGon-pa-ber-nag-can-bka-sdod-ma, bka'-srung-brag-lha-mgon-po, Brahmana Rupa Mahakala, Brahmana-

Rupadhara-Mahakala, Bram-Zehi, Bu-ston-lugs-dpal-mgon-beng-dmar, Camarimukha-Traksad-Mahakala, Canda-mukha Caturmukha-(Sri-Mahakala), Caturbhyja-Mahakala, Caturbhuja-Sri-Mahakala, Caturmukha-Karmayoga-Mahakala-Cjos-Skyong-Mahakala, Cintamani-Rakta-Mahakala, Cintamani-Sita-Mahakala, Dai-Ko-Ku, Dakamukha-Guhyasadhana-Traksad-Mahakala, Dam-tshing-gi-dbang-mo, Danda-Mahakala, Danda (Dhara)-Mahakala, dByings-Khis-ma-mo, Dhana-vardhana-Pita-Caturmukha-(Sri-Mahakala), dpal-ldan-lha, mo-dMaog-zor-ma, dpla-ldan-mgon-po, dpal-ldan-mgon-po, nag-po-chen-po, dpal-rdo-rje-nag-po-bsrung-yongs-rdzogs, dpal-ye-shes-mgon-pa-mahakala-dpa' bp-chenpo-Drag-shad-mGon-po, Dur-khor-bdag-po-lcan-dral, Dur-Khrod-mgon-po-yab-yum, Dvags-pohi-lugs-Traksad-Mahakala, Ekavira-Kartaridhara-Mahakala, Garudapaksa-Vat-Kilapade-panjara-maha-kala, gNod-sbyin-chen-po-zengs-kyi-beg-tse-can, gNod-sbyid-sgrol-gying-bshan-pa, gNas-lugs-(mahadeva), Gom-Kar, Guhya-nidhi-dhara-Sri-Mahakala, Htshal-lugs-Caturbhuja-(Jnana)-Mahakala, Janana-Krama-Navatmaka-kartaridhara-Mahakala, Kartaridhara-Traksad-Mahakala, Kasmir-maha-pandita-(Skyasri)-Krama-Kartaridhara-Mahakala, Krsna-Taksad, Ksati-tarka-Nila-Caturmukha (Sri-Mahakala), Ksiprakara-Sadhuja-Janana-Mahakala, Lha-Nub-mgon-po-gri-gug-dmar-po, Ljan-lungs-saptadas-atmaka-Tamara-Kartaridhara-Mahakala, Lugs-griyis-gcig-tu-bsgril-ba' i-ye-shes-mgon-po-phyag-bzhin-pa, Mahakala-gur, Mahakala-mGon-dpar, Mahakala-mGon-po-zas-lha-dmar-po, Mahakali-Remati, Mahapandaka-Karma-Mahakala, Maharakt Mahakala, Mahasiddha-santigupta-Krama-Caturbuja-(Jana)-Mahakala, Mamo-srid-pa'i-rgyal-mo-mgon-po-makala, mGon-dmar-dban-gi-rgyal-po, mGon-ljang-tshe-bdag-mGon-po, mGon-po-Bram-Zehi-gZungs-can, mGon-po bzhi-sbregs, mGon-bye-rog-gdong-can, mGon-po-dkar-po, mGon-po-dmar-po, mGon-po-gzag-ldan, mGon-po-jag-lha mGon-po ljang-klu, mGon-po-mgron-lha, mGon-po-phyag-drug-pa, mGon-po-phyin-kha, mGon-po-ser-po, mGon-po-srog-lha-dkar-po, mGon-po-traksad-brogn-zhal-can, mGon-po-trak-sad-seng-zhon-jo-bo'l-lugs, mGon-po-yid-bzhin-nor-bu, mGon-po-yid-bzhin-nor-bu, mGon-po-zas-lha-dlar-po, mGon-Ser-nor-srung-blo-phel-zhal-gsum,-phyag-drug-pa, Nagarjuna-Krama-Caturbhuja-(mahadharmapala)-Janana-Mahakala, Narayana-Mahakala, Nagar-Juna-Karma-Samatrka-Panjara-Mahakala, Matha-Mahakala, Nidhi-Dandadhara-Mahakala, Nikama-Varsi-sita-Mahakala, Pedatika-Traksad-Mahakala, Pandaka-Traksad-Mahakala, Panjara-Mahakala, Phur-Ideks-ma, phyis-kyi-mgon-po, Pu-tra-lcam-dral, Rakta-Karta-ridhana-Mahakala, rGva-lo-(tsa-ca)-hi-lugs-Caturbhuja-(Janna)-Mahakala, rGva-lo-(tsa-ba)-htshal-lugs-Caturbhuja-(Janana)-

Mahakala, rNog-lugs-Ekanta-panjara-Mahakala, Sadbhuja-Janana Mahakala, Sadbhuja-Mahakala, (sadhuja-Trimukha)-Mativardhana-(Dhanapala)-Pita-Mahakala, Sadhana-Kala-Sambaddha-Caturmukha- Sri-Mahakala, Sa-ra-ha'i-mgon-po, Sarva-vigha-Vinayaka-Mahakala, Seva-Kala-Samhaddha-Caturmukha-Sri-Mahakala,-Shailadeva-Mahakala-sha-za-ce-spyang-gdong-can, Sinhasana-Ganapati-Mahakala-Simhavahana-Taksad, Sita-Chintamani-Mahakala, Tuksad-Mahakala, Tamra-Kartaridhara-Krsna-Cola-Mahakala, Trakshad-Mahakala, Tshal-lugs-kyi-ye-shes-mgon-po-phyag-bzhi-pa, Tshogs-bdag-mgon-po-seng-ge';-gdan-can, Varana-Vasamkara-Rakta-Caturmukha-(Sri-Mahakala), Vyaghravahana-Mahakala, Yang-gsang-dpal-mgon-dug-ri-nag-phyag-bzhi-pa, ye-Shes-mgon-po-phyag-bzhi-pa-rGva-lo-i-lugs.[2]

Forms of mGon-po

Normally mGon-pa has the following characteristics[3]:

Face: One, most wrathful; *arms/hands* : two, right holds a wood/ hook cankusha, lcags-Khus; *body* : garment of black silk, trimmed in green, golden girdle; *legs :* two, stands on a male and female gshin-rje; *colour :* black; *Ornaments :* five skull crown, wristlets, anklets, necklace, garlands and belts of skulls or freshly anklets, severed heads, tiger or elephant skin as a body covering, an apron of carved human bones; *Vahana :* lotus throne; *companion :* two rDor-rje-kun-grun-ma, and gNod-sbyin-zhang-blon-rdo-rje-bdud-dul.

In Gon-Khang of the Phyang Monastery nine forms of mGon-po are depicted on the walls. Here follows the details:

1. mGon-po-dkar-po:

(Tib.: aka-chi-bdag-joms-pa; skt. Mahakala) : "The white Gon -po", "the vanquisher of the death lord ". A dharmapala and a form of mGon-po, or Mahakala (Skt.) *Face:* One; fierce, three eyes, bared fangs; *Arms/ hands:* four, holding a crystal vase/vessel (kalasha, bum-pa) filled with nector of life and knowledge (amrita), ritual chopper (Kartirika, grig-gug), skull cup (Kapala, thod-pa), *body:* loin cloth of a tiger skin; *legs:* two; *ornaments :* five skull crown, wristlets, anklets, necklace, garlands and belts of skulls or freshly severed heads, tiger or elephant skin as a body covering, and apron of carved human bones; *colour :* white; *Vahana :* lotus throne; *Shakti :* Ye-shes-mkhi-gro-ma; "The Shakti of mGon-po dKar-po". "The white mGon-po". *Face:* One, fierce, three eyes, bared long; *Arms/hands:* two, holding a ritual chopper (kartirika, grig-gug) and a skull-cup (kapala, thod pa) filled with blood; *Body :* loin of tiger skin, *legs* : two; *Ornaments :* garland of freshly severed heads, snakes, bones; *Colour :* White.[4]

In Gon-Khang mGon-po-dkar-po is depicted in yab-yum form.

2. mGon-Po-mar-po

A dharmapala, mGonpo or Mahakala (Skt); *Face:* one, fierce, bared fangs, three eyes; *Arms/hands :* four, holding goad/hook (ankush, lcags-kyi), flaming ritual chopper (Kartirika, grig-gug), skull-cup (kapala, thod-pa) and trident (trishula, rtse-gsum); *Body :* loin cloth of a tiger skin; *Legs:* two; *Ornaments:* five, skull crown, wristlets, anklets; necklace; garlands and bells of skulls or freshly severed heads; tiger or elephant skin as a body covering, and apron of covered human bones; *colour :* red; *Vahana :* lotus throne, *Companion;* include red yaksas and yaksis who hold wish granting jewel (chintamani, yel-bzhin-norbu); *Ornaments:* three-skull crowns.[5]

3. mGon-po-Ser-po

A dharmapala and a form of mGon-po or Mahakala (Skt.). *Face:* One, fierce three eyes, flame-like hair; *Arms/hands :* four, holding a jewel (ratna, nor-bu), human skull-cup (kapala, thod-pa) flaming sword (khadga, ral-gri) and trident (trishula, rtse-gsum); *body:* mature; *Legs :* two, *colour:* yellow, *Ornaments*; five-skull crown, wristlets, anklets; necklace; garlands and belts of skulls or freshly severed heads[6].

In Gon-khang mGon-po-Ser-po is not depicted with tiger skin body cover.

4. Danda-Mahakala

(Tib. : mGon-po-Beng). One of the deities pictured in the "three hundred" (Tib.: sku-brnam-brgya-phrag-gsum or sku-brnam-sum-brgya) with preface by Lcan-skya. Outugtu Rol-pahi-rdo-rje (1736-1795). A dharmapala and a form of mGon-po, or Mahaka (Skt.) *Face :* One, fierce bared fangs, three *eyes; Arms/hands :* Two, a staff/stick rest across on the crook of both arms; in general right hand holds ritual chopper (Kartirika, grig-gug), left holds skull-cup; *Body:* Loin cloth of a tiger skin; *Legs:* two, standing on human corpse; *colour :* blue, asana alidhasana, *Ornaments:* five-skull crown; wristlets-anklets, necklace, garlands and belts of skulls or freshly severed heads, tiger or elephant skin as a body covering, and apron of carved human bones; *Vahana :* human corpse; forms of mGon-po or Mahakala.[7]

In the monastery Danda Mahakala has one face, fierce; three eyes;

Arms/hands: Two, holding a staff/stick rest across the crook of both arms; *Body:* Loin red scarf, standing posture; wearing Ladakhi type shoes "Pabu", covered the body by woollen coat which has border of tiger skin coloured cloth; inside wearing Ladakhi type green Goncha; *throne* : lotus.

5. mGon-po-Phing-kha

A dharmapala, a form of mGon-po or mahakala (Skt.); ornaments include five-skull crown, wristle, anklets, necklace, garlands and belts of skulls of freshly severed heads, tiger or elephant skin covered the body, and apron of carved human bones.[8]

In Gon-Khang, mGon-po-phin-kha holding ritual chopper (Katirika, grig-gug) and a vessel; Ornaments include five-skull crown, wristlets, necklace; In right hand holding kalasha (bum-pa), filled with nector and left hand has skull-cup, a trident (trishula, rtse-gsum); *Body:* mature; *Legs:* two; *colour:* dark blue; lower portion of body covered by tiger skin; *Asana:* Latitasana on-a human corpse; *Vahana:* Lotus, throne; In yab-yum form; Sakti: Right hand holds thunderbolt (Vajra, rdo-rje); Hands/Arms two, *Face:* one, fierce.

6. mGon-po-ljan-klu

A dharmapala, a form of mGon-po or Mahakala (Skt.). *Face* : One, fierce, three eyes, flame like hair, *Arms/hands:* four, holding sword (khadag, ral-gri), human skull-cup (kapala, thodapa), ritual chopper (Karittrika, gri-gug) and trident (trishula, rtse-gsum), *Body:* mature; *Legs*; two, *colour:* green; *Ornament* : five skull crown, wristlets, anklets, necklace, garlands and belts of skulls of freshly severed heads, tiger or elephant skin as a body covering and apron of carved human bones; *companion:* Bye-rog-gdorg-pa.[9]

In Gon-Khang, mGon-po-ljan-klu holding sword (khadga, ral-gri), ritual chopper (Karitirika grig-gug) and a vessel (kalasha, bum-pa) filled with nector in right hands and left hand hold skull-cup and a trident (trishula, rtsa-gsum), *Body:* mature, *colour:* bluish; *Hands/Arms:* four, *Ornaments:* five skull crown, wristlets, anklets, necklace, lower body covered by tiger skin, *Eyes:* three, *Face:* one, fierce, flame like hair. *Asana* : Lalitasana on human corpse; *Vahana* : lotus, throne; In yab-yum form; *skti* : Green colour; *Ornaments* : three skull crown, wristlets, anklets, necklace, *nude body*; *Hands/Arms* : two, hold: Thunderbolt (Vajra, rdo-rje) in right hand.

mGon-po-Phyang-bZhi-pa

Caturbhuja Mahakala (Skt.): One of the Dharmapala like image found in Chu-Fa-Pu-sa-Sheng-Hsiang-Tsang; *Face:* one, fierce; three eyes, flame like hair; *Arms/hands:* four, principal hands hold ritual chopper (Kartirika, grig-gug) and human skull-cup (Kapala, thod-pa) right hand holds sword (Khadga, ral-gri), left hand holds parasol Catapatra, guduga); Body: Corpulent; legs: two; Asana : alidhasana; colour: black (?) (Mahakala's colour not noted in the source); ornaments : five skull crown, wristlets, anklets, necklace, garlands and belts of skulls or heads, tiger or elephant skin as a body covering and apron of carved human bones; *Vahana*: prostrate human forms[10]

In Gon-Khang, mGon-po-Phyag-bZhi-pa holds sword (khadga, rla-gri) and thunderbolt (Vajra, rdo-rje) in *right hands* and a trident (trishula, rtsa-gsum) with three skull and skull-cup in *left hands*; *Arms/ hands*: four; *colour:* dark blue; *eyes:* three, *Ornaments:* five skull crown, wristlets, anklets, necklace, *body:* loin cloth of a tiger skin, *garland:* snake; *Legs:* two, *face:* one, fierce: *Vahana:* prostrate human form.

8. mGon-po-Phyang-drug

This mGon-po generally has the following characteristics-*Face:* one, fierce, three eyes, flame like hair: *Arms/hands:* Six, right hands hold ritual chopper (Kartirika, grig-gug), rosary (Male, phreng-ba), and human skull-drum (damaru, thod-rnga), left hands have human skull-cup (kapala, thod-pa), trident (trisula, rtse-gsum) and noose snare (posha, zhags-pa); *body:* corpulent; *Legs:* two; *Asana :* pratyalidha-sana; *Ornaments:* five-skull crown, wristlets, anklets, necklace, garlands and belt of skulls of freshly severed heads, tiger or elephant skin as a body covering and apron of carved human bones, *colour:* blue, *Vahana:* two human corpses, *emanation;* form: Paca Buddha.[11]

mGon-po-Phyang-drug in Gon-Khang of Phyang monastery has one fierce face, three eyes, flame-like hair, *Arms/hands:* six; right hands hold rosary mala (phrangba), human skull-drum (damaru, thod-rnga) and vessel filled by nector of life and acknowledge (amrita), left hands hold human skull-cup (kapala, thod-pa), trident (trishula rtse-gsum) and noose/snare (pasha, zhags-pa): *body:* corpulent; legs: two; *Asana:* Pratyalidhasana: *Ornaments:* five-skull crown; wristlets, anklets, necklace; *body:* loin-tiger skin, and backside body covering elephant skin, garland: snake; *Legs:* two; colour: dark blue; *Vahana:* human corpse.

9. Mahakala (yab-yum) :

According to Tibetan sources Mahakala in Yab-yum form has the following characteristics:

Face: one, fierce, three eyes, flame-like hair; *Arms/hands:* four, right hands hold ritual chopper (Kartirika, grig-gug), and a vessel filled with nector of life and acknowledge (amrita). Left hands have human skull-cup (Kapala, thod-pa), and trident (trisula, rtse-gsum); *Body:* Loin-tiger skin and corpulent body; *Legs:* two, *ornaments:* Five-skull crown, wristlets, anklets, necklace; garland; skull of freshly severed heads, *Vahana:* lotus throne; *colour :* Dark blue; trampling a man at his feet; In Yah-yum form shakti has one fierce face; *Hands/Arms :* two; right hand holds thunderbolt (Vajra, rdo-rje) and left holds human skull cup (kapala, thod-pa); *Ornaments :* three-skull crown; wristlets, anklets and necklace.

Distribution of mGon-po murals in Gon-Khang of Phyang Monastery

The murals of mGon-po are shown in Fig. 10.1. However, they can be further explained in the following way:

(i) On the Right Side Wall Along the Door: Here I have seen only one mGon-po in yab-yum form called 'Green Mahakala'.

(ii) On the Wall Above the Door: There is no painting of mGon-po. However, two Dolma figures can be seen with beautiful paintings. Both these Dolmas partially or impartially protect the monastery and the sect of which it belongs through their spiritual powers.

(iii) On the Left Side Wall Along the Door: Here two forms of mGon-pos are depicted with their traditional costumes. They are Danta Mahakala and Mahakala in yab-yum form of blue colour.

(iv) On the Northern Wall : There are three mGon-po murals along with other Buddhist deities on the northern wall of the Gon-Khang. Here they are:

1. Red Mahakala (in yab-yum form).
2. White Mahakala (in yab-yum form).
3. Four–hand Mahakala.

(v) On the southern wall: Here three forms of mGon-po are depicted. They are:

(i) Mahakala (single)

(ii) Blue Mahakala (in yab-yum form).
(iii) Yellow Mahakala (in yab-yum form).

In conclusion the Gon-Khang of the Phyang monastery has twenty–one murals of different Buddhist deities with their mandalas, out of them nine murals belong to various forms of mGon-po Privious page.

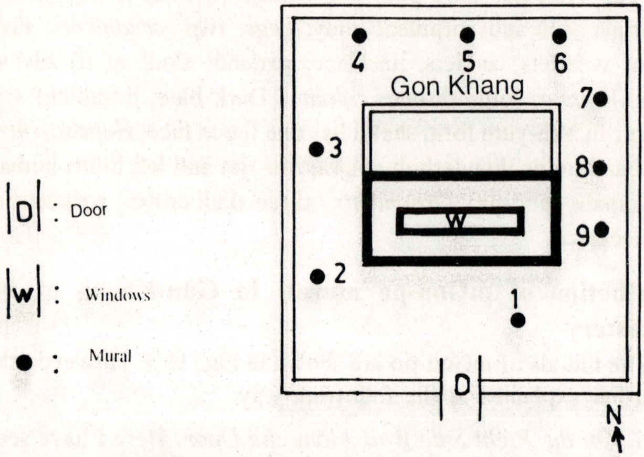

Fig. 10.1 : Murals in Gon-Khang of Phyang Monastery

1. mGon-po (in yab-yum form): Green Mahakala
2. Danta Mahakala
3. Mahakala (in yab-yum form), Colour: Blue
4. Red Mahakala (in yab-yum form)
5. White Mahakala (in yab-yum form)
6. Four–hand Mahakala (without yab-yum)
7. Mahakala (single)
8. Blue Mahakala (in yab-yum form)
9. Yellow Mahakala (in yab-yum form).

REFERENCES

1. Bunce, Fredric W : *An Encyclopaedia of Buddhist Deities, Demigods, Godlings, Saints and Demons*, Vol. I., D.K. Print World (P) Ltd., New Delhi, 1993, pp. 208-595.
2. *Ibid.*
3. *Ibid.*

4. *Ibid.*, pp. 341, 628.
5. *Ibid.*, p. 342
6. *Ibid.*, p. 343
7. *Ibid.*, p. 114.
8. *Ibid.*, p. 343.
9. *Ibid.*
10. *Ibid.*, pp. 86-87.
11. *Ibid.*, p. 808.

PERSONALITY

12

RASSUL GALWAN: A GREAT ADVENTURER OF LADAKH

Abdul Ghani Sheik

A silent war was fought between British India and Czar of Russia in the deserts, snow-bound mountain passes and desolate plains of Central Asia, Pamir, Tibet, Iran and Afghanistan for about one hundred years, which is known as the 'Great Game' in the history.

In the sixties of eighteenth century, this silent war was shifted to Chitral, Hunza, Ladakh and Chinese Turkistan (At present Shinjiang).

In 1878, a Russian column of 2,500 men with six guns actually left Margilan for Northern Area of India and it was reported that in 1885, when British India's relations with Russia were strained, the council at Kashghar in Chinese Turkistan made arrangements for collecting supplies and transport for a force whose destination was said to be Leh.

At one stage Czarist Russia and British India were on the verge of war.

The latter was worried of the expansionist policy of the Czarist Russia and was pushing forward its armed forces on the border of undivided India. It sent scientific, commercial, political missions, surveyors, explorers as well as spies to Central Asia and Tibet. The Dogra rulers of Kashmir also sent spies to Central Asia to assess the situation.

Leh was a key base for launching these expeditions. Tibet was closed to Europeans those days and the world knew very little about geography of Tibet.

An officer of the Survey of India, Captain T.G. Montgoemrie

during his stay in Ladakh observed that Ladakhis moved freely between Leh and Chinese Turkistan and Tibet without any restriction. He therefore planned to detail trained spies to Tibet in the guise of Ladakhis under the pretext of trade and pilgrimage. These adventurous expeditions brought sensational and interesting facts in public view.

The British India sent a British officer at Leh named as British Joint Commissioner for summer months though a senior officer was posted at Srinagar known as Resident.

Tibet had great fascination for Europeans. Besides the moveable archaeological remains of the missing old towns of the Gobi desert Central Asia had attraction for many Europeans.

For this purpose, they needed porters, guides, interpreters and ponymen which Ladakh provided. The region had resourceful, hardy and adventurous personnel suited for those expeditions in the inhospitable regions. They mainly belonged to Arghon clan. The Arghons are descendants of Kashmiri and Central Asian fathers and Ladakhi mothers.

There is a maxim that the high peaks of the Himalayas cannot be scaled without the cooperation of the Sherpas. The same maxim applied to the Arghons of those days.

Many have praised them in their books. These included Lord Dunmore, Captain Deasy, Seven Hedin, Frederic Drew, Colonel Younghusband, Major Godwin Austen, A.E. Ward, Filippo de Filippi, Arthur Neve, etc.

Some of these Arghons attained great reputation as Caravan Bashi (Leaders). Among them one prominent name is Rassul Galwan. He started his service as a coolie and poneymen and was elevated to caravan leader by dint of his diligence, honesty and experience. Later, he was appointed as Aqsaqual (trade Officer) for Central Asia at Leh.

He had a nodding acquaintance of English and wrote his autobiography entitled *Servant of the Sahibs* in his broken English. Other than this, Rassul spoke Turki, Urdu and knew Kashmiri and Tibetan enough for the purpose of communication.

Rassul's autobiography gives an account of his early life and journey undertaken with some Sahibs. It was the first autobiography in English written by a Ladakhi and Kashmiri. He wrote it on the persuasion of an American named Robert Barrett, with whom Rassul Galwan had travelled to Central Asia. The former was impressed by his account of journeys undertaken with various Europeans from very young age.

The book was published in Cambridge by Heffer and Sons Ltd in 1923. Sir Francis Younghusband has written the introduction. He has described Rassul as a 'Born story-teller'.

Rassul Galwan wandered about with European and American explorers and tourists in Tibet, Central Asia, China, Pamir, Aksaichin, Siachan Glacier, etc.

Most of these Europeans travelled to these regions once in their life and gained reputation. On the other hand, Rassul was destined to visit these regions year after year.

He was a born traveller. The zest for travelling was ingrained in his psyche. He mentions his reasons for travelling as follows:

> My relations in Chinese Turkistan were against my travelling. Offering financial help, they persuaded me to give up the hard life of a traveller, but I spurned their offer and told them that I find immense consolation in wandering.

Younghusband describes Rassul Galwan in these words:

> He is very diligent, hardy and strongman. Any mountaineer will be proud of his great achievements. I have never seen such a man in all my life. He is clearly a popular singer and has a great delight in banjo playing.

The exploits of Rassul Galwan were highlighted by All India Radio, New Delhi, BBC, Radio Pakistan and Doordarshan Srinagar in recent years. All India Radio, Delhi in its Urdu programme has repeatedly broadcasted a talk about Rassul.

Rassul Galwan's full name is Ghulam Rassul Galwan, but he is known as Rassul Galwan. He was born at Leh. According to Robert Barett, on the publication of his book in 1923, he was forty–five years old. By this reckoning, he was born in 1878. He was employed by Younghusband for his Central Asian trip in 1890, when he was barely 12 years old. Earlier, he had travelled to Kashmir with Dr Trall, an Anthropologist.

Rassul was grandson of Khira Galwan, who gave sleepless nights to the Sikh Governor of Kashmir. Khira was a daring and notorious robber, but a kind-hearted person. Treading into the footsteps of the legendary Robin Hood, he distributed his looted money and goods to the poor. Finally, he fell in the trap of Sikh Governor Mihan Singh, (1834-41) by the intrigue of his one confidant and was hanged. It was followed by the victimization of other Galwans.

Rassul's grandfather Mohammad Galwan fled to Baltistan and settled there. Rassul's mother was born in Baltistan. Later, she migrated to Leh and married Shukur Galwan, a relative and member of her clan. Shukur left her and went to Chinese Turkistan. She married another man named Ibrahim and Rassul was born.

Rassul Galwan travelled from very young age. He was employed by Younghusband in 1890 for his Central Asian expedition. Younghusband was of Captain's rank in those days and had been detailed by the British India to explore the Pamirs and Central Asia and to gather intelligence. The Pamirs formed a sort of no-man's land surrounded by British, Russian, Chinese and Afghan dependencies and the region had turned into a hot bed of the intrigues of these countries.

Younghusband encountered a Russian army officer Captain Grombtchevsky. He had come up to Shabidullah, an important station on the way to Ladakh. Captain Grombtchevsky told Younghusband that one day Russia would invade India, which would precipitate a revolt by people of India against the British rule.

Grombtchevsky was eager to visit Ladakh and requested Younghusband to recommend to Resident at Srinagar for issuing of a permit in his favour in this regard.

In 1892, Rassul Galwan went to the Pamir with Lord Earl of Dunmore. Dunmore's visit to the Pamir was identical to Younghusband's mission.

During this journey, Rassul came across some Russian soldiers. Sensing him a stranger, the soldiers interrogated him. Rassul was ready-witted and satisfied the soldiers with his answers. The soldiers offered him cigarettes. Rassul saw some dead bodies of Afghans killed in the skirmish with the Russians.

Rassul informed Dunmore about the presence of Russian soldiers and described his meeting to him. Dunmore was pleased and gave him reward.

During this journey, the caravan strayed from the recognized route in Aksaichin due to mist and bad weather and reached a difficult terrain. The spectre of death haunted every member of the expedition.

It was a challenge for an adventurous youngman like Rassul. He went in search of a route and reached a ravine, where he located a new route, which passed through the ravine. He rushed back and led the whole caravan though the ravine. Dunmore was pleased with Rassul Galwan and named the valley after his name as Galwan Nullah. This place was the scene of operation during Indo-Chinese war in 1962 and Galwan Nullah extensively figured in media reports.

While paying his tribute to Rassul Galwan and other Ladakhis, Dunmore, in the foreward of his book *The Pamir*, writes:

> It will ill become me to close this preface without paying a just tribute of praise to those excellent and hardworking Ladakhis headed by Ramzan Ali who formed the personnel of the caravan and accompanied the expedition on foot for 2,200 miles crossing 69 rivers and 41 mountain passes, many of them being among the highest in the world.

Later Dunmore submitted a paper before the Royal Geographical Society, in this paper he said:

"A better set of men, hardier or more willing, I have never met."

Dunmore's more willing man was Rassul Galwan and he described him as 'Old Francatelli'. Commenting on it, Professor (Dr) Henry Osmaston writes:

"The reason is obscure. At one time Francatelli was chief to Queen Victoria."

To travel in desert and desolate mountainous land of Central Asia and Tibet was tiring and arddous. The bulk of transport animals died from extreme cold and snow storms. There was always threat of highway men and robbers. Many daring persons lost their heart under such circumstances.

Referring his journey in the Gobi desert in 1877 Younghusband writes:

> That was the most despairing time of my whole journey, and many times that night I accused myself of being the greatest fool yet created and swore by all the Gods I would never go wandering about the wild places of the earth again. These periods of depression must occur to every traveller. He can't help asking himself now and then, 'what is good of it all?

The work of a porter and pony man was more arduous. He had to wash clothes, handle animals, prepare food, make camps and sometimes carry goods on his back. He normally travelled on foot. Some Europeans beat up and punished them on minor faults.

There is no doubt that the basic motive behind the travel of an Afghan was of economic compulsion, but the spirit of adventure and lust for wandering was an important factor.

Younghusband in his introduction to the book *Servant of Sahibs* writes:

> These men love adventures just as much as their employers. .... Why Himalayan people should be as ready as they are to undergo hardships and run risk of the most serious nature, in the service of any stray traveller who appears among them is not easy to understand. The payment they receive is small. They have to work for much more than an 8 hours a day. And they have no insurance against accidents, yet they readily work through long and arduous day, and willingly risk their lives. And, most wonderful of all, they are full of gratitudes to their employer when they leave his service.

In 1895, after traversing difficult terrains in Tibet, they reached near Lhasa together with British traveller George Littledale. He was the caravan leader in this journey. They penetrated Tibet from the north, covering 43 miles of Lhasa, before the Tibetans succeeded in stopping them. Mentioning this incident Rassul writes in his book that they were surrounded by about one thousand armed Tibetan horsemen and without inflicting any harm, led them to camp, wherefrom they were forced to retreat.

However, Rassul made his return journey to Ladakh from westward of Tibet. The journey though interesting, yet no European passed through Tibet before him.

Rassul put on a Tibetan dress and another caravan man and his old companion Galam Rasul personated as a lama. They posed as representatives of the Dalai Lama. The simple Tibetans were defrauded and they offered essential commodities and yaks for transportation of goods free of cost.

They reached Leh after a couple of months. After passing one night at Leh, Rassul had to accompany Mr and Mrs Littledale to Kashmir as in view of advance winter the closure of snow-bound Zojila on Leh-Srinagar Pony track was imminent. On the other hand, his newly-wed wife averse to his departure to Srinagar so soon. Rassul writes:

"With heavy heart, I had to leave for Kashmir next morning."

Rassul Galwan did not take much rest in Kashmir, the same year he travelled to Baltoro and Siachen Glaciers with Dr Arthur Neve. The next journey was with Philips and Church looking for big game. On their return to Leh, Rassul was offered a turban at a function by the duo in appreciation of his services. That was followed by a succession of journeys with a number of Sahibs including Martine, Professor Ronald Dixon, Robert Barrett and Filippo De Filippi.

In his book *Servant of Sahibs*, Mrs Robert Barrett under the caption of 'Editor's introduction' observes:

> Rassul's manners are perfect, the most polished gentleman could do no more than equal them. He is a very good person, and a father to his men. He is very black, very handsome man, graceful in all his movements, his smile most charming. His voice is the sweetest man's voice I ever heard. The woman lives not who would not fall in love at first sight but his standard of moral is very high. The women are afraid of him as of a saint.

Rassul and his companions loved nature and were very fond of visiting new places and to learn the customs, culture and mode of living of difficult people. They loved to relate their observations and experiences to others at Leh.

Rassul wrote every thing in his diary, and never hesitated even in writing broken and faulty English, as he writes:

> I was hurry for be old. And in head all times in night made rich, made meet with big man and was many countries with Sahibs.

Younghusband was very much impressed by Rassul's nature loving behaviour. He writes:

> He was sensible of the beauty of great mountains when he was one of those stupendous peaks which cluster round the second highest mountain in the world and it may have been 'K' itself.

Rassul Galwan, Galam Rassul , Shukur Ali and other friends were fond of dancing and singing and enhanced the splendour of the archery and other social festivals of Leh by their jokes! They introduced Chinese romantic 'Amban and boat' and dragon dances in Ladakh which were regularly showed till 1947 in festivals as an important item of culture. At first, 'The Amban and boat' show was presented on marriage ceremony of Rassul by Galam Rassul. They had watched these shows at Kashghar.

The most characteristic feature of Rassul Galwan's autobiography is his plain speaking, simplicity and his truthfulness.

Rassul Galwan portrays his poverty during his childhood in the following words:

> I wore loqpa (goat's hide). I used to get dung. When found good luck, then bring four baskets, bad luck time only two.

Rassul always kept very primary things with him. For example, he kept a big needle and thread with his person to sew his torn shoes.

In fact, Rassul Galwan was highly desirous to learn reading and writing. There was not any school at Leh in those days. The rich people engaged teachers at their houses to impart education to their children. He expressed his desire to his mother for his studies. Mother discouraged him and told that the education was preserved only for rich people. When Moravian Mission opened a school at Leh in 1887, Rassul went there and got little education of primary standard.

Rassul Galwan was a God-fearing man. He had blind faith in faquirs and shrines. Younghusband writes:

> The most notable point of all in Rassul's book is his touching faith in God. It was his standby in all hardships, trials and disappointment. And this habit of reverence was undoubtedly what made him the gentleman he is.

Rassul and most of the caravan men were overawed by the colonial power and felt proud in the service of Europeans in general and the Britishers in particular.

In his later years, Rassul was appointed as '*Aqsaqal*' or Chief Assistant of British Joint Commissioner, Leh. *Aqsaqal* is a Turkish word which means a man having white beard or respectable elderly man. It was a respectable assignment and/held in esteem. An *Aqsaqal* was also appointed at Kashghar in those days.

Today Rassul Galwan is not in this world but he is still sleeping eternally in the Muslim cemetery of Leh. This great adventurous traveller breathed his last on 13th March, 1925, leaving behind his wife and two minor children. The government donated a piece of land at Leh to his children for their subsistence.

REFERENCES

Abdul Ghani Sheikh: Rassul Galwan (Mashaheer Number) (in Urdu); Hamara Adab, J & K Cultural Academy, 1977-78.

Abdul Ghani Sheikh : Some well-known Adventurers of Ladakh : Recent Research on Ladakh; 6, 1997, pp. 231-38.

Mohammed Yusuf Teng (ed.) : Rassul Galwan-Arz-e-Kashmir Ka ek nāmwar sapoot; *Daily Aftab,* Srinagar.

Peter Hopkirk : The Great Game.

Rassul Galwan : *Servant of the Sahibs.*

Sir Walter Lawrance (ed.) : *Imperial Gazetter of India.*

The Earl of Dunmore : *The Pamirs.*

Younghusband : *The Heart of the Continent*

Younghusband : *The Northern Frontier of Kashmir.*

13

PREM SINGH JINA: A RESEARCH SCHOLAR OF LADAKH STUDIES

Mrs Manju Jina

Prem Singh Jina was born on 26th June 1956 at Dogaon village near Nainital, Uttar Pradesh. He belongs to a poor family. His father was a primary school teacher. He got his primary education from 'Chopra' a village primary school. During those days there were very few schools in UP Hills, so he passed primary education after travelling 16 kms daily. In 1965 he went to Nainital and got admission in C.R.S.T. College. But he left the college in 1970 and sought admission in Government Inter college. From this college he passed Intermediate and then went to Thakur Dev Singh Bisht Govt. P. G. College for further higher studies. In 1977, he passed M.A. in Economics.

His father never favoured him and once said:

"You have got M.A. degree, but what for, you haven't knowledge even upto Class Vth level student. How can you get a Govt. job. I did a blunder to give you a chance for higher studies. It would be better for me if you remain uneducated and help me in agriculture works."

When till the end of 1977 he did not get any Govt. job, his father finally decided to send him back to Dogaon village for cultivating his agricultural land. He was then sent to G.B. Pant Agricultural & Tech. University, Pantnagar for Agricultural training. After completing Agricultural training from Pantnagar University in 1979, he returned to Nainital. But his father did not want that he should stay at Nainital, so he was bound to go to Dogaon village and lookafter 'the agricultural activities there'.

In 1980 he came to Nainital and met Prof Maya Ram and expressed his desire for doing research work. He accepted his proposal and in the same year he got registration for Ph.D. degree in Kumaon University Nainital. Now he was looking after agricultural work in Dogaon village as well as doing his research work. After some time he saw an advertisement for the post of Lecturer in Economics in the *Times of India,* News paper. He applied for the post, and in October, 1980 he was called for interview at Leh. He went Leh, but the interview was cancelled. In June 1981 he was again called for interview for the same post. This time interview was held in Delhi. He was selected and on 25th June 1981 he decided to go to Leh and join his duty. This time again his father did not approve him and said:

"Please don't go there. How much salary will you get there? If you'll wholeheartedly work in the village you may get more than your salary".

He disagreed with father's arguments and went to Leh. On the 1st July, 1981 he joined his duties as a lecturer in Economics in the Central Institute of Buddhist Studies, Choglamsar; Leh-Ladakh. He did not like Ladakh but felt that the job in Ladakh would be better than the agricultural work in the village Dogaon. So, he unwillingly stayed in Ladakh. After some time he thought of writing something on Ladakh. Then he started writing articles for *Dinman*, *Sheeraja—Jammu*, *Yojana—Jammu*, *Newslatter—Delhi*, *Prakashitman—Delhi*, *Hindu Chetan—Delhi*, *Yojana—Delhi* and *Navaneet—Bombay*.

In 1982, he thought to finish his half done Ph.D work. So, he worked day and night and submitted his thesis to the Kumaun University, Nainital in 1983 and in 1985 he was awarded Ph.D. degree.

After completing Ph.D. work, he kept busy in writing articles on Ladakh for 'the different Indian and foreign magazines. Here follows a brief list of his contribution on Ladakh studies:

1. *Ladakh Aur Paryatan* (Hindi); Proceed of the 1st National Conference; C.I.B.S., Leh-Ladakh; 1981.
2. Santi Stupa Ladakh ke; *Yojana*, Jammu, 1982.
3. *Seemant Sanskrit ka Kumauni Sanskriti me Prabhav;* News-letter, Delhi, 1982.
4. Sect Kal me Leh Ghati (Hindi), Seeraja-65, J & K Academy of Arts and Culture Languages, Jammu, March, 1983.
5. Foreign tourists and their impact upon Ladakh, Proceed of the Third National Conference; C.I.B.S., Leh-Ladakh; 1983.

6. Boudh Bikshus of Ladakh; In : Proceed of All India Conference on Buddhist and Jain Monasticism, Deptt. of Buddhist Studies, Delhi University, 1983-84.
7. Buddhism in Ladakh and World Peace, In : 10th International Buddhist Conference on Buddhism and World Peace, Japanese Temple, Bodh Gaya, Vol. X, 1984.
8. Ladakh me Ringcell Ka Mahatava (Hindi); *Seeraja*-71, J & K Academy of Arts and Culture languages, Jammu; Vol. 2-3, June-Sept. 1984, pp. 23-25.
9. Foreign tourist traffic in Ladakh; *Himalayan Research and Development,* Nainital, 1984.
10. Kashmir me Bodh Chitrakala evam Murtikala tatha uska Ladakh me Prabhav (Hindi); Fifth National Conference Proceed; CIBS Leh-Ladakh, 1985.
11. A Brief Introduction of Ladakh Gompas; In : All India Conference, Kashmir University, Srinagar, Deptt. of Centre for Central Asian Studies, Proceeding, Ladakh Life and Culture; 1986.
12. A Survey of Buddhist Community in Ladakh Himalaya, In: 12th International Buddhist Conference on Buddhism and Social Harmony, Japanese Temple, Bodh Gaya, Vol. XII, 1986.
13. Pasture Land of Leh and its effect on Ecology; National Workshop on Nature Conservation, Trishul, Leh-Ladakh, 16th-25th June, 1986.
14. Socio-Economic and cultural relations between Ladakh and Lahul-Spiti, National Conference, Keylong, 1986.
15. Ladakh ki Sanskriti me Stok Rajvans (Hindi); *Culture* (Quarterly Journal), Delhi, 1986.
16. Pasture land of Zangskar and its effects on Ecology; National Seminar-cum-Workshop on 'Development of the Cold Desert of Ladakh', Desert Development Agencies Leh and Kargil; 23rd-25th September, 1986.
17. Leh tab aur Abb. (Hindi); *Navneet* (Hindi Digest), Bombay, April, 1987.
18. Monasteries in the Economy of Leh-Ladakh; In : All India Conference on Buddhism Monasteries of Himalayan Region : Various Aspects; 9-13th August, C.I.B.S., Leh, 1988.
19. Bodh Dham Leh-Ladakh (Hindi), *Hindu Chetana*; Vol. 7, New Delhi, 1988, pp. 21-25.

20. Ladakhi Rajao Ke Bodh Dharam me Yogdan (Hindi), *Hindu Chetana*; Vol. 10, Sept. 1988, pp. 19-20.
21. Eco-Environmental Study of Tourism in Ladakh Himalaya, All India Conference; Kashmir University; Srinagar; 1989.
22. Logar in Himalayas; Proceeding of All India Conference.
23. Himalayayi Sanskrati-2; Shimla, 1989, pp. 115-18.
24. Buddhism and Human Values in the History of Ladakh Himalaya; In : International Buddhist Conference, Japanese Temple, Bodh Gaya, India, 1990.
25. The Pashmina Economy in Ladakh Himalaya, *Yojana* (English); Delhi, December, 1990, pp. 16-31.
26. Pasture Ecology of Leh, Ladakh, In: Internales Kolloquium, Herrnlul Herausgegeben und redigiert vom Lydia Lcke-Schwalbe und Gudrun Meier, 'Wissenenschaftsgeschichte und Gegenwartige Forschungen in 'Nordwest-Indian, Staatliches Museum Fur volker-kunde Dresden Forschungsstelle, Vol. 9, Bis 13, Marz, 1987, 1990, pp. 171-84.
27. Ladakh: History and Growth of Education; *Himalaya Today*, September-November, Vol. III, No. 2, 1991, pp. 16-18.
28. Ladakh me Bodh Kala Ka Udha aur Vikash; *Seeraja,* Vol. 6, Feb-March, 1991, pp.12-14.
29. Ladakhi Shirobhusa-Perakh (Hindi), *Seeraja*, Vol. 6, Feb.-March, 1992, pp. 20-23.
30. Ladakh Ki Mahila Prasasak-Putith Wangmo; *Hamara Sahitaya*; Usha Viyas (ed.); J&K Academy of Arts, Culture and Languages, Jammu, 1992, pp.104-106.
31. Impact of Tourism on Ladakhi Society and Culture; In : All India Conference Proceedings, J.N.U., New Delhi., 1993.
32. Impact of Tourism on Ecological set-up of Ladakh Himalaya, In : International Conference on Ladakh Studies (Sixth Collquium), August 16-20, Leh, 1993.
33. Poultry Industry in Ladakh, *Himalaya Today*, Sept. 92, Vol. IX, Nos. 6 2 & 3, Feb. 1993, p.7.
34. Buddhism in Ladakh and its Approach to Material World, In: International Buddhist Conference, Japanese Temple, Bodh Gaya, 8-10 Dec., India, 1993.
35. Tourist Industry in Ladakh, *Himalaya Today,* Vol. V, No. 2, Jan-March, 1994, p. 20.
36. Bhikshunis in Ladakh (Nuns in Ladakh); In : International Conference Proceed; Keylong (H.P.); 14 -15 July, 1994.

37. Kesar : A Great Epic (Hindi); *Seeraja*, Vol. 2, (June-July), 1994, pp. 17-20.
38. Tourism in Ladakh Himalaya, Indus Publishing Company, New Delhi, 1994, p. 252.
39. Phyang Monastery of Ladakh, Indus Publishing Company, New Delhi, 1995, p.152.
40. Famous Western Explorers to Ladakh, Indus Publishing Company, New Delhi, 1995, p. 152.
41. High Pasturelands of Ladakh Himalaya, Indus Publishing Company, New Delhi, 1995, p. 142
42. Ladakh : The Land and The People, Indus Publishing Company, New Delhi, 1996, p. 288.
43. Recent Researchers of the Himalaya, Indus Publishing Company, New Delhi; 1996, p. 252.
44. Tibetan Manuscripts and Inscriptions of Ladakh Himalaya, Sri Satguru Publication, Delhi, 1998, p. 98.
45. Some monasteries of Drigungpa order in Central Ladakh, (in press); Sri Satguru Publications, Delhi.
46. Ladakh ki Kala Avam Sanskriti (Hindi); Indira Gandhi National Centre for Arts & Culture; New Delhi (in press).
47. Changing face of Ladakh Himalayas, Om Publication, Faridabad; Haryana; (in press).
48. Lamayuru monastery of Ladakh Himalaya; Om Publication, Faridabad; Haryana; (in press).

In conclusion Dr. Prem Singh Jina like A.H. Francke, Moorcroft, Csoma De Koros, Cunningham, etc., is fully dedicated in Ladakh studies, but he needs moral and financial support by the governmental and non-governmental institutions for further studies.

TRADITION AND SOCIETY

14

BUDDHIST TRADITIONS AND LADAKH

Geshey Konchok Namgyal

Buddhism is very fortunate not to be ridden by any major destabilizing divisions. This is strength that we are to employ for making the world benefit from Buddhism.

The three traditions of Buddhism that we find in the present time are peacefully coexisting. There are no conflicting differences among them in so far as fundamental philosophical beliefs are concerned. Hinayan, Mahayan and Zen Buddhism all share the basic foundation of the Vinaya rules governing the life of ordained monks. We can look back on the history of the growth of Buddhism with a great sense of pride that there were no occasions of any confrontations among the different traditions of Buddhism.

In Ladakh we are following Mahayan tradition of Buddhism based on Tibetan practices. Our monasteries are built in accordance with the rules prescribed by the Vinaya Sutra and our monks lead monastic lives strictly according to the Vinaya. It is natural that because of the separate cultural and geographical features of Ladakh, our tradition of Buddhism has developed its own distinct characteristics so far as the monks' cells and robes are concerned.

It is, of course, not the right forum, for me to throw light on the Vajrayan practices followed in our monasteries in Ladakh. However, one can see such practices almost in all the monasteries at their Gon-Khangs. Besides, Tantric Buddhist deity murals are beautifully decorated on the walls of the monasteries in Ladakh.

We have the greatest respect for the Theravad tradition of Buddhism followed in many South-East Asian countries. In the last few years, we have come much closer to these countries by exchanges of visits. In fact a chapter on Buddha's Light International Centre has actually been opened in Ladakh. Our people have benefited a lot from it. Ven. Sangha Sen is presently the head of this centre. Like monasteries and such religious centres, thus, made a few programmes of direct social uses. Through these institutions we can integrate the intact Buddhist Communities with monastic set-ups.

In our age of easy means of communication, various Buddhist traditions have come into contact with one another as never before. My own experience has been that the more we interact with one another, the clearer it becomes that in the matters of belief in the Sutra we have no difference at all. In our tradition also the study of Abhidharma is very essential. Differences due to local conditions are small and insignificant.

It is the measure of the greatness of the Dharma that a number of people in the industrialised countries follow our Dharma. If, there is one religion that can go hand in hand with the fast advancing scientific mode of thinking it is our Dharma. Like the many chapters of Buddhist Light International Centre in Ladakh, there are many Tibetan Mahayan Buddhist Centres which are quietly working in Ladakh. Through these we are bringing the teachings of the Buddha to all the places in Ladakh as much as we can.

I deem it necessary to say that Ladakh has become a very popular international tourist destination because of the people's culture which wholly based on their faith in the practice of Buddhist learning.

In conclusion Ladakh is a centre of Mahayan Buddhism, but monastic set ups and vinaya rules are not having much difference from the other cycles of Buddhism like Hinayan, Zen, etc.

15

THE SOCIAL ECONOMY OF BUDDHIST MONASTERIES IN LADAKH

Prem Singh Jina

Ladakh was first influenced by Buddhism in second century AD. During this period a chorten was built at Sani in Zangskar after the name of Kushan Emperor Kanishka. Later during eighth century Padamasambhava spread Buddhism in Tibet and Ladakh. The rock engravings on the numerous sites of Ladakh are associated with this. At that time, Bon religion was very much popular in Tibet. Therefore in order to spread Buddhism he instead of fighting with the deities of Bon religion or keeping them away, decided to assimilate them along with Buddhist deities. Slowly Buddhism got its roots in Tibet. In tenth century Rin-Chen-bzan-po was born in Guge, later he went to Kashmir and West Bengal to study Buddhism under the guidance of Indian Buddhist scholars. But when he heard about his father's death, he returned to Tibet. Later he started a movement to construct chortens and monasteries throughout in Tibet and its adjoining regions. In Ladakh, he constructed chortens near Thikse, Lamayuru, Alchi, etc. and monasteries at Alchi, Wanla, Atiche, Lamayuru etc. Hence, began the strong revival of Bonism which re-established Buddhism throughout in Western Tibet including Ladakh.

In tenth century AD Ladakh came under Lha-Chhen-pal-gyi-gon, a descendant of Tibet Royal Dynasty. He was Buddhist and encouraged Buddhism in his kingdom. As the centuries rolled on, the other sects of Buddhism also started to establish their monasteries in Ladakh.

Monasteries in Ladakh thus, became a key centre of cultural

heritage. The Lamas of these monasteries gradually started taking active part in politics. Many lamas of them became the advisers of king of Ladakh. Today Ladakh is an integral part of India and still has rich cultural heritage, monasteries perform rituals in old tradition. There are beautiful paintings statues of Buddhist deities, Gurus, religious books and rituals items, etc. Prominent among them are :

1. Tathagat Buddha
2. Padmasambhava
3. Avalokitesvara
4. Gonpo
5. Mandalas
6. Different forms of Yab-yum
7. Traditional lamas of the concern sect
8. Indian and Tibetan Gurus
9. Maitreya
10. Manjusri

In Ladakh monasteries are deeply attached with the Buddhist society. Lamas of these fulfil the ritual demands of Buddhists. Each Buddhists family has its own Chot-Khang, and lamas are called for perform rituals in it. (Fig. 15.1)

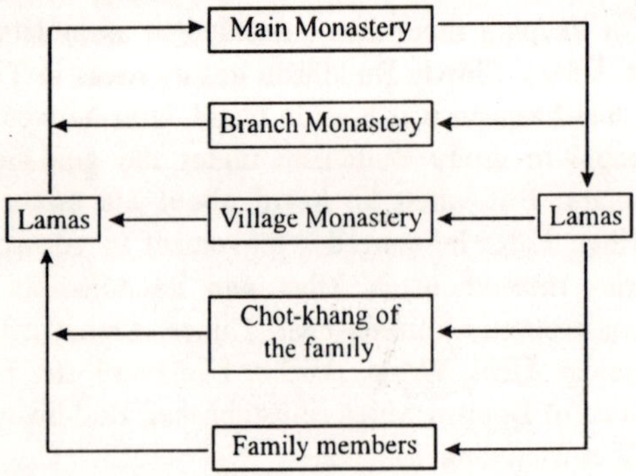

Fig. 15.1 : Socio–cultural structure of monasteries in Ladakh.

Thus ritual practice is the main source of earnings of the monasteries. Every monastery has some villages under its religious control. And villagers of these whenever in need approach only that monastery under which they come and follow ritual tradition according to the sect of the monastery.

Table 15.1 shows the details.

TABLE 15.1

NUMBER OF VILLAGES ATTACHED TO THE MONASTERIES IN LADAKH

Sl. No.	*Name of the Monastery*	*No. of Villages Attached*
1.	Hemis	100
2.	Thiksey	25
3.	Likir	10
4.	Phyang	14
5.	Spituk	13
6.	Stakna	12
7.	Matho	05
8.	Takthok	02

Source: Jina, Prem Singh : 'A brief introduction of Ladakh Gonpas', In : *Ladakh Life and Culture*, 1985, pp. 39-50.

The Table indicates that :

1. Monasteries are closely woven with the socio-eccnomic fabric of Ladakhi society.
2. Hemis monastery has good control over Buddhist population in Ladakh, as about sixty per cent villages are under its supervision.

Besides, monasteries have hundred acres land. During olden days lamas of their respective monasteries cultivated the lands. Now this practice is not prevalent, instead they give their lands on rent to villagers and in return get foodstuff, apricot oil, fuel wood, etc. (Fig. 15.2 and Table 15.2):

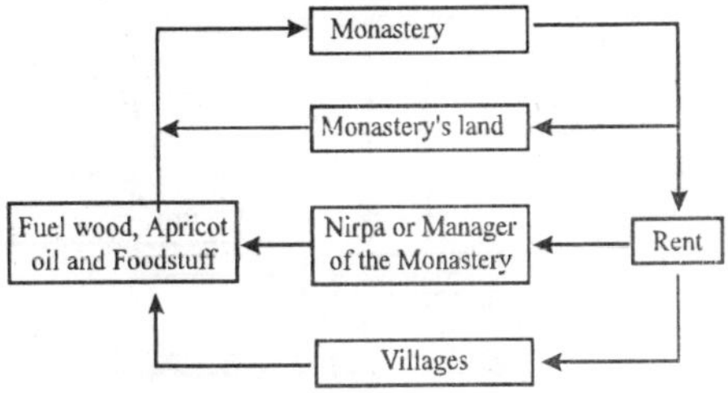

Fig 15.2. Monastery's land management system in Ladakh.

TABLE 15.2

LAND HOLDING OF DIFFERENT MONASTERIES IN LADAKH

Sl. No.	*Name of Monastery*	*Landholdings (in acres)*
1.	Hemis	1998.3
2.	Thiksey	1327.3
3.	Likir	0263.3
4.	Phyang	0360.0
5.	Spituk	0375.8
6.	Stakna	0516.7
7.	Matho	0400.0
8.	Takthok	0043.3

Source: D.C. Office, Leh, Ladakh.

The table 15.2 reveals that :

(i) Hemis monastery is a number one rank for landholding in Ladakh. It has land not only in Leh district, but in Kargil district also.

(ii) Land is the other source of income for the monastery after ritual practice.

Since beginning, monasteries have been educational centres for lamas. Here they get religion and philosophical education from their senior lamas (Fig 15.3). Later on the basis of philosophical and ritual knowledge they get the posts in the monasteries. A lama can reach up to the Deputy head lama after working in the post of Komner, Gyeskas, Lonpo, Champspon, etc. However, those who are interested in professional training (i.e. Painting, wood carving, etc.) can also get training in the monasteries.

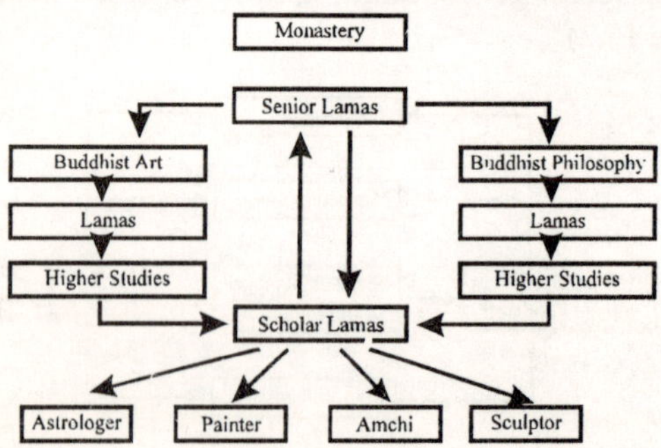

Fig. 15.3 : Education Structure of monasteries in Ladakh

During the olden days monasteries were also the source of public recreation. Ladakhis, who used to be busy during summers in their fields, have had sufficient leisure time in winters. Therefore, monasteries celebrated their annual festivals in winters, so that maximum Ladakhis could participate in the festival. Now this trend has been changing due to tourist rush, monasteries are now shifting their festivals in summers.

In the annual festival, lamas of the respective monastery gather at the 'Chamra'. Thereafter with some ritual offerings, they with their colourful dresses and masks come at the ground and play 'Cham' dance in groups for two days.

It has been noticed that monasteries in Ladakh celebrate their annual festivals every year not only for the welfare of Ladakhi people, but also they arrange the festivals for the welfare of all living beings of the world. Now these festivals are becoming source of entertainment among foreigners and thus encouraging tourism in Ladakh (Fig. 15.4).

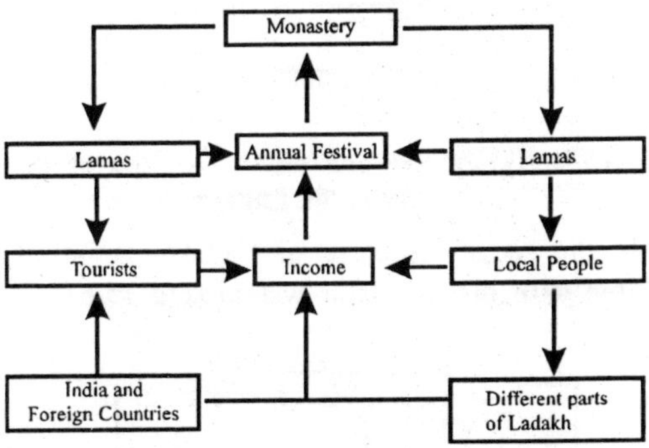

Fig. 15.4: Tourists and local people attractive relationship with monastic festivity in Ladakh.

Besides, some monasteries in Ladakh annually send their lamas to Leh and other parts of Ladakh to celebrate special festivals. For example, the Takthok monastery sends lamas to Leh for Dos-Moche festival and looks after the religious works like 'Onpo' and 'Tak-las'.

Though lamas of the monasteries are not practically engaged in fields for the cultivation of foodstuff, yet with the help of villagers they grow horticultural and agricultural products, to look after the agriculture and allied activities, monasteries employ 'Nirpa' and 'Chang-Jot'. Thus, the produced food products collected by lamas and Chomos (if they are) in presence of 'Nirpa' or 'Chang-Jo'. And later sale these to the nearby market if so require. Sometimes, neighbouring villagers purchase these directly from the monastery's authority (Fig. 15.5).

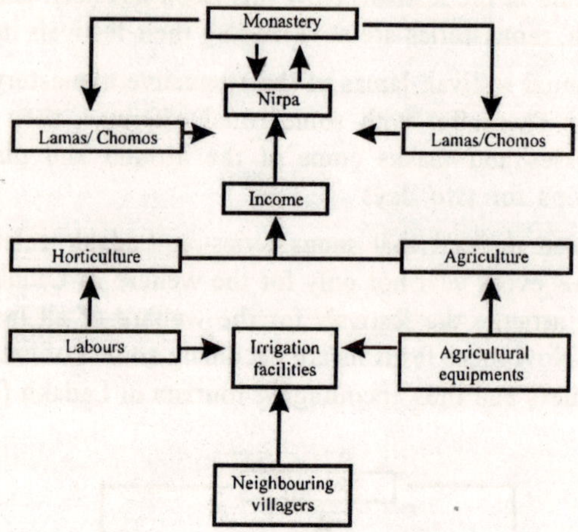

Fig. 15.5: Agriculture and allied activities of the monasteries in Ladakh

In Ladakh, the social structure of Ladakhi Buddhist people is closely associated with the monastic system (Fig 15.6).

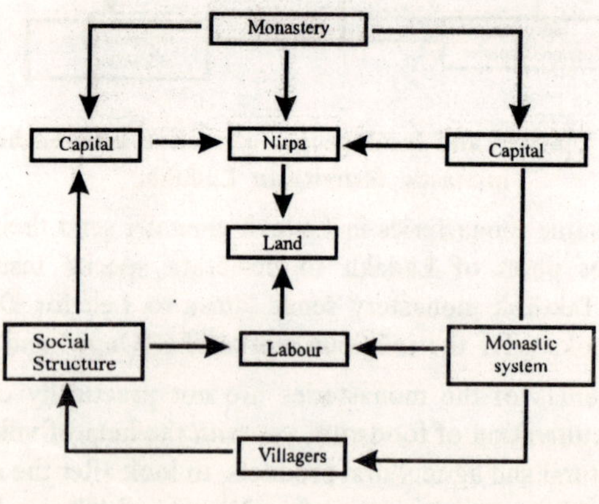

Fig. 15.6: Coordination between villagers' social structure and monastic system in Ladakh

The redistribution of the food products is also done with the help of lamas and villagers.

According to this, redistribution of perishable foodstuffs involve the movement from the site of production to monastery and vice-versa. Hence, this system is a symbol of interdependence between site workers (villagers) and monastery community which ensure the subsistance of produce (Fig. 15.7).

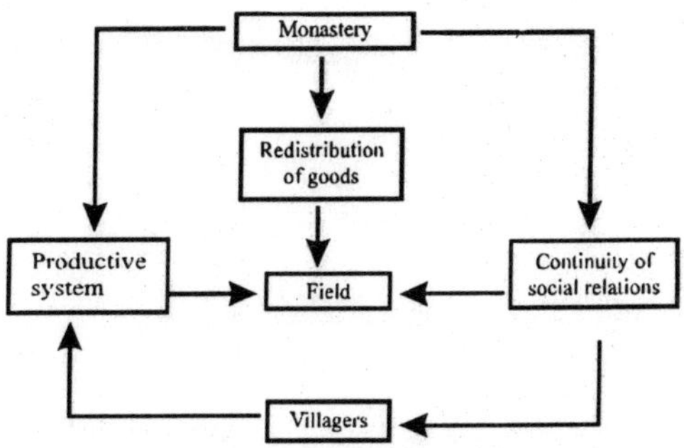

Fig. 15.7: Redistribution of goods for the subsistance produce within the monastic system.

In conclusion monasteries in Ladakh have established very strong socio-economic relations between lamas and laymen Buddhist community (Fig 15.8).

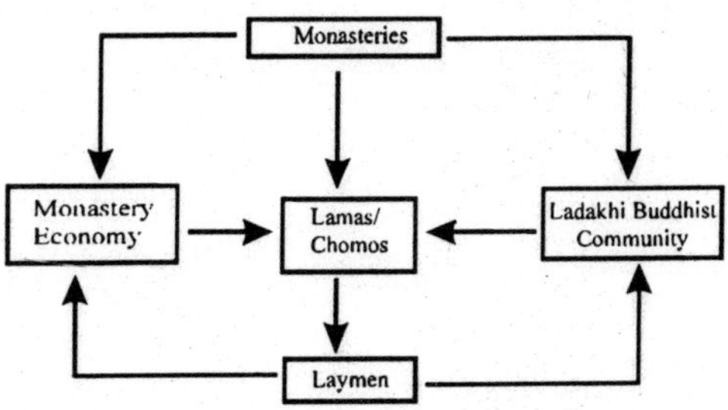

Fig. 15.8: Socio-economic structure of monasteries in Ladakh

REFERENCES

1. Grimshaw, Anna: 'Celibacy, Religion and Economy activity in a monastic Community of Ladakh', In : 'Recent Research on Ladakh', Band I, 1983.
2. Jina, Prem Singh: 'A brief Introduction of Ladakhi Gonpas', In: *Ladakh Life and Culture*, Srinagar, 1985.
3. Jina, Prem Singh: 'Buddhism in Ladakh and world peace', In: The Proceed of 10th International Buddhist Conference, Vol. X, 1984.

POLITICS

16

CHANGING HORIZON OF LADAKHI POLITICS

Prem Singh Jina

Ladakh is a part of Jammu and Kashmir state. In the tenth century AD King dpal-gyi-gon, the son of a descendant to Tibetan Royal Dynasty, became the first King of Ladakh. Since then Ladakh was ruled by Buddhist kings. In 1834, when Wazir Zorawar Singh forcibly occupied Ladakh and annexed it with Jammu and Kashmir, Ladakhis were ignored by higher authorities of state. Even during British regime, they were not given proper justice. When Britishers recognised democratic system in Jammu and Kashmir state, they recognised the political system and made Assemblies on the basis of population or rather to say on the religious grounds as Muslim and Hindu Constituencies. The Praja Sabha or the Kashmir Assembly was therefore constituted along the religious grounds and Buddhists of Ladakh did not get representation in the Kashmir Assembly.[1]

In 1930s, besides religious ground state politics, Ladakh obtained two seats for its Buddhist Community in the Praja Sabha. Muslims who were slightly less than 50 per cent population did not get representation in the Praja Sabha. This event caused little differences among Buddhist and Muslim political leadership. To settle down the grievances Glancy Commission of Enquiry was constituted in November 1931. But nothing was given to Muslims in the Praja Sabha. The commission considered Ladakh as a Buddhist dominant region. Thus Glancy Commission's report was the green signal for Buddhists. Consequently the Youngman's Buddhist Association was founded in 1934. This association was renamed 'Ladakh Buddhist Association'. Its primary aim was to protect and promote the interests of Buddhists in Ladakh (Appendix-1).

Hence, Buddhists got their representation in the State Assembly, but in the Muslim dominated State Assembly they could not do better for the Buddhists in Ladakh. In the mean time Kushok Bakula, head lama of Spituk monastery emerged as a new leader of National Conference (a political party of Jammu and Kashmir State). But his appearance in politics left a deep impact on other sects of Buddhism.

In 1960, when first time election was held in Ladakh, Kushok Bakula faced 'Social boycott' by the patrons of Drukpa Kargut pa order, however, he succeeded in his political mission.[2]

The other group who opposed Kushok Bakula leadership during those days had argued that Bakula Rinpoche declined Scheduled Tribe status for Ladakh in 1950 when it was offended by Pt. Nehru, because he felt it meant lowering the status of Ladakhis. But this argument does not have sufficient evidence.[3]

In state level politics Muslim leaders had a dominant role, they ignored the Buddhist culture and Buddhism in Ladakh. Therefore, Ladakhi Buddhists were not happy with the Jammu and Kashmir government. So, they were of the view that the Central Government should take Ladakh under direct control. When Kushok Bakula ceased to be a Minister in the G.M. Sadiq Government in 1963, the demand for central rule in Ladakh gained momentum. It was also argued that the funds which had been alloted by Central Government for the development of Ladakh should not be routed through the Jammu and Kashmir Government. Charges of misappropriation of the funds were levelled.[4]

In 1975, Sheikh Abdullah became Chief Minister of Jammu and Kashmir state, he considered the grievances of Ladakhis and admitted that his party National Conference failed to give proper representation to Ladakhis. He included Sonam Norboo in his cabinet. Sonam Norboo was a dynamic leader, under his leadership Ladakh, achieved considerable economic development. After his death Sheikh Abdullah appointed his son as Deputy Minister, but he failed to do better for Ladakhis. He could only represent a section of population in Ladakh. By and large he could not influence Ladakhis in general. Therefore, Sheikh Abdullah joined hands with Bakula in 1975.[5] However, Kashmir Government did not change its partial attitude for Ladakh and discriminated amongst Ladakhis. The facts in the connection are as follows:[6]

1. Ladakh, the third most important region within the Jammu and Kashmir State, does not have a single representative in the State's, 30 membered Council of Ministers.

2. Although, in area, it is far larger than Jammu and Kashmir Valley, but it has only two members in the State Assembly of seventy–five.
3. There is no sound education policy for Ladakh. Even this massive region does not have a degree college.
4. The government has systematically dismantled all the important forums of development such as the Ladakh Affairs Department in the State Secretariat and the Ladakh Development Board.
5. The meagre funds allocated to the region are wasted on ill-designed works like Stakna project, a 4 MW hydel project, that took 25 years and crores of rupees, only to prove a failure in the end.

Apart from such general discrimination the Kashmir Government through various policies favoured the Muslims (Appendix-2).

Such calculation as made by the State Government created disturbances in Ladakh. In 1989, Ladakh Buddhists were unable to tolerate State Government partial attitude for Buddhists in Ladakh. Therefore, they went on an agitation to declare Ladakh a Union Territory. Bakula not only supported the movement, but demanded to declare Ladakhis as Scheduled Tribes.[7]

Thus, viewing the mounting pressure upon State Government, the State Government created 'The Ladakh Affairs Department' under the interest that, 'It would have a representative from the region as the incumbent minister, and would function as the nerve-centre for Ladakh's betterment and development.[8]

However, in Ladakh, people were not very happy with this, they felt that :

> Besides creating 'Ladakh Affairs Department,' the successive Kashmir Governments from Baksh's to Farooq's have never felt comfortable with this special provision. With Dr. Farooq's coming back into power, the Ladakh Affairs Department was virtually turned into a defunct department."[9]

However, Dr. Farooq did not agree with this argument. In his interview with *Frontline* in 1989 he said:

"The Development Commissioner for Ladakh Affairs in the State Secretariat and to all intents and purposes, Ladakh is deemed to be a separate division in the state."

About funds allocation for Ladakh region according to him: The State Government had been ploughing in more money in the region over the years. He further pointed out that the Sikri Commission appointed by the State Government, to inquire into the question of regional imbalances and which submitted its report in August 1980, has held that as far as Ladakh is concerned, there is no imbalance except under certain developmental heads. On the basis of this the Government has issued order to rectify the imbalances.

In Leh district, Ladakhis made complaints against the plan allocation. According to them : Leh and Kargil roughly have the same population, but both districts received the same funds for the developmental work. Whereas Leh district is four times bigger in size and the transport costs to Leh from Srinagar are double that for Kargil. Therefore, Leh district should be given more funds than Kargil."[11]

Thus, Ladakh Buddhist Association called a meeting in order to discuss the various aspects of Ladakhis problems. After this discussion an action committee was formed. It was headed by Kushok Bakula, then member of the Minorities Commission. It demanded the creation of a Ladakh division and allocation of funds on the basis of area rather than population.[12]

This was crucial period in the Ladakhi politics. Because all Buddhists in Ladakh were ready to fight the government for fulfilling their demands. Hence, Kushok Bakula also raised the following two demands:[13]

(*i*) That Ladakh be granted internal autonomy;
(*ii*) That Ladakhis be treated as Scheduled Tribes.

In 1989, young leadership came forward in Ladakh. Thupstan Chhewang became the President of Ladakh Buddhist Association. Thereafter, under the leadership of Thupstan Chhewang, Ladakh Buddhist Association started strong agitation against the discrimination of Kashmir Government and for Scheduled Tribe status to Ladakh. This movement was successful in convincing the Kashmir Government authorities about their demands. Ladakhis were then declared Scheduled Tribes and the region as Scheduled Tribe Area. Then with this declaration Ladakhis have had new hopes as they could get good opportunities in educational institutions and government jobs. Thus it gave new opportunities to Ladakhis for the development in educational pursuits and governmental assistance expanding its developmental activities. In this connection a mini census and a survey had been conducted in 1986. This survey established that the ethnic groups in Ladakh such as : Bodh, Balti, Drogpa, Purigpa and Chang-pa were distinct tribes as understood under the constitution. The Central Government passed on the above recommendation to the State Government for Notification under the State Constitution.[14]

Although during 1989, the major grouse was over by declaring Ladakhis as Scheduled Tribes but the discrimination in the Plan allocation to Ladakh by State Government remained at the same position. Therefore, Ladakh Buddhist Association continued its agitation, unfortunately during the agitation differences between Buddhist and Muslim communities took place, consequently social boycott took place for local Muslims. Then late Agha Hyder reacted on this and in an interview he said:

"We are all Ladakhis, we all suffer under the Kashmiris. We Should fight them together, instead of each other."[15]

Kacho Mohammed Ali Khan, administrator and scholar from Kargil also then favoured the Agha Hyder's statement. Thus, Ladakh Buddhist Association conducted an emergency meeting and in the meeting maximum Buddhist members considered the feelings of Muslim leaders of Ladakh. Hence, the social boycott lifted in November 1992.[16]

In 1993, a joint meeting of Buddhist and Muslim leaders of Leh district was organised. In the meeting they decided that leaders of both communities would work jointly for declaring Ladakh an Autonomous Hill Council. Thereafter on 10th and 11th of June 1993, the representatives of Ladakh Buddhist Association and Ladakh Muslim Association under a single delegation went to Srinagar and talked with the State Government officials on the structure and constitution of the Leh Council. This time the government side was led by Chief Secretary Sheik Ghulam Rasool, while the Ladakh Buddhist Association and Ladakh Muslim Association team were headed by Thupstan Chhewang and Akbar Ladakhi respectively. Besides, several rounds of talks were held in Jammu, Srinagar and Delhi in relation with Autonomy for Ladakh. In each meeting green signal was given from the government side, thus in meeting after meeting progress had been noticed by the Ladakhi leaders. Finally, the government agreed in principal to grant Hill Council status to Ladakh region (i.e. both the Leh and Kargil districts). But the Kargil delegates then turned down the offer, stating that they would rather wait till a popular government is established in the state. Since then the talks about Autonomy was centered between the delegates of Leh district and the Government. Thus, while talking with the Chief Secretary in June 1993 the Ladakhi delegation gave the following description of the Autonomous Council:

"The Council will be a two-tier structure comprising a General Council (GC) and Executive Council (EC). The 'G.C.' will have 30 members, four of whom will be nominated by the Governor to ensure representation of minorities, women and specialists. The 'EC' will comprise five members, one of whom will be from the principal minority group (Muslims). The chairman of 'EC' will be elected by the General Council.

The power structure in the proposed council has many parallels with that in the state : for instance, the Chief Executive Councillor will be somewhat like the Chief Minister in the State. The Vice-Chairman (proposed) will act as a speaker in the 'GC', which itself will be equivalent to the State Assembly. The twenty six members will be like MLAs and MLCs in the state, and the four members Executive Council like the state cabinet.

The Development Commissioner (DC), who will be the Chief Executive Officer of the Executive Council (comparable to Chief Secretary in the state) will manage all development, financial and administrative activities. But he/she will be independent of the council in the exercise of magisterial powers.

However, the budget and all decisions about the utilization of grants, etc. will be made in the General Council. The DC will be a senior Indian Administrative Service (IAS) officer and through him the council will control the whole official machinery. It is important to note that the D.C. will be accountable and answerable to the council, and his Annual Confidential Report (ACR) will also be recorded by the Chief Executive Councillor."[17]

Though the delegation from Leh had long discussion about the formation of Leh District Autonomous Council with State Government side officers, yet the following points remained unsolved:

1. The name of the council
2. Vice-Chairman
3. Placement of Government Employees.

About the name of the council, Ladakh delegation (i.e. delegation from Leh district) insisted on word 'Autonomous' in the name of the council. But the Jammu and Kashmir government officials did not appreciate the term 'Autonomous' and they preferred to give little 'Leh Planning and Development Board'.[18]

The Ladakhi delegation also raised the need for appointment of Vice-Chairman in order to work out council activities in democratic order. According to the spokesman of the delegation:

"There should be a post of Vice-Chairman in the council and a member of the executive council should be appointed as Vice-Chairman who will act like a speaker in the Assembly. This will be very important to make the council democratic and its members participative, because if things go properly there should be ruling wing and an opposition wing in the council and it will be for the Vice-Chairman/Speaker to control the proceedings democratically."[19]

But the State Government did not agree with this argument (i.e. about the post of Vice-Chairman). However, discussion was continued. The Ladakhi delegation then pointed out on the issued of the placement of Government Employees and made the following argument:

"Officials up to the rank of Deputy Director to be subject to the council, i.e., their placement, promotion, transfer and punishment, etc. should rest with the council. Officers about this rank including the DC would be taken on deputation from the state with a mechanism of choice, sending penels of 3 or 4 preferred names to the State Government."[20]

Again the State Government did not agree with Ladakhi delegation on the issue of Government officers and employees placement.

Thus, after the meeting the spokesman of the Ladakhi delegation said that the meeting was partially successful, as they have achieved their two objects halfheartedly. [21]

1. Originally it was proposed that the council budget will be presented to the State Assembly for approval and the final decision in case of differences be kept with the council. This objectives could not be achieved, meaning that the State Assembly can make modifications in the council budget. However, in the event of a major dispute between the State Government and the Council, the final decision will rest with Governor of the State.

2. The second demand was that grant-in-aid from centre should be directly placed at the Council's disposal, without being channeled through the State Government. Although the state had no objection to

this, they said that technically it was not possible. Hence the alternative agreement upon is that the state will make no changes whatever in the Central Grants earmarked for the district, and that all such grant will be non-lapsable. This does not seem to be a bad arrangement, the only problem they say is that it will leave the council at the State Government's mercy regarding prompt processing, etc.

The last round of tri-partie talks held in New Delhi on October, 1993 with Union Home Minister S.B.Chavan. During this meeting Kashmiri lobby was opposing to include the word 'Autonomous' with Hill Council. In this connection they made the following argument :

"If the word 'Autonomous' will be included with the council, a day may come when Ladakhis would demand to separate them from the Jammu and Kashmir State."[22]

Besides, Kashmiris objection about the word 'Autonomous' the Ladakhi delegation remained strict on their stand and had strongly demanded that 'Autonomous' word must be included with the council.

Finally, both the Ladakhi delegation and the state officials left the decision to the Home Minister, who without hesitation agreed that 'Autonomous' should be in the name of the council.[23]

On 9th May, 1995, President of India finally approved the 'Ladakh Autonomous Hill Development Councils Act' (Appendix-3). Laying a copy of a statement on the table of the Lok Sabha, Rajesh Pilot, then the Minister of State for Home said:

"The President of India on May 9 approved the 'Ladakh Autonomous Hill Development Council Act'. The Act envisages at Autonomous Hill Development Council for each district of the region. Leh and Kargil and an inter-district advisory council for the Ladakh region as a whole with the State Government may constitute in consultation with the councils of Leh and Kargil.

Under the law, the Government can appoint different dates for the constitution of the district council. In pursuance of this, it is proposed to constitute the council for Leh district in the first place. The district council is to comprise 30 members to whom 26 shall be elected. The remaining members are to be nominated by the Governor from among the principal religious minorities and women in the district.[24]

About the powers of council, Rajesh Pilot further said:

"The council will have executive powers in the districts in relation to allotment use and occupation of and, formation of development scheme for progress of development schemes, formulation and finalisation of budgets, plan as well as non-plan, laying down guidelines for implementation of schemes at grass root level. The council shall also have the powers to collect taxes under the law within the district.

The members of the council shall elect a Chairman, who will also be the Chief Executive Councillor of a five member executive council and shall be responsible for conduct of the business. The four other Executive Councillors shall be nominated by the Chief Executive Councillor."[25]

After declaring Ladakh Autonomous Hill Council, elections were held in Leh district during the month of August. 23 Congress (I) candidates were elected unopposed. Thus, election was held only in three constituencies—Phyang, Martseland and Saspol (Appendix-4). The Phyang, and Saspol seats went to independent candidates, but they also joined the Congress (I), with this all 26 seats went to Congress (I).

On 3rd September, 1995 swearing ceremony was held at Leh Polo ground in presence of Gen. K.V. Krishna Rao, the then Governor of J & K State. The four members were nominated by Governor. The name of these members are:

1. Ms. Tsheshu Lhamo,
2. Mr. Mohd. Ashraf Barcha,
3. Mr. Mohd. Shafi, and
4. Ms. Spalzes Wangmo.

During the oath taking ceremony all the four nominated members were present in Polo ground. They also took oath along with 26 elected members. Thereafter, Thupstan Chhewang elected the Chief Executive Councillor and Sonam Dawa, Akbar Ladakhi, Thiksey Rinpoche and Rigzin Jora as Executive Councillors. But after a month or so Thiksey Rinpoche gave his resignation because of some differences in the council meeting, and in 1996 another Executive Councillor, Akbar Ladakhi passed away. Thus, the absence of two Executive Councillors was a great setback to the Hill Council.

Not only this some people even did not hesitate to criticise the function of Hill Council in the following grounds:

1. That the Ladakh Autonomous Hill Council, Leh is unable to take any bold step for the development works.

2. That the allocation of funds to Leh district is still routed through State Government. And, Hill Council failed to give pressure upon the Central Government to send funds directly to the Hill Council.

Keeping in view the above criticism a delegation from Leh district met with State Government higher officials and discussed the above matter. But State Government did not agree with them. Consequently, differences between Hill Council and State Government took place. Later these differences became so deepen that the Chief Executive Councillor and his executives collectively submitted their resignations, in the beginning of 1997. But their resignations were not accepted. However, the State Government accepted their main demand and approved the revised budget of Rs. 32 crores, which was earlier 25 crores only.

In the middle of 1997, Hill Council again sent a delegation to Srinagar under the leadership of Rev. Thiksey Rinpoche to talk to chief Minister Farooq Abdullah about giving the state cabinet minister rank/status to the Chief Executive Councillor. The chief minister made two proposals, i.e., either Rev. Thiksey Rinpoche should become Chief Executive Councillor or the present Chief Executive Councillor should change his party and come to National Conference. If any of the above proposal is accepted by the Hill Council, he may consider the proposal given by Rev. Thiksey Rinpoche. But Thupstan Chhewang did not agree with Dr. Farooq Abdullah. Later in April 1998, Dr. Farooq Abdullah nominated Rev. Thiksey Rinpoche for Member of Parliament (Rajya Sabha).

In conclusion Government did right action by declaring Ladakh as a Autonomous Hill Development Council, this step of decentralization of powers will definitely help to accelerate the developmental activities in the region.

REFERENCES

1. Beek, Martijin and Bertelsen, Kristoffer Brix.: 'Ladakh: Independence is not Enough,' Vol. 8, No. 2, March/April, 1995, pp.1-15.
2. *Ibid.*
3. *Ibid.*
4. Ganju, O.N.: 'Lessons from Ladakh' *Frontline*, July 28-Aug. 4, 1989, pp. 15-16
5. *Ibid.*

6. A booklet on 'Ladakh people's movement for Union Territory status,' p. 5.
7. Ganju, O.N., *op. cit.*
8. A booklet on 'Ladakh people's movement for Union Territory status; *op. cit.*
9. *Ibid.*
10. Ganju, O.N., *op. cit.*
11. Menon, Appan: 'The political overtones', *Frontline,* July 22-Aug. 4, 1989, pp. 16-17.
12. Ganju, O.N., *op. cit.*
13. *Ibid.*
14. Menon, Appan, *op. cit.*
15. Beek, Martijin and Bertelsen, Kristoffer Brix., *op. cit.*
16. *Ibid.*
17. Ladakh Melong, Trial Issue—Summer, 1993, pp. 6-7.
18. *Ibid.*
19. *Ibid.*
20. *Ibid.*
21. *Ibid.*
22. *Ibid.*
23. Ladakh Melong, Trial Issue, No. 2, 1994, pp. 11-12.
24. *Tribune*, 10th May, 1995.
25. *Ibid.*

APPENDIX-I

CONSTITUTION OF LADAKH BUDDHIST ASSOCIATION LEH (LADAKH)

Chapter-1

1. Name of the Association shall be 'Ladakh Buddhist Association'.
2. The registered office of the Association shall be at Leh.

Chapter-II

Aims and Objects of the Association

(i) To preserve and promote the religious and cultural traditions of Ladakh;

(ii) To disseminate and promote the teaching of Buddhism;

(iii) To assist promotion of the philosophical system and methods of their teachings;

(iv) To work for laying a firm foundation for promotion and propagation of Buddhist meditation and other practices;.

(v) To establish, develop, maintain and manage institutions for pursuit of the aforesaid objects;

(vi) To frame rules, regulations and bye-laws for control and supervision of activities of the Association;

(vii) To organise symposia and seminars to sum centres interested in promoting the aims and objects of the associations;

(viii) To constitute committees necessary and other bodies as may be deemed necessary and to prescribe their powers and functions;

(ix) To acquire, hold and dispose of property in a lawful manner and to construct, improve, alter, demolish;

(x) To eradicate social evils prevailing among the Buddhists;

(xi) To open, maintain and develop industries, hotels, shops, monasteries, gardens and farms;

(xii) To give scholarships and loans to poor, promising students for technical trainings and higher studies;

(xiii) To promote the Bodhi language;

(xiv) To subscribe to, or become member of or to co-operate with any other organisations, institutions or associations having objects wholly or partly similar to those of this association and to aid and assist such existing institution in such manner as the working committee may deem fit;

(xv) To collect subscription, donation, rents, sale proceeds or other income in accordance with the rules and regulations that may be framed from time to time;

(xvi) To deposit all such money in such bank or banks as the working committee may so desire;

(xvii) To raise funds or to borrow money with or without securities or on the security or a mortgage, charge, hypothecation or pledge of the immovable or movable properties belonging to the association or in any manner whatever.

(xviii) To draw and to make available instruments and for this purpose to sign, execute and deliver such assurances and deeds as may be necessary for the purposes of the association;

(xix) To enter into an arrangement or contract with the State or the Central Government or any society or individuals to obtain any rents, donations, concessions, grants-in-aid desirable and to use the same for the purposes of the association;

(xx) To perform the religious ceremonies entrusted to the association; and

(xxi) To support and promote such other objects and purposes as may be conducive to the attainment of the aims and objectives of the association.

Name, Addresses and Occupations

The names, addresses and occupations of the first members of the working committee referred to in these rules, to whom the rules of the Association refer and as required under Section 2 of the Societies Registration Act-VI of 1998 the management of Affairs of the Association has been entrusted, are as under:

1. Ven Kushok Stakna, Head Lama Stakna Gonpa, President Ladakh Buddhist Association, Leh.
2. Shri Tashi Tundup, Contractor; Vice-President Ladakh Buddhist Association, Leh.
3. Shri Norboo Gialchan, Advocate; Secretary Ladakh Buddhist Association, Leh.

4. Shri Tsewang Norboo, Farmer; Joint Secretary, Ladakh Buddhist Association, Leh.
5. Ven. Lama Lobzang, Member, High Powered Panel of Minorities, Scheduled Castes and Scheduled Tribes, Govt. of India, New Delhi.
6. Ven. Gergan Sonam, Phyang Gonpa, Leh-Ladakh.
7. Shri Sonam Gialson, Advocate, Leh-Ladakh.
8. Shri Tsering Samphel, Travel Agent, Leh-Ladakh.
9. Shri Sonam Wangyal, Contractor, Leh-Ladakh.
10. Ven. Lobzang Norboo, Lama, Samkar Gonpa, Leh-Ladakh.
11. Rev. Lama Yontan, Lama, Likir Gonpa, Leh-Ladakh.
12. Shri Tsetan Namgyal, Contractor, Leh-Ladakh.
13. Shri Tashi Targias, Contractor, Leh-Ladakh.
14. Shri Sonam Gialson, Ex.Govt. Employee, Leh-Ladakh.
15. Shri Murup Namgyal, Govt. Employee, Leh-Ladakh.
16. Shri Lobzang Dorje, Shopkeeper, Leh-Ladakh.
17. Shri Tsering Wangdus, Shopkeeper, Leh-Ladakh.
18. Shri Wangyal Kidar, Businessman, Leh-Ladakh.
19. Shri Sonam Gonbo, Shopkeeper, Leh-Ladakh.
20. Shri Tashi Tsering, Shopkeeper, Leh-Ladakh.

Chapter-III

Members of the Association

The Association shall have the following category of members:

(*a*) Member
(*b*) Life Member
(*c*) Honorary Member

(*ii*) Every Buddhist male or female above 18 years of age shall be a member of the Association on payment of an admission fee of Rs. 5/ (Rs. Five only) in the first instance and a membership fee of Re. 1/ (Re. one only) per year as prescribed by the Association.

(*iii*) Every such member as pays Rs. 1000/- (Rs. one thousand only) will become a life member.

(*iv*) Every such person as is not a member of the Association but who is interested in the aims and objects of the Association and in the achievement thereoff shall be invited to the Association.

Bodies of the Association

The following shall be the bodies of the Association:

(*a*) General Body

(*b*) General Council

(*c*) The Central Working Committee and Unit Association.

General Body

(*a*) All members of the Association shall constitute the General Body. The General Body shall be split up in Unit General Bodies for election and administrative purposes. The Unit General Body shall elect the office-bearers of the Unit Associations and members of the General Council, each member shall have one vote in every election.

(*b*) The Unit General Body shall have all such powers at the Unit level as the General Council at the Centre.

General Council

(*a*) There shall be a General Council formed by the prescribed number of members duly elected by the Unit General Bodies.

(*b*) Each Unit General Body shall elect its representatives for the General Council on the basis of one representative for every 300 primary members.

(*c*) The General Council shall be the controlling authority of the Association.

(*d*) The General Council shall have powers to amend the constitution and to pass the annual plan and the Budget estimates.

(*e*) Meetings of the General Council shall be held atleast twice a year.

(*f*) Special meetings of the General Council shall be called by the General Secretary with the approval of the working committee or on a written demand of fifty members of the General Council.

(*g*) At least one month's notice for the six-monthly meeting and 15 days notice for a special meeting of the General Council shall be served by the Unit Association along with the agenda for such meeting.

(*h*) Every meeting of the General Council shall be presided over by the President or in his absence by the Vice-President or in absence of them both, by any senior member of the working committee present at the meeting of the council.

(*i*) The quorum for such meeting shall be one-fifth of the total members of the General Council.

(*j*) A decision in a meeting shall be taken by the majority of votes. The President shall have a casting vote in case of a tie.

(*k*) The General Secretary shall maintain the minutes of the meetings of the General Council and shall present the same in the Council for confirmation.

(*l*) The General Council shall elect the President, Vice-President and General Secretary.

Treasurer and other members of the Central Working Committee

The Central Working Committee

(a) The office-bearers of the Central Working Committee elected out of the members of the General Council shall be the following:

(*i*) President

(*ii*) Vice-President

(*iii*) General Secretary

(*iv*) Joint Secretary

(*v*) Treasurer and 16 members (inclusive of one representative each from the Gompa Association, Nyansor. Sabha and the Lamdon Social Welfare Society);

(*b*) In all matters, the Central Working Committee shall be answerable and responsible to the General Council;

(*c*) All affairs of the Association shall be administered, managed, directed and controlled by the Working Committee in accordance with the provisions of the constitution and the rules and regulations framed thereunder;

(*d*) The Working Committee shall control and account for the funds, movable and immovable properties of the Association;

(*e*) It shall have full powers to fix, enhance or reduce rents of the immovable properties of the Association;

(*f*) It shall prepare and implement the annual plans and the Budget estimates in furtherance of the aims and objects of the Association;

(*g*) The committee shall be competent to create posts in the interest of the efficient working of the Association as also to lay down terms and conditions of the services of its employees;

(*h*) It shall have full powers to enter into a contract, agreement of loan, sale, mortgage, and any other deeds with any other third party on behalf of the Association through its President or its authorised representative;

(*i*) It shall have the powers to appoint such committee or committees as it may deem necessary for the attainment of the aims and objects of the Association;

(*j*) The Central Working Committee shall have the powers to make rules, regulations and bye-laws, which shall not be inconsistent and derogatory to the provisions of the constitutions;

(*k*) The Central Working Committee shall supervise, direct and control all the offices of the Unit Association;

(*l*) The President, Vice-President and General Secretary shall tour the Units from time to time;

(*m*) Every meeting of the Central Working Committee shall be presided over by the President or in his absence by the Vice-President or in absence of both, by a senior member present in the meeting;

(*n*) All meetings of the Central Working Committee shall be convened by the General Secretary notifying the date, time, place and agenda. In absence of the General Secretary, meetings may be convened by Joint Secretary;

(*o*) A matter not included in the agenda of a meeting may be discussed with the permission of the chair;

(*p*) At least 10 days notice shall be given to convene a meeting of the Central Working Committee;

(*q*) An emergency meeting of the Central Working Committee shall be convened at short notice;

(*r*) The Central Working Committee shall hold at least one meeting in a month and the quorum for such meeting shall be one-third of the total members of the committee;

(*s*) Each member of the Working Committee shall have one vote and in case of equality of votes the President shall have a casting vote;

(*t*) A member of the Working Committee shall cease to be a member of the Committee if he does not attend three consecutive meetings of the committee on receipt of the notice for the meeting without proper permission of the President or the Vice-President; and

(*u*) A member of the Working Committee may resign from the committee by submitting his resignation in written to the President, but the same shall not take effect unless accepted by the Working Committee. Any vacancy so caused shall be filled in accordance with the procedure prescribed in this constitution.

President

(*a*) The President shall be the Chief Executive of the Central Working Committee and shall preside over all the meetings of the Working Committee and the Central Council;

(*b*) All the rules, regulations and the bye-laws passed by the Central Working Committee shall become effective on receipt of assent of the President;

(*c*) Income of the Association shall be deposited in the Bank in the name of the Association which shall be jointly operated by the President and the Treasurer;

(*d*) The President shall have powers to supervise, direct and control the Central Working Committee and its employees;

(*e*) He shall be the custodian of funds, properties and records of the Association;

(*f*) He shall have powers to make appointment, to sanction leave/promotion and to take disciplinary action against employees of the Association.

Vice-President

In absence of the President the Vice-President shall exercise all the powers, functions and duties of the President.

General Secretary

(*a*) The General Secretary shall be responsible for the administration and other day-to-day working of the Association;

(*b*) He shall exercise such powers as may be delegated to him by the President;

(*c*) He shall prepare the Annual Plan and the Budget estimates in consultation with the Central Working Committee, and present the same to the General Council for approval;

(*d*) He shall record the minutes of the meetings of the Central Working Committee and the General Council and shall have the same confirmed at the next meeting of the Central Working Committee and the General Council;

(*e*) He shall maintain an up-to-date Membership Register of the Association;

(*f*) He shall issue notice of the meetings of the General Council and Central Working Committee;

(*g*) He shall be responsible for implementation of the decisions of the Central Working Committee and the General Council; and

(*h*) The General Secretary shall conduct correspondance with the unit Associations and shall also issue directions and circulars for their proper working.

Joint Secretary

(a) The Joint Secretary shall assist the General Secretary in the day-to-day working of the office and shall discharge such duties which may be assigned to him by the President and the General Secretary; and

(*b*) In absence of the General Secretary he shall perform the duties and functions of the General Secretary.

Treasurer

(*a*) The treasurer shall collect the membership fee and the annual fee from members of the Association against proper receipt along with donations, if any;

(*b*) He shall be responsible for collection of rents of the Association;

(*c*) He shall maintain the accounts of receipts and expenditure of the Association on proper registers;

(*d*) He shall get accounts of the Association audited annually by the internal audit party to be constituted by the Central Working Committee; and

(*e*) He shall deposit all incomes to the Association in the Bank Account of the Association and that no money shall be withdrawn otherwise than through a proper cheque jointly signed by the President and the Treasurer.

Unit Association

(*a*) There shall be a Unit Association in every circle of the region to be demarcated by an Adhoc Committee, which will be appointed by the General Council, the following shall be the Unit Headquarters:-

	Unit Association	*Headquarters*
1.	Changthang	Nyoma
2.	Sakti	Sakti
3.	Tangtse	Tangtse
4.	Nubra	Deskit
5.	Leh	Leh
6.	Sham	Saspol
7.	Illaga Line	Khalse (Khal-tse)
8.	Skurbuchan	Skurbuchan
9.	Kargil	Mulbek
10.	Zanskar	Padam

(b) Members of the Unit General Body shall elect members of the Unit Working Committees;

(c) The Unit Secretary shall be responsible for running of the office of the Unit Association as well as implementation of decisions and directions of the Unit/Central Working Committee;

(d) He shall maintain a list of members of Units sending a copy thereof to the General Secretary for the Central Working Committee;

(e) Admission fee annual membership fee and donations shall be collected by the Unit Association and one-half thereof shall send to the General Secretary within a month after the said collection;

(f) The Unit Secretary shall submit a quarterly expenditure/ progress report on the activities of the Unit Association to the Central Working Committee;

(g) The Unit Association implements all directions of the Central Working Committee for attaining the aims and objects of the Association;

(h) The Unit President, Vice-President and the Secretary shall be the members of the General Council; and

(i) The Unit Treasurer shall maintain account books according to the directions of the Central Working Committee and shall get the same audited by the Central Working Committee.

Chapter–IV

Special Provision for the District Level Buddhist Association, Kargil

In view of Kargil being a separate district, the Unit Association of that district shall have also a district level Association of which Kargil shall be the headquarter. The District Level Association of Kargil shall function on the lines of Ladakh Buddhist Association, under the directions and guidance of the Central Working Committee of Ladakh Buddhist Association, Leh.

Election

(*a*) Members of the Unit Working Committee and the General Council shall be elected after every three years from amongst members of the Unit General Body;

(*b*) Members of the Central Working Committee shall be elected from amongst members of the General Council;

(*c*) All elections shall be conducted through non-transferable secret ballot system;

(*d*) Elections shall be conducted by Chief Electoral Officer duly appointed by the Central Working Committee for different Polling Stations;

(*e*) The Chief Electoral Officer shall supply necessary nomination papers to the Returning Officers;

(*f*) Members of the Central/Unit Working Committees shall be eligible for re-election;

(*g*) Dates of elections shall be fixed by the Working Committee at least 40 days in advance; and

(*i*) Expenditure on account of elections shall be borne by the Central Working Committee.

Annual Plan and Budget Estimates

(*a*) The Central/Unit Working Committees shall prepare the annual plans and the budget estimates which shall be presented for approval to the General Council and the Unit General Body as the case may be; and

(*b*) The financial year of the Association shall be the same as that of the Government.

Chapter–VI

Popular Control

A motion of non-confidence against any member of the Working Committee shall be dealt with in the following manner:-

(a) A motion of non-confidence against any member of the Central/Unit Working Committees shall be moved in a meeting of the General Council and Unit General Body respectively;

(b) Such a motion shall be entertained only on receipt of a written demand of at least fifty members of the General Council or the Unit General Body as the case may be;

(c) At least one month notice shall be given for moving such a motion;

(d) Such a motion shall require one-third majority of the General Council or the Unit General Body as the case may be;

(e) In the event of carrying out such a motion, fresh election shall be conducted within 30 days from the date of adoption of the said motion; and

(f) In case a non-confidence motion is passed against the Central/ Unit Working Committee as a whole, the General Council or the Unit General Body as the case may be, shall appoint an adhoc Committee of three members in the same meeting in which such a motion is passed to organize a fresh election to carry on the work of the Working Committee temporarily for a period not exceeding 45 days.

Chapter–VII

Amendment of the Constitution

(a) The Constitution of the Association may be amended, altered or substituted at any time by a resolution passed at a special meeting of the General Council of the Association by a one-half of the total membership of the General Council; and

(b) Motion for amendment of the Constitution shall require to be got circulated through an agenda at least one month in advance.

Chapter–VIII

Suits by or against the Association

All suits, complaints and applications by or against the Association in any court or office whatsoever shall be instituted or filed in the name of the Association. Such suits, complaints, applications and replies shall be taken and shall stand and be deemed to stand in the properties of the Association shall be executed for and on behalf of the Association by the President or any member of the Central Working Committee duly authorised by a resolution passed by the Committee in a meeting convened for the purpose.

Dissolution

In the event of the dissolution of the Association, all its properties, movable and immovable, shall vest in the Chokhang Buddha Vihar, Leh.

Source: Booklet of Constitution of Ladakh Buddhist Association, pp. 1-20.

APPENDIX-2

COMMUNITYWISE GOVERNMENT EMPLOYEES IN DIFFERENT DEPARTMENTS IN LEH DISTRICT OF LADAKH (1987-89)

Name of the Department	*Category of Post*	*Buddhists*	*Muslims*	*Muslims of Kargil*	*Others*
(1)	*(2)*	*(3)*	*(4)*	*(5)*	*(6)*
Animal Husbandry	Gazetted	03	01	-	08
	Non-Gazetted	25	25	03	15
	Class-IV	51	49	01	-
Agriculture Deptt.	Gazetted	-	-	-	-
	Non-Gazetted	-	-	-	-
	Class-IV	69	38	-	-
Tourism Deptt.	Gazetted	01	-	-	-
	Non-Gazetted	06	04	06	-
	Class-IV	15	14	01	-
Tehsil/Agri	Gazetted	01	01	-	-
	Non-Gazetted	04	01	01	01
	Class-IV	-	01	01	01
I.T.I. Deptt.	Gazetted	-	-	-	-
	Non-Gazetted	02	02	01	01
	Class-IV	-	02	-	-
Cultural Academy	Gazetted	02	-	-	01
	Non-Gazetted	06	02	01	01
	Class-IV	02	01	-	-
Police Deptt.	Gazetted	-	02	-	01
	Non-Gazetted	100	45	75	54
	Class-IV	-	-	-	-
State Archives Repository	Gazetted	-	-	-	-
	Non-Gazetted	02	04	-	01
	Class-IV	-	02	-	-
Mechanical Div., Leh	Gazetted	01	01	-	-
	Non-Gazetted	24	19	02	19
	Class-IV	13	16	01	02
District Treasury, Leh	Gazetted	-	-	-	01
	Non-Gazetted	01	06	-	-
	Class-IV	01	01	-	-

(Continued on next page)

(Appendix 2 Contd.)

Handicraft	Gazetted	-	01	-	-
Centre	Non-Gazetted	17	11	01	02
	Class-IV	05	03	-	01
Public Works	Gazetted	-	01	-	-
Deptt.	Non-Gazetted	12	04	-	04
	Class-IV	07	-	-	-
District	Gazetted	-	-	-	-
Library, Leh	Non-Gazetted	03	01	-	-
	Class-IV	02	-	-	-
Co-operative	Gazetted	-	-	-	-
Bank	Non-Gazetted	01	-	-	02
	Class-IV	01	-	01	-
Stationary	Gazetted	-	-	-	-
Depot	Non-Gazetted	02	-	-	-
	Class-IV	-	-	-	-
Tehsil Office	Gazetted	-	-	01	-
Leh	Non-Gazetted	15	08	-	01
	Class-IV	08	07	-	-
SICOP,	Gazetted	-	-	-	-
Leh	Non-Gazetted	01	01	-	-
	Class-IV	02	-	-	-
N.A.C., Leh	Gazetted	-	-	-	-
	Non-Gazetted	03	02	-	-
Class-IV	03	20	05	-	
Electrical	Gazetted	01	02	-	02
Div., Leh	Non-Gazetted	21	18	02	04
	Class-IV	54	10	03	01
P.W.D., Circle	Gazetted	-	-	-	02
Leh	Non-Gazetted	05	05	-	01
	Class-IV	03	01	-	-
Civil Const.	Gazetted	01	-	-	03
Div., P.W.D.	Non-Gazetted	07	13	01	05
	Class-IV	16	-	-	-
Land	Gazetted	-	-	-	-
Development	Non-Gazetted	01	-	-	-
Bank					
	Class-IV	-	01	-	-
Social Welfare,	Gazetted	01	01	-	01
Leh	Non-Gazetted	06	07	-	02
	Class-IV	03	04	-	-
Distt. Rural	Gazetted	02	-	-	01
Development	Non-Gazetted	-	01	-	04
Agency, Leh	Class-IV	03	04	-	-

(Continued on next page)

(Appendix 2 Contd.)

Desert	Gazetted	-	-	-	02
Development	Non-Gazetted	03	02	-	01
Department	Class-IV	02	01	-	-
Co-operative	Gazetted	-	-	-	-
Department	Non-Gazetted	27	13	-	03
	Class-IV	08	08	-	-
Fisheries	Gazetted	01	-	-	-
Department	Non-Gazetted	09	07	-	-
	Class-IV	01	-	-	-
R & B Div.	Gazetted	-	02	01	01
Leh	Non-Gazetted	33	17	09	12
	Class-IV	16	09	-	01
Employment	Gazetted	01	-	-	-
Exchange	Non-Gazetted	01	09	01	08
	Class-IV	-	02	01	-
Investigation	Gazetted	01	-	02	-
Div.	Non-Gazetted	07	09	01	08
	Class-IV	06	02	01	-
District	Gazetted	-	02	-	02
Industries, Leh	Non-Gazetted	28	25	-	04
	Class-IV	07	05	-	-
Deputy	Gazetted	-	02	-	03
Commissioner's	Non-Gazetted	34	18	-	04
Office, Leh	Class-IV	10	14	-	-
Medical Deptt.	Gazetted	11	03	-	04
(Excluding	Non-Gazetted	79	68	-	27
SNM	Class-IV	61	33	02	-
Hospital)	Gazetted	01	-	-	-
Forest Deptt.,	Non-Gazetted	43	19	04	-
Leh	Class-IV	21	07	-	-
Food and	Gazetted	-	01	-	-
Supplies,					
Leh	Non-Gazetted	19	14	01	-
	Class-IV	18	15	-	-
Public Health	Gazetted	-	03	-	-
Engg.	Non-Gazetted	25	15	01	26
	Class-IV	03	05	-	-
Education	Gazetted	-	03	-	05
Department	Non-Gazetted	01	01	-	-
	Class-IV	04	-	-	-
Information	Gazetted	-	01	01	-
Office	Non-Gazetted	12	09	-	-
	Class-IV	09	02	-	-

(Continued on next page)

(Appendix 2 Contd.)

Igoo-Phey Div.	Gazetted	01	01	-	03
	Non-Gazetted	11	17	-	10
	Class-IV	14	16	06	-
A.C.T.R's Office	Gazetted	01	-	-	-
	Non-Gazetted	06	01	-	-
	Class-IV	06	03	-	-
Sub-Judge	Gazetted	-	-	-	01
	Non-Gazetted	01	01	01	01
	Class-IV	02	03	-	01
Weights and Measures Office	Gazetted	-	01	-	-
	Non-Gazetted	01	01	-	-
	Class-IV	-	02	01	-
Sheep Husbandry Office	Gazetted	01	02	-	05
	Non-Gazetted	31	24	18	05
	Class-IV	77	30	05	02

Source: *Booklet of Ladakh People's Movement for Union Territory Status*, pp. 11-14.

APPENDIX-3

Registered No. DL-33004/95

The Gazette of India

Extraordinary

Part - II - Section I

Published by Authority

No. 24

New Delhi, Tuesday, May 9, 1995/Vaisakha 19, 1917 Separate paging is given to this Part in order that it may be filled as a separate compilation

Ministry of Law, Justice and Company Affairs

(Legislative Department)

New Delhi, the 9th May, 1995/ Vaisakha 19, 1917 (Saka)

The following President's Act is published for general information:

The Ladakh Autonomous Hill Development Councils Act 1995 No. 1 of 1995 Enacted by the President in the Forty-Sixth Year of the Republic of India.

An Act to provide for the establishment of Autonomous Hill Development Councils and an Inter-District Advisory Council in the Ladakh region of Jammu & Kashmir.

In exercise of the powers conferred by Section 3 of the Jammu Kashmir State Legislature (Delegation of Powers) Act, 1992, the President is pleased to enact as follows:

Chapter 1
Preliminary

1. (1) This Act may be called the Ladakh Autonomous Hill Development Councils Act, 1995 — short title extent, and

(2) It shall come into force on such date as the Government may by notification in the

Government Gazette appoint and different dates may be appointed for different provisions of this Act. commencement

(3) It shall extend to the whole of the districts of Leh and Kargil in the State of Jammu & Kashmir.

APPENDIX-4

CONSTITUENCYWISE CANDIDATES FOR LADAKH AUTONOMOUS HILL DEVELOPMENT COUNCIL LEH

Sl. No.	*Candidates*	*Constituency*	*By Election or Unopposed*	*Party*
(1)	*(2)*	*(3)*	*(4)*	*(5)*
1.	Sonam Dawa	Sakti	Unopposed	Congress(I)
2.	Thupstan Chhewang	Lower Leh	Unopposed	Congress(I)
3.	Akbar Ladakhi	Chushot	Unopposed	Congress(I)
4.	Norbu Gyaltsan	Khalsi	Unopposed	Congress(I)
5.	Tsering Motup	Tangtse	Unopposed	Congress(I)
6.	Thiksay Rinpoche	Thiksey	Unopposed	Congress(I)
7.	Nima Stanzin	Skurbuchan	Unopposed	Congress(I)
8.	T. Gurmet	Korzok	Unopposed	Congress(I)
9.	Tsewang Dorje	Igoo	Unopposed	Congress(I)
10.	Rigzin Namgyal	Chushul	Unopposed	Congress(I)
11.	Nawang Rigzin	Basgo	Unopposed	Congress(I)
12.	Tsewang Rinchen	Sku-Markka	Unopposed	Congress(I)
13.	Tsering Dorje	Upper Leh	Unopposed	Congress(I)
14.	Ghulam Mohd. Chatapa	Turtuk	Unopposed	Congress(I)
15.	Sonam Targias	Hundar	Unopposed	Congress(I)
16.	Tsultim Phunchog	Diskit	Unopposed	Congress(I)
17.	Padma Rigzin	Tigar	Unopposed	Congress(I)
18.	Tsering Norbu	Panamik	Unopposed	Congress(I)
19.	Tundup Sonam	Temogam	Unopposed	Congress(I)
20.	Rigzin Spalbar	Lamayuru	Unopposed	Congress(I)
21.	Rigzin Namgyal	Nyoma	Unopposed	Congress(I)
22.	Sonam Phunchok	Lingshed	Unopposed	Congress(I)
23.	Rinchen Tondup	Suspol	by Election	Independent
24.	Tashi Chotak	Phyang	by Election	Independent
25.	Gonbo Chemet	Kyngyam	Unopposed	Congress(I)
26.	Tsering Angdus	Martselang	by Election	Congress(I)

Notes: 1. Rinchen Tondup and Tashi Chotak later joined Congress(I)

2. Tsering Dorje, Councillor from upper Leh was later elected MLA

from Leh and in place of him Lobzang Rinchen (Congress (I)) elected as councillor.

3. In place of Thiksey Rinpoche, Tundup Sonam was appointed Executive Councillor.
4. In place of Akbar Ladakhi, Ashraf appointed Executive Councillor.
5. After the Thiksey Rinpoche resignation election was held and Nawang Phendey (National Conference) was elected.
6. After the death of Akbar Ladakhi election was also held for Chushot seat, and Dr. Saukat Ali (National Conference) was elected.

Part–II

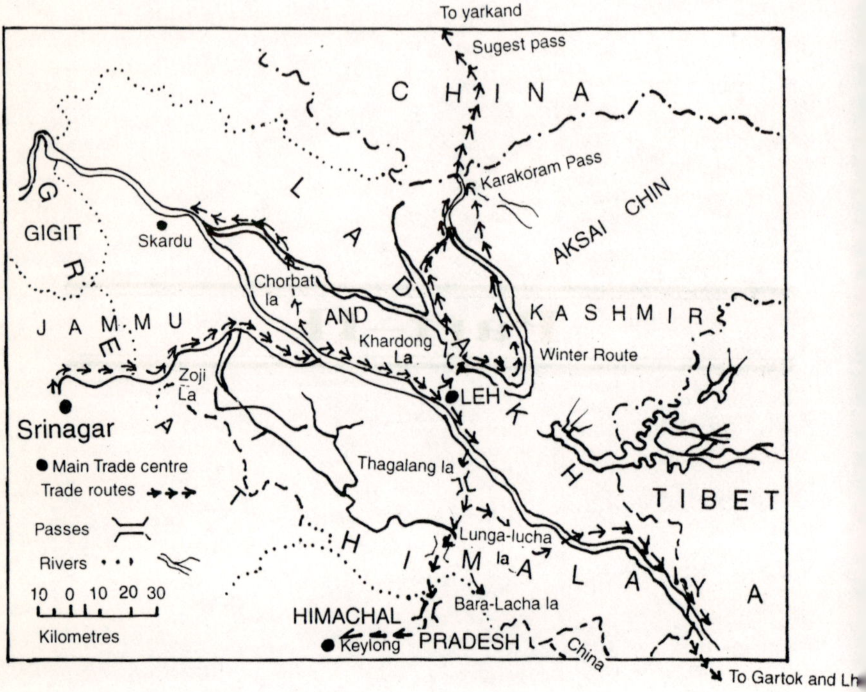
To yarkand
Sugest pass
CHINA
Karakoram Pass
AKSAI CHIN
GIGIT
Skardu
Chorbat la
AND
KASHMIR
JAMMU
Khardong La
Winter Route
Zoji La
LEH
Srinagar
Main Trade centre
Trade routes
Passes
Rivers
Thagalang la
TIBET
Lunga-lucha la
10 0 10 20 30
Kilometres
HIMACHAL
Bara-Lacha la
Keylong
PRADESH
China
To Gartok and Lh

1

LADAKH PROFILE

Location

Ladakh, interwoven with a complex network of nude Himalayan ranges, that extend between the latitude of 30 to 35° North and longitude 70 to 80° East, constitutes the northern most part of India where the altitude above mean sea leavel of inhabited places is between 2440 m and 4270 m. The highest inhabited place in the world, if alone accounted for 95,876 square kilometres before 1947, but has only 58,321 square kilometres now as it lost Skardu and some of its parts in the east in the Pakistani and Chinese aggressions respectively.

Ladakh has high mountains which vary in height from 5,000 to 7,000 metres on an average. Leh is the chief town, itself situated at 3,507 metres enclosed by the Karakoram and the Great Himalaya, the world's mightiest mountain ranges. Beyond the Karakoram, the desolate high plains were once the trade routes of Central Asian traders. Leh to Sinkiang in China was an important trade route. To go to China from Leh, traders climbed three passes: Khardung La (5,605 m) just after Leh over Ladakh range, Saser La (5,382 m) over the Karakoram range, and the Karakoram Pass (5,575 m) over the Aghil range. The other routes passed along the Indus Valley through Leh to Gilgit in the west, and Kailash Mansarovar in the east.

Formation

According to geologists, Ladakh was formed only a few million years ago by the buckling and flooding of the earth's crust as the Indian sub-continent pushed with irresistible force against the immovable mass of Asia. The name Ladakh brings to mind the daunting high mountain peaks, the piercing wind, the ground under the foot, especially at night, like muddy slabs of ice.

Weather

The days are quite warm for nearly half the year. During winters, temperature in some parts of Ladakh goes down as low as –40° C to –50° C. Life then seems to be difficult; however, when sun shines it becomes bearable. Yet dryness makes even these months a hazard for life. Each sign of moisture in the body has to be carefully guarded against the dehydrating action of the dry winds and hot sun.

The vast, barren, high plateau, intermittent sandy storms, scanty rainfall and rare atmospheric conditions with low percentage of oxygen at the high passes, can sometimes become a serious problem to a person who drives to a high altitude over uneven tracks or roads without proper rest at Leh. While trekking in such a zone, one becomes sluggish, as such high attitudes tend to tire the mind along with the body.

How strange! In winter, when you throw an egg up, it comes down and strikes ground like-ball, but with only a few cracks! Meat and vegetables get frozen, as hard as a rock. If you want to make them edible, you have to boil before using to your taste. How difficult reaching supplies to Ladakh in as trucks stop on the way, when the fluid in the batteries and diesel in the tank freeze due to the sever cold. When snow it Ladakhis feel happy, as snow fall helps irrigation, the villages being situated at the base of glaciers. Siachen among them is the largest glacier in the world about 72 kms. long.

Food and Fuel Availability

On account of the rocky nature of its mountains, procurement of timber and fuel is very difficult it. The percentage of Buddhist marriages are on an increase, consequently the barren lands, earlier, given to other on rent, are being cultivated among themselves, the number of houses too have increased. In order to increase agricultural production Ladakhis, particularly the Baltis, have been constructing long channels cutting along the granite mountains and gravel slopes.

Barley, the popular foodgrain is roasted and ground to become *sattu,* and is eaten with salted butter. Tea is called *gur-gur*. The consumption of rice, chicken, and food of other parts of India is on the rise nowadays.

Apricot, a hardy plant, can be grown up to 14,000 feet, and is useful since it can be preserved by drying for later consumption. The dry and sour apricots are called *chuli*; sweet and dry ones are called 'phating' and have nation-wide demand. The apricot kernel yields oil, useful both for application and for burning votive lamps. Mulberry, apple, walnut and grapes are grown at lower altitudes.

The fuel problems of the past are now being solved at private and State Government levels. Every year the State forest department plants lakhs of new trees, along channels, water-locked areas, forest reserve zones, gardens and so on. Willow and poplar are the popular ones among them. Besides these, people grow juniper for religious purposes.

Landscape and Population

Today the landscape of Leh town has been changed drastically. In October, 1980, when I came to Leh, there were only a few shops and guest houses, 10 to 15 taxies, 10 to 20 State Government buses, 20 to 25 trucks, 4 to 5 restaurants and 2 to 3 public schools. Now their number has increased considerably. The agricultural land around Leh has been converted into guest houses or hotels, human and animal population has increased; the cement production, the buildings in Leh and its surrounding areas, the increasing number of buses and taxies have swallowed up the greenary, peace and tranquility of the town.

The happiness of the secluded town is slowly dying, losing its natural beauty. Its border is as busy as any European town. The environment has been polluted, the water that flows through town is not suitable for drinking even for animals. Vehicular traffic has polluted the atmosphere to an even greater extent. With the increase in mobility to and from Ladakh and intermingling of different groups from other parts of world through introduction of airways and roadways, there has been a corresponding change in the lifestyle, language, behaviour, customs and religious practices of the people of Ladakh. Today they are not only dealing with old traders like Yarkandis, Turkis, Kashmiris, Hindustanis, Lahulis, Punjabis or Hoshiarpuris are conducting, but business with Europeon and American tourists, high class army officers, wholesale businessmen, State and Central Government officers, etc.

In shops, there is a visible change in the merchandise. Once they had riding boots, saddles made of Sinkiang, large and genuine pieces of turquoise, papier matche boxes from Peking and salt from Chang-Thang. Now these have been replaced by readymade garments, playing cards, torches, battery cells, cameras, cigarettes, matches, packets of tea, Chinese shoes, Chinese flasks, Ludhiana made jackets, sleeping bags and a dozen other things of tourist interest. Except a few things, all are brought from the plains of the country. The market is now expanding towards the new bus stand, Skara, Agling and Choglamsar.

Dress

The faces in the street, however, are still the broad Mongoloid Bhots or the slightly narrower and refined ones of the Muslims of Kargil. In the eighties; they mostly wore traditional dresses—embroidered fur caps with long unwashed hair gathered inside it or decending from it in a long pigtail; the ankle length woollen coat—gathered at the waist with a rope of hair; necklaces of multicoloured beads or a woollen hood decorated with turquoise. The style of dressing and appearance of the locals has undergone lot of change. More and more of the local people are now seen in shirt and trouser in styles imported from the plains; some even sport a neck tie; young boys wear tight jeans, cut their hair short and are clean shaven; boys and girls—are a smart set, who probably fancy themselves as local heroes; Ladakhis of the old generation wear army rejected dress; young girls wear tight jeans, *salwar* and *kurta,* and cut their hair like English ladies; and finally boys have long hair like girls.

Religious Following, a Chapter from History

Ladakh has four administrative centres Leh, Nubra, Kargil and Zangskar. Leh and Kargil have two big mosques in the heart of the city, an evidence of the influence of the West Asian Islamic culture which came here through neighbouring Muslim territories. At first, Syed Hamdani came to Ladakh in 1394 AD and spread the message of Islam peacefully. Later it was propagated by the aggressive attitude of Muslim Badshas. In fifteenth century Zain-ul-Abidin of Kashmir made two invasions and plundered many Buddhist monasteries. Thereafter in September, 1532, the Kashgar army under the command of Mirza Haider entered Nubra, plundered Buddhist property and forced Buddhists to embrace Islam. Ali Mir during King Jamyang Namgyal's reign invaded Ladakh and forced the King of Ladakh and his army to surrender. However, King Jamyang Namgyal was released under the condition that he would marry Ali Mir's daughter, Gyal Khatoon, and give his full assistance to propagate Islam in his kingdom. Though Aurangzeb, the Mughal Emperor also gave threat to Ladakh, but king of Ladakh in order to avoid war, sent his proposal for peace agreement to Kashmir. The Mughal Emperor, agreed with the peace agreement, on some conditions:

"The peace agreement would only be followed if the king of Ladakh renounces Buddhism and embraces Islam. Besides, the king has to give tribute to the Mughal emperor, the tribute being fixed by the authorities of the Mughal emperor in due course of time."

Ladakhi King Del-dan Namgyal accepted the above conditions and saved Ladakh from the big battle. Thus, Ladakh, which was earlier a Buddhist dominated country, was divided into two parts i.e. Leh and Kargil because of the Muslim aggressions between the fourteenth and eighteenth centrury A.D. Consequently, Leh is dominated by Buddhists whereas Kargil by Muslim Shias.

Aggressions

When the Muslim aggression stopped, the threat this time came to Ladakh from the Dogras and the British. In 1819 A.D. Kashmir camo under the rule of Maharaja Ranjit Singh. He turned to Ladakh to extract tribute, as Ladakh had the famous market for Pashmina wool. The Maharaja's interest was to control the wool trade. On the other hand, the British India Government sent William Moorcroft to Ladakh to study trade activities. In May, 1821, he drew up a trade agreement on behalf of the British merchants allowing them to trade with Ladakh and then with Chinese, Western Turkistan. But Maharaja Ranjit Singh had strong objections to this agreement, and ordered his officers to prevent any active interference by the Britishers in Ladakh.

In 1821, the British authorities approached Raja Gulab Singh to allow them to trade with Central Asian countries through Ladakh. But Gulab Singh did not accept the proposal, and kept his eyes wide open on the commercial potentialities of Ladakh. His interest was that the King of Ladakh should divert only a portion of the pashmina wool to Punjab via Kulu. But the King of Ladakh did not follow Raja Gulab Singh's ideas. Differences took place when Raja Gulab Singh accused the King of Ladakh with favouring the British. He ordered his army chief, General Zorawar Singh to conquer Ladakh. Zorawar Singh along with an able army of 5000 soldiers crushed the Ladakhis and emerged victorious. In 1834, he conquered Ladakh and in 1841 marched further ahead towards Tibet. He wrested Taklakot, Garo and Rudok from the Tibetans. Later, as he marched to the Mansarovar lake, the Tibetan army surrounded his army from all directions. Due to severe cold of December and the altitude of 13,000 feet many of his soldiers died. Zorawar Singh was left with only a few soldiers, but he fought bravely against the Tibetan army. He fought bravely till the last when he was left all alone as all his soldiers were killed. A shell hit him on his shoulder and he died on December 12, 1841.

After the death of Zorawar Singh, the Tibetan army recovered all the territories they had lost during the war. At the defeat of his army by Tibetans, Raja Gulab Singh immediately sent a huge army under the command of Dewan Hari Chand and Wazir Ratanu. In May 1842, they reached Leh, and fought a fierce battle with the Tibetans at Chemrey. The Tibetans lost the battle, and later encamped near Chushul. By that time winter was approaching. The Dogras remembered the cause of Zorawar's defeat and decided not to fight with the Tibetans in winter. Consequently they agreed to a peace treaty which took place on September 17, 1842. This time the British attitude was no longer hostile, and British agent J.O. Cunningham acted as a mediator for establishing an agreement between the Dogra and the Tibetan army, and renewed the shawl, wool trade.

On March 16, 1846, Raja Gulab Singh signed the treaty of Amritsar with the British, where he became the Maharaja of Jammu and Kashmir for ever, with independent possession of all the hilly territory east of the Indus river and west of the Ravi including Chamba came under the Jammu and Kashmir *Riyasat*. In lieu of this territory, Maharaja Gulab Singh was to pay a sum of rupees one crore to the Company. Later a remission of rupees twenty-five lakh was allowed as compensation for the Kulu and Mandi districts which were taken back by the British. Thus, Maharaja Gulab Singh became an independent ruler of Jammu and Kashmir, Ladakh, Baltistan and Hazara. Ladakh came under Dogra supremacy and when the British brought all of India under its rule, Ladakh too came under the British Raj. In 1947, India attained independence, Ladakh became a part of Indian Republic and merged with Jammu and Kashmir State.

Today Shia Muslims are in majority in Kargil district, but the predominant religious landmarks are the dozens of white 'chortens' which dot the brown rock of the areas talk of the past when Ladakh was under the influence of Buddhism. Leh district and Zangskar tehsil of Kargil district are still the seat of the Mahayani Buddhist culture and religion. The important monasteries viz. Hemis, Thiksay, Daktok, Phyang, Lamayuru and others celebrate their annual festivals during summer. These festivals are not only of religious but tourist interest also, with the tourists taking part and enjoying the Lama cham dance.

Topography

The ranges which enclose the valleys of Ladakh are pierced by a number of passes at varying heights. Across a broad saddle between Lahul-Spiti and the routes of the arc, lies the Bara-la-cha which gives both Lahul and Spiti access to each other and to Ladakh. Although it is the gentlest of the passes in this area, it is the second highest pass on the Leh-Manali road, and is the earliest to become snowbound. Closer to the middle of the arc, Lahul and Spiti are separated from each other by a short offshoot of the middle-Himalayan range, the Kunzum ridge, with a pass of the same at 15,000 feet. This is the next to be shut down by snow. The Leh valley itself is surrounded by very high passes such as Chang-la (17,350 feet), Khardong la (18,380 feet) and Taglang la (17,500 feet). The Zoji-la is the gateway of Ladakh, located at 11,300 feet, and is popular for traffic. However, Rohtang and Bara-la-cha from the south-east is a safer route to penetrate Ladakh than the Srinagar-Leh road from Zoji-la. The area between Dras to Kargil is under the target of Pakistani forces, and any time Pakistani shelling may occur. The Leh-Manali road is comparatively safer with the added advantage of being close to a railway station. Since 1998 Kargil has been a target of Pakistani forces, many people including locals losing their lives. May 1999 witnessed a new violent turn in this process as an undeclared war was imposed on India by Pakistan army and Pakistan backed mercenaries who unlawfully occupied territory beyond the Line of Control. A bloody battle is on between India and Pakistan forces with India appreciably exercising great restraint in spite of great provocation from Pakistan.

Road and Air Connections, Then and Now

Leh is connected by air from Srinagar, Jammu, Chandigarh and Delhi. The journey from Srinagar which by mule-caravan takes a fortnight, by bus two days, is now completed in 25-30 minutes by air. But the slightest mistake or a miscalculation in the pilot's cabin could make this one's last journey.

Till, the sixties, it was a difficult task for pilots to land their aircrafts in at Leh, because the airport then was short and sandy. That is why, a set face, vigilant eyes and hands which alertly darted every now and again from knob to needle and back to the stick. Behind the pilot sat the navigator, droning out a constant stream of instructions while alternately he pored over a largescale map and a pair of magnifiers built into the floor of the aircraft. In 1981, being all uneasiness and clouds of fear as soon as our aeroplane Boeing 737 of Indian Airlines landed safely on Leh airport, I offered prayer and thanked to the pilots who flayed our aircraft.

Pran Chopra says :

> The airfield at Leh used to be a very rudimentary affair, with a runway much shorter than was needed. The only aircraft it could take were unable to fly at the altitudes one could have considered sufficiently high to be safe, because at a lower height there was always the risk of collision with the treacherous hillsides. Unable to fly higher, the aircraft in which we flew had to stick dangerously to narrow and winding valleys, flanked by steep mountains which rose to a few thousand feet above us on both sides. The pilot took sharp twists and turns, like a scooter driver on a congested road and even then he appeared nearby to graze the walls of the valley.

How vastly different was the second flight to Leh, about ten years later! We took off from Chandigarh, not Srinagar, the distance was twice as long, the route entirely different and yet the time taken was almost the same. We did not iand at what would barely have passed for an airfield, its landing strip only a patch of the dusty plain which the local population had just cleared of stones. It was a double track runway of perforated steel plate.

Buddhism

Though landing and take off is a difficult job, yet as we meet the inhabitants, we forget all our past problems and enjoy the cheerfulness and hospitality of every simple, honest and religious villager. As one approaches the villages inscriptions like *Om-Mani-Padme-Hum*, *Om-Vajrapani-Hum* welcome the visitors. Every Buddhist, rich or poor has full and strong faith on these mantras. They chant these mantras whenever they get time—whether walking along the roadside, travelling by bus or flying by Indian Airlines or while resting when they have no work.

Ladakhis are very cultured people. They have cultural, racial and spiritual affinities with Tibet. For several centuries, the flow of Buddhist culture was from Kashmir via Ladakh to Tibet. Many Kashmiri Buddhist scholars visited Tibet and China. After the fourteenth century, when Kashmir came under Muslim rule, cultural relations between Kashmir and Ladakh or Tibet came to an end. By this time Buddhism in Tibet was in full glory. Ladakhi Buddhist scholars then established relations with Tibet. With the help of Tibetan scholars and *gurus,* many Buddhist monasteries and learning centres came up in Ladakh. Later these developed according to the lamastic form of Buddhism. Till the sixteenth century many rival influences prevailed in Ladakh, especially those of Tibet and Kashmir, and later of Skardu and Baltistan. Towards the end of the sixteenth century, Tsewang Namgyal annexed the western stretches of Tibet; Singhe Namgyal further extended his territory and built the Leh palace. Thereafter his successors, directly or indirectly, propagated Buddhism throughout Ladakh, and helped monasteries extend their functions to the grassroot level and strengthen the hold of Buddhism in Ladakh. The relics of Buddhism continue to be a real source of attraction for tourists and research scholars.

Agriculture and Horticulture

About eighty per cent of the people of Ladakh depend on agriculture. The principal crops grown are barley, gram and wheat but owing to the high altitude, extreme cold, lack of oxygen and humidity, the agricultural season is limited to the May-October period. The agricultural produce of this season is not sufficient for the local population. Every year about 300 to 400 metric tons rice, 200 to 400 metric tons of flour, 200 to 300 metric tons of ration is supplied through ration depot. In the olden days people had to depend on their limited product. Today, due to scientific advancement, Indian scientists have developed new agricultural methods and high yielding varieties of vegetables and food crops. In 1819-25, Moorcroft and Trebeck visited Ladakh on an official tour and were very impressed by the superb quality of the fruits especially apricot and apple. They then recommended to East India Company that some of these strains should be introduced in European horticulture. With a view to develop agriculture and horticulture Field Research Laboratory (FRL) was established in Leh in 1960 when it was under the administrative control of the Indian Council of Agricultural Research. It was later transferred to Defence Research and Development Organisation (DRDO) in 1962.

Field Research Laboratory: Contribution

Since then the FRL is waging war with nature in an attempt to make the hostile terrain of Ladakh reasonably green by developing its agro-animal resources not only to sustain the meagre population but also the military and para-military forces deployed there. The FRL has its rear base in Chandigarh and field stations at Ranbirpura (11,800 ft); Partapur (9,500 ft) and Kargil (9,200 ft). Here follow some of its important contributions:

1. Standardized cold desert technologies of more than 40 types of vegetables and 40 types of flowering annuals.
2. Identified suitable varieties of important vegetable crops, wheat, barley, maize, mustard and alfalfa.
3. Demonstrated commercial cultivation of broccoli, Jerusalem artichoke, Brussels sprouts, shubarb and beetroot.
4. Popularized protected cultivation of leafy vegetables during the icy winters.
5. Early production of vegetable nursery under soil trench and polyhouse, transferred to the fields of farmers.
6. Demonstrated production of cucurbits in the cold desert, using plastic mulch.
7. Seed production of vegetables including True Potato Seed (TPS) production.
8. Developed, demonstrated and introduced into service protocol for underground storage of potato in bulk during frozen winters.
9. Demonstrated and disseminated fodder (alfalfa) production, processing and baling technologies to the growers, for supply to the services.
10. Documented flora of Ladakh highlighting medicinal and edible plants.
11. Developed and demonstrated solar heated underground poultry production technology, including hatching for cold desert. Provided brooded chicks to farmers.

12. Package for rearing high yielding crossbred cows in Ladakh terrain has been developed and successfully demonstrated.
13. Provisioning of propagating material of poplar, willow, seabuckthorn, vegetables, medicinal plants and other crops.
14. Explored possibilities of Maintaining Meat on Hoof (MOH) during winter season.
15. Experiment on development of self-sustaining village.

The Field Research Laboratory has achieved a breakthrough in raising maize and wheat crops even in harsh conditions. Experiments on trenches, boxes and glass houses are being conducted for stretching the agricultural season. Army scientists not only conduct research and supply the seedlings but also visit private farms. I have been invited several times by them and they have informed me that FRL has successfully introduced high-yielding varieties of potatoes, tomatoes, cabbage, cauliflower, turnip, radish, knolkhol, peas, etc. I visited the experiment unit side and found vegetables of extraordinary sizes viz. cucumber, pumpkin, cauliflower, cabbage, radish, turnip, knol-khol weighing 9 to 20 pounds. I was also informed that agricultural scientists invite peasants to the laboratory and hold discussions with them about how to increase their agricultural production. Scientists have succeeded in keeping poultry warm in the freezing surface temperature in underground houses. In September 1998, when I visited FRL, they told me that they had a good demand for broilers; unfortunately the demand could not be fulfilled by them. Therefore, in case a private entrepreneur comes forward he can definitely earn good profit from poultry rearing. FRL has made a successful attempt to improve agricultural production as well as the environment of the neighbouring villages of Ladakh.

Impact of FRL on Ladakh

The impact of FRL on Ladakh can be summarized as:

1. Greening of Leh valley resulting in eco-environment improvement.
2. Availability of off-season vegetables during summer for the common man and the soldier which is a luxury.
3. Greening of Leh market during winter season (polyhouse vegetable production).

4. Alfalfa (fodder) production surplus to the requirement of farmers and its supply to the Army as baled hay.
5. Production of surplus potato in the valley.
6. Successful underground poultry production.
7. Availability of high yielding milch animals and an increase in their population.
8. Vegetable seed production in Leh valley.
9. Improvement in the economic conditions of tribal farmers.
10. Storage of fresh vegetables for use during long winters.

In 1975, a seven-member delegation of the Indian Council of Agriculture Research (ICAR), led by its Deputy Director-General D.R. Bhumba, conducted a study of the 'nature of research and development effort required for the development of agriculture and allied fields in Ladakh'. The team proposed to introduce a new breed of pashmina goats from USSR. In 1979, a scheme had been launched under which the local breed was crossed with the Goran Alataskyia breed in order to increase the pashmina wool.

In October 1977, Dr C.K. Atal, Director of the Regional Research Laboratory (RRL) conducted a systematic study on various aspects of the utilization of apricot fruit which is grown in abundance. Some of the varieties are of a high quality. Dr Atal said that scientists of RRL tried the solar drier for three seasons between 1975 and 1977 and its efficiency under field conditions was ascertained, stabilised and demonstrated. The high quality of apricot is indicated by its sweet taste and by the fact that after drying its flavour does not change a phenomenon popularly known as 'phating'.

Recently after the nineties Shere Kashmir University of Agriculture and Technology, Srinagar, opened its Regional Research Centre at Leh and appointed Aziz Mir as Associate Director. Under his direction this unit has introduced many high yielding crops in Ladakh, particularly along the Indus valley. The demonstration units of this centre will definitely help to increase agriculture and fodder production in Ladakh.

Today, as said earlier, changes are taking place in all the spheres in Ladakh. Tourism and agriculture are the principal source of income which during the last two decades has increased considerably. As there is great stress laid on Buddhist culture and religion which attracts thousands of tourists every year, there is need to develop and upgrade the Central Institute of Buddhist Studies. The scholars and lecturers should be given better grades. This will encourage and enable good research work in Ladakh and further the promotion and sustenance of Buddhist culture and religion.

REFERENCES

1. Brochure—FRL, 1998.
2. Chopra, Prans: *On an Indian Border*, Asia Publishing House, 1964: pp. 2-40.
3. Datta, C.L.: *Ladakh and Western Himalayan Politics: 1819-48*; Munshiram Manoharlal Pub., New Delhi, 1973.
4. Jina, Prem Singh: 'Ladakh: The Land and the People', Indus Pub. Co., 1996.
5. Kak, B.L.: *Chasing Shadows in Ladakh,* Light and Life Pub., Jammu, 1978.
6. Kapoor, M.L: 'History of Jammu and Kashmir State', Jammu.

2

THE TREATY HIGH ROAD TO LEH BEFORE INDEPENDENCE

Ladakh, a large mountainous tract of country, has always been a place of attraction for traders. It was the chief trade centre of the Tibetans, the Yarkandis, the Kumaonis, the Kashmiris, the Turks and Hindustanis soon. Before independence the Hindustani and the Kashmiri traders used 'The Treaty High Road to Leh' for trade the details of which are as follows:

Trade Politics

Ladakh consisted of Rupshu, Zangskar, Middle Ladakh, Nubra and the plateau south of Karakoram before independence. It was under the administrative control of the *Wazir-i-wazarat* who, during summer, came to Leh and, in winter, returned to Skardu. Kargil, Skardu and Leh are three tehsils of Ladakh district.[1]

Ladakh was important for its strategic location. Leh, the capital of Ladakh acted as a great entrepot where merchants gathered and exchanged commodities.[2]

In 1681, religious disturbances took place in Tibet. As a result trade in central Asia through Ladakh was affected. The King of Ladakh then decided to favour Red sect of Buddhism. Consequently the other groups of Buddhism were annoyed with the King. These differences later became serious and ended in war. Dalai Lama entrusted the command of the Tibetan forces to Ga-den-tshe-wang-pal-sang-po. He marched towards Ladakh and soon reached Mansarovar. Thereafter they came to Basgo, defeating Ladakhi army.[3]

Faced with the prospect of fight facing the Tibetan Army the King of Ladakh Deldan Namgyal asked assistance from Aurangzeb and warned if Tibet occupied Ladakh, Kashmir might lose its monopoly over the pashmina wool trade. This proposal was received by Ibrahim Khan, the Governor of Kashmir, who also thought if the disturbances continued in Ladakh, the flow of shawl-wool into Kashmir would be adversely affected and this would hamper the shawl industry in Kashmir. Therefore, he advised Aurangzeb to accept the King of Ladakh's request.

Accordingly Aurangzeb, the Mughal Badshah sent a huge army to Ladakh to help King Deldan Namgyal. The Ladakhi forces, with the help of the Mughal army, defeated the Tibeto-Mongol troops. A peace treaty was signed and under the commercial agreement, the flow of Pashmina wool to Kashmir was resumed as earlier.

To look after the wool supply from Ladakh, four Kashmiri merchants were deputed at Spituk village near Leh. Thus, entire wool from Tibet as well as from the Chang-Thang region was exported to Kashmir. Besides, Ladakh and Tibet agreed to exchange trade missions. These missions were of commercial and religious nature. Under the Cha-ba trade mission a few hundred horse loads of tea came to Ladakh from Tibet. On the return they carried apricots, saffron, sugar and such commodities. On the other hand, Ladakhi caravans were allowed to carry large quantities of all the other necessary commodities for trading purpose, under the Lapchak trade mission.[4]

During the eighteenth century, Britishers made an attempt to divert the flow of shawl-wool into their areas. But the Dogras were not interested in diverting pashmina wool through British territories. Thus a quarrel across between the British East India Company and the Dogras. In 1820, Moorcroft was deputed to Leh to study trade activities. The Dogras were not happy with Moorcroft as he made an agreement with the King of Ladakh for establishing commercial intercourse with British merchants and for their passage through the country of Ladakh to Chinese Turkistan. Here follows a brief of the agreement:

> William Moorcroft was deputed on the part of British merchants of Calcutta to establish a commercial intercourse with the north-western parts of Asian Leh. The British merchants should have a free commercial communication with Ladakh as traders from other places. Besides twenty to fifty soldiers shall be accompanied with the caravan of Turkistan by the way of Yarkand for safeguard.[5]

William Moorcroft was able to please the ruler of Ladakh and according to his advice, the authorities of Ladakh agreed to impose a heavy duty of up to 70 Mahmood *Shahee* rupees on the traders of Central Asia and only 10 Mahmood *Shahee* rupees for British merchants, as indicated below:

> The duty on merchandise entering Leh is thirteen Mahmood *Shahee* rupees on seventy *munwattees*, the munwattee being one and a half to the Yamboo of China. However, due to friendly relations with Ladakh, the authorities will charge only 10 Mahmood *Shahee* rupees on British merchants.[6]

In the mean time, Gulab Singh became Raja and Administrator of Jammu hills. He later appointed Zorawar Singh as his *Wazir*. In 1823, he got the information that the Britishers would control Central Asian trade with the help of the Ladakhi king. Much annoyed with the British intervention in Ladakh, he decided to teach a lesson to the King of Ladakh. In July 1834, he ordered Zorawar Singh to conquer Ladakh. With 5,000 soldiers Zorawar Singh attacked Ladakh and defeated the Army on all fronts. Ladakh came under the control of the Dogras. The King of Ladakh had to pay a yearly tribute of Rs 20,000 and Rs 50,000 as war indemnity. The king immediately released Rs 37,000 partly in cash and partly in jewels for this purpose. After this war the Dogras had effective control over Ladakh.[7]

In 1840, Zorawar Singh wanted to conquer Yarkand so that the Dogras would have full control over Central Asian trade. In December he advanced towards Taklakot and fought a pitched battle with the Tibetan Army. The war continued for five days till December, 12. Finally, near Do-Yo-a shell struck in the Zorawar Singh's right shoulder. He fell from his horse. Fighting bravely, this great warrior lost his life.[8]

After the death of Zorawar Singh, the Tibetan Army marched ahead with full power, recaptured Gartok, Rudok, Tholing, Dapa, Tsaparang and other areas, from the Dogras. Raja Gulab Singh then sent 5,000 soldiers under the command of Dewan Hari Chand to Ladakh. A pitched battle was fought near Chemrey. This time the Tibetans lost the battle. By the time winter started, Hari Chand did not want to repeat the same mistake as Zorawar Singh did. So he agreed to peace, on October 17, 1842 a peace treaty was signed. The boundary of Ladakh and Tibet remained the same as it was earlier. Article II shows the details :

> The boundaries of Ladakh and Lhasa shall be constituted as formerly. The commodities viz. tea and Pusham shawl-wool shall be transmitted by Ladakh road.[9]

On the other side, in Jammu, differences between Britisher and Sikhs arose. Gradually it became serious, and in 1846, war broke out. Raja Gulab Singh did not take part, but after the battle of Sobraon, he acted as a mediator and succeeded in stopping the war.

British Government in India was very pleased with Raja Gulab Singh's role and transfered Kashmir to him for the sum of Rs. 75 lakhs through a treaty which was signed on 16th March, 1846. According to the treaty, Raja Gulab Singh was declared Maharaja of Jammu and Kashmir and, excluding Lahul and Spiti, he would have independent possession of Kashmir. Article-I reveals :

> The British Government transfers and makes for ever, in independent possession, to Maharaja Gulab Singh and the heirs male of his body, all the hilly or mountainous country, situated eastward of the river Indus and westward of the river Ravi, including Chamba and excluding Lahul, being part of the territories ceded to the British Government.[10]

After the agreement Maharaja Gulab Singh despatched Dewan Lakhpat Rai to take possession of Kashmir, but Immam-ud-Din defeated his army and killed the General. The Maharaja then applied to Sir Henry Lawrence for possession. He studied the treaty, and accordingly helped Maharaja Gulab Singh to take possession of Kashmir. Here follows the details:

"Maharaja Gulab Singh will refer to the arbitration of the British Government any disputes or questions that may arise between himself and the Government of Lahore or any other neighbouring State, and will abide by the decision of the British Government.

"Maharaja Gulab Singh engages for himself and heirs to join, with the whole of his military force, the British troops, when employed within the hills, or in the territories adjoining his possessions.

"Maharaja Gulab Singh engages to respect, in regard to the territory transferred to him.

"The British Government will give its aid to Maharajah Gulab Singh in protecting his territories from external enemies."[11]

After taking possession of Kashmir, Maharaja Gulab Singh started to present annually one horse, twelve goats and three pairs of shawls in token of the recognition of British supremacy as mentioned in the Article X:

"Maharaja Gulab Singh acknowledges the supremacy of the British Government, and will in token of such supremacy present annually to the British Government one horse, twelve perfect shawl goats of approved breed (six male and six female), and three pairs of Cashmere shawls."[12]

Besides the above treaty, the Britishers did not stop to intervene the Central Asian trade activities in Leh. As a result traders of British territories like Nurpur, Kulu and Mandi received a shawl, wool from Ladakh side particularly from Chang-Thang and West Tibet. Maharaja Gulab Singh made strong objection on the diversion of wool from Ladakh to British territories and asked British government to define the northern boundary between British and his territories. British government considered his objection and immediately appointed P.A. Vans Agnew and Captain A. Cunningham to demarcate the boundary between British and Gulab Singh's territories.[13]

Meanwhile Maharaja Gulab Singh ordered his officers in Ladakh to stop the intervention of Britishers, accordingly Gulab Singh's officials stopped the export of wool from Ladakh to Bashahr. As a result Bashahr trade got severe set-back. Raja Bashahr informed to the British officials that his trade suffered a lot because of boundary dispute. The demarcated boundary had been several times violated by Dogras as well as by Tibetans, even in 1847, some Chinese officials arrived up to Gartok to check the boundary mark. To know these incidences British-Governor-General had appointed second commission of three persons--captain Alexander Cunningham, Lieutenant Henry Strachey and Dr Thomas to demarcate the Ladakh-Tibet boundary. In addition the commissioners territories of British India and Central Asian countries. After enquiring various aspects of trade relations they came to the following conclusion:[14]

1. Ladakh enjoyed the monopoly of Tibetan shawl-wool trade after the 1842, treaty.
2. The clause under reference had operated injuriously to the interests of Kinnaur trader and were not favourably looked upon by the Chinese themselves.
3. Dogras imposed heavy duties on British hill state traders through check posts called *chowkis*.

4. Sometimes *kardars* of the Maharaja Gulab Singh even did not allow the British hill state traders in Ladakh to carry on their usual commercial speculations with Yarkand.

Therefore, to solve the above problems Vans Agnew from British India government side had pleaded with Maharaja Gulab Singh to remove prohibitory duties, onto reduce the duty from Rs 49.50 to Rs. 3.00 per maund. But, Maharaja Gulab Singh did not accept his plea.[15] Then Britishers made new trade politics and planned to encourage Russian traders and their goods in Ladakh and discouraged the supremacy of Yarkandi and Tibetan goods. Moreover, Harding felt some hesitation to do that and asked boundary commissioners to give detail of the regions of Central Asian countries which were involved in trade through Ladakh.

On 29th August 1847, the above commissioners reached the Tibetan frontier. But no Chinese or Tibetan agents reached for the discussion. Hence, commissioners failed to come to any conclusion, on the other side Dogras had already rejected to participate in any kind of discussion related with trade.[16] However, Strachey in his report in 1848 said that Britishers could promote their trade with Tibet through friendly contacts with local Tibetan agents.[17] Consequently in 1867. Coyley was appointed as the first British Joint Commissioner. He tried to establish fruitful trade relations with Tibetan agents. But Maharaja of Kashmir was not interested to give independent charge of Ladakh affairs to British Joint Commissioner. He said that Ladakh affairs should be looked after jointly by British and Kashmir Government Joint Commissioners. Thus, a commercial treaty between the British Government and the Maharaja of Kashmir was made in 1870. Under the Article-I of the treaty British Government appointed Joint Commissioner at Leh to survey the trade-routes through the Maharaja's territories from the British frontier of Lahul to the territories of Yarkand. The State Commissioner, on the other hand was responsible through the Tehsildar and his subordinates including the police force of about a dozen constables, under the Head Constable, to look after the proper functioning of the Res system of men and ponies, on the Treaty Road.[18]

After the treaty, Maharaja Runbeer Singh allowed all travellers and traders to use Highway Treaty road freely in perpetuity under Article II. However, for the supervision and maintenance of the road in its entire length through his territories and for the settlement of disputes of traders or others using the road, two Commissioners one from British

Government and other by Maharaja were appointed. The powers of commissioner had been described in detail in Article VII. But, in brief the commissioners were responsible for supply depot at suitable places on the road. Through these depots ration was supplied at fixed rates to traders and others. They were also responsible to fix the rent for the use of rest house or *serais* which were established on the road. Under the Article III of the treaty, thirteen clauses were formulated for the assistance of Joint Commissioners. According to clause I commissioners could stay only during summer (*i.e.* from 15th May and to the end of Ist December) in Leh because of unfavourable climatic condition. In their absence the Wazeer of Ladakh decided the cases (clause II). However, they did not interfere with any such case which effecte the trade (clause IV). Thus, they were responsible for the necessary supply of fuel, or wood for building purposes. In this connection the Wazeer of Ladakh helped them according to their instructions as described in clause IX.[19]

In 1870, for smooth trade through Treaty High road Maharaja Runbeer Singh gave Rs 5,000 for the construction of roads and bridges; Rs 2,000 per annum sanctioned for the maintenance of roads and bridges. He also agreed to give Rs 100 per annum for the repairs of each *serai*. In this connection he ordered the officers in Ladakh and in British territory to use their best endeavour to supply labourers on the indent of the commissioners at market rates and no tolls were levied on the bridges on this line of road (clause XII).[20]

Therefore, the Treaty High road was very much popular among traders. It was the easiest and best approachable road from Kashmir, Skardus, etc. On the way traders got good facilities like *serai*, guest house, supply of grass, fuel, etc. Besides it remained open for traders up to November whereas Kulu-Leh closed two months earlier (*i.e.* in the month of September). Nevertheless to improve trade through Kulu-Leh route, British Government took numerous steps, but only a few Lahuli traders used to go to Rudok via Rupshu (in Chang-Thang) for *pashmina* wool and collected about 20 per cent of the total exported wool trade through Ladakh which they sold into the hands of Kulu shawl manufacturers. However, the rest wool was exported to Kashmir via High Treaty road. Therefore, as said earlier British Joint Commissioner at Leh was responsible for the construction and maintenance of Dak Bungalows and *serai*. E. Joldan says:

The British Joint Commissioner was responsible for the construction and maintenance of the 14 Dak Bungalows and 14 *serais* (rooms and stables for the animals). Any traveller could stay in the *sarai* free of charge, but a room in the Dak Bungalow would cost one Rupee for 24 hours. There was a paid local *chowkidar* to look after both the buildings."[21]

The Treaty High Road to Leh

This was a pony transport route which officially closed from October to the middle of May, however, unofficially this was opened till December. Expert traders during this period crossed Zoji-la before day light and in early morning. It was also recommended that to keep Dras ponymen as they were sturdy and hard.[22]

There were small dak huts on the way at frequent intervals to keep the traffic open in winter. However, the rates of ponies and coolies were little higher than the summer. The detail is shown in Table 2.1.

TABLE : 2.1
RATES ON HIGH TREATY ROAD TO LEH-LADAKH

Sl. No.	*Stages*	*Per Poney (As)*			*Per Cooly (As)*		
		Summer	*Winter*	*% increased*	*Summer*	*Winter*	*% increased*
(1)	*(2)*	*(3)*	*(4)*	*(5)*	*(6)*	*(7)*	*(8)*
1.	Srinagar to Ganderbal	14	17	21.42	07	09	28.57
2.	Ganderbal to Kangan	11	14	27.27	06	08	33.34
3.	Kangan to Gund	14	17	21.42	07	09	28.57
4.	Gund to Sonmarg	15+1=16	20	25.00	8+2=10	13	30.00
5.	Sonmarg to Baltal	09	-	-	05	-	-
6.	Baltal to Matyan	15+1=16	-	-	8+4=12	-	-
7.	Matyan to Dras	12	-	-	06	-	-
8.	Dras to S. Kharbu	22	36	63.63	11	26	136.36
9.	S. Kharbu to Kargil	16	25	56.25	8+2=10	13	30.00
10.	Kargil to Mulbekh	22	36	63.63	11	20	82.00
11.	Mulbekh to B. Kharbu	15	24	60.00	08	12	50.00
12.	B. Kharbu to Lamayuru	15+1=16	24	50.00	8+2=10	13	30.00
13.	Lamayuru to Nurla	17+1=18	25	38.89	9+3=12	12	-
14.	Nurla to Saspol	14	-	-	7+1=8	-	-
15.	Saspol to Nimu	11	-	-	06	-	-
16.	Nimu to Leh	18	-	-	09	-	-

Source: Arora, R.C.; *op. cit.*, p. 293.

Table 2.1 reveals that during winter due to cold and snowfall per pony and coolie rate increased from 21 per cent to 64 per cent and 28 per cent to 136 per cent respectively. Because of the most difficult route between Matyan to S. Kharbu the rates per pony and coolie had been little higher than the normal.

The rates for crossing Zoji-la, the most difficult and snow covered pass, were Rs 10 per pony and Rs. 5 per coolie during 15th April to 15th May (or till the date on which the pass was officially declared open). During this period the contractor was entitled to take a commission @ nine paise per pony per stage, and Rs. 6 per pony and Rs. 4 per coolie were charged for halts at any intermediate state when transport was not arranged through the contractor.[23]

The general rates for Ladakh vary between Rs. 6 to Rs. 10 (Table: 2.2). And without the proper permit no traveller and trader was allowed to enter Ladakh. The permits were issued by the Resident of Kashmir.[24]

TABLE : 2.2
GENERAL RATES FOR PONY AND COOLIE IN LADAKH

Sl. No.	*Pony and Coolie*	*Rates (Rs.) per Mile*
1.	Riding pony	010
2.	Pack Pony	009
3.	Coolie	008

Source: Arora, R.C., *op. cit.*, p. 294.

The road between Leh and Srinagar was known as the Treaty road as a result of a treaty between the Kashmir State and British India and had 19 Marches (Table : 2.3) But one could cover this distance in 12 or 13 days by horse back.[25]

TABLE : 2.3
THE STAGES OF SRINAGAR TO LEH TRADE ROUTE

Stage	*No.*	*Height Above the Sea Level in Feet*	*Miles from Last Stage*
(1)	*(2)*	*(3)*	*(4)*
Srinagar	0	5,235	—
Gandarbal	1	5,230	14
Kangan	2	—	12
Gūnd	3	—	14

(Continued on next page)

(Table 2.3 Contd.)

(1)	(2)	(3)	(4)
Gagangir	4	—	09
Sonamarg	5	8,650	10
Baltal	6	—	10
Matāyan	7	—	16
Dras	8	10,144	15
Tashgām	9	9,390	15
Chānegund	10	8,675	18
Kargil	11	8,790	06
Shargol	12	10,290	20
Kharbu	13	11,200	18
Lamayuru	14	11,300	16
Nurla	15	—	18
Saspol	16	—	17
Nimu	17	—	13
Spituk	18	—	13
Leh	19	11,500	05
			259

Sources: (1) Drew, Frederic; *op. cit.*, pp. 531-32.
(2) Zoji-la; 11,300 feet lies between Nos 6 and 7.
(3) Nomika-la; 13,000 feet lies between Nos 12 and 13
(4) Fotu-la; 13,400 feet lies between Nos 13 and 14.

Besides there was an alternative route between Lamayuru to Leh (Table: 2.4).

TABLE: 2.4
ALTERNATIVE ROUTE BETWEEN LAMAYURU TO LEH

Stages	*Height above sea level*	*miles in feet*
Lamayuru	11,520	-
Khalsi	-	12
Timisgam	-	10
Tarutse	-	17
Nimu	-	10
Leh	11,500	18

Source: Drew, Frederic; *op.cit.*, p. 532.

Traders from Kashmir marched to Leh in summer when the above said road remained fit for laden ponies. This time they got sufficient supply of ration and green fodder for their animals. Here follows the details:

1. Srinagar to Ganderbal

Ganderbal, a small village is situated 12.5 miles away from Srinagar. Traders were using the following routes while marching towards Ladakh:

(1) Via Shadipur through the river Jhelum

(2) Via Mar Canal

(3) By motor road.

The first route was interesting for travellers because they could see Wular lake. The second was a direct water route and through third route they came across Anchar lake.[26]

2. Ganderbal to Kangan

Traders up to Wayil covered 5 miles through metal road then via Parao came to Kangan, in this way covered 11.5 miles between Ganderbal and Kangan.[27]

3. Kangan to Gūnd

It was bridle path of 13 miles. Traders throughout the way enjoyed the beautiful mountain scenery. Gūnd then had sufficient fuel, ration, etc., facilities for traders.[28]

4. Gūnd to Sonamarg

The route between Gūnd to Sonamarg was 14.5 miles. It was a hilly and zigzag track.[29]

5. Sonamarg to Baltal

It was a lovely path of nine miles consisting of meadows and good scenery up to Baltal.[30]

6. Baltal to Matāyan

It was a difficult route of 15 miles steep ascending up to Zoji-la then descending gradually eastward to Matāyan. However, this became more difficult for traders when snow bridges occurred. At Matāyan, villagers had a few huts but, traders could get necessary commodities.[31]

7. Matāyan to Dras

It was a 12.5 miles route gradually descending up to Dras, an open valley. Villagers at Dras had many huts but they were settled down in different groups, and spoke Dardi and Balti languages. Ladakhis called them Hembabas.[32]

8. Dras to Shimbha Kharbu

This was a 20 miles narrow road with bends north-eastward.[33]

9. Shimbha Kharbu to Kargil

Here the route was 15 miles ascending over a spur. But it was in bad shape over Chāngegund. Travelling further at right side along the Suru river one could reach Kargil. In those days it was the capital of Purik and came under the administrative control of Baltistan.[34]

10. Kargil to Mulbek

The 22 miles long route was narrow and full of scenic beauty. The long march could be halved at Lotsun, whence a difficult track carried to the Indus below Dah via Bula-la. Thereafter, road was good up to Shergol, thence traders reached Mulbek. This village is located at the foot of rock, now it is spread on the upper side of the road also. The track between Kargil to Mulbek would be of great interest for geologists, as there are sandstone rocks along the route.[35]

11. Mulbek to Bod Kharbu

The 14.5 miles road was fair. After crossing Wakha-chu valley, traders had to ascend gradually to Namika-la, thence descending along the Sangeluwa-chu stream to Khangra, further ascending a few miles they reached Kharbu.[36]

12. Bod Kharbu to Lamayuru

The 14.5 miles route ascending up to Kanji valley, thereafter from Fotu-la descending to Lamayuru.[37]

13. Lamayuru to Nurla

The road about 18 miles was down the ravine and finally into the Indus valley near Hangru. Thereafter, traders after travelling reached Khalsi, a large village had all necessary facilities for them. Khalsi to Nurla was an 8 mile journey, the route was rough but levelled.[38]

14. Nurla to Saspol

The 11 miles road via Bazgo[39] had group of villages at Nimu with sufficient fodder, fuel and ration supply for traders.[40]

15. Nimu to Leh

The route is of 18 miles, at first ascending along the plateau, then descending gradually up to Phyang, travelling further the route again ascending from Spituk to Leh.[41]

The Treaty High Road had villages at every stoppage. The State Government then provided encamping ground, fuel, forest rest house, grass, grazing ground, etc., facilities to traders or travellers at each stoppage (Table: 2.5). This is present in page no. 228.

Benefits of Trade to Ladakhis along the Treaty High Road:

1. On demand Ladakhis provided ponies on hire basis to traders and to increase their income.
2. The inhabitants of Ladakh usually sell their agricultural products viz. vegetables, grass to traders in cash and kind.
3. Through traders Ladakhis sent their letters or other necessary informations to their relatives or friends in Leh or other places.
4. Sometimes through traders Ladakhis were able to get things according to their need.
5. Those traders who stayed in the government guest houses and *serais* were invited for breakfast, dinner, etc., by Ladakhis at their houses and earned handsome money.
6. Sometimes traders stayed at Ladakhis guest houses and gave boarding and lodging charges to them which increased their income.
7. Along the route Ladakhis cultivated fodder grass and fulfilled the fodder demand of traders in exchange of money.
8. To increase their income many Ladakhis had opened restaurants at the different stages along the roadside for traders.
9. Sometimes Ladakhis along the route exchanged their commodities with *dal*, rice, etc.

Benefits to Traders along the Treaty High Road

1. Traders did not feel any problems while travelling through the Treaty High Road as they got sufficient facilities at every stage by the State Government as well as by the Ladakhi families.
2. Sometimes traders got free service by Ladakhis in loading and unloading their goods.
3. Traders could get yak, horses, etc., from Ladakhis at noninal rates.

TABLE 2.5
FACILITIES AVAILABLE AT THE STAGE ALONG THE TREATY HIGH ROAD TO LEH

Atage/Village 1	Height 2	C 3	DB 4	Dispy 5	E 6	F 7	G 8	PO 9	RH 10	S 11	T 12	TO 13	SC 14
Ganderbal	-	-	-	✓	-	-	-	✓	-	-	-	✓	-
Kangan	-	✓	✓	-	-	-	-	✓	-	-	-	-	-
Gund	6,500	✓	-	-	-	-	-	✓	-	-	-	-	-
Matayan	10,430	✓	-	-	✓	✓	✓	-	-	-	-	-	✓
Dras	10,144	✓	-	-	✓	✓	✓	✓	✓	✓	✓	✓	-
S. Khasrbu	9,250	✓	-	-	✓	-	✓	-	-	✓	✓	✓	✓
Kargil	8,790	✓	-	✓	✓	✓	✓	✓	✓	✓	✓	✓	-
Mulbek	10,500	✓	-	-	✓	✓	✓	-	✓	✓	✓	-	-
B. Kharbu	11,200	✓	-	-	✓	✓	✓	-	-	✓	✓	-	-
Lamayuru	11,300	✓	-	-	✓	✓	✓	-	✓	✓	✓	-	-
Khalsi	9,700	✓	-	-	✓	✓	✓	✓	✓	✓	✓	✓	✓
Nurla	9,900	✓	-	-	✓	✓	✓	-	✓	✓	✓	-	-
Saspol	10,200	✓	-	-	✓	✓	✓	-	✓	✓	✓	-	-
Nimu	11,250	✓	-	-	✓	✓	✓	-	✓	✓	✓	-	-
Leh	11,500	✓	-	-	✓	✓	✓	✓	✓	✓	✓	✓	-

Source: Arora, R.C.; *op. cit.*, pp. 63-163.

REFERENCES

1. Arora, R.C.: *In the land of Kashmir, Ladakh and Gilgit*; Jay Kay Book House; Jammu, 1940:152.
2. Datta, C.L: *Ladakh and Western Himalayan Politics*: 1819-1848; Munshiram Manoharlal Pub.; 1973:18.
3. Basgo = Bazgo and Datta, C.L., *op. cit.*
4. Datta, C.L., *op. cit.*, pp. 65-66.
5. *Ibid.*, Appendix-C, p. 208.
6. *Ibid.*, p. 209.
7. *Ibid.*, pp. 111-12.
8. *Ibid.*, p. 140.
9. *Ibid.*, Appendix-E, p. 214.
10. Drew, Frederic: The Jummoo and Kashmir Territories; Cosmo Pub. (Reprint 1976); Appendix-V; p. 546.
11. *Ibid.*
12. *Ibid.*
13. *Ibid.*, p. 189.
14. *Ibid.*, p. 192.
15. *Ibid.*
16. *Ibid.*, pp. 196-98.
17. *Ibid.*, p. 198.
18. Joldan, E: *Harvest Festival of Buddhist Dards of Ladakh and Other Essays;* Kapoor Brothers, Srinagar; 1985, p. 67.
19. Drew, Frederic; Appendix-V; p. 552.
20. *Ibid.*
21. Joldan, E.; *op. cit.*, p. 64.
22. Arora, R.C., *op. cit.*, p. 158.
23. *Ibid.*, p. 204.
24. *Ibid.*, p. 282.
25. Joldan, E., *op. cit.*, p. 65.
26. Arora, R.C., *op. cit.*, p. 64.
27. *Ibid.*, p. 94
28. *Ibid.*
29. *Ibid.*

30. *Ibid.*, p. 95.
31. *Ibid.*, p. 159.
32. *Ibid.*
33. *Ibid.*
34. *Ibid.*
35. *Ibid.*, p. 161.
36. *Ibid.*
37. *Ibid.*, p. 162.
38. *Ibid.*
39. Bazgo = Basgo.
40. Arora, R.C., p. 163.
41. *Ibid.*

3

BISCOE'S JOURNEY TO LADAKH — 1896

C.E. Tyndale Biscoe started his journey from Srinagar to Ladakh in the summer of 1896, with the permission of Captain Cheveneux Trench, the then Commissioner of Ladakh. After travelling seventeen miles a day he and his party along with Ladakh's Commissioner reached Leh.

Hill Station of Srinagar

Travelling across the Kashmir valley, Biscoe and his party reached Sonamarg in the evening. It is the last point in Kashmir valley and is situated at the height of 10,000 feet surrounded by beautiful stretch of grass and flowers. According to Biscoe,

"Sonamarg is surrounded by peaks of 18,000 feet, and three glaciers at the head of their respective valleys can be seen looking down upon one from the east. Sonamarg means 'the meadow of gold'."[1]

In those days travelling over high Himalayan passes in moonlight was considered safe, therefore, Biscoe made his journey to Ladakh in moonlight from Sonamarg.

Zoji-La: A Rocky Pass

Biscoe crossed Zoji-La in June 1896, at night. It was considered the gateway of Central Asia for traders, but was difficult and almost impossible for ponies. As a result many traders lost their ponies. According to Biscoe:

"Zogi-La (Zoji-La) is not a high pass, being only 11,500 feet, but a steep road, and dangerous for ponies on account of the hard snow and ice slopes. At the top of the pass on the watershed there was snow for some miles. It was not unlike a frozen-rough sea, the snow having drifted into small hillock like waves and breakers, and therefore, not easy going".[2]

Dras: A Small Country

Biscoe crossed Zoji-Laat in midnight. He was extremely exhausted and when he saw rocks and grass he got down and lay down by the side of the road for some rest. The other men also took rest for sometime. Later they proceeded for Dras also known as Him-babs. It is situated next to Zoji-la, and was annexed to Ladakh in 1758 by King Bra-shis-r Nam-rgyal. Unfortunately it was not properly looked after by the king, so the Raja Hazara looted it several times. On 16th October, 1822, when William Moorcroft was passing through Dras with his fellow-traveller, he acknowledged:

"A party of eight hundred men lead by Raja of Hazara who later plundered Dras. He also came to know that another group from Hazara came to Matayan and stole several horses of the villagers."[3]

Thus, during the nineteenth century the journey through Dras was risky as there were frequent robberies in Dras and its adjoining areas. But, Biscoe did not face any such incident.

Corruption in Kargil

After travelling further Biscoe and his party halted in Kargil, the capital of Purik. While staying in Kargil he got complaints from the public that the Governor of the province denied to supply foodgrain to them, therefore, they want to enquire this case seriously. Captain Trench who was with Biscoe accepted public demands and made an inquiry against the Governor. Biscoe explained the details of inquiry proceedings in the following way.

"The Governor of the province called on us. He was a Kashmiri Brahman, a little man, but from the size of his lower chest he evidently had done himself well. Captain Trench asked him to show him his statement of grain accounts, as there was a threatened shortage of food that autumn. He had received orders to keep large stores of grain in case of emergencies, the old fort on the hill having been requisitioned for such a purpose. The books were brought, and from them Captain Trench saw that his orders had been faithfully obeyed, and the fort was just bulging with grain, like the Governor's lower chest. Captain Trench was so pleased to hear of the great supplies that he told the Governor he would like to see how he had managed to store so much, and would visit the fort that very afternoon at 3 p.m.

At 2.30 p.m. the Governor with his suit arrived at our camp again, to invite the Commissioner Sahib and all his party to take tea with him at his house, but as it was such a hot day surely it would be more comfortable for the ladies if they and all the party came up later, say 4.30 p.m. Captain Trench accepted for the whole party, but said that he at any rate would visit the fort first and afterwards come on to tea. So we all climbed the hill towards the fort, and as we neared it the Governor again pressed Captain Trench to come straight to his house for the tea and afterwords visit the fort, for was it not very hot ?— and the evening would be cooler, etc. Captain Trench would not give in, and made straight for the fort, we all following him.

"When we all entered through the large gateway into the quadrangle, Captain Trench asked the Governor to have the door opened, whereupon he called a *peon* to go and bring the keys. The *peon* remained absent a long time, so the Governor again asked Captain Trench to come to his house for tea while the keys were being fetched. But no, Captain Trench was firm on the point, he would see the store first, and asked the Governor to hurry up his *peon.* So another was sent after the first. At last the servant arrived, breathless, with a huge bunch of large keys, and commenced trying to—or, to be truthful, pretending to open the great lock. He went through the whole lot, but no key would fit it. So the Governor again broached the subject of tea, and apologised for the foolishness of his servant, explaining that the man with the right set of keys had left the office with the keys. So Captain Trench asked the Governor to send a man after him and fetch the keys. He said that he would, but this servant with the keys lived a long way off, and it would all take time, and again mentioned tea first.

"Captain Trench's patience was beginning to give out, and he said: 'Do not bother about the keys: We will soon burst that door open with that big beam,' pointing to one leaning against the wall.

"The Governor begged him not to do that, for he would send a man running to fetch the right keys. In an extraordinarily short time. considering the great distance this man was supposed to have covered, the man arrived, puffing and blowing, playing his part well, with another (?) great bunch of keys, though uncommonly like the first bunch which had proved useless.

"The keys were applied, but the lock refused to be opened. Again the Governor expressed his sorrow for the delay battering-ram again was mentioned, and Captain Trench made a move towards it. Then the Governor, seeing his game was up, gave a sign, and the key turned the lock and the door swung open. Captain Trench went in; the great store-room was entirely empty! not a single sack of grain was there.

Captain Trench came out and said to the Governor: "Why did you bring me to this empty store-room ? I want to see your stores of grain, and not empty rooms " The Governor apologised to Captain Trench, and swore at his servants for having made fools of them all, and ordered them at once to open those store-rooms where the grain was. The servants' faces were a study, and their hands and knees literally shook, as they did not know which orders they were to obey the ones given by the Governor before the arrival of Captain Trench or the ones now given. However, the Governor pointed to another door, and ordered it to be opened. Again there was going to be the same waste of time over the keys, when Captain Trench cut it short by stepping towards the battering-ram and asking me to help him.

"Then the door was opened, and we found this store-room also absolutely empty. At last the play was over the chief actor, forgetting all his greatness, fell on his knees before Captain Trench, and with hands in the attitude of prayer pleaded for mercy. Captain Trench told him to go home, and he would see him at the Public *Durbar* next day. So our tea with the Governor was off."[4]

Central Asian Caravans

While moving towards Leh from Kargil, Biscoe saw some traders with their loaded animals. The sheep were in large number because in those days sheep were used for two purposes, i.e., as carriers and for food. Biscoe says:

"It was an interesting sight to watch the caravans from Central Asia and China passing, with the loads carried often on yaks and some even on sheep's backs, the sort of sheep which grow a broad fat tail, which swings about most uncomfortably as the animal walks. The idea of loading sheep is a very practical one, for when the food which is carried by the sheep is eaten up, then there is no need of the carrier, so it is then eaten, the fat tail being considered a great delicacy."[5]

Large Rock Carved Image at Mulbek

At Mulbek, Biscoe first saw a Buddhist monastery, near which there was a large rock carved image, according to him it was Buddha's image, about thirty feet in height. When I visited the site during 1981, I saw the image and confirmed that the image was not of Buddha but of Maitreya or Chamba. During his visit to Mulbek, Biscoe saw a lama dance at the monastery. He described the lama ceremony as under:

"There was a sort of maypole erected in front of the figure, decked with colour paper or rags. Then the troops of thirty children appeared, dressed in bright 'garments' wearing crowns of flowers, and they were dancing round the pole and singing, reminding one of the maypole dance. Then came a monk, dressed in a white garment like a surplice, with a red fool's cap on his head. In one hand he carried a Kashmiri fire-pot full of live charcoal and some narcotic mixture of hemp or opium. These fumes he kept inhaling, which made him become very excited. In his right hand he carried a carved sword, which he flourished about in a most dangerous manner. He commenced to dance round the pole, followed by the children. He shouted louder and louder, and twirled about his body faster and faster, while his sword was flashing and slashing about in all direction."[6]

Inscription at Mulbek

Biscoe found an inscription of King Ides on a stone plate on 'mane' near the Mulbek monastery. According to him: "There is an inscription of King Ides abolishing living sacrifices. This was not, however, obeyed, and the people continued to sacrifice goats before the pre-Buddhist altars, tearing out the heart of the living animal."[7]

Polo

Polo was the main source of entertainment of villagers in Ladakh. In every big village one could see a Polo ground, which was generally kept in good order, the grass being kept green by irrigation. According to Biscoe's description:

"The chief features in which the game differs from Western polo are: Firstly, there are two long stone walls, about three feet high, built along with both sides of the ground, against which the ball is made to rebound; they are also used, by the way, for squeezing your, adversary's pony, and if possible the leg of the rider, against the jagged stones, to his great discomfort. Secondly, all the players start at a gallop from one end. The leader then throws the ball into the air and strikes up a joyful noise, accompanied by plenty of drums. The riders play and players receiving terrific whacks, and blood flowing profusely; and sometimes the onlookers receive wounds from standing too near the wall. It is a very ancient and honoured game in these regions."[8]

Mane

Travelling inside the Buddhist country in Ladakh, Biscoe saw many 'Mane walls' along the roadside, as he says:

"On the road one passes walls from 100 to 300 yards long, about eight feet high and eight feet broad, with a pent roof of flat stones of all sizes, on which are carved the same words,' *Om mane Padme Hun*, on the lotus or, as it has been interpreted to me: 'May my soul, O God, be like the jewel of water lies on the lips of the lotus leaf just as it is going to fall into the lake and be lost in the ocean of water (i.e., be lost in Nirvana).

Monks roam over the country doing this pious carving work for those who will pay them. Merit not only comes to men who place these stones on the wall, but to all those travellers who pass on the left side of the wall, and curses on those who pass on the wrong side."[8]

Along 'Mane', Biscoe saw numerous *chortens* of different sizes. He remarks:

"On the road one continually passes *chortens*, stone pagodas generally white-washed, and not only on the road, but dotted about in the fields and up the mountainsides. They are of all sizes from three to forty feet high. They are hollow, and in them one will often find clay medallions vulgarily called potted lamas, for they are composed of the ashes of the monks, which have been stamped with the monastery stamps, like prettily stamped pats of butter. Some of the stamps are very decorative, generally with the figure of Buddha in the centre of a circle with writing around."[9]

Religious Flag

In Buddhist villages and houses one can see religious flags on the tops of their houses and on trees, passes, etc. Biscoe says:

"On the tops of the houses and on trees one sees bunches of flags made of coloured rags on which is inscribed this same prayer. When the flags flutter in the breeze this prayer ascends for the good of the individual who placed these rags to be moved by the wind."[10]

Prayer Cylinder

Buddhists are simple and religious people. One can see 'Prayer Cylinder' at inn places or near monasteries. Biscoe says:

"As we pass through a village we see little paper wind-mills on the roofs which work a prayer wheel inside the house. This is a metal cylinder crammed full of paper on which is written hundred times this one prayer: *Om mane Padme hun.*

Along the walls of certain houses and always at the monasteries are found these cylinders of wood let into the wall at a convenient height from the ground to allow passer-by's to pat them and make them revolve. In some villages they have huge prayer wheels worked by water, which pray automatically night and day, year in and year out for all the villages. Lastly, you meet both men and women walking on the road carrying these wheels of metal, which they keep on the spin by the twist of the wrist, for a lead ball is attached to this cylinder by a metal chain, which adds considerable momentum. Some of these hand prayer wheels are beautifully ornamented with silverwork."[11]

Ladakhi Dress

Ladakhi Buddhists wear long woollen garment called *Goncha*, head dress *Pirak,* etc. Biscoe describes:

"The people one meets are most picturesquely dressed. The men and women wear a long woollen garment generally of red, but often of green or some other colour. The men have a leather girdle into which they stick a regular ironmonger's shop of goods, such as one or two knives, a brass opium pipe, a tinder-box, a metal purse, a long metal pen-box with metal inkpot attached, a whip of three thongs, the handle of which is always most simple. They fill their cup with cold water, and then pour the flour and stir it with their first finger, and when it becomes a sort of watery paste they drink it. It is a most unappetising food and gives them indigestion continually. Most of them also add an ikon to their belt collection. It is an image of Buddha made of silver or gold in a casket of some metal, and a pocket communion set of copper or silver with much ornamentation.

"This pocket set is a most neat and clever arrangement, for the paten and stand are so made that they fit beautifully into the metal pot which is the chalice. Every Buddhist can be his own priest and give the elements to himself.

"Many wear a chatelaine attached to their leather belt, on which hang most of the things mentioned, and thus their belt is left free for other goods and chattles. Their shoes are generally felt top-boots, often of gaudy colours.

"The head-dress is a cloth cap, not infrequently of the same colour as their dress, but it is perhaps a little like a Balaclava cap or a helmet with flaps. It is most picturesque and odd-looking. The whole costume seems to suit the Mongol features excellently, especially with the long bigtail hanging down the back, which always covers the back of the cloak with black grease. The women dress much like the men, only their head-dress is different. They wear a 'Pirak'—that is a piece of red cloth about six or eight inches wide, which starts from the forehead and continues down the back nearly to the waist. It is covered with rows of precious stones, chiefly rough pieces of turquoise, and silver ornaments. This system of carrying their wealth on their head shows how honest these people are then on each side of the face, and sewn on to this strip of cloth, are two pieces of astrakhan, which are made of to stick out at right angles to the face some six inches like black wings. Altogether it is most becoming."[12]

Buddhist Women

In Ladakh Buddhist women are very frank. One can see them working in government and private offices more than thirty per cent. They do not hesitate to go outside Ladakh for higher education. Some occupy good offices like that of: Director, Block Development Officer (BDO), Police officer, Doctor, Air Hostess, etc. Biscoe also acknowledged these characteristics, as he says:

"The women in this country are not 'Purdah' and are treated on equal terms with the men. It is most refreshing. They are not the least shy or bold. They are just their smiling jolly selves, like their menfolk."[13]

Lamayuru Monastery

After Mulbek, Biscoe crossed two passes: Namika-la (12,200 ft) and Fotu-la (13,432 ft.), thereafter he entered Lamayuru. It is a big village, monastery on the top of some low cliffs, and worth a visit. One can see beautiful murals, tanks, images of Avalokitesvara, Gonpos, Maitreya, etc. It is situated at 11,300 ft., when Biscoe and his party reached this monastery, lamas and villagers welcomed them in traditional way, he remarks:

"As usual, as we approached Lamauru (Lamayuru), we were met by much noise and dust as they approached. We were taken round the monastery by the head ecclesiastic. We climbed the stone stairway to the monastery, which, as usual, was situated on the top of a cliff, but on it is such a way that it was not easy to see where rock ended and the building commenced. Along the side of the stairway were rows of prayer wheels let into the wall, which we set spinning in the orthodox manner. At least I hope we did spin them the right not the wrong way. The chapel was full of interesting objects, and one did not know quite what to look at, for there seemed to be, and there was, such a crowd of interesting objects which I had never seen before. The building was like a hall, the roof supported by wooden pillars, with a gallery all round, from which hung a profusion of silk banners of Chinese design, chiefly dragons. On one side of the hall was a row of coloured figures, life-size of Buddha and sainted lamas, which were arrayed in rich silk. Before each figure was a table or altar of very curious design, coloured with bright red, green, yellow and gold, carved with dragons and sacred symbols.

"On the tables were metal cups and goblets, and on each table was a basin of holy water, an oil lamp burning. The chalice for the *Chang* (cider) and paten for the bread, a *dorje* (a prettily carved brass or silver dumb-bell-looking article used by the priest during part of the service), also a little drum often made of a human skull sawn off at the top to allow for the skin to be stretched. There were also some goblets made of human skulls, and a human thigh-bone used as a trumpet.

"Down the middle of the chapel are low benches in lines, end on to the row of figures, on which the monks kneel facing the altars as they read their sacred books. On the left side of the chapel are rows of copper beakers full of *chang*, from which the monks refresh themselves when they become sleepy over their much reading. Then on the left wall are shelves in which their books are kept. These are long strips of paper or parchment manuscripts.

"There are five chapels kept each day when any great person dies the monks are paid to read through a certain number of their holy books. They each take so many pages, and read through them aloud, all together, each one reading something different, so there must be a fair volme of sound."[14]

When Biscoe visited Lamayuru monastery, he found a separate building for nuns, today there is no nun and the nunnery is in ruined condition. Speaking about nuns Biscoe says:

"There are nuns who live in separate buildings. Many of them are so like the monks that it is difficult to tell one from the other at least to an unpractised eye."[15]

Leh

As soon as Biscoe and Commissioner of Ladakh arrived in Leh, they were warmly welcomed by the Ladakhis and lamas in their traditional style, Biscoe remarks:

"The reception given to the Commissioner Sahib at Leh was the culmination of great doings. Seven miles from Leh, in the valley of the Indus; a large sandy plain, there meet us a great cavalcade of grand folk dressed in most weird costumes, uncommonly like a well-got up pantomime.

"There were men dressed in Chinese silks, with their smart and gold caps with tassels, Ladakhi officials of various grades, from the Joint-Commissioner, a fine-looking Mohammedan, to his fat babu who sat on his pony like a monkey, his stirrups being so short that his knees and fat stomach met.

"When we arrived through the fine gateway into the main street we found both sides lined with H.H. the Maharaja's troops and the crowds of citizens behind them. The monastery band was in full view on the roof of one of the buildings and made the usual joyful sound."[16]

Trade Centre

Leh is 11,500 feet above the sea level, needs a little time to get acclimatized. In olden days it was one of the important centres of Central Asian trade. Traders carried goods from east and west, therefore, the population of Leh which was 3,000 in the winter of 1896, rose to 6,000 in summer. The Commissioner's chief duty was then to look after the trade, because in those days greatest part of Ladakh's national income came from the caravans crossing the country between Tibet or Turkestan and Srinagar through the Zoji-La.[17]

Polo Game in Leh

After the traders of Central Asia sold their goods they played polo game in the main street of Leh bazaar, as Biscoe says:

"This main street of shops has a fine avenue of popular-trees, which give most grateful shade in the hot summer weather.

"As it is very broad, it is the polo ground. It seemed most strange to see the players dashing up and down the main street, often hitting the ball into the shops. Fortunately the shops in Leh do not possess glass windows, otherwise polo in that street would be an expensive amusement."[18]

Khardong-La

After staying a few days in Leh, Biscoe climbed Khardong-La, the highest pass in Ladakh of 18,380 ft. It was a difficult pass for traders as annually many traders lost their animals. According to Biscoe:

"Kardang (Khardong) pass, of some miles from Leh, the one of which there is so much loss of life of luggage animals. The air is so rare that the pony and donkey men often slit up the noses to their animals to allow easier breathing. The traders use yaks to a great extent on this pass, which they ride to save themselves from mountain sickness."[19]

Hemis Monastery

Biscoe went up to Khardong-La only and returned back to Leh. Next day he went to Hemis and reached there after two days. About the Hemis he says:

"About twenty miles from Leh is a very large and important monastery called Hemis. It took us two days to reach Hemis. The monastery is situated in a very narrow valley on the side of a mountain and not on the top as is usually the case. This monastery is a very rich one and possesses stores of rich Chinese silks and jewels.

"The play took place in a very fine courtyard, the monastery towering above one like a huge castle, a very impressive building. It contains three hundred monks, who wear yellow robes and are superior to red-robed ones. The play lasts for the whole day and till noon on the second day, with no interlude, and is wearing to a degree. The idea of the play is to teach the people the power of the monks in future life. They act all the known, or rather unknown, horrors of hell and the only way of salvation through the holiness of the monks. Not a word is spoken; it is taught entirely by right.

"The acting is guided by the monastery band as to time, fervour, quietness, tempest, hell fire or death. The band is directed by the precentor, and he by a big book in front of him. There is a fire burning in the centre of the court. Then there enter monks, dressed up in hideous masks with faces of various animals, such as dogs, tigers, dragons, etc. They carry large three-pronged forks, and a clay figure of a man into the flames. The devils commence dancing round, pretending to stick their forks into the figure, and seem to be enjoying the sport of tormenting their victims. This scene continues for what seems to be an interminable time, when in come a party of monks from the great door of the monastery, dressed in coloured silk garments, wearing huge masks, and commence to march round and round hell fire, making various passes with their arms towards the flames. They begin with painfully slow steps, which are so monotonous that they get on one's nerves, the band playing softly but in terribly slow time.

"Then the music quickens slightly, and then a little quicker, then quicker, until these holy monks fairly spin like dancing *dervishes*. The band works itself crazy with the screeching of its pipes, crashing cymbals, bellowing giant trumpets and resounding drum. Then all of a sudden there is dead silence, and we are all thankful for the respite. Then the whole dance commences over again from the very beginning, with one step every three seconds, and again working up to the whizz-bang. By this time this lot of holy men are tired out with their exertions and they disappear through the same great door from which they came. Immediately come in a second lot with a different set of great masks, some of them wearing most benign faces. They with the help of the band try their charms in marching and dances, and so one party succeeds another all through that day and part of the next without any success, for the flames of hell still burn on and the devils have it all their own way until a party of super-holy monks arrive, who come with holy water, with which they conquer the flames, and then the devils one and all rush out of the arena amid a tempest of crashing and shrieking; but above it all is the sound of a mighty wind caused by all the monks whistling their loudest, and the whole band of devils, pitchforks and all, disappear into the monastery well, it was a great show. People had come from long distances to see their religion acted."[20]

Conclusion

Though Biscoe's visit to Ladakh was for short duration, the information he collected has historical importance, particularly for cultural history, i.e., about monastic ceremonies and trade in general.

REFERENCES

1. Biscoe, C.E. Tyndale: *Kashmir in Sunlight and Shade*, Sagar Pub., New Delhi; 1971 (Reprint), p. 198.
2. *Ibid.*, pp. 198-99.
3. Calloc'h, Bernard Leh: 'Historical Background of Csoma De KoRōs sojourn in Ladakh (Zanskar) between 1822 and 1826'; In : *Recent Research*

on Ladakh 4 and 5; Osmaston and Denwood (ed.); Motilal Banarsidas Pub., Delhi, 1995, p. 365.

4. Biscoe, C.E. Tyndale; *op. cit.*, pp. 203-06.
5. *Ibid.*, pp. 207-08.
6. *Ibid.*, p. 208.
7. *Ibid.*, p. 210.
8. *Ibid.*, p. 211.
9. *Ibid.*, pp. 211-12.
10. *Ibid.*, p. 212.
11. *Ibid.*, pp. 212-13.
12. *Ibid.*, pp. 213-14.
13. *Ibid.*, p. 214.
14. *Ibid.*, pp. 216-17.
15. *Ibid.*, p. 218.
16. *Ibid.*, pp. 218-19.
17. *Ibid.*, p. 218.
18. *Ibid.*, pp. 219-20.
19. *Ibid.*, p. 223.
20. *Ibid.*, pp. 227-28.

4

A JOURNEY TO TYAKSHI-PACHATHANG IN NUBRA VALLEY

Leh to Nubra Road

On 30th May 1998, at 10 a.m., we stated for Nubra from Leh by buses. After travelling for about 5 kms., we reached Ganglas. After crossing the T.C.P. barrier, the buses were climbing slowly towards Khardong-La. Fortunately there was not much snow on the road up to Khardong-La. But as we started other side of the Khardong-La, the road had snow and it was very slippery. Our bus drivers were driving the buses very gently on the instruction of the men who were sprinkling soil over snow. Here, after about a one hour struggle we were able to cross the snow covered zone and at 2 p.m. reached Spang Chenmo.

After little refreshment at Spang Chenmo, we marched and about 6 p.m. reached at Deskit via Khardong, Khalsar, etc., villages.

Thus, on 30th May we covered about 123 km. between Leh and Deskit in one day. The details are as follows (Map 1):

Leh (11,500 ft.) : District headquarter of Leh

↓

Ganglas (Micro Hydel Project of M.E.S.)

↓

Khardong-La (18,380 ft.) : Highest pass on this route

↓

Spang Chenmo (15,230 ft) : Dok of Khardong village

↓

Khalsar (10,060 ft.)

↓

Deskit : Headquarter of Nubra Sub-Division

Trekking Route

Nowadays Nubra is a very popular trekking route especially among foreigners. The route taken by the trekkers is as follows:

Leh: District headquarter of Leh district.

Sabu: A village near Leh, bus service is available for this village.

Dogerla

Digor

Khalsar (10,060 ft.)

Deskit: Headquarter of Nubra Sub-Division

Summer Trade Route

During olden days, summer trade route between Leh to Yarkand via Nubra was very popular among traders. Before leaving to Yarkand, traders made all arrangements of transport at Leh. The Khardong pass, which was dangerous for ponies, remained open from mid June to November. Here follows the details:

Stage (1)	*Inter Miles* (2)	*Nature of Journey to Next Stage* (3)
Leh; 11,500 ft.	—	Road rough and ascending pass. Ganglas, 5 miles
Leh Polu; 15,252 ft.	10	Ascend to Khardong pass, 18,380 ft. Descend about 1,200 ft. Over snow belt. Pass Khardong Polu, 15,300 ft., 9 miles.
Khardong village; 13,350 ft.	15	Village. Descend through ravine to 7 miles and then in Shyok valley. River troublesome in summer.
Khalsar; 10,060 ft.	12	Village. Cross Shyok river. 3 miles. Pass Thirit, 6½ miles. Road rough from Nubra-Shyok confluence to Liakzun, 11 miles. Cross Sumur Lungpa.
Tegur; 10,250 ft.	15	Village on Nubra river. Pass hamlets. Road fair.
Panamik; 10,600 ft.	16	Village. Granary. Cross Thulanbutichu, 8 miles. Ascend 2,000 ft. and descend.
Umlung; 12,250 ft.	12	Cross Thulanbuti chu, 2 miles. Leave here left bank road.
Tut-yailak; (Pang-dangsa) 14,150 ft.	11	Camp opposite Moraine of Mamostang (Murgistan) Glacier to west road rough Pass Skyangpochu, 15,070 ft., and Sartang. Ascend saddle glacier on watershed between Shyok and Nubra valleys cross Saser Pass 17,480 ft. 11 mile.

(Continued on next page)

(Table 4.1 Contd.)

(1)	(2)	(3)
Saser Brangsa; 15,200 ft.	16	Ruined hut on Shyok river, cross Shyok valley early. Ascend over plateau to Chong-Tash lake, 8 miles. Descend to Murgo.
Murgo (Chalan Chumik); 14,600 ft.	12	Camp at Murgo-Shyok confluence. Road rough ascending.
Kizil-langar; 16,400 ft.	24	Upstream, ascend to 17,780 ft. cross Depsang plains. 6 miles. Ford Chip Chap river, 13 miles. Pass Daulat Begoldi, 15 miles. Then ascend.
Karakoram Polu; 16,900 ft.;	17	Road rough through stoney valley. Ascend Karakoram pass. 18,300 ft.
Balti Brangsa; 17,000 ft.	22	Road gradual descending and easy.
Baksam bulak; 16,700 ft.	10	Continue descending downstream across plateau.
Malik Sai (Aktagh); 15,450 ft.	20	Road fair and gradual ascending east of Aktagh hill.
Chibra; 16,400 ft.	10	Track upstream pass Sugetdawan; 17,618 ft., then descend.
Suget Karaul; 12,300 ft.	21	Summer residence of a Chinese official. Road fair down Karakash river.
Shahidulla; 11,900 ft. old fort.	08	Kirghiz camps. Road fair down Karakash river. Ford Toghra-Su, 11 miles.
Kilian Kurghan; 11,400 ft.	18	Track down Karakash river. Then up Tugur Manlik-Su. Road fair.
Bostan	06	Road fair up Tugur Malik-Su.
Karachaglan	14	Ascend Kilian down pass 17,910 ft. and descend. Both way steep.
Chush-Kum; 11,620 ft.	16	Track fair down Kilian river.
Akshor; 8,250 ft.	12	Track fair down Kilian river.
Kilianbazar; 7,000 ft.	24	Village, road through cultivation and sandy soil.
Bash-Langar	14	Village, Road through cultivation and gravel.
Oil-toghrak; 5,760 ft.	10	Village, Road through cultivation and gravel.
Bora; 5,340 ft.	12	Journey across Tiznaf valley. Pass Be harikoasis, 14 miles.
Karghalik; 4,430 ft.	22	Town. Residence of Amban. Road good through cultivated country.
Posgam; 4,200 ft.	22	Village. Residence of Amban. Road good through cultivated country.

(Continued on next page)

(Table 4.1 Contd.)

(1)	*(2)*	*(3)*
Yarkand; 4,430 ft.	18	Large town and centre of trade. Residence of Amban. Road good through cultivated country.
Kok-rabat; 43,80 ft.	25	Village. Track through desert; Oases frequent.
Kizilbazar; 4,410 ft.	27	Village, track through desert; Oases frequent.
Yangi-hissar; 4,250 ft.; Fort.	30	Town, frequent cultivation in sandy track
Kashgar; 4,380 ft.	24	Capital of Chinese Turkestan, Centre of trade, residence of British Consulate General and Taotai.

Source: Arora, R.C.: *In the Land of Kashmir, Ladakh and Gilgit*, Jay Kay Book House; Jammu; 1996; pp. 167-72.

Deskit: The Headquarter of Nubra

On reaching and getting accommodation in Dak Bungalow at Deskit and meeting my friend Naib Tehsildar Namgyal who was of great help in putting me up there, we decided to take a round of Deskit. We went towards S.S.B. side, where I saw a big 'Mane'. It had many stone plates ingraved with *Om Mane Padme Hum* mantra. This mantra embodies the compassion and blessing of all the Buddhas and Bodhisatvas, and invokes especially the blessing of Avalokitesvara, the Bodhisatva of compassion. Avalokitesvara is a manifestation of the Buddha in the Sambhogakaya, and his mantra is considered the essence of the Buddha's compassion for all beings. Just as Padmasambhava is the most important master for the Tibetans, Avalokitesvara is the most important Buddha, and the karmic deity of Tibet.[1]

It is said that Avalokitesvara vowed not to attain enlightenment until all the other thousand princes had themselves become Buddhas. In his infinite compassion, he vowed to liberate all sentient beings from the suffering of the different realms of *samsara*. Before the Buddha of the ten directions, he prayed: "May I help all beings, and if ever I fire in this great work, may my body be shattered into a thousand pieces."[2]

First, it is said, he descended into the hell realms, ascending gradually through the world of hungry ghosts, up to the realm of the gods. From there he happened to look down and saw, aghast, that though he had saved innumerable beings from hell, countless more were pouring in. This plunged him into the profoundest grief; for a moment he almost lost faith in that noble vow he had taken, and his body exploded into a thousand pieces. In this desperation, he called out to all the Buddhas for help, who came to his aid from all directions of the universe, as one text said, like a soft blizzard of snowflakes. With their great power, the Buddhas made him whole again. From then on Avalokitesvara had eleven heads, and thousand arms, and on each palm of each hand was an eye, signifying that union of wisdom and skilful means which is the mark of true compassion. In this form he was even more resplendently empowered than before to help and again he repeated this vow before the Buddhas: "May I not attain final Buddhahood before all sentient being attain enlightenment."[3]

It is said that in his sorrow at the pain of *samsara*, two tears fell from his eyes; through the blessings of the Buddhas, they were transformed into two Taras. One is Tara in her green form, who is the active force of compassion, and the other is Tara in her white form who is compassion's motherly aspect. The name Tara mean's "She who liberates": she who ferries us across the ocean of the *samsara*.[4]

It is written in the Mahayana Sutra that Avalokitesvara gave his mantra to the Buddha himself, and Buddha in turn granted him the special and noble task of helping all beings in the universe towards Buddhahood. At this moment all the gods rained flowers on them, the earth shook, and the air rang with the sound *Om Mani Padme Hum*.[5]

The teaching explain that each of the six syllables of the mantra '*Om Mani Padme Hum*' has a specific and potent effect in bringing transformation at different levels of our being. The six syllables purify completely the six poisonous negative emotions, which are the manifestations of ignorance, and which causes us to act negatively with our body, speech, and mind, so creating *samsara* and our suffering in it. Pride, jealousy, desire, ignorance, greed, and anger are transformed, through the mantra of the six Buddha families that become manifest in the enlightened mind.[6]

So when we recite *Om Mani Padme Hum* or ingrave on stone plates or rocks, the six negative emotions, which are causes of the six realms of *samsara*, are purified. Thus through this mantra one may get relieve from the rebirth of realms, and also dispels the suffering inherent in each realm.[7]

Lifestyle of People in Deskit

I went to villages and fields at Deskit. Farmers were ploughing their fields and sprinkling manure. We were lucky enough to breathe in the peaceful and pollution free atmosphere. People were not busy like Leh, they enjoyed their time in gossiping and working in their fields.

Deskit is the only town in Nubra valley. It has a few shops. There is no rush in the market. As a matter of fact it is a beautiful valley on the roof of the world. Villages along the Shyok river lie against the spectacular background of rows of tall willows and poplar trees. Water is plentiful here. Women are simple.

State Govt. Livestock Farm

At the State Government farm one can see Jersy cows and double hump camels. They are in good condition. Though there are only nine camels, yet they are beautifully reared. In olden days they were abundantly used by traders.

A farm man informed: "These are very costly animals nowadays. One camel may cost you Rs. 9,000 to Rs. 10,000. There are some camels, reared by local people, but they do not have much use, so they take least care. Consequently they are now becoming rare."

Images of Maitreya Buddha

On 31st May afternoon, the S.D.M. Nubra gave me a letter appointing me Presiding officer at Tyakshi-Pachathang polling station. The next day, I departed for my station along with my polling officers Ali Hussain, Sonam Rigzin and Norboo.

When we passed through Hundar village, I saw the carved image of Maitreya Buddha (Chamba) on the rock near the monastery, along the banks of the stream. I did not see the other image, but Rohit Vohra found Me'me' Thuba on the opposite side of the stream, as he says, "There was a second image of Me'me' Thuba on the opposite bank and the two were like a pair. (Meme' Thuba) was destroyed, as it stood in the way of the construction of a canal. These images would date them to the late Gupta period."[8]

In Turtuk

In the evening at about 5 pm we reached Turtuk via Hundar, Parta, Skamphuk, etc. The details are given below:

Deskit (Headquarters of Nubra)
↓ 6 km
Hundar (9,900 ft.)
↓ 7 km
Parta village
↓ 3 km
Skamphuk village and Gonpa
↓ 5 km
Thoise (Airport)
↓ 3 km
Therche village
↓ 2 km
Kharu village
↓ 5 km
Udmaru village
↓ 10 km
Nine post
↓ 10 km
Bogdang village
↓ 4 km
Chalunka or Calungka (C.P.)
↓ 20 km
Turtuk or Turtok (9,000 ft)

Ancient Trade Through Turtuk

In the olden days, some traders of Khapalu used the trade route via Turtuk. Every June they reached Turtuk, and in mid July returned from Leh. The following routes were popular among traders:

(a) By the left bank of the Shyok;
(b) By Abadon and the left bank of the Shyok;
(c) By Abadon and Biagdangdo; and
(d) Via Chorbat La.

Route by Left Bank of the Shyok

This route was constructed in 1912. Kharding la was the highest pass, difficult to cross between late November and June. Traders crossed the Shyok river by skin-rafts between Khapalu and Sogo. However, the river was fordable in winter at Khapalu, Pachathang and at the Nubra-Shyok confluence. Following are the details.

Stage (1)	*Inter miles* (2)	*Nature of Journey to the Next Stage* (3)
Khapalu (8,400 ft.)	—	Khapalu, the capital of lower Shyok and a group of hamlets, is situated on a long slope. It was the residence of the local Raja whose mansions were situated to the west with a polo ground nearby. Ascend plateau. Descend to Surmo, 7 miles. Road rough.
Lunkha (8,500 ft.)	14	Village pass Dou, 4 miles. Cross Kustang, 10 miles, Road rough.
Piun (Paxfain) (8,650 ft.)	14	Village and Mosque. Route bifurcates for Chorbat-La. Road liable to slips.
Siari (8,740 ft.)	13	Village opposite Prahnu. Descend to river. Pass Tyakshi, 9 miles. Ascend and descend to Turtuk.
Turtuk (9,000 ft.)	13	Large village. First 5 miles sandy and stoney but path fair, and then up and down, cross Tebe Lungma and Malakcha Lungma.
Malakcha Lungma camp (9,400 ft.)	18	Path undulating and rough.
Yaglung Lungma camp (9,700 ft.)	09	Path shadeless but fair through valley. Cross Pachathang Lungma.
Kharu (9,800 ft.)	13	Buddhist village path fair. Pass Pakhura and Spanpuk (Skamphuk)
Hunda (9,900 ft.)	13	Village. Path fair but stoney and sandy. Pass Deskit, 6 miles; Thirit, 13 miles.
Khalsar to Leh	—	Same as said in the trade route Leh to Yarkand.

Source: Arora, R.C.: *In the Land of Kashmir, Ladakh and Gilgit*, Jay Kay Book House; Reprint 1996, p. 216.

Trade Route by Abadon and the Left Bank of the Shyok

Traders crossed the Shyok river over the bridges at Prahnu and Thiret between Chogogron and Abadon. At other places the river was crossed by skin-rafts. The details are given below:

Stage (1)	*Inter miles* (2)	*Nature of Journey to Next Stage* (3)
Khapalu	—	Up to Surmo-cross Shyok at Chogogron.
Abadon (8,450 ft.)	11	Village, cross several stony streams.
Marcha (8,550 ft.)	11	Village, Ascend and descend to Partuk. Ascend to kalan, 8 miles, and decend.
Prahnu (8,850 ft.)	14	Village, Path down Shyok river.
Turtuk	15	Next join the Turtuk to Leh route.

Source: Arora, R.C.; *op. cit.*, pp. 216-17.

Trade Route by Abadon and Biagdangdo

From Biagdangdo, there was short cut to Hunder by staging at Hotuny where the rivers were forded. Before taking up this route, enquiries should be made at Biagdangdo whether river is fordable beyond Waris. If impractical, animals should go south-east of the pass through the steep and sandy track.

From Chalunka, there was a route up the Korisa glacier, Chulung la, Chulang glacier to Goma in the Saltoro valley. Following are the details of trade route between Khapalu to Leh via Chalunka.

Stage (1)	*Inter miles* (2)	*Nature of Journey to Next Stage* (3)
Turtuk	—	Up to Turtuk, see Khapalu to Turtuk route via Abadon. Path rough. Cross Shyok at Turtuk and ascend.
Chalunka	10	Village, Ascend cliffs and descend.
Biagdangdo (11,700 ft.)	09	Village, Ascend Biagdangdo Lungma. Pass Shupa, 4 miles. Cross steep Lagopa La; 13,143 ft. and descend.
Zdong-polas (12,500 ft.)	09	Buddhist village. Track up and down to Waris nala.
Waris	05	Hamlet, Path difficult.
Unmaru	20	Village, Path sandy.
Mondari	08	Village, Cross river by skin raft.
Hundar	11	Join Hunder to Leh route via Khalsar

Source: Arora, R.C.; *op.cit.*, p. 217.

The route via Saltora can be seen at the end of this chapter[9].

Trade Route via Chorbat-La

This trade route followed by traders via Goma Hanu to Khalatse and then joined Srinagar-Leh road. Following are the details:

Stage (1)	*Inter miles* (2)	*Nature of Journey to the next stage* (3)
Khapalu (8,400 ft.)	—	Cf. op. cit.
Lnnkha, op.cit.	14	op. cit.
Piun (8,650 ft.)	14	Track stoney. Cross river banks at 2 and 7 miles. Then up grassy valley of Chorbat Lungma.
Chunga (14,500 ft.)	12	Hamlet. Track up Chorbat Lungma. Cross Chorbat La. 16,700 ft. Descend.
Goma Hanu (upper)	19	Village group. Pass Nabi Brangsa. Track stoney. Cross Broglon nala and Skirbuchan bridge at Achinathang.
Skirbuchan	18	Village. Track stoney and rough. Cross ravines, spurs and Dumkhar chu.
Khalatse (9,700 ft.)	16	Join Srinagar-Leh Road.

Source: Arora, R.C.; *op. cit.*, p. 218.

Landslide-Prone Zone

The road between Deskit and Turtuk is good except at a place before the narrow bridge near Bogdang village. When we reached the landslide-prone zone, our bus driver said: "Please get down from the bus, because the road ahead is not clear. It is landslide-prone zone, and it is difficult to drive the bus on such a narrow path."

All the passengers came out from the bus and walked for 5-10 minutes. Two labourers were on duty throughout the day to clear the road. While crossing the landslide zone, I saw that small particles of rocks were constantly sliding down to the road; and when at full momentum they reached a speed of about 60-80 km/hour.

At Bogdang Village

This is the first village which the Indian Army recaptured in the 1971 Indo-Pak war. When we reached there, the Turtuk inhabitants asked the driver to stop the bus for some time and complained that the ration shop in Turtuk had no stock of kerosene.

My polling officer and some men went to the Ration shop in Bogdang village, and brought 20 litres of kerosene.

Bogdang is a Balti Muslim village population of this village is about one thousand. From the motorway it looks small, but it has large terraced wheat and barley fields. People do not have any awareness of modern education, eighty per cent of them being illiterate. To educate them the Indian Army has especially deployed teachers. Besides, the State Government has opened a middle school for them.

Chalunka Village

This is the second village to be brought under the control of the Indian Government in the 1971 Indo-Pak war. It is also a Balti Muslim village with, population of 900 and is a very sensitive area on the border.

Turtuk

This is the third village, which was recaptured by the Indian Army in 1971 Indo-Pak war. It has 2,000 Balti Muslim population. Here I met Lama Lobzang Skyabdo; senior teacher of Deskit Higher Secondary School. Like me he came to Turtuk on election duty, and was staying at the Turtuk Dak Bungalow. He accompanied me for evening walk. We entered the Turtuk village via a wooden village, and enjoyed seeing lush green wheat and barley terraced fields, surrounded by apricot bearing trees, Willow and poplar trees were also in abundant numbers. Some poplar trees near the I.T.B.F. office were as high as those one sees in Srinagar. When I asked the cost of one tree, the I.T.B.F. man replied, that "Though he did not have the exact idea, each might cost around Rs. 10,000/-."

The climate of Turtuk is a little warmer than the valley of central Ladakh; people here grow two crops in a year. Among vegetables- cauliflower, turnip and carrots are common. To increase their annual crop and vegetable production, farmer, use chemical fertilizer and also rotate their crops.

In the olden days, Turtuk had trade relations with Khapalu, Skardu (now in Pakistan) and Ladakh. The people exchanged salt from Changthang traders with apricots, mulberry and food items. Traders from Khapalu and Skardu after crossing Chorbat-la, took rest at Turtuk. Consequently it was popularly known as 'Dhurdiuk' meaning 'stay here'. Later, through the ages, the name became corrupted to 'Turtuk' as :

Dhurdhuk * Dhurdtok

Dhurdtok * Dhurdtok

Dhurdtok * Durtok

Durtok * Turtok

Turtok * Turtuk

A Centre of Cottage Industries

The inhabitants of Turtuk are good artisans. They make 'doltok' (a stone item which is used in making Ladakhi bread), 'Thumbu', (Figs. A & B.)

Fig. 4.1 (A) : Dotkot

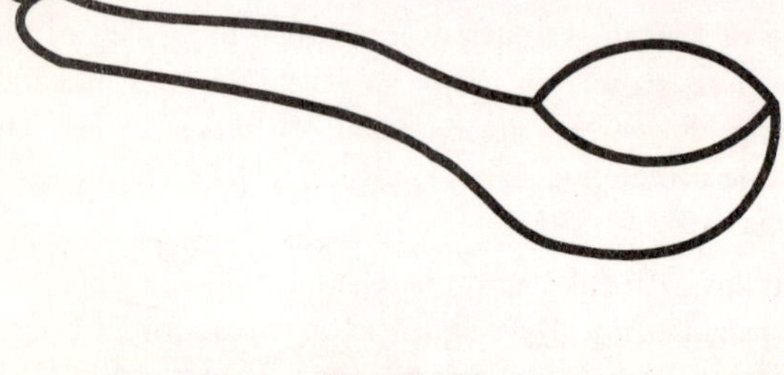

Fig. (B): Thumbu

The stone vessels, doltok and stone lookers are quite popular throughout Nubra. The taste of food cooked in doltok adds flavour to the fun of marriage parties in Turtuk.[10]

Marriage ceremony

Except the Nikah-Namah, the rest of the ceremonies are almost the same as in other in Ladakh. Nyewopas (the boy's party) have to go through several interesting feasts at the house of the girl, before she agrees to marry the boy. During the wedding people here sing 'stodlu' and dance to the tune of musical instruments like the 'daman' and 'surna' till late night. Besides, they sing different songs for different occasions such as the 'rgyanglu' or the 'zhunglu', noros and 'dhaphok' harif.[11]

Polo

Turtuk is one of the homes of polo. Every year at the polo ground of Turtuk, a tournament is organised by the people of Turtuk in which team from the neighbouring villages also participate. I visited the Turtuk polo ground. It is not very wide but is long enough. During the tournament people from the neighbouring villages come with 'Daman' and 'Surna' and play these musical instruments in rhythm with the 'Dhaphok' harif to encourage their players. There is an interesting folklore related to polo.

Once a Skardu chief, Magspon Cho Yakub Sheik, banned a very talented player, Ali of Turtuk, from playing in the annual polo event in Skardu. Ali was banned because his presence in the match meant sure defeat of Skardu at the hands of Turtuk.

Ali was not even allowed to enter Khapalu—the border area between Turtuk and Skardu. However, Ali managed to enter Skardu in the guise of a poor peasant. and tricked his way into the Turtuk team on the eventful day. The match began. In polo it is a rule that no team wins until nine goals are scored. Turtuk was goalless till the other team had scored eight. At this point, Ali scored a goal and earned a 'Dhaphok' that he turned into another goal. One after another, he scored nine goals amidst thunderous applause from the spectators. The Turtuk team won the match. Ali received the valley of Hanjor as prize.[12]

People

The women of Turtuk are comparatively more hardworking than the men. They get up early in the morning and, after finishing their work in the kitchen, proceed to the fields. Except ploughing, they work with their hands at all jobs in the fields.

In 1971, when Turtuk was recaptured, it had a population of around 500. Now the population has risen to more than two thousand. The population density is high, that is, around 50 persons per sq. km.

Almost all the Baltis in Turtuk are engaged in agriculture. Besides, there are a number of artisans who make a variety of kitchen items. The majority of menfolk are connected with cottage industries or are engaged in grazing their animals, driving to 'Doksas' in the morning and returning in evening.

Poultry like chicken and ducks and domestic animals like sheep and donkeys are a soul of livelihood to the people of Turtuk.

The houses are built of stone. They are flat-roofed, two-storyed high but very low in height. Except for the reception room, which is always kept neat and clean, the rest of the house is not so. When a visitor comes to the house, he is welcomed warmly and provided *fating* (dried sweet apricots) and salted tea in Chinese style cups. On the ground floor the animals are kept. On the upper storey there are big rooms for kitchen, reception and so on. They do not have glasses and have small windows only in the upper rooms.

Tyakshi-Pachathang

Next day, on June 2, after breakfast at 8 a.m. we departed for Tyakshi. It is about 10 km. from Turtuk. After climbing for about half an hour from the main road, we reached Tyakshi. Pachathang is another village a little ahead and below Tyakshi. Both these villages were recaptured in 1971.

Population

The population of Tyakshi-Pachathang together is about eight hundred. This polling station has 420 voters. Of these, 72 per cent cast their votes in the Ladakh Parliamentary election on June 3, 1998.

Su-Malik songs

The Su-Malik songs are sung during festive occasions in Tyakshi-Pachathang and in almost all the villages of the Chorbat area. Su-Malik was a great ruler of Gilgit during 1335-1390 A.D. The following song is popular among Tyakshi-Pachathang and the surrounding villages.[13]

Su-Malik where have you come from?
Su-Malik where will you go?
Su-Malik, water, earth and three trees (chang-ma, shuk-pa and chu-li)
Three mountains of earth.

Three mountains of stone.
Su-Malik, where have you come from?
Su-Malik came from the mountain.
Like the smell of incense in the smoke of the red mountain came su-Malik
Su-Malik came with a bull.
What will you do with the meat which is like medicine?
Divide it among the people.
Red earth on top of the mountain.
Who is coming
A horse is coming with a trader.

This song is also sung by the Buddhist Dards of Ladakh in the villages of Moa and Garkun. It indicates that people inhabiting Chorbat are possibly of Dard stock ethnically. They migrated from Gilgit and when Su-Malik become a strong leader, he converted them into Islam.

Apricot

Tyakshi-Pachathang, Turtuk and other villages in the Chorbat area are famous for horticulture. Their inhabitants grow apricot trees. The apricots are sweet.

Thang

It was the last village which was reoccupied by the Indian army in the 1971 Indo-Pak war. This village has a population of about 150 and only 50 voters. From this village one can see the Pakistani village of Pharan at a distance.

Indo-Pak War, 1971

On December 11, 1971, the Indian army marched ahead from Udmaru and Largyap covering Bogdang from all directions supported by heavy artillery. On December 12, they recaptured Bogdang and Chalunka post from Pakistan. In the meanwhile, when the inhabitants of Turtuk came to know of this they immediately called a meeting and decided that if Indian army entered their village, they would surrender before them under the condition that no harm be done by the Indian soldiers and that they be given the same treatment as was given to their own people. When the Indian army entered Turtuk and Tyakshi villages, the demand was put forward. The Indian army officers accepted their request. After that they marched up to Thang, when cease fire was called. Thang village became the last Indian post in Chorbat area (Map 1).[14]

REFERENCES

1. Sanghasena, Bikkhu: *Om Mani Padme Hum*, 1995; p. 7.
2. *Ibid.*, pp. 7-8.
3. *Ibid.*, pp. 8-9.
4. *Ibid.*, p. 9.
5. *Ibid.*, pp. 9-10.
6. *Ibid.*, p. 10.
7. *Ibid.*, p. 11.
8. Vohra, Rohit: 'Ethno Historical Notes on Nubra in Ladakh', in: *Ladakh, Himalaya Occidental Ethnologie, E'cologie*, Claude Dendalitche' (ed.); Pau, France; 1985; p. 247.
9. It was long and tiresome march. The stages of the trak is shown below:

Stage (1)	*Inter miles* (2)	*Nature of Journey to Next Stage* (3)
Khapalu; 8,400 ft.	—	Large village. Ascend plateau and descend to river near Surmo, 7 miles. Cross to the bank of Shyok by skin raft at Chogogron. Descend, cross a spur and ascend to Saltoro valley.
Paron	21	Travel along right bank of Saltoro. Pass Kundus and Dansam, 4 miles.
Palit; 10,050 ft.	12	Path was fair. Pass Goma, 9 miles; last village. Ford Saltoro Pass and ascend Ghyari Nala.
Ghyari; 12,400 ft.	16	Track ascends over Saltoro Pass or Bilafond Pass and was troublesome.
Naram; 14,400 ft.	06	The track was up the Bila, found glacier, crevasses, sometimes dangerous.
Ali Brangsa; 16,500 ft.	07	Cross Saltoro Pass, 18,200 ft. Rope in ascending and decending was preferred.
Siachen glacier; 16,000 ft.	15	Camp under cliff

Source: Arora, R.C.; *op.cit.*, pp. 214-15.

10. Morup, Tashi: 'Turtuk'; Ladags-Melong; March-April 1998, p. 29.
11. *Ibid.*, pp. 29-30.
12. *Ibid.*, p. 30 and The prize Hanjor has historical importance. It is said that during olden days 'Hanjor' was the prestigious prize of polo of the Skardu Polo Association and was given to only those players who played polo during the tournament in an extraordinary manner.

The 'Hanjor' prize is named after the hunting ground of Skardu. It is said that during those days hunting was a popular game like polo. Hunting was an important source of livelihood besides agriculture. Through hunting they could get meat, leather or skin, which has used for making caps, gloves and other useful items.

13. Vohra, Rohit: *Early History of Ladakh: Mythic Lore & Fabulation* (A preliminary note on the conjectural history of the Ist millennium A.D.); In 'Recent Research on Ladakh 4 & 5'; Osmaston & Denwood (ed.); Motilal Banarsidass Pub., New Delhi; 1995; pp. 230-31.

14. On October 26, 1947, Maharaja Hari Singh of Jammu and Kashmir signed a note of accession to the Governor-General of India. With this formal accession, Ladakh became a part of the Indian Union on October 27, 1947. But Pakistan did not accept Maharaja Hari Singh's decision and attacked Ladakh. They captured Kargil, Basgo and advanced up to Taru village near Leh and in Nubra they reached up to Bogdang. As the Pakistanis began converging on Leh, an urgent appeal for help was made to the Indian army. The Ladakhis built a small airstrip at Leh to enable the Indian troops to land. Then the Indian army sent troops directly by air to Leh and recaptured Basgo and Kargil and thus broke the enemy lines near Zoji-La and re-established Ladakh's link with Kashmir.

    In Nubra valley late Col. Rinchen who was then only seventeen years old, got military training in the garrison at Leh. Then with the request of the garrison officer, he took thirty rifles and a sufficient quantity of ammunition and returned to Nubra. Later along with 300 volunteers, they dug a defensive position at different villages—Skuru, Waris, Udmaru, etc. Through their counter attack the Pakistani forces could not march further from Bogdang. Like Leh, the inhabitants of Nubra valley provided all help such as food, clothing and so on to the Indian army.

    In 1965, too the Pakistani army made an unsuccessful attempt to capture Kashmir, but failed.

    In 1971, Pakistani forces infiltrated into Indian territory. But the Indian army was fully prepared to defend the country from the enemy. This time the Indian army's main mission was to keep the supply line running to Leh and Nubra valley with sufficient food, fuel, arms and ammunition. These were stored at different points of supply. Thus with the help of heavy artillery gun firing and gallant action under the command of late Col. Rinchen, then major and Major Singh's command of Gorkha regiment, the Indian forces recaptured five villages—Bogdang, Chalunka, Turtuk, Tyakshi—Pachathang and Thang from Pakistani forces.

5

'RES' SYSTEM IN LADAKH BEFORE INDEPENDENCE

Introduction

Ladakh is derived from the Tibetan word La-tags, means country of 'La' or 'pass'. Earlier it was known 'Mar-yul', the lower lying portion of western Tibet.[1]

Maharaja of Jammu and Kashmir State, was a good administrator and an able man to annex Ladakh with the state in 1834. But after an agreement with British India Government in 1846 Spiti and Lahul earlier were detached from Ladakh and annexed with the Kulu sub-division of Kangra district of the Punjab, as said. Gya peak was then defined as the boundary between Ladakh of Jammu and Kashmir and Lahul and Spiti of British Indian Government territories. The details are given below:[2]

(a) Boundary between Lahul and Zangskar

The boundary demarcated the snowy range dividing the drainage of the Bhaga and Chandra Bhaga from that of the Zangskar river.

(b) Boundary between Lahul and Ladakh

Here a boundary stone called Phalang Danda was considered as the limit between Lahul and Ladakh. The details are given below:

"There was an old well-known boundary stone called Phalang Danda found beyond the Bara Lacha to the eastward, or located in the midst of an open plain on the right bank of the Yunam river. But there was no recognised boundary mark on the other side of the stream, therefore, commissioners of both the territories selected a remarkable cream-coloured peak, called Turam, as the northern limit of the British territory on the left bank of the river. As this peak, situated at the end of one of the spurs of the great snowy chain, already determined as the northern limit of the Lahul district."[3]

(c) Boundary between Spiti and Ladakh

The Yunam river was considered the boundary between Ladakh and Spiti. Here follows the details:

"Spiti is at the eastward of the Phalang Danda and Ladakh on the westward. So, a straight line was drawn from the Phalang Danda to the junction of the first nala on the right bank of the Yunam, from which point the Yunam river forms the boundary as far as the junction of the Ts-arap river."[4]

(d) Boundary between Tibet and Ladakh

In 1872 the boundary line was drawn from the village of Narbu Sumdo along the ridge to the Gya peak and was considered the boundary line between Tibet and Ladakh.

Therefore, the boundaries between Ladakh, Tibet and Lahul-Spiti of British India were well marked till 1912, even then some doubts remained as the boundary between Ladakh and Tibet from the head of the Chang-Chenmo valley to the south and south-west till Gya peak, and at the neighbourhood of Pangong lake were not well demarcated.[5]

Res System

It was a system under which a village or a group of villagers were asked by the administrator of Jammu and Kashmir State to supply transport[6] at a certain stage on a certain road. They were also asked to maintain number of ponies for certain periods.[7]

Hence the arrangement for supply of ponies and coolies to traders/travellers was known Res or Begar system. The number of ponies varied between 20 to 50 at each stage. E. Joldan says:

> The supply of ponies and coolies to travellers was known Res or Begar. 'Res' in Bodhi means 'by turn'. In practice it would mean that all the surrounding villages, in turn, would be responsible for supplying a fixed number of ponies at a particular stage. The maximum number of 50 ponies would be available only when the Joint Commissioners would be travelling. On other days, 15 to 20 ponies would always be there, at every stage, during summer seasons.[8]

In Ladakh the undivided house is known as Khang-chen, under the Res system a man and a pony from every Khang-chen according to turn had to remain on every stage. Taking the example of Nimu village E. Joldan says.

"Nemo (Nimu) was the first stage on the Treaty Road from Leh. A man and a pony from every main house (Khang-chen) from the neighbouring villages of Nye and Bazgo (Basgo), Nemo (Nimu) itself and Phiang (Phyang), in turn, had to remain on duty at Nemo (Nimu) Serai with ration for himself and the pony, for one month, every four months. In one year it would be three months of Begar duty, away from home. However, by mutual and unofficial agreement only a dozen or so, would actually be there during winter months."[9]

All the Government officials travelling on duty, British Army officers and Haj pilgrims also had Res facility. E. Joldan remarks:

"Government officials travelling on duty. British Army officers coming to Ladakh for hunting and Haj pilgrims would also avail themselves of the facility of Res ponies. The traders would usually send their goods from Leh to Srinagar direct with ponywallas known as *kira-kash*, belonging to Kargil and Dras areas. It would be cheaper from 5 to 8 rupees per pony."[10]

The State Government however fixed the amount of transport for different stages (Table 5.1)

TABLE 5.1
The Maximum Limit of Res Transport for Different Stages in 1912

Stages	*Ponies or Zo (No.)*			*Coolies (No.)*		
	Summer	*Winter*	*(-) % increase (-) % decrease*	*Summer*	*Winter*	*(+) % increase (-) % decrease*
(1)	*(2)*	*(3)*	*(4)*	*(5)*	*(6)*	*(7)*
Dras	80	–	—	20	125	(+) 525.00
Kharbu	45	–	—	20	30	(+) 50.00
Kargil	50	30	(-) 40.00	20	30	(+) 50.00
Mulbek	40	20	(-) 50.00	20	20	—
Nimu Leh	50	30	(-) 40.00	20	20	—
Kherdong to	25	10	(-) 60.00	10	10	—
Panamik Kharal	15	10	(-) 33.33	15	10	(-) 33.33
Olding	15	10	(-) 33.33	15	20	(+) 33.33
Tarkatti to Skardu	06	05	(-) 16.67	45	40	(-) 11.11

Source: Sectt. Political Deptt. File No. 218/p-156, Year 1912.

(a) Zo is a cross breed of yak and cow and is used for carrying loads.

(b) Winter, officially from 15th October to 15th May during this period the road was impracticable on account of heavy snowfall or avalanches. This period still continues as winter period.

(c) For Dras and Kharbu: During the months of January and February there was hardly any traffic. It would not be necessary to keep 125 coolies and 80 ponies respectively during these months. However if any one required transport he could it get after a week's notice to the Tehsildar of Kargil.

Table 5.1 reveals that

1. Regardless of it being winter State Government did not give any 'Res' facility, except Dras and Kharbu all the other stages had 'Res' facility. However, the number of transport (i.e. ponies or Zo) would be 30 to 60 per cent less than that of summer.

2. State Government gave special attention to the snow bound villages viz. Dras and Kharbu in order to face any kind of emergency. In 1912 Maharaja Sahib Bahadur had given instructions to Tehsildar of Kargil to keep 125 coolies and 80 ponies ready round the clock, particularly coolies. As a result the number of coolies increased 525 per cent more than the summer season.

3. The Maharaja Sahib Bahadur also gave instructions to the concerned Tehsildars to keep good number of coolies at Kargil and Olding stages.

4. During summer the percentage of ponies increased by 17 to 60 and coolies by 11 to 33 at every stage.

'Res' Rules

Maharaja Sahib Bahadur made some rules for 'Res' system. According to them—Public servants, bonafide travellers whether Europeans or others and Central Asian traders could use 'Res' transport for carrying their personal baggage and merchandise in case of traders.[11]

The 'Res' transport rule further explained that Public Servants[12] were entitled first to have 'Res' facility, after them travellers, and lastly traders. Besides individuals could claim for 'Res' facility in order of their arrival at the stage. But this facility was not given to Public Works Department (P.W.D.) for carrying timber and other materials from place to place. Similarly no Public Servant was allowed to carry Public Works Department's stores and materials.[13]

Load for Pony and Coolie

Under 'Res' system maximum weight load for pony and coolie was fixed in the following way[14]:

Pony load = 2.5 maunds

Coolie load = 35 seers (in summer)

Coolie load = 25 seers (in winter)

or Three coolies load = one pony load (in summer)

or Four coolies load = one pony load (in winter)

Under the 'Res' transport rules no one could use transport until he/she gave the full payment. The wages for carrying load on the Treaty High Road were fixed by the British Joint Commissioner and other roads by the Wazir Wazarat.[15]

The British Joint Commissioner during his visit to Leh, inspected the Dak Bungalows, Serai, Supply facilities, etc. Normally commissioner covered the distance between Srinagar to Leh in 15 or 16 days. His party consisted of clerks, several Ladakhi peons, jamadar, etc. E. Joldan says:

"On his annual visit, usually in June, the British Commissioner with his 2 clerks, several Ladakhi peons (with their family members) headed by a *Jamadar* would travel one stage a day, with an additional stay at Spituak—only 8 kilometres from Leh. Thus, it would take the Commissioner's party 15 or 16 days to reach Leh from Srinagar."[16]

When Commissioner arrived at Leh all the important citizens, merchants, officers, students, soldiers, etc., warmly welcomed him and his party. E. Joldan has beautifully explained in the following way:

"A number of prominent citizens, the Tehsildar, the charas officer, his head clerk, the Zaildar and several big Yarkandi merchants would go on horseback to say their 'Salam' to the Commissioner at Spituk, and again on the following morning to bring him to the Residency, in a procession, through the Leh Bazar which would be gaily decorated with welcome archways. Near the Balkang gate, a contingent of 30-40 sepoys of the State Government with a Jamadar, holding a drawn sword, would present arms. He would inspect the two row of soldiers and a little further on, Master Sultan, the Drill Master of the Govt. Middle School would say General Salute, Present arms, and the boys standing in two lines on either side of the bazar, would put their sticks forward, in both hands, followed by three cheers for the Commissioner.

"About the middle of the bazar, the musicians and the professional lady-dancers would give the Joint Commissioner the traditional welcome."[17]

The British Commissioner after one or two-day rest at Residency visited Dak Bungalow, Serais, etc., for inspection, Aksakal also accompanied him and translate the petitions if so into Urdu/English. According to Joldan:

"The British Commissioner after or two-day of rest would inspect the Dak Bungalow and the 2 Sarais and order repairs, where necessary. A delegation of Yarkandis would meet him at the Residency and he would listen to their petitions, in a sort of 3 way channel— in Turki to the Aksakal, who would translate it to the Khan Sahib (Munshi Mohammad Din) in Urdu, and English to the Commissioner."[18]

The State Joint Commissioner, called Wazir Wazarat came to Leh for 6 month's stay from Skardu. He was also welcomed in similar way as British Joint Commissioner. Both the Commissioners during August organised party and *Tamasha*. Joldan says:

"Some time in August, the Commissioner would give his big tea party and the *Tamasha* which would be arranged by the Charas office staff, under the overall direction of the Khan Sahib. This and the State Commissioner's party would be a great event in summer for the mirth-loving Ladakhis."[19]

Galwan Rasul Bahu-ud-Din Khan, Afzal Turki, Khwaja Abdullah Shah, Jonathan Tharchin were some Aksakal before independence who were appointed to look after the needs of the Yarkandis, settle their disputes and collect taxes. Joldan remarks:

"The other function was to supply to the Yarkandis as much barley grain from the state granaries located to Leh, Saspol and Lamayuru as they required, for their horses, at fixed rate. The farmers of Ladakh were required to pay part of their land tax in grain, and deposit them at those places. The Aksakal at Leh was the representative of the British Commissioner to look after the needs of the Yarkandis and settle their disputes. The Aksakal usually had a clerk whom he paid from his own pocket. However, the two Serai keepers at Leh, and the 14 others on the Treaty Road, and the 2 Road Overseers were also under the British Commissioner and were paid by him."[20]

'Res' Availing Categories

Under the 'Res' system facility besides public servants/travellers/traders, any person could avail the above facility, but this facility would be available only for one day at each stage.[21]

Limits for the Use of 'Res' Transport

'Res' transport was not allowed for use beyond the next stage on the road on other side of the starting point, with the exception that the 'Res' at Dras could be used up to Gund in the direction of Kashmir.[22]

'Res' Transport and Travelling Allowance

The state officials were entitled to use 'Res' transport, but they could not claim for travelling allowance. Moreover, if they travelled on duty and used the main road/roads within the Jammu and Kashmir territory, would be entitled to use 'Res' transport without payment for their personal baggage and state things which they usually carried with them. However, if they used riding ponies, they had to give the payment from their own pocket.[23]

State officials who were on duty but did not have authority letter from Wazir Wazarat or Tehsildar, were not entitled to use the facilities of 'Res' system. However, there had been some limits for using the 'Res' system for officials, for example : *Patwaris* and Menials could use the services of one coolie only and that of two for officials of superior grade for their personal luggage. In case Wazarat visited Ladakh, the carriage of personal luggage of the Wazarat *chaprasis* being given along with travelling allowance from contingencies.[24]

Voluntary Rates

If government official/trader/traveller could not wait for the special arrangements from government side or for 'Res' system, then they would be allowed to make their own arrangements at voluntary rates.[25]

Responsibility by Group of Villages

In case a large group of traders/travellers/officials camp outside the village where no regular stage was available, the villages surrounding the area gathered at one place and after discussion would provide the same facilities as mentioned in the 'Res' transport rules.[26]

'Res' Transport not for Personal Service

Under 'Res' rules no official was allowed to use Res-Respas[27] for personal services at the headquarter of Tehsils or in camps.[28]

'Res' Transport was not Responsible for the Supply of Grain

According to 'Res' rules and regulations, there was no provision to supply grain to traders. However, State Government established Kothis at different stage to supply foodgrain to traders/travellers. The following villages had Ration Kothis along the Treaty High Road to Leh:[29]

1. Dras
2. Kargil
3. Lamayuru
4. Saspol[30]
5. Leh
6. Panamik

On the Skardu road, the State Government had *kothis.*[31]

1. Kharal
2. Olding
3. Tarkati
4. Kharmang
5. Parkuta
6. Skardu
7. Thor

Normally above kothis had wheat and grains besides they had sufficient stock of flour. But for dal, rice and other things traders/officials/travellers had to purchase these from the shops at Dras, Kargil, Leh and Skardu at bazar rates.[32]

State *kothis* supplied cereals only to those officials who were on duty and 'Respas' were not responsible to supply above items to anybody.[33]

Supply of Firewood and Grass

All the officials who travelled on duty were entitled to get firewood and grass under 'Res' rules free of charge.[34]

Other Supplies

Under the 'Res' system the following articles were not supplied to visitors/traders:[35]

1. Butter
2. Milk
3. Fowls
4. Eggs
5. Sheep
6. Oil
7. Grass
8. Firewood.

Visitors/traders could get the above articles from *Parao Thekedars* at every stage on the road. These 'Thekedars' were given contracts to supply the above items by the British Joint Commissioner.

Supply of Miscellaneous Articles

The 'Res' system was not responsible to supply oil for light, utensils and beds. Therefore, these things were arranged by the traders/travellers/officials from their own resources.[37]

Complaints

In June 1914 some complaints received to His Highness the Maharaja Sahib of Jammu and Kashmir, who ordered the concern officer to revise the 'Res' system, to equalize the strength of each *parao*. Accordingly the revision of the 'Res' agreements had been made with great care. And the number of villages attached to each *parao* based upon the number of *assemies* and the beast of burden available.[38]

The objections of the zamindars were also considered even when they were received during the course of 'Res' system revision. Later it was decided that the number of *paraos* previously fixed should be increased by one and the new *paraos* should be created at Kharbu. But villagers of Choukial, Tungus and Jagund made objection for the creation of new *parao* at Kharbu. They argued that Kharbu could not supply grass as it did not have sufficient grass fields.[39]

Advantages and Disadvantages of 'Res' System

The advantages of 'Res' system can be summarized as below:

1. Ladakhis could earn good deal of money as they had limited sources of income.

2. The concerned authorities of the Treaty High Road recommended to give certain concessions for grazing transport animals.
3. To increase the number of transport animals at the different stages, the State Government allowed to give subsidy on loans for purchasing animals to the villagers along the Treaty High Road.

There were many disadvantages:

1. It had been seen that during trading season the demand of transport animals was very high, but during off-season the demand was almost nil; whereas during summer the supply of fodder grass was sufficient but in winter there was a great shortage of grass. As a result villagers were unable to rear large number of animals, and many animals died for want of fodder. In this connection the settlement officer of Ladakh made the following report:

> "The increasing trade requirements far exceed the limited number of livestock available for transport during certain months in the year. Unfortunately with the increase in trade there has been a corresponding decrease in the number of transport animals, owing to a large number of ponies having died for want of fodder. In some cases ponies have been sold by their owners, who could not resist the temptation when offered a good price. The result is that the number of ponies kept at the stages is very small and quite unable to come with the rush of traders especially in the month of Asar and Sawan. The traders are thus detained at each stage for some days and persistent complaints reach the higher authorities. At such times of high pressure no regard is paid to the fixed turns and all the adjoining villages are compelled by local authorities to supply necessary transport. Thus, the villagers are put to a good deal of expenses and trouble, and the overworked animals become disabled and unfit for further service."[40]

2. As the Treaty High Road opened for traders in the month of May till October, large parties of traders travelled to Leh during these months. Therefore, villagers had to supply their services under 'Res' rules. This caused a great loss to Ladakhi families. Because in Ladakh only one crop can be grown, which could be possible during summer. As most of the able males were engaged with 'Res' system, females and old persons would look after the agricultural activities. This caused less crop production and many other related problems.

3. Under 'Res' rules State Government had allotted numbers of

coolies and ponies for each stage. So, the villagers at the surrounding villages had to remain on duty throughout the season with their entire strength and transport animals. This on one hand seriously effected the agricultural operations and on the other hand without earning, they had to arrange ration as well as fodder for their animals throughout the period of their duty.[41]

Suggestions

Suggestions for removing the difficulties of villagers caused by 'Res' system and to improve 'Res' System:

1. To improve the number of transport animals, viz., ponies, yaks, etc. The settlement officer of Ladakh tried to induce the Zamindars in several villages to purchase ponies. He made the following report in this connection:

> I tried to induce the Zamindars in several villages to purchase ponies but the average Zamindar cannot affort to do this and almost all the villages have applied for advances to purchase ponies. I have submitted proposals to higher authorities for advancing Rs. 7,500 for the villages on the Treaty road. I have further proposed that sale of ponies 'purchased from these advances should be prohibited.[42]

2. During summer, transport animals could get green grass, but this was unavailable during winter season. So, owners of the transport animals should be given concession on grazing fees. The settlement officer of Ladakh gave the following report in this regards.

> I intend to recommend certain concessions on grazing fees as levied on transport animals, and in view of these concessions I would propose a prohibition against the sale of such animals, the concession and the prohibition being restricted only to one transport animals per holding.[43]

3. To allow limited number of traders/visitors/officials at a time from Kashmir so that villagers would provide them all facilities under 'Res' system. The settlement officer made the following comments in this regards.

> To equalize the strain of transport the concerned authority in Srinagar is requested to issue a notice to the traders leaving Srinagar not to come up in very large parties. Besides some other similar precautions should be considered by the higher

authorities. However, British Joint Commissioner made all possible help to improve the present position of 'Res' system.[44]

4. Large exemptions in each village by competent and incompetent authorities hampered the Res arrangements by reducing the number of men liable to *Kar-begar*. Gonpas, leading men had been given exemptions by 'Darbar' and others were given by Wazirs, Tehsildars and even by Kardars. Besides a number of village officers and servants were exempted by the villagers themselves. As a result under these circumstances Begar or 'Res' system might be a problem for poor villagers. Thus there was urgent need to check the criterion under which exemptions were given.

5. Exemption from the payment of land revenue should be carefully examined. Chaudhri Khushi Mohamad, settlement officer, Ladakh said that in the following cases exemption should be given:

(a) On production of a sanad granted by the Durbar.

(b) In case of Kardars and Lambardars as long as they continue to hold that office.

(c) In case of widows, infirm old men, minor and persons permanently disabled by disease, etc., provided they have no able-bodied male relations living with them and assisting them in agriculture.

(d) Persons taken into State Service should personally be exempted from Begar, but their holdings should remain subject to Begar, unless they prove their inability to manage their holdings by the help of relations and karindas, etc.

(e) No exemption should in any case be given from expenses of the village excluding those incurred in supplying labour or transport unless the person exempted from Kar-begar is proved to be unable to pay such expenses.

Note: These common expenses correspond to the 'Malba' expenditure in the Punjab but are, as a rule, incurred to a much larger extent in this country.

(f) In case of persons exempted by united consent of the villagers such as Larje (physician), Gara (blacksmith), Mon (musician).

Further, the settlement officer, Ladakh had requested the higher authority to give him power to issue exemption certificates, otherwise no exemption should be given by local officers below the rank of Wazir-i-Wazarat and that such exemptions should, as a rule be given in accordance with the above provisions.

In conclusion under 'Res' system villagers living in and around the stages, during the trade season were ready to provide their services to traders/travellers/officials, who enjoyed the State Government patronage. Ladakhi villagers also benefited by trade except a few problems—they could not participate in agricultural and other home affairs, during summer when they rendered their services to traders/ public officials/ travellers, or that there was no provision to give them some remuneration or incentives from State Government.

REFERENCES

1. Ramsay, H.L.: 'Western Tibet: A practical dictionary of language and customs of the districts included in Ladakh Wazarat: 77 and quoted by Datta, C.L.: *Ladakh and Western Himalayan Politics: 1819-1848*, Munshiram Manoharlal Pub. 1973: 1.
2. Datta, C.L.; op cit.; 5 and Arora, R.C.: *In the land of Kashmir, Ladakh and Gilgit*, Jay Kay Book House, Jammu, 1996 (Reprint); 15 and Gazetteer of Kashmir and Ladak; Vivek Pub. House, Delhi, 1974 (Reprinted): 4.
3. Gazetteer of Kashmir and Ladak; *op. cit.*; 4.
4. *Ibid.*
5. *Ibid.*
6. *Transport*: The word "Transport" means — 'Means that includes men and animals used for carrying passengers and animals from place to place'.
7. Cief Sectt. Political Deptt. File No. 218/p. 156, 1912.
8. Joldan, E.: *Harvest Festival of Buddhist Dards of Ladakh and other Essays*, Kapoor Brothers, Srinagar, 1985, p. 65.
9. *Ibid.*
10. *Ibid.*
11. Cief Sectt. Political Deptt., File No. 218, *op. cit.*
12. *Public Servant*: The term Public Servant includes Public Works Department contractors.
13. Cief Sectt. Public Deptt., *op. cit.*
14. *Ibid.*, weights and measurers—

    1 maund = 40 seers

    2.5 maunds = 100 seers

15. Treaty High Road: The road between Srinagar and Leh was called Treaty High Road. According to Arora (Cf. Arora : 294) are :
    Riding Pony : Rs. 0 1 0 per mile
    Pack Pony : Rs. 0 0 9 per mile
    Cooly : Rs. 0 0 6 per mile.
16. Joldan, E.; *op. cit.*, p. 66.
17. *Ibid.*
18. *Ibid.*, p. 67.
19. *Ibid.*
20. *Ibid.*, pp. 67-68.
21. Cief Sectt.; *op. cit.*
22. *Ibid.*
23. *Ibid.*
24. *Ibid.*
25. *Ibid.*
26. *Ibid.*
27. Respas: Coolies.
28. Cief Sectt.; *op. cit.*
29. *Ibid.*
30. Saspol = Suspol
31. Cief Sectt.; *op. cit.*
32. *Ibid.*
33. *Ibid.*
34. *Ibid.*
35. *Ibid.*
36. *Ibid.*
37. *Ibid.*
38. *Ibid.*
39. *Ibid.* No. C/191/, Srinagar, 13th : June 1914 and Petition of Villages Choukial, Tungus and Jagund, 26/9/1914.
40. Mohamad, Chaudhri Khushi: 'Preliminary Report of Ladakh Settlement', 1908, p. 25.
41. *Ibid.*
42. *Ibid.*
43. *Ibid.*
44. *Ibid.*

6
TRADE MISSIONS

Leh was the important trade centre of Central Asian countries before independence being the gateway, of Indo-Central Asian exchange of materials through the ages. Ladakhis trade in agricultural products with the Champas of Tibet and Skardu. Salt was largely exported to Skardu and in a less degree to Kashmir, being exchanged for grain, apricots, tobacco, madder and ponies. The chief mission was the Central Asian trade between Yarkand and India.[1] However, Jammu and Kashmir State Government's main intention was to give support to Kashmiri merchants so that they could have their full control over wool trade. And through Ladakh some trade missions were sent to Tibet. Here follows the details:

1. Lo Phyag Trade Mission

In 1684, a treaty was signed between Ladakh and Tibet. Among other clauses, the treaty reached an agreement that annually both countries would send their trade missions between Leh and Lhasa, and was known as Lo Phyag trade mission. Thus the wool received from Lhasa was totally exported to Kashmir.[2]

2. Cha-pa Mission

Chaba or cha-pa literally means 'tea' carrier (i.e. tea merchants).[3] According to Ramsay, the Leh officials called the Lhasa commercial agent as 'chaba' which was the corruption of 'chhaba', the correct Tibetan pronunciation would be cha-pa meaning 'tea man'. The correct title of this official was the 'Zhungtsong pa', meaning the merchant of the 'Deyva Zhung' (the Dalai Lama) of Lhasa.[4] Under the terms of the 1684 treaty, the Cha-pa mission carried 200 animal-loads of brick tea from Lhasa once a year to Ladakh and returned with dry apricots, saffron and sugars, etc.[5]

The Cha-pa Trade mission was commercial and religious in nature. This mission while passing through Ladakh enjoyed Ula[6] or, free transport and many other cognate facilities. Since the treaty was regulated after 1684 at Tingmosgang, Kashmiri merchants made some trade stipulations, one of which the wool, thus imported in Ladakh through Cha-pa mission which was later entirely exported to Kashmir. To have had firm monopoly over wool export, four Kashmiri merchants settled at Spituk. They undertook the collection of all wool so received either by Cha-pa mission or from the Chang-Thang and later supplied to Kashmir.[7]

3. Lapchak Mission

Under the treaty in 1684 the Ladakhi kings who recognised the religions as well as commercial mission and was known as Lapchak or Lopchok. Like Cha-pa mission every year from Ladakh, the Lapchak mission was to send to Lhasa and carried some presents from kings of Ladakh for His Holiness the Dalai Lama. In other words, Lapchak means ''yearly salaam.'' This mission while marching in the territory of Tibet enjoyed Ula or Begar facilities as traders of Cha-pa mission got in Ladakh like free transport, accommodation, etc.

The Lapchak mission or commercial embassy was a trade mission from Ladakh to Lhasa. It was not a political mission. After Dogra conquest some modifications were considered. In 1842 A.D. a treaty between Ladakh and Lhasa was made which determined the existing north-east frontier of Ladakh and began peaceful relations between the two countries. Under the treaty every three years a *kafila* had to leave Ladakh to Lhasa, consisting of 270 horse or yak loads of goods, and conducted by a representative of the Maharaja chosen by the Governor of Ladakh. In the mission the Maharaja's representative should be chosen from Ladakh Raja's family. The representative or the post of leader of the Lapchak had much value, as it generally enriched the family, which shared the profits of the trade with the Maharaja's government. Girdlestone says:

''In 1842 A.D., when a treaty between Ladakh and Lhasa was made which determined the existing north-east frontier of Ladakh and began the peaceful relations between the two states which have subsisted ever since. The arrangement is that every three years a *kafila* should leave Ladakh for Lhasa, consisting of 270 horse or yak loads of goods, and conducted by a representative of the Maharaja chosen by the Governor of Ladakh. For just that number of loads is carriage provided by the Lhasa authorities from Gah to Lhasa on the outward journey, and from Lhasa to the first village or encampments in Ladakh on the return journey. The Maharaja's representative is always taken from a Ladakh family of eminence, as no other person, not even a Dogra of high rank from the Maharaja's own court, would be welcomed, probably indeed would not be received into the grand lama's capital. The post of leader of the Lapchak, though held only for one turn, is much valued, as it generally enriches the family, between whom and the Maharaja's government the profits of the trade are divided. The goods sent from Ladakh are dried apricots, which constitute the most bulky part of the consignment, currants, saffron, kottzchin, and textile fabrics from European and Indian looms; on the return the chief goods are shawls, wool and tea.''[8]

At the time of sending Lapchak mission from Ladakh to Lhasa, the Governor of Ladakh sent complimentary letters to the grand lama and his ministers, and to the heads of certain monasteries with some small gifts. The mission returned after a gap of one year to Ladakh reciprocating with letters and gifts. Girdlestone writes:

''...Complimentary letters signed by the Governor of Ladakh are sent to the grand lama and his ministers, and to the heads of certain of the monasteries, and with each of them goes a small present, the nature of which is laid down and does not vary. The embassy, which is absent nearly a year, brings back corresponding letters and gifts. The leader transacts his business with the ministers, but pays ceremonial visits to the grand lama. It appears that he is always well treated, and that the arrangements for his journey are carefully made. Besides this triennial embassy, of which the last set out from Ladakh in 1871, and the return compliments by Lhasa, there is a yearly *kafila* from Lhasa, consisting also 270 loads, for which carriage is found by the Maharaja's government within his border, the reason for this additional party being that as only about a quarter of the whole route lies in the Maharaja's territories, and as the cost of carriage falls heavier in proportion on the Tibetan government, the latter looks to reimburse itself by a more frequent ventures. The same formalities are observed on either side in regard to this, as to the triennial embassy.''[9]

After 1834, when Dogras got their full control over Ladakh, the Lapchak mission lost its religious influence, as this trade mission was managed by Kashmiri Muslim traders who settled in Leh and earned large profits in the transaction.[10] However, in order to accelerate the trade relations with Tibet the Maharaja advanced Rs. 1,920 to the mission every third year. Later on when independent Dogra rule was established throughout the Jammu and Kashmir State, Maharaja Pratap Singh continued to follow the practice of exchanging trade missions every third year. And like his predecessor advanced a sum of Rs. 9,000 to the agent in return for which he was expected to bring Rs. 18,000 worth goods from Tibet.[11]

The Lapchak mission had to pay *sahtal* or ground tax to the treasurer of Lhasa at the rate of Rs. 8 per gold dust bag, Rs. 50 for 1.5 seers of saffron and Re. 1 for each piece of native cloth. The treasurer was appointed by the Deva Jung who paid into the Deva Jung treasury. Elias writes:

"It is difficult to estimate precisely how far the *sahtal* paid or presented to the treasurer of Lhasa is regarded by the Tibetan authorities as *nazar* or tribute, but by the government of Kashmir it is certainly looked upon in the light of a present of ceremony only, and as a return for the provisions, etc., with which the agent and his party are applied during a part of their stay in Lhasa. Further, the last of my informants as this subject (the man who acted as Lapchuk to Lhasa in 1877-78) says that no mention is made of the Min Sar Jagir, either in presenting the *sahtal* to the treasurer or the presents to any of the other authorities. The treasurer is a servant of the native government and is appointed by the Deva Jung, or grant lama, not by the Chinese officials, and his receipt sets forth' that the *sahtal* has been paid into the Deva Jung's treasury.

The facts:

(i) of the treasurer giving a formal receipt, while the other recipients of presents give none;

(ii) that he sends no return present; and

(iii) that the ward *sahtal* means literally 'land tax' would be reasons in favour of regarding the present or payment made to the Lhasa treasurer as tribute paid by the Maharaja's government to Chinese Tibet.

But against this must be placed the following considerations:

(i) that so far as those best acquainted with the contents of the agreement of 1842 are aware, no mention is made of tribute in return for the Min Sar Jagir;

(ii) that *sahtal* or similar value, etc., was given by the Lapchuks for many years before the agreement was made, and

(iii) that is those (third) years when no Lapchuk goes to Lhasa, no *sahtal* is paid by the Maharaja's government, though the revenue of the jagir is collected as usual."[12]

Though the Lapchuk mission had to carry some presents as well as to pay taxes to the treasurer of Lhasa. But the purpose of taxes as levied on the mission was not clearly designated. Elias says:

> The distinction between presents of ceremony or friendship on the one hand, and tribute as a sign of dependence or vassalage on the other, is frequently very loosely drawn by Asiatics, and the name of their taxes, duties, etc., do not always designate accurately the purpose for which they are levied. Thus, as far as I am able to judge from such enquiries as I have made, I am inclined to think that neither the present nor the *sahtal* sent by the Maharaja's government to the Lhasa authorities can rightly be regarded as tribute (or *nazar*) either for the Min Sar Jagir or for any other consideration; and further, that the Min Sar Jagir is viewed by the Lhasa authorities as a local matter concerning the Gartok province only, and entirely separate from the agreement regarding the Lapchuk.[13]

Through Lapchak mission traders exchanged commodities like wool, pashmina, gold dust, turquoise, coral, etc. In 1906, Sven Hedin saw chests full of silver, gold dust, turquoise, coral, etc., in a Muslim merchants commercial house, his name was Haji Nazer Shah who had monopoly over Lapchak mission and earned a profit of about Rs. 25,000 a year. Maharaja of Kashmir entrusted him the duty to carry out the Lapchak mission.[14]

Nazer Shah and Haider Shah were well-known traders. In Ladakh their families were regarded as aristocratic families. Both these families have had good command over Lapchak mission. The members of the former traded with Lhasa, while the latter with Sinkiang. Besides Abdul Hamid Khan served for many years as British Akshal in Yarkand and was given the title of Khan Bahadur, which was second only to knighthood in the British Empire in those days. Gulam Rashul of the Shah family also received the same title, mainly for rendering assistance to the well-known explorer Sven Hedin. Thus, Lapchak mission during Dogra period and later in British Empire was being fully dependent upon Muslim traders.[15] Kashmiri Muslims involvement was marked by their settlements at Leh as well in Tibet where they were settled till 1959, with about 129 such families having about 600 members.[16]

REFERENCES

1. Imperial Gazetteer, p. 93.
2. Bray, John: Episodes in Frontier Diplomacy during British Rule in India; In: *Recent Research on Ladakh* 4 and 5; Motilal Banarsidas Pub., New Delhi; 1995; 256 and quoted from Luciano Petech, "The Tibetan-Ladakhi-Moghul War of 1681-1683." *India Historical Quarterly* 23(1947), pp. 169-99; The kingdom of Ladakh (Rome : Istituto Italiano per il Medio ed Extremo Oriente, 1977). Zahiruddin Ahmad, "New Light on the Tibet-Ladakh-Mughal War of 1679-1684". *East and West* 18(1968), pp. 340-61.
3. Datta, C.L.: *Ladakh and Western Himalayan Politics: 1819-1848*, Munshiram Manoharlal Pub., New Delhi, 1973, p. 65 and Quoted from Cunningham, J.O.: 'Notes on Moorcroft's Travels in Ladakh, etc.', *JASB*, XIII, pt. I, 1844, p. 217.
4. Datta, C.L.; *op. cit.*, p. 65 and Ref. from Ramsay, H.L. "Western Tibet: A practical of the language and customs of the districts included in the Ladakh Wazarat, Lahore, 1890, p. 20.
5. *Ibid.*; pp. 65-66.
6. Ula = 'U lag and in Treaty High Road to Leh from Srinagar as Kar Begar or Begar or 'Res' system.
7. Datta, C.L.; *op. cit.*, p. 65.
8. Gazetteer of Kashmir and Ladakh, Vivek Pub. House; 1974, p. 558 and quoted from Girdlestone, Memorandum on Kashmir and some adjacent countries.
9. *Ibid.*; pp. 558-59.
10. Warikoo, K.: Gateway to Central Asia the Trans Himalayan Trade of Ladakh, 1846-1947; In: *Recent Research on Ladakh*, 4 and 5, 1995, p. 239.
11. Jina, Prem Singh: Ladakh and Central Asian Trade during 1825-1925; In: Recent Researches on the Himalaya; Prem Singh Jina (ed.); Indus Pub. Co., 1997, p. 137.
12. Gazetteer of Kashmir and Ladakh; *op. cit.* p. 559.

13. *Ibid.*
14. Warikoo, K.; *op. cit.* and referred Sven Hedin, *Trans Himalaya*, London 1909, Vol. I. pp. 57-59.
15. Joldan, E.: *Harvest Festival of Buddhist Dards of Ladakh and other Essays*, Kapoor Brothers, 1985, pp. 61-62.
16. Warikoo, K.; *op. cit.*, p. 239 and referred for details see note given by the Ministry of External Affairs, New Delhi, to the Embassy of China in India, September 24, 1959 (India, Ministry of External Affairs) Notes, Memoranda and letters exchanged between the Governments of India and China, September to November 1959, White paper II, New Delhi, pp. 88-96.

7

TRADE BETWEEN LADAKH AND YARKAND

The people of Sinkiang or Eastern Central Asia who came in Leh called Yarkandis. There were many other Yarkandis who came in Ladakh from other parts of the Central Asia but Ladakhis generally addressed them as Khoja or a Haji. They were partially or fully involved in trade. However, they can be classified in two categories—the traders and caravan. The traders came in Ladakh with caravan but did not have many horses, whereas caravan carried the commercial commodities on their pack animals mostly on big Yarkandi horses on payment, from Sinkiang to Leh and back.[1]

Some Yarkand traders were well-known throughout Central Asia big mundies, viz., Gartok, Lhasa, Leh, Khotan, Kasgar, etc. They were called Bias, (millionnaire). Popular among them were Hussain Haji, Mohammad Omar Khan, etc. E. Joldan writes:

"The top class among the traders were known as Bias, (millionnaire) in their language. Hussain Haji of Khotan would come in this category, others like Mohammad Omar Khan and Khan Bahadur Nur Mohammad Khan were from Peshawar and Persia respectively."[2]

The Yarkandi traders had a caravan of 30 to 40 horses each, each horse carried two to two and half maund. The caravan had servants to look after the horses. Annually about three to four caravans fulls went to Laddakh E. Joldan remarked:

"A caravan would consist of 30 to 40 horses with a caravan Bash (leader) and 5 to 8 servants, known as chakars—5 horses under one servant. As pack animal would carry a load of two and a half maunds (92 kg.)—the maximum weight fixed by convention. 4 caravans of say 150 horses would bring 300 packed loads which would be staked in 2 or 3 tiers in the upper compound of the serai in a complete way."[3]

There were a few Yarkandis who reached Leh for the purpose of going to Mecca for Haj. They also carried less bulky but high in value goods such as gold and silver bars and coins to cover the expenses of the long journey to Mecca. E. Joldan writes:

"The other category of Yarkandis who would reach Leh were the Haj pilgrims on their way to Mecca. They would come in small groups. Sometimes there would be women and children in a group. Each person would have his own horse and all his belongings—clothes, bedding, edibles, some petty items of trade and some grain-feed for the horses, all stufled in a big saddle-bag, would be loaded on the animal, and himself or herself on the top of it. But they would also have to carry several things less bulky but high in value such as gold and silver bars and coins, to cover the expense of the long journey to Mecca."[4]

Yarkand was one of the trade centres and was in the east of Chinese Central Asia. In 1877 China reoccupied the area between Kashgar to Yarkand and named it Sinkiang. E. Joldan writes:

"Chinese Central Asia, is a vast area, stretching about 1500 miles from west to east and at its widest part measures 400 miles. It is as big as France and Austria put together with an area of about 465,000 square miles. Kashgar in the west and Yarkand in the east were the two main centres of trade. The Chinese renamed it as Sinkiang (New Province) after it was reconquered from Yakub Beg in 1877."[5]

Yarkandis went every year to Senirechia and Ferghana, and covered the trade of 150,000 pounds in a year. However, Yarkandi who went for trade to Badakshah brought horses, pista, gold, carpets, etc., and from India cotton goods, watches, jewellery, etc. Referring to the book of Henry Lansdell, E. Joldan writes:

"(Henry Lansdell) valued Sinkiang's trade with Senirechia and Ferghana at 15,000 pounds during that year (1888). From Badakshan they brought horses, pistachionuts and took back Nasha (probably charas) gold and carpets. From India via Ladakh were brought cotton goods muslins, watches, jewellery and Mohammedan books and took back Nasha, gold, silver, wool carpets and felts. He noticed cloth manufactured by Macdonald of Manchester."[6]

Roads from Leh to Yarkand

There were four roads leading from Leh to Yarkand across the Karakoram:[7]

1. Ordinary summer route: The road leading from Leh across the Khardong pass, up the valley of the Nubra river, and thence across the Saser and Karakoram passes to Sháhidúla.

2. Winter Route: The road leading from Leh across the Digar pass into the valley of the Shyok river, and thence across the Karakoram.

3. Winter Route: The road leading from Leh up the valley of the Indus, and thence across the Changla pass and to Shyok village and up the Shyok valley to the Karakoram pass and Sháhidúla.

4. Old Changchenmo Route: The road leading from Leh up the valley of the Indus, and thence across the Changla pass to Tankse and over the Changchenmo and Lingzi-thang plains of Aktagh and Sháhidúla.

Besides Dr. Cayley discovered western Changchenmo route from the Lingzithang plain down to the valley of the Karakash river to Sháhidúla.

The direct route over the Karakoram via Nubra was difficult route. According to Shaw:

"Beyond the Indus there are two sets of roads to Yarkand, which may be classed under the heads of the Karakoram line and Changchenmo line when I had the honour, in 1869, of submitting to His Excellency the Viceroy a memorandum on the routes, the comparison lay between the old or Karakoram route and that via Changchenmo across the high plateaux of Lingzithang and the Soda plain."[8]

However, Dr. Cayley's new route followed by Foryth's returning party from Yarkand was superior to the old Changchenmo route. Shaw remarked:

"Instead of four high passes* two of them covered with glaciers and three minor, though difficult ones, we have four passes altogether,**

---

*(1) Khardong 17,900 ft.; Digar 17,930 ft or Changla 17,590 ft. (2) Saser 17,820 ft. (3) Karakoram 18,550 ft. (4) Suget 17,610 ft.

**(1) Changla 17,590 ft. (2) Marsemik 18,400 ft. (3) Changlang 18,910 ft. (4) Karatagh 17,710 ft.

The heights may be varied as per the locations of the measurement.

which are a par with the easiest of those by the old route, and one none of which are snow or ice to be found in the summer. Instead of the difficult and dangerous fords of the shyok (at only one of which a boat can be used),*** we have no water higher than the kee to cross. Instead of four and a half days from grass to grass. The new route has first one camp without grass and after an interval of four days one or possibly two more occasions alone there is a chance of the horses going on an entire day without grazing. The difference in point of roughness and laboriousness between the two routes cannot be expressed by a contrast of numbers. It must, moreover, be remembered that the old route passes through gorges where it is difficult, and over glacier passes where it is impossible to keep the road in order, while the course of the other is chiefly over plains or through wide villages. While firmly believing in the superiority of the improved Changchenmo line over the old route, one must admit that traffic is the only final and decisive test in comparing two roads. Assessing the artificial advantages, the best of the routes will certainly, in the end, be picked out by those who habitually use them. But we are far from having reached that stage yet. Not a single native caravan has yet traversed the latest line via Changchenmo. There has not yet been time for them to do so. Thus the only Changchenmo route as yet practically known to merchants is that which due to the neglect of certain Kashmir officials laid strewn with the dead bodies of some 200 horses during Forsyth's upward march. But even setting aside this terrible and unnecessary mortality, the state of all the new routes till date has been this. Each merchant and caravan has had to discover the route afresh, partly assisted, it is true, by hearsay descriptions, and partly by half-obliterated traces of predecessors. In those wind-swept regions of shifting sand or of gravel, there are no marks to direct the traveller,

***On the summer route the Shyok is crossed only twice, viz. once between Khardong or Digar and Satti, and once again at north base of the Saser pass. At the former place a ferry-boat has been in use for a long time. At the latter place a ferry boat was started by Mr. Elias in 1882 or 1883. Both boats are now in use. The boatmen are paid out of the Joint Commissioners' fund. The Saser boatmen get Rs. 90 per season, the Satti boatmen Rs. 60 per season. The ferry-boats do not carry baggage animals, these have to swim, but even during the time the Shyok is in flood, viz, July and August, they are very seldom drowned in the attempt; they are washed away and land lower down the stream.

In the winter the shojok is frozen over. Mr. Shaw's remark must have been applied to the winter route during the first and last month it is open, when the ice has not formed or has broken. Then the Shyok has to be forded frequently, and this is at places very dangerous.

who must feel his way along, nearly at random. Even if he succeeds in taking the right line, it is odds but he misses the right camping ground, near the grassy side-valley or hill-slope, which affords the only chance of grazing for his cattle for the next 20 miles."[9]

The above new route no doubt was superior than the well-known old route by the Karakoram where traders got sufficient grass supply facilities as well as for their animals they had grazing fields on the way, but it was not developed. Shaw says:

"Let us compare (the new route) with the case of the well-known old route by the Karakoram, where custom has made the traders at home in every yard of the way. Each blade of grass within grazing distance contribute to the support of the animals, camping grounds are so arranged as to make the most of the few advantages of the road. It is obvious that until the traders' knowledge of the new route in some measure comes up to their knowledge of the old, the former will not have a fair chance. For this purpose both road and camping grounds must either be distinguished by unmistakable and permanent marks (a difficult thing in such a country), or else each party must be accompanied by men thoroughly acquainted with the route. Again, another point on which the artificial advantages are not equal is the assistance afforded to the caravans by the country people. The men of Nubra reap an annual harvest by sending their yaks, with provisions, across the Saser pass to meet the traders. On the new route this mutually advantageous traffic have not yet sprung up* and the losses incurred by the villagers whose cattle were employed. Thereafter, in 1870 they, will not encourage them to begin. Again, till such time as the Tankse and Pangong** people find out the

---

*The two cases differ, and it is doubtful whether such a traffic would spring up on the changchenmo route.

In the case of the Karakoram route we have the Saser pass close to the low-lying and fertile valley of Nubra, and there are villages and cultivated lands 80 miles beyond Leh and within 26 miles of the Saser pass.

On the Changchenmo line, villages and cultivation cease a few miles above Tankse, which is 55 miles from Leh. There is a small patch of cultivation at Lukung on the Pangong lake, but for practical purposes the country beyond Tankse may be said to be uninhabited, save by a few Tartar shepherds, who wander about from place to place grazing their cattle.

**Village on south side of Pangong lake, about 12 or 15 miles from Lukung camping ground.

advantage of doing it themselves, the Joint Commissioners must take their place in providing supplies in the Changchenmo valley.*

In short, it seems that we have the choice between an inferior but frequented road, and a superior but undeveloped and (at present) unfrequented road. If the Joint Commissioners are confined to the former, the trade loses the prospective advantages promised by the adoption of a better line. If the letter is exclusively chosen, their jurisdiction would, at least for some years, be confined to an empty tract, while the trade would be flowing unprotected through a parallel channel. One horn of the dilemma is entirely avoided, and the other partially, by fixing on a line which, while taking is the whole of the better route, also includes the terminus,** or a most important point of the old and usual road. At the same time, it would probably be wise to reserve liberty of changing on to the other road if at a future time it be found that the great test of traffic withholds its sanction from the new route."[10]

As said earlier mostly traders preferred the Karakoram route as it was comparatively 76 miles shorter than the Changchenmo and for this route traders could hire yaks to carry their loads and they paid Rs. 2 per yak from Leh Khardong village; from Panamik to Shyok Rs. 4 per yak and Rs. 6 per horse load was being expended on yak between Leh and the Murghi 'nala'. Ramsay remarked:

"The Karakoram route is, however, preferred by most traders. It has the great advantage of shortness from Leh to Sháhidúla via the Khardong-Saser passes, being 240 miles; while via Changchenmo the distance is 316 miles, and where grain has to be carried for the feed of animals. The only people who really use the Changchenmo route are the Punjab mule-men, who do not feed their animals on grain, but let them subsist on such grass as they can pick up; the mass of trade is, however, carried on ponies, and they being fed on gram, distance becomes of primary consideration. On this route traders are obliged to hire yaks to carry their loads over the Khardong (glacier)

*The provision of supplies along a regularly frequented road is a mere matter of time and money, but the point for consideration is, could supplies be furnished along the Changchenmo route at prices which traders could afford to pay, i.e., without resolving not to come again by that road? I am inclined to think they could not at any rate at places more distant than Gogra.

**In the middle of summer, when the Sigar pass is free from snow, they might go via Digar instead of via Khardong, but the Digar is very steep on the Leh side, and as a matter of fact, traders always prefer, if possible to go by Khardong to hire yaks for the two marches between Leh and Khardong village.

pass these yaks are hired at Leh and discharged at Khardong village, and the hire paid is Rs. 2 per yak. From Khardong to Changlung or Nubra) the road is fairly easy; the next two marches, viz., to Tutyalak over the Changlung pass (also called Karawal Diwan), and to the Shyok river, over the Saser pass, are along, hard marches. Laden horses can and do pass over this road,* but, as a rule traders wish to spare their horses as far as possible, so that they may be better able to endure the fatigues of the onward journey from the Shyok to Shāhidúla. For this reason yaks are hired at Panamik, one march on the Leh side of Changlung, which is a very small village, where yaks are not obtainable.

For the journey from Panamik to the Shyok the hire is Rs. 4 per yak. It may, therefore, be considered that in going by the summer road, Rs. 6 per horse-load is expended on yak hire between Leh and the Murghi 'nala'. When coming from Yarkand to Leh the case is difficult, for no yaks remain for hire at the Murghi 'nala', and traders are therefore obliged to make their horses carry their loads over the Saser pass; but on arrival at Khardong village, they hire yaks at Rs. 2 each to carry their goods to Leh. Thus the total expenditure on yak hire for the double journey to and from Yarkand via the Saser route is Rs. 8 per horse load."[11]

The distance between Leh to Yarkand was 525 miles and on horseback this distance could be covered in 29 days. Aziz Din also visited Yarkand and covered the above distance in 29 days via Panamik and Karakoram route. The details given by him were as follows:

1.	Leh to Panamik	4 days
2.	Panamik to Saser	2 days
3.	Saser to Chongthash	1 day
4.	Chongthash to Morgo	1 day
5.	Morgo to Depsang	2 days
6.	Depsang to Karakoram	2 days
7.	Karakoram to Suget Karol	5 days
8.	Karol to Shaidulla	1 day
9.	Shaidulla to Sanju	5 days
10.	Sanju to Karghalik	4 days
11.	Karghalik to Yarkand	2 days
	Total	29 days

*The Saser glacier is not very difficult for horse to cross, as it is not very steep, and is covered with snow.

Frederic Drew summarized the Leh to Yarkand routes in the following:[13]

1. Summer Route via Karakoram

Stage	*No.*	*Height (ft.)*	*Miles from Last Stage*
(1)	*(2)*	*(3)*	*(4)*
Leh	0	11,500	—
Camp	1	15,000	12
Khardong	2	13,500	15
Khartsar	3	10,430	12
Tigar	4	10,030	13
Panamik	5	—	14
Chonglung	6	11,500	13
Tutiyalak	7	13,000	13
Sar-i-Hauz-i-khoja	8	15,500	12
Brangsa Saser	9	15,400	09
Bulak-i-Murghai	10	15,100	22
Burtse	11	16,000	12
Kizil Angūr	12	16,700	11
Daulat Beguldi	13	17,200	18
Brangsa	14	16,500	23
Wahāb-jilgāh	15	16,000	19
Malikshāh	16	15,300	15
Chibrā	17	16,480	12
Suket	18	13,000	18
Shāhdūla	19	11,500	12
Yarkand	35	4,000	240
	Total		515

The Passes crossed are:

(1) Between stages 1 and 2, the Khardong pass 17,500 ft.
(2) Between stages 8 and 9, the Saser pass 17,500 ft.
(3) Between stages 13 and 14, the Karakoram pass 18,300 ft.
(4) Between stages 17 and 18, the Suket pass 18,200 ft.
(5) And afterwards the Sānju pass 16,760 ft.
(6) And the Chuchu pass 11,800 ft.

The Shayok river is crossed by boat between stages 3 and 4, or in certain seasons it may be forded a few miles above or below the ferry.

This road is traversed by laden ponies, but it is usual to have the aid of yaks to carry their loads over the Saser and the Sanju Passes. The road keeps open for four to five months in the year.

From stage 8 to 17, there is very little grass to be got, at some stage none at all; and at some fuel also is wanting.

2. Leh via Karakoram to Yarkand; Winter Route

Stage	*No. of March*
1	*2*
Leh	0
Sabu	1
Digar	2
Agyām	3
Pakra	4
Chimchāk	5
Lamakyent or Shayok	6
Chungjangal	7
Dungyalāk	8
Mandarlik	9
Kutaklik	10
Sultān Chushkum	11
Duhn-i-Murghi	12
Bulak-i-Murghi	13
Burtse	14
Kizil Angur	15
Daulat Beguldi	16
Brangsa	17
Wahāb-jilgah	18
Malikshāh	19
Kafalong	20
Jindbalghūn	21
Bukharuldi	22
Kirgiz-jangal	23
Yarkand	36

From stage 13 to 19 this route coincides with stages 10 to 16 of summer route.

The Passes crossed are:

(1) Between stage 1 and stage 2, the Digar Pass

(2) Between stage 16 and stage 17, the Karakoram pass 18,300 ft.

After the Yangi Pass, and the Tup Diwan, this road is fit for laden ponies; it is open from November till February. There are many places where grass and fuel are scant, and somewhere they are absolutely wanting.

3. Leh via Changchemo to Yarkand: Western Route

Stage	*No.*	*Height (ft.)*	*Miles from Last Stage*
(1)	*(2)*	*(3)*	*(4)*
Leh	0	11,500	—
Tikse	1	—	13
Chimre	2	—	16
Zingral	3	—	11
Tsultak	4	—	13
Durgo	5	—	16
Tanktse	6	12,500	07
Camp	7	—	11
Lukung	8	14,086	11
Charkang	9	16,700	14
Gunle	10	16,140	13
Tsolu (near Pamzal)	11	14,760	12
Gogra	12	15,500	14
Camp	13	16,500	21
Camp	14	17,000	20
Sumdo	15	17,000	25
Shinglung	16	16,700	11
Kizil Jilgah	17	16,500	14
Khushk Maidan	18	15,600	18
Shor Jilgah	19	15,900	14
Karatagh Lake	20	16,900	17
Malikshah	21	15,300	25
Shahdula	24	11,500	54
Yarkand	40	4,000	240
Total			610

The Passes crossed are:

(1) Between stages 3 and 4, the Chang Pass about 18,000 ft.
(2) Between stages 9 and 10, the Masimik Pass 18,200 ft.
(3) Between stages 13 and 14, a Pass 18,000 ft.
(4) Between stages 16 and 17, the Kizil Pass 17,800 ft.
(5) Between stages 19 and 20, the Karatagh Pass

Afterwards, the Suket Pass 18,200 ft.
The Sanju Pass 16,760 ft.
And the Chuchu Pass 11,850 ft.

This was the road indicated by Dr. Cayley and traversed by Mr. Forsyth's pary on their return journey, it is thought to be the easiest of roads to Yarkand; it can be traversed by camels of the two humped species; fuel and grass are wanting at two or three stages only. It would be closed in the winter.

4. Leh Via Changchenmo to Yarkand; Hayward's Route

Stage	*No.*	*Height (ft.)*	*Miles from Last Stage*
(1)	*(2)*	*(3)*	*(4)*
Leh	0	11,500	—
Gogra	12	15,500	151
Chonglung	13	—	17
Nischu	14	—	15
Lingzhithang	15	—	21
Burtse	16	—	10.5
Karasu	17	—	10
Kizil Jilgah	18	—	14.5
Khushk Maidan	19	—	16
Shor Jilgah	20	—	10
Oglok	21	—	21
Wahabjilgah	22	—	10
Aktagh	23	—	15.5
Yarkand	36	—	235
Total			546.5

This road was found out and recommended by Hayward.

5. Leh via Changchemo to Yarkand: Eastern Route

Stage	*No.*	*Height (ft.)*	*Miles from Last Stage*
(1)	*(2)*	*(3)*	*(4)*
Leh	0	11,500	
Gogra	12	15,500	151
Chonglung	13	16,700	17
Nischu	14	17,700	15
Lingzhithang	15	17,300	21
Tsothang	16	17,100	18
Lokzhung	17	17,200	16
Thaldat	18	16,300	15
Yangpa	19	16,200	30
E. Karakash valley	20	15,000	24
Shahdula	27	11,500	81
Yarkand	47	4,000	240
Total			628

This was the road over the great plateaus; it was taken by Adolphe Schlagintweit and imperfectly described by Muhammad Amin his guide; afterwards Johnson traversed, it on his way to Khutan and gave a detailed itinerary (*Journal R. Geographical Society,* 1867). The details of distances and heights are given as follows.

A diversion from or loop in this route was made by Dr Cayley; the distances and heights are as follows:

Stage	*No.*	*Height (ft.)*	*Miles from Last Stage*
Tholdat	18	16,300	—
Patsalung	19	16,400	20
Camp	20	15,900	2i
E. Karakash Valley	21	15,000	12

6. Leh via Shahidula to Yarkand (Summer Route)

This route had little different halting places, the details are as follows:

Sl. No.	*Stage*	*Intermediate Distance (miles)*	*Total Distance (miles)*
(1)	*(2)*	*(3)*	*(4)*
1.	Leh	—	—
2.	Polu Digar	10.0	10.09
3.	Digar (13,080 ft.)	14.0	24.0
4.	Satti (10,500 ft.)	17.0	41.0
5.	Taghar (10,500 ft.)	15.0	56.0
6.	Panamik (10,840 ft.)	13.0	69.0
7.	Changlung (10,760 ft.)	11.0	80.0
8.	Tutyalak (13,000 ft.)	11.0	91.0
9.	Saser Polu (15,204 ft.)	15.0	106.0
10.	Bulak-i-Murghai or Murghai (15,190 ft.)	10.0	116.0
11.	Kizil Langar (26,700 ft.)	16.0	132.0
12.	Daolat Beguldi (16,880 ft.)	20.0	152.0
13.	Balti Brangsa or Brangsa Karakoram (17,180 ft.)	22.0	174.0
14.	Malikshah or Aktagh (15,590 ft.)	28.0	202.0
15.	Chibra (16,480 ft.)	10.0	212.0
16.	Suget (12,970 ft.)	21.0	233.0
17.	Shahidula Khoja (11,780 ft.)	08.0	241.0
18.	Yarkand (via Sunju pass)	202.4	443.4

(+) Gazetteer of Kashmir and Ladakh, Route No. 37; *op. cit.*, pp. 968-71

Description of the Halting Places of the Above Route

1. Polu Digar

Camping ground and a few huts and south base of the Digar La, small stream; a little pasture, but no ful.

2. Digar

This village situated between Digar La and Shyok river; ascent of pass steep and rough; cross a narrow gap and reach crest of Digar La (17,900 ft.), down a long, stoney slope, covered with snow patches at the end of June, to Polu camp at 9 miles. Then across bogs and peat beds and down a moorland 5 miles to Digar. The pass was very difficult and yaks were used to cross this pass.

3. Satti

It is situated at the right bank of Shyok river; at 5 miles reach Shyok, and proceed down left bank and cross by boat opposite Satti. Traders were advised to cross Shyok river with baggage animals who could swim over.

4. Taghar

It is situated at the left bank of Nubra. This village has barley and luccrn cultivated grounds and a good many trees. Proceed down right bank Shyok in the rich valley of that river, to Tirit, 7 miles; then up left bank Nubra passing Lukhjung, there is a flourishing village at the confluence of the Shyok and Nubra; the valley of the Shyok is here some 4 miles wide, and of the Nubra 2 to 3 miles; it is in parts sandy and shingly, and in parts covered with jungle. There is cultivation, fruit trees, and hamlets in places.

5. Panamik

Large village left bank Nubra; extensive cultivation; traders while passing through this village collected barley and luccrn for their onward journey. Midway crossed a rocky ridge abutting on the stream, with the populous village of Chirasa on the opposite bank. Pass Popchi, a large village, at 7 miles; hot springs at 12 miles.

6. Changlung

Small village left bank Nubra; the last inhabited place in Ladakh by this route. Hot springs here, and a little cultivation; road across patches of turf and bruhwood jungle. 3½ miles pass Takcha, and cross the Tutyalak, a rapid stream, by a timber bridge.

---

*Cf. Gazetteer of Kashmir and Ladakh; *op. cit.*; pp. 968-71.

*7. **Tutyalak***

Camp on gravelly flat close under a glacier, left bank Tutyalak; fuel scarce, pasture plentiful. This place is called Pangdongsta by the Tibetans; steep zig-zag ascent of 4,000 feet to the Karawal Dawan ridge, 3 miles. Then down a steep hill slope and cross Tutyalak river by ricketty Spar bridge, and proceed up left bank 3 miles to camp.

8. Saser Polu or Brangsa Saser

Here traders did not get any kind of supply, viz., fuel, grass, etc. Camping ground and a few huts at north-east base of Saser Pass and on right bank of Shyok river. Proceed north through a narrow defile; path very rough. At half-way pass Sartang camp (also called Sar-i-Kanz-i-Khoja-Fateh) at foot of Saser Pass. Glaciers all round. Path now winds under a huge glacier, which it eventually crosses; leading over it for 3 miles; passage dangerous; this is the submit of the Saser Pass (17,500 feet); it is covered with perpetual snow, and is the most difficult of all the passes on either the summer or winter route. The ascent and descent were nearly always impracticable for laden horses, and yaks must be employed to carry loads over it. Path leads down.

From Brangsa Saser there were other routes to Daolat Beguldi, which were only practicable in winter, here follow the details:

(a) To Kundan: Brangsa Saser to Kundan is eight miles distance up a wide river channel, through a very narrow and winding strait between a great glacier and opposite cliffs and along the river course. The passage of the strait was done on the ice, or through the stream where it was broken, a difficult road under any conditions.

(b) To Gapshan, 9 miles: Across a bank of loose pebles, through a narrow strait where the river bed was almost blocked by a vast glacier which had slid down across it, and up the bed of a stream, in and out of the water repeatedly.

(c) To Daolat Beguldi, 15 miles: Across an undulating ravine-cut plateau.

*7. **Bulak-i-Murghai or Murghai***

Camping ground right bank of a tributary of Shyok. Opposite to Shyok is Saser. Proceed down left bank for a mile, and then due east up a deep gully to Chungtash camp, 8 miles, at a great erratic boulder on a turfy flat; thence proceed down dry stoney gully to Murghai.

8. Kizil Langar

Camping ground on left of a tributary of the Shyok, flowing down south from the Dipsang plain. No fuel or forage procurable. Road very narrow and difficult, and risky from stone avalanches. Follow up course of stream and cross it repeatedly by narrow fords; it flowed as a raging torrent, rolling over great boulders in a fight winding gorge, then quit the river, and pass over projecting bluffs, joining it again at 11 miles and follow it up to Kizi Langar. At 13 miles pass Bartsi or Borsa camping ground on a gravelly talus shelving to the stream.

9. Daolat Beguldi

Camping ground at north-west corner of Dipsang plain. Continue upstream, path still difficult, and at 6 miles ascend up steep and stoney gorge to the Dipsang plain (17,800 feet), about 18 miles broad, cross this bleak, barren, undulating plateau, from which the world around subsides, the highest hill tops only appearing above the horizon. Soil soft, and spongey, gravel and clay mixed, and water-logged at places, boggy, breathing distressed. From plateau descend into a wide deep gully. Cross shallow stream with muddy bottom, in which cattle stick, and from it ascend to the Daolat Beguldi plateau.

10. Balti Brangsa or Brangsa Karakoram

Camping ground at north base of Karakoram pass, and left of a sandy ravine. Large rock here used as a shelter by travellers. No grass or fuel. Gradual rise to foot of Karakoram (18,550 ft.), which was crossed at 11 miles. Breathing difficult, surface bare gravel and clay, ascent sudden and steep. Descent also short and steep, and then gradual down a shingly gulley to Balti Brangsa. Pass Chajosh Jilga camp at 12 miles. Near the summit of the pass three streams rise, one runs down to the west and south, the second to the south, and the third was the source of the Yarkand river; snow in winter only on the pass; road nearly always open. Many beasts of burden (ponies and horses) succumbed to fatigue and difficulty in breathing. The pass was throughout passable for laden horses.

11. Malikshah or Aktagh

Camping ground righ^t^ bank Yarkand river. No wood or grass and no water from end of October to end of April. Road followed down course of a wide shingly gulley. Pass Kiziltagh, Chadartash, and Wahab Jilga camps. Later at 14 miles, where the Aktagh stream flowed through a cutting in slate rocks. Vegetation was most scanty is herbal tufts; a few antelopes found. From this down stream was the winter route via the Yang Diwan and Kugiar to Yarkand. The Changchenmo route joined in at Malikshah. On this march this road was good, and there was little snow in winter.

12. Chibra

A few stone enclosures in which travellers rest for the night at foot of Suget Pass; cold usually intense; no grass or fuel; water scarce. Proceed north over an elevated, arid, stoney plateau, a desert, gradually ascending. Breathing oppressed on this march. This whole region is a bleak, desolate and inhospitable waste.

13. Suget

Camp ground, right bank Suget stream, close to its junction with the Karakash, in an open wide valley. Grass and wood abundant; the grazing ground was much used by traders. Ascent gradual for 6 miles to top of Suget Diwan Pass (17,610 ft.). Snow covered from September to April; and the breathing of men and animals were much affected. Descent at first steep into a ravine. Then over high moraine banks of granite boulders and across slope of a hill to Suget. Pass Kutas Jilga at about 6 miles.

14. Shahidula Khoja

Camping ground, left bank Karakash. Small fort with garrison was there. Fuel and grass here, and Kirghiz camps around. The road from Suget followed the course of the Suget stream, crossing it several times; at 4 miles it joined the Karakash, crossed and then kept the right bank of the latter to opposite Shahidula. The Kugiar route could be joined from here by following up the stream that flowed down east from the Kirghiz pass. It was 2 marches to Kirghiz jungle.

This route was open for 4 to 5 months.

Facilities Available at the Stages of Leh to Yarkand Route

Stage	*S*	*T*	*F*	*G*	*E*	*W*	*C*	*P*	*Scanty*
1	*2*	*3*	*4*	*5*	*6*	*7*	*8*	*9*	*10*
Shahidulla	✓	✓	✓	✓	✓	✓	—	—	✓
Kilian kurghan	—	—	✓	✓	✓	✓	—	—	—
Bostan	—	—	✓	✓	✓	✓	—	—	✓
Karachaglan	—	—	—	—	✓	✓	—	—	—

(Continued on the next page)

Continued

1	2	3	4	5	6	7	8	9	10
Chush-kum	—	—	—	✓	✓	✓	—	—	✓
Lamlung Mazar	—	—	—	✓	✓	✓	—	—	✓
Akshor	—	—	✓	✓	✓	✓	—	—	—
Kilianbazar	✓	✓	✓	✓	✓	✓	—	—	—
Bash-Langar	—	—	—	✓	✓	✓	—	—	—
Oi-toghrak	—	—	—	✓	✓	✓	—	—	—
Bora Oasis	—	—	—	✓	✓	✓	—	—	—
Karghalik	✓	✓	✓	✓	✓	✓	✓	—	—
Posgam	✓	✓	✓	✓	✓	✓	—	—	—
Yarkand	✓	✓	✓	✓	✓	✓	✓	✓	✓

R : River; M : Miles; C : Caravan Serai; E : Encamping Ground; F : Fuel; G : Grass, Grazing; S : Supplies; T : Transport; PO : Post Office.

Import from Yarkand

The chief imports from Yarkand were woollen products such as items made from lambs wool, camel hair, dried sheepskins for cloaks, a small quantity of shawl-wool, fine tea, yambo silver, steel for the formation of chakmaks, boots, Russian leather, brocades, velvets, broadcloth of Russian manufacture, horses and drugs. The greater portion of these imports were for Punjab.[14]

Yarkand or yar-kiang situated beyond the Pamer or Karakoram mountains at the bank of river was of considerable importance, being the centre of commerce among Turkistan, China, Tibet and Russia. In 1820 A.D. it had population between fifty to sixty thousand consisting of Muslim Tajiks, Turks and Uzbeks. Before 1760 A.D. it was under Uzbeks thereafter it was occupied by China. During the first quarter of the nineteenth century the imports of shawl-wool in Kashmir via Ladakh varied between 1.5 lakh lbs to 3.0 lakh lb. annually. This wool was imported from Tibet, Ladakh (The Chang-Thang region) and Yarkand. The average daily earnings of shawl weavers ranged between Rs. 1.5 to Rs. 5. Thus the shawl produced from this wool had very good demand in European countries such as France, England, etc.[15]

Alexander Cunningham of British East India Company, Calcutta visited Ladakh in 1846 mentioned in his book *Ladak* (physical, statistical and historical) that a considerable quantity of shawl-wool, tea, charas, tobacco and silver in ingots or bars was annually brought into Ladakh by Yarkandis as shown below:[16]

		Import from Yarkand	
1.	Shawl-wool	Rs.	28,000
2.	Tea	Rs.	48,000
3.	Tobacco	Rs.	64,000
4.	Charas	Rs.	24,000
	Total	Rs.	164,000
	Add: Ponies, sugar-candy, drugy, skins, turquoises	Rs.	16,000
		Rs.	180,000

Each silver ingot called yambu or kuru was worth Rs. 166, constantly being brought into Ladakh from Yarkand which was after exported to Bisahar paying half a rupee per ingot duty in Ladakh. Further details of Import duty on Yarkandi goods during 1846-47 is shown below:[17]

Sl. No.	*Imported Articles from Yarkand*	*Import duty* *Rs.*	*A*	*P*
1.	Charas, per maund	2	4	0
2.	Wool	2	4	0
3.	Tea	0	8	0
4.	Cloth	0	8	0

Notes: Rs = Rupee
A = Anna (one Anna was equal to 6 paise and 16 Annas was equal to one Rupee)
P = Paise

Charas

In India it is popularly known as *Bhang*. It had very good demand in Hindustan. About 500 maunds were annually imported in Ladakh from Yarkand which valued Rs. 24,000 or £ 2,400. Surprisingly that sixty per cent was consumed in Ladakh and only 40 per cent was further exported to the neighbouring countries. In my opinion the reason of such big consumption of charas in Ladakh was due to the presence of Indian traders, Dogras, etc.[18]

Tobacco

Like Charas tobacco was also consumed in a big way in Ladakh. Therefore, it was imported largely from Yarkand, the annual supply was 4,000 maunds or 1,28,000 lb. in 1846. The average price of tobacco at Leh was one rupee per seer and the value of the whole import was Rs. 64,000 or £ 6,400 in 1846.[19]

Opium

It was the chief article of trade between India through Ladakh to Yarkand. The annual supply was 500 maunds. In 1846 it had valued Rs. 1,20,000 at the rate of Rs. 15 per seer.[20]

Shawl

The finest shawl was manufactured in Kashmir but some coarse material shawls of cheap rate about Rs. 50 per pair could be imported.

Export to Yarkand

Indian articles were mostly carried to Yarkand through Ladakh. Alexander Cunningham made a list of those articles which were exported to Yarkand.[21]

1. Laki, goat-skins dyed red, the article was exported to Yarkand from Nurpur through Ladakh
2. Cottons, flowered (chicken)
3. Cottons, coarse (ghara)
4. Cottons, thin (gaji)
5. Chintzens of all kinds
6. Silk, lungi of Multan
7. Shawls, mostly coarse
8. Jamawar or Shawl-cloth
9. Brocades, mostly coarse
10. Turbans
11. Opium
12. Indigo
13. Heron-plumes, kalgi, generally of the feathers of the jugul fowl
14. Shoes from Nurpur
15. Pearls of all sizes up to one hundred rupees each
16. Other skins
17. Turmeric
18. Cardamoms
19. Ginger

20. Cloves
21. Black pepper
22. Honey
23. Tamarinds, dry
24. Sherbet, lemon
25. Coarse Sugar, Gur
26. Narcachor, the root of a reed, used both as a scent and as a medicine. It is the common Narket or Nalkand (Curcuma Zerumbat), in Hindi we call it Narkat and in Sanskrit Nalkand.
27. Turban, convolvulus Turpethum, or Turbith, a purgative root
28. Habilistan
29. Khurma chhuhara, dates
30. Salt.

Laki

Nurpur leather products had good demand in Yarkand. The red bright coloured leathers were generally exported to Yarkand from Nurpur via Ladakh. For the manufacture of boots bridles and trappings of horses, about 200 maunds skin was annually imported into Ladakh. In 1846 it worth Rs. 6,400. Half of this quantity was later exported to Yarkand.[21]

Spices

India was famous for spices throughout the world. Spices to the value of about Rs. 1000 were annually imported in Ladakh of which 80 per cent were exported to Yarkand.[22]

Saffron

Kashmir was the centre of saffron. Annually 20 maunds at the rate of forty rupees per seer of the worth of Rs. 12,800 was exported to Yarkand through Ladakh.[23]

Cloth

Annually 100 maunds cloth of the value of Rs. 10,000 came to Ladakh and 90 per cent was exported to Yarkand.[24]

Export Duty

All the articles which were exported through Ladakh had to pay export duty in Ladakh. In 1846 the export duty was charged in the following way:[25]

Sl. No.	*Articles Exported through Ladakh*	*Export duty* *Rs.*	*A*	*P*
1.	Cloth, Laki per maund	0	4	0
2.	Opium	0	4	0

Thus, Ladakh was a border country and was very important for export and import from India to Yarkand. Yarkand was a famous mundi for carpet industry, besides charas, tobacco, opium, wool were exported to India and its neighbouring countries. The important items of export consisted of: leather, cotton, shawls, sugar, gur, etc. These articles were exported from India through Ladakh to Yarkand.

REFERENCES

1. Joldan, E.: *Harvest Festival of Buddhist Dards of Ladakh and Other Essays*, Kapoor Brothers, Srinagar, 1985, p. 68.
2. *Ibid.*
3. *Ibid.*
4. *Ibid.*, p. 69.
5. *Ibid.*, p. 60 and quoted from the book of Henry Lansdell who travelled through Sinkiang to Leh via Russia in 1888.
6. *Ibid.*
7. Jina, Prem Singh: 'Ladakh and Central Asian Trade during 1825-1925', In: *Recent Researchers on the Himalaya*, Prem Singh Jina (ed.), Indus Pub., Co. New Delhi, 1997, pp. 130-31 and *Gazetteer of Kashmir and Ladak*, pp. 563-64.
8. *Gazetteer of Kashmir and Ladak*, p. 564.
9. *Ibid.*, pp. 564-65.
10. *Ibid.*, p. 565.
11. *Ibid.*, p. 566 and quoted from Ramsay, H.L., *Western Tibet: A Practical Dictionary of the Language and Customs of the Districts Included in the Ladakh Wazarat*, Lahore, 1890.
12. Joldan, E.; *op.cit.*, p. 62.
13. Drew, Frederic.
14. Moorcroft, W & Trebeck, George : *Travels in Hindustan*; Sagar Pub., New Delhi (Reprint in India 1971), p. 356. Moorcroft was in Ladakh during 1820-21 A.D.
15. *Ibid.*, pp. 165-366.

16. Cunningham, Alexander: *Ladak,* Sagar Pub., New Delhi, (First Print in 1854), pp. 252-53.
17. *Ibid.*, pp. 249-53.
18. *Ibid.*, p. 241.
19. *Ibid.*
20. *Ibid.*
21. *Ibid.*
22. *Ibid.*
23. *Ibid.*
24. *Ibid.*, p. 247.
25. *Ibid.*, p. 249.

8

HINDU TRADERS IN LADAKH AND CENTRAL ASIAN COUNTRIES

The Hindu traders from Hoshiarpur in Punjab carried on trade to Yarkand and Turkistan through Ladakh. During 18th century they had business with China and carried their goods through the silk route to China. The Lalas who were in this business were Lala Shadi Lal Sud, Dina Nath, Bishembar Das, Biharilal Rulia Ram, Het Ram, Bansi Lal, Gori Mal Gohal, Fakeer Chand, Rai Sahib and Butamal Dogarmal. They brought their commodities from Karachi and Calcutta to Ladakh and then exported to Yarkand other Chinese territories. Among the articles which they exported to Yarkand were:

1. Cottons of different varieties.
2. Sewing machines
3. Dyes
4. Clothes.

They exchanged the above commodities with gold and silver. In those days gold was imported in the shape of dust, gold dust and pashmin wool were imported from Tibet. The gold dust had more than 75 per cent purity. They later carried the imported items to Amritsar for manufacture of shawl and ornaments. Thus Karachi, Calcutta, and Amritsar were the main *mundies* in Hindustan plains, whereas Tibet and Yarkand were the main markets in Central Asia. Till 1947 Sadilal Dawarkanath was the main firm which had large scale import and export business with Yarkand, Lhasa and even with some territories of China. It had offices at Leh, Srinagar, Amritsar and at Yarkand. The following officials were the head of the respective offices:

1. Sitaram Dawarkanath at Amritsar
2. Pt. Om Prakash and Pt. Kisorilal at Srinagar
3. Pt. Hirdaram and Pt. Hakuram at Leh
4. Pt. Biharilal at Yarkand

Besides Lala Hetram, Lajpat Rai, Lala Cintram, Khushi Ram, Sadilal, Nanakchand Devraj Sethi also came for business during the late nineteenth century or in the mid twentieth century. Thereafter some more Hindu traders came from Jammu. Among them Agrawal traders were famous.

In 1939 for the welfare of Hindu traders Shadilal firm constructed a Dharmshala at the heart of the Leh. It is called 'Hindu Dharmshala'. According to E. Joldan, Lala Nand Lal of Hoshiarpur had trade with Sinkiang and Yarkand, traders. He remarks:

"Central Asia Traders would get their foreign goods such as dyes, cloth, etc., either direct from Bombay, the port of landing, or from Amritsar from wholesale dealers and send them to Srinagar in big packages, through their commission agents. Take, as an example, Lala Nand Lal of Hoshiarpur who trades with Sinkiang through his two employees, Bishambar Das and his son Dina Nath. They were called Gumashtas. Nand Lal sends 50 maunds of invoice goods to Srinagar, where Dina Nath is waiting for them in the Yarkandi Serai, at Safakadal. When the goods and papers pertaining to customs duties are received, he repacks the goods into smaller bundles, each weighing one maund and ten seers, because as already stated, the maximum pony load is 2½ maunds (92 kilograms). He sends, these 50 bundles of invoice goods on 20 ponies and himself proceeds to Leh on the Res ponies"[1]

In those days Charas officer checked the goods for exporting them to Central Asian countries such as Sinkiang, Yarkand, etc. As said earlier Lala Nand Lal was having good business with Sinkiang. Remembering one incident of Lala Nand Lal, trade activities at Leh, Joldan says:

"When he reaches Leh, he goes to the Charas officer to inform that he would be leaving for Yarkand soon, with 80 bundles of invoiced goods. In the meantime, a caravan of 20 horses has arrived from Sinkiang and Dina Nath negotiates with the Caravan Bash to carry his goods to Yarkand after a week. One or two days before departure for Sinkiang Dina Nath goes to the Charas officer again to inform that the caravan is ready and they would be leaving on 28th of August. He is accompanied by Bishambar Nath who runs a shop in Leh. Dina Nath requests the Charas officer to issue the required certificate to Bishambar Das soon. Charas officer after ascertaining from the North Gate clerk that the goods have left for Sinkiang, issues the certificate to Bishambar Das. He sends it to Nand Lal at Hoshiarpur, who in due course, collects from the concerned authorities the amount of custom duty back. Such foreign made goods which were actually exported to Central Asia were known as invoice or custom bound goods. This concession was meant to encourage trade with Central Asia."[2]

Later according to the negotiation with Bash, Dina Nath's ten bundles were loaded on six Yaks. E. Joldan writes:

"Dina Nath being an orthodox Hindu, carries his pots and pans as he would be doing his own cooking during the journey. The caravan has provided Dina Nath a yak to ride on the High Khardong pass. He would require 6 yaks to transport the 10 bundles of Dina Nath upto Panamik. So he has hired 6 yaks."[3]

Khardong pass is 18,380 ft. from the sea level, so sometimes traders from Punjab or Indian plains felt mountain sickness and to protect their eyes from sunlight reflection by snow, it was advisable to carry some tablets of Asprin for headache and sun goggles for their eyes. Keeping in view these facts, Dina Nath carried Asprin tablets and sun glasses with him while marching towards high mountain trade route from Leh to Sinkiang. E. Joldan said about his experiences with Dina Nath:

"There is nothing like a ride on the sure-footed yak, lead by the owner, by its nose string. The pace is slow but steady. Near the top it is windy so Dina Nath puts on his eye goggles and takes 2 Asprin tablets as he feels headache. It is what we call mountain sickness. As the sun sets, they reach Khardong village on the other side of the mountain."[4]

On the way to Yarkand, Yshyok river at Koyak in Nubra was a big problem for Dina Nath and his other members as there was no bridge. Before 1920 caravans passed through the bridge, but due to the mighty Khomdan flood in the late 1920s it washed away. However, after 1933 bridge was reconstructed. Dina Nath used two big boats to cross the river, but the horses forded easily as the river was not swollen. Thereafter Dina Nath's caravan halted for 2 or 3 days and made the final preparation for the long journey ahead. In those days at Leh there were good demands of *Nals* (horse shoe) as all the traders needed *Nals* for their horses. Here each servant of the carvan had been alloted various duties such as to look after Nals and prevent them from straying, etc. E. Joldan remarked:

"At Panamik the caravan makes a halt for 2 or 3 days to rest and make final preparations for the long and bleak journey ahead. Each of the servants would mend the saddery, etc., of the 5 horses under his charge and with the help of another man examine all the hoofs of the horses. If a shoe is missing, he would shod a new one with six nails. The hoof would first be placed on a small wooden board and with a big file he would file away some parts, here and there. With a sharp-edged instrument he would chip away small pieces to fit the horse-shoe well. Then with his small hammer he would drive in the nails in the holes, at a slightly oblique angle, so that the nails would come out of the hoof in the middle. The ends of the nails would be cut away with another instrument. The horse would now have a new shoe. When a camping site is reached, after unloading, the horses would be tied in pairs in opposite directions— one's head and the other's tail, ensure that they do not stray away and drink water which sometimes make them sick. When the perspired body is dry, each horse is fed barley grain in a goat-hair bag called *Tobra*, with its muzzle in it. As there is no human habitation after Panamik till the caravan reaches Suget Karol on the other side of the Karakoram, the horses are mainly fed on grain. Even if there are some pastures, the Yarkandi horses are not used to grazing when the grass is poor."[5]

The journey between Panamik to Depsang plateau was four days, thereafter two days continuous ascending journey, Dina Nath reached at the foot of Karakoram, then to the top of the pass of 19,000 feet. Finally after 12 days marched from Suget Karol, he and his party reached Hinu Serai at Yarkand where his officials welcomed him. Dina on his returning journey to Hoshiarpur brought 10 bundles charas on 5 horses and sold them to licensed dealers. E. Joldan narrates:

"After 12 days march from Suget Karol, Dina Nath reaches the Hindu Serai in Yarkand. Dina Nath is welcomed by another Panjabi employee of his master who stays there more or less permanently, to look after the trade—mainly to collect charas, which constitutes the main item of their export to India. He has purchased in small quantities the narcotic drug from farmers, graded them into three qualities, got them processed and packed them in strong donkey hides, ablong in shape, each bundle weighing more or less one maund and ten seer. The processed charas is rather a sticky brownish substance with a peculiar smell. The number of bundles collected in Yarkand is 6. Dina Nath purchases 4 more bundles at Karghalik to make the total 10 for 5 horses. Also 22 horse-loads of raw silk thread and carpets. By June, 1932 he is ready to leave for Leh with a caravan of 20 horses."[6]

Hindu traders were involved in charas, silk and carpet business, they imported these things from Yarkand, Karghalik and Sinkiang and sold them to the wholesale dealers in Hoshiarpur, which was under Punjab State. In Ladakh, Panamik and Leh were the main check posts where charas clerk inspected the charas bundles and issued a chit, thereafter charas officer issued a certificate. E. Joldan explains the details as:

"At Panamik, the charas clerk inspects the 10 bundles and issues a chit. Reaching Leh, while Dina Nath gets all the details of his goods entered in the register by the North gate Munshi, his father Bishembar Das and the caravan men take the charas bundles direct to the charas office premises, and unload them there. The charas officer, two clerks, a weigh man, 4 peons and a chowkidar (were in the charas office). The office was probably opened during the early years of this century. The charas officer ordered to inspect the 10 bundles. If any bundle is found damaged he would get it mended by grafting fresh patches of sheep skin by semi-skilled coolies, at the expense of Dina Nath. Each bundle would be weighed by the charas weigh-man, in the big wooden pass attached with iron chains to the tripoled scale. All the bundles would now be stored in the godown."[7]

The import of charas was controlled by the British Commissioner. The Punjab Government deputed charas officers in order to help British Commissioner to control the possible theft of narcotic drug. In this connection from 1920 onwards Punjab Government deputed the following charas officers.[8]

1. Byramji (a Parsi)
2. Khan Bahadur Ghulam Mohammed
3. Mian Amir-Din

4. Khan Bahadur Ashraf Khan
5. Mr. Gautama

When the charas bundles reached Hoshiarpur, they were stored in a government warehouse and thereafter sold to concern dealers. E. Joldan writes:

"The ten bundles of charas would ultimately reach Hoshiarpur where they would be stored in a government warehouse. Nand Lal would sell a bundle to a licensed dealer in narcotic who would pay the cost to the owner but the custom duty to the Government which according to Shadi Lal Gohal would be more than a 1000 rupees."[8]

In the charas office there were two gates known as the North and the South gates, two Munshis were at these gates checked the import and export items. E. Joldan made the following details:

"There were two Munshis at the North and the South gates, the traders or their agents or the pony-owners were required to give them the details of the merchandise. The two Munshis submitted a date-wise monthly report, on fullscape sheets of paper, in red and blue ink to the charas office which maintained the record of all trade passing through Leh to Central Asia and coming down from there."[9]

Normally the register of import and export was maintained in the following way:[10]

Sl. No.	*Date*	*Item*	*Import/Export*	*Belonging*
1.	Ist Sept. 1928	14 bundles of raw silk thread	Import from Sinkiang	Karim Haji through Sabir Akhoom Caravan Bash.
2.	Ist Sept. 1928	8 bundles of raw silk thread	Export to Punjab via Kulu/Srinagar	Rullia Ram

Source : Joldan, E.; *op. cit.*, p. 77.

The above register then submitted to the British Joint Commissioner with complete details of six months statement.[11]

In Punjab, Hoshiarpur was a well-developed market, where cotton cloth dealers, dyers, confectioners, grainsellers, and turners in wood were involved in large scale business with India and foreign (i.e. Central Asian) countries. The maximum Punjab trade of import and export with Central Asian countries were looked after by Hindu traders. Willian Moorcroft and George Trebek who visited during 1820-24 write:

"Hoshiarpur is a large and populous town surrounded by a brick wall, separated from another town, Bahadarpur, by a few fields only; the latter, however, is nearly uninhabited. The population of Hoshiarpur consists chiefly of weavers, dyers, confectioners, grainsellers, and turners in wood. The weavers are almost all Mohammadans, and are an orderly and industrious set of people. They are employed extensively in the manufacture of cotton cloths and muslins, which are sent to distant markets in various directions; as white cloths to Delhi, white and red to Jaipur and Bikaner; coarse cottons to the Punjab and Kabul and the finer sorts to Herat, Balkh, Bokhara and Yarkand. The water of Hoshiarpur is said to be of great efficacy in whitening cloths."[12]

Hindu traders carried merchandise from Ladakh to Hoshiarpur. From Tibet they chiefly transported wool through Ladakh and used well trained ponies and sheep. Moreover, sheep were preferred for carrying grain. Moorcroft and Trebeck write:

"The inhabitants of this part of the country are much employed as carriers between Chamba, Kulu and Ladakh, transporting merchandise from the latter country, chiefly wool, on ponies about thirteen hand high, well made, strong and well trained to the peculiarities of mountain carriage. Sheep are also used to carry grain and goods. The hire of a pony from Tandi to Le' was ordinarily eleven rupees, each carrying two paka maunds; we were made to pay thirteen rupees. Although the charge was high, yet, as supplies were not likely to be abundant on the road, and grain is ordinarily dear in Ladakh. I laid in a considerable quantity of wheat flour at Tandi, and engaged carriers and ponies for its transport."

The Hindu traders of Hoshiarpur normally followed the Keylong to Leh route through Rupshu. The route was opened from June to October. Yaks were recognised the best transport for the journey. Traders were given all kinds of assistance by the British Commissioner at Leh. Keylong was the tehsil and during summer Wazir resided here to look after the trade affairs. Here follow the details:

Keylong to Leh Route

Stage	*Iter miles*	*Nature of Journey to Next Stage*
(1)	*(2)*	*(3)*
Keylong; 10,100 ft.	—	Road zig zag and ascends up the western side of the Bhaga valley.
Jispa	13.5	Road fair, Pass Keda Tokpo Br. and Keylong m 10. Pass Darcha.
Patseo; 12,464 ft.	10.25	A market for Kulu, Tibetan and Lahul traders. Road up Bhaga valley.
Zing-Zingbar; 14,000 ft.	6.25	Reach Surajdul lake, m 4. Ascend Baralacha La, 16,200 ft. m 6. Descend to Yuman Tso.
Keylong; 15,120 ft.	12	Road easy. Descend through open Yunan valley
Sarchu; 13,950 ft.	11	Track down Tsarap valley.
Rachog-ba; 13,400 ft.	10	Track through Tsarap valley. Pass Gian, m.2.
Sumdo; 15,520 ft.	9	Ascend Lacha lung la; 16,600 ft. m. 4. Further descend.
Pang; 15,200 ft.	16	Cross another pass; 16,630 ft. Descend. Walk over more plain.
Rogchin (Rukchin); 15,300 ft.	19	Sometimes Changpa camp. Path up Debring valley.
Debring; 15,780 ft.	14	Changpa camp. Yaks from here for further journey. Ascend up Debring ravine to Tangalang La; 17,500 ft. m. 4. Descend to Gya:
Gya; 13,500 ft.	15	Village. S (granary). Track through Gya ravine. Pass Latho, m. 4, and Miru, m. 10.
Upshi; 11,900 ft.	16	Village. Pass Ugu, m. 5. Cross Shang Br.
Marsalang; 11,500 ft.	10	Village and Hemis Monastery 2 miles further inside ravine. Road through sandy plain.
Shushot; 10,750 ft.	13	Village. Sometimes journey tiring, cross Indus at Choglamsar, m. 8.

Source: Arora, R.C.: '*In the Land of Kashmir; Ladakh and Gilgit*; Jay Kay Book House; (Reprint 1996), pp. 178-79.

Facilities Provided along the Keylong to Leh Route

Stage	*S*	*T*	*F*	*G*	*W*	*RH*	*E*	*C*	*PO*	*TO*	*Dispy*	*Scanty*
	1	*2*	*3*	*4*	*5*	*6*	*7*	*8*	*9*	*10*	*11*	*12*
Keylong	✓	✓	✓	✓	✓	✓	✓	✓	✓	✓	✓	—
Jispa	✓	✓	✓	✓	✓	✓	✓	—	—	—	—	—
Patseo	✓	✓	✓	✓	✓	✓	✓	—	—	—	—	—
Zing-Zingbar	—	—	✓	✓	✓	—	✓	✓	—	—	—	✓
Kinlung	—	—	✓	✓	—	—	✓	✓	—	—	—	✓
Sarchu	—	—	—	✓	✓	—	✓	—	—	—	—	✓
Rachog-ba	—	—	✓	✓	✓	—	✓	—	—	—	—	✓

(Continued on the next page)

(Continued)

	1	*2*	*3*	*4*	*5*	*6*	*7*	*8*	*9*	*10*	*11*	*12*
Sumdo	—	—	—	—	✓	—	✓	—	—	—	—	—
Pang	—	—	—	—	✓	—	✓	—	—	—	—	—
Rukchin	—	—	✓	✓	✓	—	✓	—	—	—	—	✓
Debring	✓	✓	✓	✓	✓	—	✓	—	—	—	—	✓
Gya	—	✓	✓	✓	✓	—	✓	✓	—	—	—	—
Upshi	✓	✓	✓	✓	✓	—	✓	✓	—	—	—	✓
Marsalang	—	✓	✓	✓	✓	—	✓	✓	—	—	—	✓
Shushot	✓	✓	✓	✓	✓	—	✓	✓	—	—	—	—
Leh	✓	✓	✓	✓	✓	✓	✓	✓	✓	✓	✓	✓

Abbreviations

Br : Bridge
TO : Telegraph Office
C : Caravan Serai
Dispy : Dispensary
E : Encamping ground
F : Fuel
G : Grass, grazing
M : Mile
PO : Post Office
RH : Rest house
S : Supplies
T : Transport

In conclusion Hindu traders had their shops at Leh, Yarkand, Srinagar. Nand Lal, Bishambar, Dina Nath and Sadhilal were among some important traders from Hoshiarpur who were involved in Invoice trade (i.e. custom bound goods). They exported cloth and dyes to Yarkand through Ladakh. From Yarkand they carried charas, gold dust, silver and silk to Hoshiarpur. Sometimes, traders gave their orders well in advance to Yarkandi weavers to manufacture carpets. Like Nand Lal; Sadhilal had offices in Leh, Yarkand and Srinagar. He had managers in these places who looked after trade and through their shops they exchanged Indian goods such as cloth, dyes, etc., with gold, silver, precious stones, carpets, silk, etc. Some Hindu traders were having good business with Tibetans. The Tibetan articles offered to them were wool, yak's tail with flour, spices, etc. Among wool item Hindu traders were mostly interested in Pashmina wool items and Posish wool. It is said that in 1947 when Pakistan attacked Ladakh, Sadhilal's firm supplied all possible things to army and even when in 1948 Indian Air Force was unable to land their aeroplanes on Leh Airport because of the invisibility of runway, Sadhilal's firm supplied white cotton for the whole runway free of charge to Air Force authorities. Thus, enabling Indian aeroplanes to land over the Leh Airport facilitating in the victory of Ladakh from Pakistani forces. Besides, Sadhilal's firm was responsible in giving state employees salary, because they normally did not get their salaries in time. However, after receiving State Government grants the firm received the same amount later on. Thus, Hindu traders had great contribution in the Ladakh economy.

REFERENCES

1. Joldan, E.: *Harvest Festival of Buddhist Dards of Ladakh and other Essays*, Kapoor Brothers, 1985, p. 72.
2. *Ibid.*, pp. 72-73.
3. *Ibid.*
4. *Ibid.*, p. 73.
5. *Ibid.*, p. 74.
6. *Ibid.*, p. 75.
7. *Ibid.*, pp. 75-76.
8. *Ibid.*
9. *Ibid.*, p. 77.
10. *Ibid.*
11. *Ibid.*
12. Moorcroft, William and Treback, George: *Travels in Hindustan*, Vol. I, p. 84.
13. *Ibid.*, p. 198.

9

TURKIS AND TRADE THROUGH LADAKH

In Ladakh Turki caravan consisted of two groups—one of Haj pilgrims and the other of traders. The Haj pilgrims would sell their goods like gold, silver and precious stones so as to meet the expenses of their ongoing journey. The Turki traders traded in their *namdas*, carpets, cotton mattresses and velvet covers. E. Joldan says:

"There were two caravan Serais in Leh the accommodation of the Central Asian Turki traders and Haj pilgrims, probably got constructed by Johnson, The Governor of Kashmir Maharaja from 1822 to 1890. The bigger one was located where the police station is built now. In the upper part of the premises there was a double-storeyed 'L' shaped building. Each of the ground floor room had a small varandha with two mud-brick plastered platforms and the Turki traders would spread their *namdas*, carpets and lightly—cotton-padded matresses with velvet covers."[1]

Among Turki traders one Aksakal was appointed by British India Government as British consulate at Leh, similarly in 1890 Aksakals were appointed in Yarkand, Kargalik, Guma in Sinkiang and in Srinagar. Aksakal is a Turki word which means white beard and hence recognised as elderly respectable officer. In Leh he was seated in the middle of the compound with his clerk on carpet under the shade of the poplar tree. Many Yarkandi traders met him there and solved their trade related problems.[2]

The Turki traders came to Ladakh through the caravan road over the Karakoram pass which was connecting Eastern Turkistan with Ladakh. However, their were three famous routes which were known as the 'Silk Route', the first route was from Kashgar to Gilgit over the Hindukush via Nagar and Hunza. The second route was from

Kashgar via Yarkand to Skardu (winter capital of Ladakh) the third being from Kashgar via Yarkand to Leh. Thus, Eastern Turkistan known as Sinkiang had trade routes with Hindustan and not with Tibet because of the Gobi desert, which was a big obstacle for the traders to cover, being without water and grass and other supply facilities.[3]

In 1873-74, Kishan Singh made 380 kilometre long route survey of Yarkand and Kashgar. He discovered that there was a direct route linking Turkistan with India which was free of snow in summer months.[4] This indicates that traders probably came to Ladakh through this route as discovered by Kishan Singh, yet, it was not well surveyed by any earlier authority. Hence, possibly when the trade route between Ladakh and Turkistan was indicated through maps, trade activities between these countries started developing. And in the beginning of twentieth century it was well developed.

In 1935, fractional fightings broke out in Sinkiang. A defeated faction along with their army leader Ma-Si-Jung came to seek refuge in India. Ladakhis called them Tungans (Chinese Muslims). They mostly came from Northern Sinkiang near Urimchi. Their numbers were about three hundred. E. Joldan remarks:

"The next one came from Sinkiang in 1935 and Ladakhis called them Tungans (Chinese Muslims) but most of them were Turki soldiers. There were factional fightings in Sinkiang again and a defeated faction, along with their army leader, Ma-Si-Jung came to seek refuge in India. They mostly came from Northern Sinkiang near Urimchi, the capital. Lu-Jang and Thung Jang were other two officers. The local clerk dealing with Tungan Affairs in Leh (said) their total number was about 300. They came with their arms and trained horses, the arms were confiscated by the state authorities on arrival in Leh. Among other things, they brought gold in dust form, in bullion, and Russian gold coins, silver bars and some final special kinds of Chinese rugs."[5]

In 1950 again revolution took place. This time Turks came for refuge from Eastern Turkistan and crossing Karakoram range they came to Ladakh. Prominent among them were Mohammed Amin Beg Bughra, Governor of Turkistan and Mohammed Isa Affendi, a Turki minister.[6]

Many Turki refugees started cobbler works along the streets of

Leh market, others married Ladakhi women and settled in Leh, and engaged in trade and adventurous jobs with European explorers. They are often are known as Argons. Whenever European explorers came in Ladakh for the unexplored parts of Central Asian countries they preferred to employ Argons in their caravan as they could speak Turki and Tibetan languages. They worked as grooms, cooks and orderlies. Most of the servants were grooms to look after the transport ponies, horses and mules, feeding and grazing them, to see that the horse's shoes are in order, shodding new ones whenever necessary, mending the saddle, for which they would always carry dangling by their sash or belt, a sharp long knife in a skin cover and big needles in another, packing, loading and unloading the ponies and pitching the tents would be other work they had to do.[7]

According to Hajmattullaha—The town of Ladakh, Leh was a market of Turkistan (Chinese) and Lhasa traders on one side and Kashmiri, Hindustani traders on the other. It was barter market. Traders from Chinese Turkistan carried Chinese namdas, cloth, silk, carpets and charas.[8] Thus the total import from the Chinese territories during 1846-47 was to the tune of Rs. 2,67,650 (Table: 9.1).

TABLE 9.1

Import from the Chinese Territories in Ladakh

Articles	*Quantity*		*Value*			*% of the total*
	Maund	*lb*	*Rate/seer*	*Rs*	*£*	
1	*2*	*3*	*4*	*5*	*6*	*7*
Shawl-wool	4,000	1,28,000	200	1,28,000	12,800	47.82
Wool	1,000	32,000	020	2,000	200	00.74
Tea	1,000	32,000	300	48,000	4,800	17.93
Charas	500	14,000	300	24,000	2,400	08.97
Tobacco	4,000	1,28,000	100	64,000	6,400	23.92
Borax	2,500	80,000	006	1,250	125	00.47
Sulphur	400	12,800	010	400	40	00.15
Total	13,400	4,28,000	—	2,67,650	26,765	100.00

Source: Cunningham, Alexander: *Ladak*, Sagar Pub., New Delhi, p. 249.

Table 9.1 reveals that during 1846-47 about 48 per cent of the annual imports belonged to shawl-wool and 24 per cent to tobacco. Thus 33 per cent charas and tobacco was imported through Ladakh to Punjab. Tea was also an imported item about 10 per cent tea of the total imports from Chinese territories to Ladakh and maximum of it was consumed in Ladakh. Every year Ladakh earned Rs. 7,350 annually from the Chinese imports. Table 9.2 shows the details.

TABLE 9.2

Import Duty of Chinese Commodities during 1846-47

Articles	*Import duty Rate/maunds*	*Rs*	*£*	*% of the total*
Shawl-wool	080	2,000	200	27.21
Wool	080	500	50	06.80
Tea	020	2,000	200	27.27
Charas	240	1,125	112.5	15.30
Tobacco	040	1,000	100	13.62
Borax	040	625	62.5	8.50
Sulpher	040	100	10	1.36
Total	—	7,350	735	100.00

Source: Cunningham, Alexander; *op. cit.*, p. 249.

Table 9.2 reveals that Ladakh earned good income from shawl-wool and tea. Around 54.42 per cent of the total import duty on Chinese commodities was earned from these two goods. The second imported item from Chinese territories was charas and earned 15.30 per cent of the total import duty.

Among exports to Turkistan and other territories of China were opium, shawls, brocades, laki, etc. Table 9.3 shows the details.

TABLE 9.3

Export to the Chinese Territories during 1846-47

Articles	*Quantity*			*Value*		*% of the total*
	Maund	*lb*	*Rate/seer*	*Rs*	*£*	
1	*2*	*3*	*4*	*5*	*6*	*7*
Opium	500	16,000	15,00	1,20,000	12,000	55.55
Shawls, pairs	500	-	100,00	50,000	5,000	23.14
Brocades pcs	400	-	50,00	20,000	2,000	9.25
Laki	100	3,200	32,00	3,200	320	1.48
Spices	-	-	-	800	80	0.37
Saffron	20	640	40,00	12,800	1,280	5.95
Cloth	100	3,200	-	10,000	1,000	4.26
Total	720	23,040	-	2,16,000	21,600	100.00

Source: Cunningham, Alexander; *op. cit*, p. 249.

Table 9.3 indicates that opium and shawls had good demand in Chinese territories. Out of the total annual exports, 55.55 per cent and 23.14 per cent belonged to opium and shawls respectively. British India Government and State Government of Jammu and Kashmir had exempted export duties on export articles in order to encourage exports. However, Ladakh earned Rs. 150 annually from the exported articles to Chinese Territories as shown in table 9.4.

TABLE 9.4
Export Duty on the Chinese Territories during 1846-47

Articles	*Duty Rate/Maunds*	*Rs.*	*£*	*% of the Total*
Opium	040	125	12.5	83.33
Shawls, pairs	—	—	—	—
Brocades, per	—	—	—	—
Laki	040	25	2.5	16.67
Spices	—	—	—	—
Saffron	—	—	—	—
Cloth	—	—	—	—
Total	—	150	15	100.00

Table 9.4 shows that in Ladakh only the opium and laki traders had to pay export duty of Rs. 125 and Rs. 25 per year. The total amount of duties thus collected from Chinese articles was Rs. 7,500. Besides small duties on Chinese silk, salt, iron and copper vessels would amount to about Rs. 18,000. This was the amount collected from duties before and after Gulab Singh's is conquest.[9]

During 1846-47 opium was exported to Eastern Turkistan through Ladakh, though in 1839 Chinese imposed some prohibition on its import, later during Yakub Beg's rule in Kashgaria, opium was not exported, however, after the death of Yakub the opium exports were resumed to Chinese Turkistan and reached Rs. 86,000 during 1878-80 period. However, charas, pashmina wool and ponies continued to be imported in Ladakh. This trade further continued till 1947.

REFERENCES

1. Joldan, E. : *Harvest Festival of Buddhist Dards of Ladakh and Other Essays*, Kapoor Brothers, 1985, p. 36.
2. *Ibid.*, pp. 63-64.
3. Ahluwalia, HPS., *Hermit Kingdom Ladakh*, Vikas Publishing House, New Delhi, 1980, p. 124.
4. *Ibid.*, p. 144.
5. Joldan, E.; *op. cit.*, p. 81.

6. Ahluwalia, HPS., *op. cit.,* p. 123.
7. Joldan, E.; *op. cit.,* p. 38.
8. Hajmattullaha, Alhas: *Tariki Jammu*, 1939, p. 415.
9. Cunningham, Alexander: *Ladak*, Sagar Pub., New Delhi, pp. 251-52.

10

KASHMIRI MERCHANTS AND CENTRAL ASIAN TRADE

Kashmiri merchants were mainly involved in wool trade. They purchased wool from Yarkand, and other countries of Chinese territories; and Chang-Thang region in Ladakh. However, maximum wool was purchased from Rudok (Ruthog) and Chang-Thang. Thus was the entrepot between Kashmir where the shawls were manufactured and the Chinese provinces of Rudok and Chang-Thang, where the shawl-wool was produced. The details are stated below:

Pashmina Wool

Pashmina wool is found in Chang-Thang and the high elevated regions. Due to extreme cold and very less moisture, pashmina wool is not only found on goats but on the yak and the shepherd dogs. Major R.E., Cunningham, states that during mid nineteenth century, the average price of shawl-wool in Ladakh was Rs. 2 seer, 1,28,000 lbs of which were annually imported into Kashmir from Ladakh. On the arrival in Kashmir, the wool was brought by a *pashm farosh*, or wool retailer, who distributed it to the women for spinning it into yarn.[1] Moorcroft who visited Kashmir 20 years before Cunningham; states the girls begin to spin at the age of ten, and that a hundred thousand females were employed in this occupation in Kashmir.

The first task of the spinner was to separate the different materials from the fleece which contained the following proportion of:

Coarse hair	--	1.5 seers
Seconds or phiri	--	0.375 seers
Dust and foreign substances	--	2.125 seers
Fine wool	--	2.000 seers
		6.000 seers or 1 trak

The cleaned wool was then spread on a board. The general earnings of an expert spinner being only Rs. 1.8 per month.[2]

In this way in order to accelerate fine wool trade between Ladakh and Kashmir the Raja of Ladakh and his minister known as khalun (kalon) personally supervised the trade activities. William Moorcroft and George Trebeck write:

"One of the most important articles of the trade of Ladakh is shawl wool of which it forms, in some degree, the source, but in a still greater, the entrepot between the countries whence the wool is chiefly supplied, Rodokh (Rudok) and Chan-Than (Chang-Thang) and that is which it is consumed, Kashmir. The wool is that of a domesticated goat, and consists of the under fleece. The fleece cut once a year, and the wool, coarsely picked either in the place from whence it comes, or at Le'(Leh), is sold by the importers to the merchants at that city, by whom it is sent on to Kashmir. The Raja and Khalun (Kalon) deal extensively in this trade, but it is also shared by merchants, both from Kashmir and Turan. About eight hundred loads are annually exported to Kashmir to which country, by ancient custom and engagements, the export is exclusively confined, and all attempts to convey it to other countries are punished by confiscation. In like manner it is considered in Rodokh (Rudok) and Chan-Than (Chang-Thang) as illegal to allow a trade in shawl wool except through Ladakh; and in the latter country considerable impediments are opposed to the traffic in wool from Yarkand, although it is of superior quality and cheapness."[3]

Sheep Wool

The sheep wool is not considered for the manufacture of shawls. Wherefore, it was exported in a small portion to Kashmir.[4]

Tusi Wool

Besides domesticated goat and sheep wool, wild goat wool was also exported to Kashmir. Moorcroft and Trebeck write:

"The wild goat, under the denomination of *Asali-tus* is exported in small quantities to Kashmir. It is of a light brown colour, and exceeding fineness, and is worked into shawls, a species of soft cloth called Tusi, and linings for shawl wool stockings, very few shawls, however, are made from this material."[5]

The shawls made from Tusi were much warmer and soft than

any other wool. A price of Tusi shawl made from Kashmir could have price Rs. 100 to Rs. 150 in 1820-21. Moorcroft writes:

"Shawls made from (Tusi wool) would be much softer, lighter, and warmer than those of ordinary fabric. When without being picked the *Asali Tus* is worked into *tusi*, it forms a warm, soft cloth, of drab or grey colour, which is much worn in the hills. A piece brought at Amritsar for ninety rupees was sold at Delhi for two hundred and fifty, but the Tusi cloth which comes to Hindustan is made from a mixture of the Asali Tus with from the difficulty of procuring the animal that produces it."[6]

Tea

It was imported from Lhasa and some finer quality from Yarkand and maximum of them exported to Kashmir. Moorcroft says:

"The next article of importance in the trade of Ladakh is tea, the consumption of which in the country is very considerable, but which is also exported in large quantity to Kashmir. The teas of China are chiefly brought through Lassa (Lhasa), but some of the finer kinds are also imported by way of Yarkand. They are brought is square masses or lumps, consisting of the leaves firmly compacted as if they had been wetted, and in that state forcibly compressed, they are covered with coarse yellow paper stamped with a seal in Chinese, characters and packed in the raw skins of yaks, the hair inwards and the joints neatly secured by a sewing of thongs. Each block called 'Dom' by the Kashmiris and 'Ponkch' by the Lassans (Lhasans), weighs about four Delhi sers, or less than eight pounds. The green is sold usually at the wholesale price of three rupees and the retail price is nearly double."[7]

Borax

In Ladakh borax and sulphur mines are found at an uninhabited spot Puga. Shepherds collected the borax and sold into the hands of Kashmiri merchants. Alexander Cunningham during 1846-47 estimated that borax worth Rs. 500 was exported to Kashmir. He writes:

"The borax and sulphur mines are found together at an uninhabited spot named Puga, on the Rulang-chu, a small stream which is full of hot springs. The borax is ejected in the bed of the stream by the numerous hot springs at various temperatures, from 80° upwards. In collecting the borax, the surface of the salt is carefully scraped and collected in bags. The quantity of this borax annually exported is stated at 500 maunds, or 16,000 lb; the value, at the rate of sixteen seer per rupee, being only Rs. 500."[8]

Dried Fruits

These consist of apricots and small seedless raisins called currants and was to Kashmir in little quantity.

Saffron

It was entirely supplied to all Central Asian countries by Kashmir.

Shawls

The finest quality of shawls were exported to European countries such as England, France, etc. But they were manufactured on order. Thus common quality of shawls were exported to Yarkand through Ladakh. During 1846-47, 500 pairs of shawls were annually exported to Yarkand. The value of these shawls was about Rs. 50,000.[9]

Hence, Kashmiri merchants mainly exported saffron and shawls to Central Asian countries through Ladakh. However, they had to pay export and import duties in Ladakh. Alexander Cunningham collected some statistics in this regards during 1846-47. Table 10.1 shows the details:

TABLE: 10.1

Export and Import Duties of Kashmiri Merchants Commodities during 1846-47

Sl. No.	*Article*	*Unit*	*Rate*		
			Rs	*a*	*p*
(1)	*(2)*	*(3)*	*(4)*	*(5)*	*(6)*
1.	Cloths	per maund	1	0	0
2.	Saffron	—	3	0	0
3.	Brocades	per piece	0	8	0
4.	Shawls	per pair	0	8	0
5.	Tobacco	—	0	4	0
6.	Ghi	—	0	4	0
7.	Sugar Candy	—	1	4	0
8.	Opium	—	2	8	0
9.	Other Skins	—	2	8	0
10.	Wool	per maund	0	8	0
11.	Tea	par dam	1	0	0
12.	Langa and Siling	per piece	0	2	0

Source: Cunningham, Alexander; *op. cit.*, p. 249.

The above table gives a complete idea of duty system on commodities which were exported or imported to Ladakh by Kashmiri merchant.

REFERENCES

1. *Gazetteer of Kashmir and Ladak*; Vivek Pub. House, Delhi, 1974, p. 71 and referred from Cunningham, R.E.
2. *Ibid.*, referred from Moorcroft's book.
3. Moorcroft, William and Treback George: *Travels in Hindustan*, Sagar Pub., New Delhi, Reprint 1971; p. 346.
4. *Ibid.*
5. *Ibid.*, p. 348.
6. *Ibid.*
7. *Ibid.*, p. 351.
8. Cunningham, Alexander : 'Ladak', Sagar Pub., New Delhi, p. 238.
9. *Ibid.*, pp. 238-56.

11
LAHULI TRADERS AND THEIR TRADE THROUGH LADAKH

The most active and enterprising commercial movement was when Lahuli merchants in every year passed through Spiti or Lahul and entered into Kulu. They carried borax, wool, etc., which were purchased by them from Ladakh and its surrounding Central Asian *mundies* viz. Rudok, Gartok, etc., on sheep and goat backs. Rupshu is a junction of routes from Kulu to Leh and Tibet, it is situated at the south-east of Ladakh, and the highest inhabited part in the world. Here inhabitants are living between 13,500 ft. and 16,500 ft. at Chang-pas. They rear sheep, goats and yaks and move from place to place in search of pasture.

There are routes from Spiti and Lahul across the lofty valley to Leh which were popular before 1947 among Lahuli traders.

Keylong to Leh

This route was opened from June to October. Yaks were considered the best transport on this route, but sheep and goats were used for carrying loads. For the assistance, Assistant Commissioner was appointed by the British India Government. Traders after halting few days at Keylong would go to Shimla via Chamba or to Kulu via Manali (Table: 11.1).

Table 11.1

Keylong to Leh Route

Sl. No.	*Stage*	*Inter Miles*	*Nature of Journey to Next Stage*
1	*2*	*3*	*4*
1.	Keylong; 10,100 ft.	—	Road zig zag and ascends up the western side of the Bhaga valley.
2.	Jispa; 10,500 ft.	13.5	Road fair. Pass Keda Tokpo Br. and Keylong m. 10. Pass Darcha.
3.	Patseo; 12,464 ft.	10.25	A market for Kulu, Tibetan and Lahuli traders. Road up Bhaga valley.
4.	Zing-zingbar; 14,000 ft.	6.25	Reach Surajdul lake, m. 4. Ascend Baralacha La, 16,200 ft. m. 6. Descend to Yuman Tso.
5.	Kinlung; 15,120 ft.	12	Road easy, Descend through open Yunan valley.
6.	Sarchu; 13,950 ft.	11	Track down Tsarap valley.
7.	Rachog-ba; 13,400 ft.	10	Track through Tsarap valley. Pass Gian, m. 2.
8.	Sumda; 15,520 ft.	09	Ascend Lacha Lung la, 16,600 ft. m. 4. Further descend.
9.	Pang; 15,200 ft.	16	Cross another pass, 16,630 ft. Descend. Walk over more Plain.
10.	Rogchin; 15,300 ft.	19	Sometimes Chang-pas camp. Path up Debring valley.
11.	Debring; 15,780 ft.	14	Chang pa camp. Yaks from here for further journey. Ascend up Debring ravine to Tagalang la, 17,500 ft., m. 4. Descend to Gya.
12.	Gya, 13,500 ft.	15	Village. S (granary). Track through Gya ravine. Pass Latho, m. 4. and Miru, m. 10.
13.	Upshi; 11,900 ft.	16	Village. Pass Ugu, m. 5. Cross Shang Br.
14.	Marsalang; 11,500 ft.	10	Village and Hemis Monastery 2 miles further inside ravine. Road through sandy plain.
15.	Chushot; 10,750 ft.	13	Village. Cross Indus at Choglamsar, m. 8.
16.	Leh, 11,500 ft.	12	Capital of Ladakh.

Source: Arora, R.C.: *In the Land of Kashmir; Ladakh and Gilgit. op. cit.*; pp. 178-79.

Sometimes traders used alternative routes—(i) Sarchu to Debring and Debring to Leh. Here follow the details:

Sarchu to Debring

Sl. No.	*Stage*	*Inter Miles*	*Nature of Journey to Next Stage*
1	*2*	*3*	*4*
1.	Sarchu	—	Descend
2.	Luntunnu	16	Ascend
3.	Takh	9	Descend
4.	Lun	18	Streams
5.	Sangtha	9	Sandy
6.	Debring	21	Ascend
	Total	73	

Source: Arora , R.C., *op. cit.* p. 179

Debring to Leh

Sl. No.	*Stage*	*Inter Miles*	*Nature of Journey to Next Stage*
1	*2*	*3*	*4*
1.	Debring	—	Ascend
2.	Gya	15	Decend
3.	Igoo	21	Fair track
4.	Thikse	15	Ascend Little up to Leh
5.	Leh	12	
	Total	63	

Source: Arora , R.C., *op. cit.*, p. 179.

Spiti to Leh Route

This route remained open from 15th June to October. Traders usually hired Spiti ponies for this route. This route is described below table 11.2:

Table 11.2

Spiti to Leh Route

Sl. No.	*Stage*	*Inter Miles*	*Nature of Journey to Next Stage*
1	*2*	*3*	*4*
1.	Spiti; 12,774 ft.	16	Up & Cross several torrents
2.	Kaja	16	Ascend steeply
3.	Kibar; 13,400 ft.	12	Track difficult
4.	Jughtha; 16,000 ft.	12	Track steep. Cross glacier and Parang La; 18,300 ft.
5.	Dutung; 16,000 ft.	10	Travel along Parang. Cross several spurs.
6.	Umdung	17	Cross several spurs
7.	Narbu Sumdo; 15,300 ft.	20	Road fair, Cross Phirsu Fu.

(Continued on next page)

(Table Continued)

1	*2*	*3*	*4*
8.	Kiandom; 14,900 ft.	11	Road fair, Cross Phirsu Fu.
9.	Karzok; 14,900 ft.	14	March northward along TSO-Moriri lake
10.	Shaksang;	11	March northward. Pass Peldo, m. 5.
11.	Polakonka La	17	Cross Nanak la. The cross polo
12.	Thugji	14	Descend gradually by Polakonka
13.	Debring	17	Road Fair. Cross Tsoka Chomo Maidan

Source: Arora, R.C.; *op. cit.*, p. 182.

Facilities available along the Keylong and Spiti to Leh Trade Route

Stage	*S*	*T*	*F*	*G*	*W*	*RH*	*E*	*C*	*PO*	*TO*	*Dispy*	*Scanty*
1	*2*	*3*	*4*	*5*	*6*	*7*	*8*	*9*	*10*	*11*	*12*	*13*
(a) Keylong to Leh:	✓	✓	✓	✓	✓	✓	✓	✓	✓	✓	✓	—
Keylong	✓	✓	✓	✓	✓	✓	✓	—	—	—	—	—
Jispa	—	—	✓	✓	✓	✓	✓	✓	—	—	—	—
Patseo	✓	✓	✓	✓	✓	✓	✓	—	—	—	—	—
Zing-Zingbar	—	—	✓	✓	✓	—	✓	✓	—	—	—	✓
Kinlung	—	—	✓	✓	✓	—	✓	✓	—	—	—	✓
Sarchu	—	—	✓	✓	✓	—	✓	—	—	—	—	—
Rachog-ba	—	—	✓	✓	✓	—	✓	—	—	—	—	✓
Sumdo	—	—	✓	—	✓	—	—	—	—	—	—	—
Pang	—	—	—	—	✓	—	✓	—	—	—	—	—
Rogchin	—	—	✓	✓	✓	—	✓	—	—	—	—	—
Debring	✓	✓	✓	✓	✓	—	✓	—	—	—	—	—
Gya	—	✓	✓	✓	✓	—	✓	✓	—	—	—	—
Upshi	✓	✓	✓	✓	✓	—	✓	✓	—	—	—	✓
Marsalang	—	✓	✓	✓	✓	—	✓	✓	—	—	—	✓
Chushot	✓	✓	✓	✓	✓	—	✓	✓	—	—	—	—
Leh	✓	✓	✓	✓	✓	✓	✓	✓	✓	✓	✓	✓
(b) Sarchu to Debring:												
Luntunnu	—	—	✓	✓	✓	—	✓	—	—	—	—	—
Takh	—	—	✓	✓	✓	—	✓	—	—	—	—	✓
Lun	✓	✓	✓	✓	✓	—	✓	—	—	—	—	✓
Sangtha	—	—	—	—	—	—	—	—	—	—	—	—
Debring	✓	✓	✓	✓	✓	—	✓	✓	—	—	—	✓
(c) Debring to Leh:												
Debring	See above											
Gya	✓	✓	✓	✓	✓	—	✓	✓	—	—	—	✓
Igoo	✓	✓	✓	✓	✓	—	✓	—	—	—	—	—
Tikse (Thiksey)	✓	✓	✓	✓	✓	—	✓	—	—	—	—	—
Leh	(see above)											

Source: Arora, R.C., *op. cit*., pp. 178-80.

Imports from Ladakh and Central Asian Countries

Pashmina Wool

Lahuli traders were bartered wool with wheat which they brought from the plains of Hindustan, Punjab. Sometimes they exchanged flour (*atta*) with the wool/pashmina wool. Mostly Lahuli traders carried their merchandise to Rudok via Chushul. Rudok was a subdivision of Chinese district of Nari Khorum during 1820-21, comprising of the country immediately to the east of the Ladakh districts of Tankse and Rupshu, including the eastern portion of Pangong lake. The whole Rudok region was a good grazing ground, suitable for pashmina goats. Therefore the shepherds of this region had good pashmina production every year. The quality of pashmina was also of high standard.

Every year in the month of September or sometimes one month earlier Lahuli and in some cases Kulu traders came to Rudok. Here they called shepherds from 'Dok' with their wool, and negotiated about exchanging their commodities in the barter trade system, for examples, Lahuli trader offered to give 1 kg flour or 1.5 kg. wheat for 1.5 to 2 kg wool and in the case of pashmina it would be slightly costlier than ship wool and the exchange rate being 1 kg. flour with ½ kg. to 1 kg. pashmina. In case agreements materialized then traders from Lahul/Kulu Rudok visited every year and called the shepherds from Dok at the same spot, where they did wool trade agreements the previous year.[1] In some cases traders visited further ahead to Gartok, where every year a great fair had taken place. On this occasion traders exchanged their commodities. About Gartok and its fair,[5] Charles A Sherring says:

"Gartok is situated at a height of 15,000 ft. and is a very cold place in the winter. For this reason it is only the summer headquarters of Garphans, and in the winter it is absolutely deserted. In fact, there are only a few substantially built houses, by far the greater portion of the inhabitants living in tents. The total population would be about fifty families (in 1904). There is an annual gathering of all officials, Jongpens, Tarjums, and nobility at Gartok at the end of August or beginning of September, coincidentally with the great fair, which has been held there from time immemorial."[2]

About the trade fair Traill, the Commissioner of Kumaon, who visited Gartok in 1854 AD wrote:

"A periodical fair takes place annually in September at Gartok the residence of the Lhasan viceroys which is principally attended by traders from Hindustan, Ladakh, Cashmer (Kashmir), Tartary, Yarkand, Lhasa and Liling or China proper; under the first description are included Bhotias at this province. At this annual gathering business, both official and merchantile, is transacted, and is blended with pleasure in the shape of horse-racing, the mounts being owned by the aristocracy and ridden by boy jokeys. Traders from Kashgar and the north prefer to face the Karakoram pass 18,550 ft. high which yearly levies a heavy toll on the lives of beasts of burden, then the difficult passes of the Kun Luns, which are almost impracticable. Central Asian caravans, after visiting Leh, pass near the Mo Gnalari lake, on whose northern and southern banks are respectively the towns of Noh and Rudok, and thence continue their way to Lhasa through the goldfields north of Thok Jalung, which at 16,200 ft., is the highest inhabited spot all the year round in the world; or go south through Gartok along the most frequented trade route in Tibet.

"The road from Gartok to Leh, a distance of 200 miles, passes through the district of the Rudok Jongpen, going via Tashigong and Demchok on the Indus river, and does not present any great difficulties. The Tibetans do a considerable trade with the inhabitants of Leh, with whom they are on excellent term. The exports to cashmer (Kashmir) from this quarter of Tibet amount to £8,000 annually, and are principally composed of wool, pashm (pashmina), musk, salt, precious stones, and tea, while the imports, valued at £5,000 annually (in 1854 AD)."[3]

The Tibetans harnessed a favourable attitude towards the Ladakhi and Ladakhi traders, this was greatly evident in the trust imbued in them, as Lahulis are enterprising people. Since time immemorial they had been engaged in trade in addition farming. Their valley lies on the traditional trade route to Ladakh, Sinkiang and beyond through which Hindustan, Punjab imported wool, borax and the precious merchandise of Central Asia. Therefore, learning from their ancestors, Lahulis did not hesitate pursuing traditional trade business with Central Asian countries. As a matter of fact they were always ready to face any kind of hazard. Because of this reason Lahulis carried wheat from the plains and their own barley to Rudok and Gartok respectively. Thus, forgetting the monopoly of Ladakhis in Tibet and the Kashmiri merchants over trade of pashmina, they directly contacted the shepherds from Dok and after negotiations carried pashmina and sheep wool to Kulu/Shimla via Kelong or Spiti.

Borax

Lahulis brought borax from Ladakh from where they took it to Kulu and Chamba, where it was refined, then it was further taken to the Punjab and Hindustan, for the use of silvermiths and braziers. In 1820-21, one maund and twenty-four seers cost one rupee in Delhi markets. Moorcroft says:

"...borax, which is brought through Ladakh from Bhot, sometimes by the Bhotias themselves, but more commonly by the people of Lahoul (Lahul), but convey it to Kulu and Chamba, where it is refined and whence it is conveyed to the Punjab and Hindustan, for the use of silvermiths and braziers. It is bought in Bhot and thirty-two battis, or one maund and twenty-four seers, Delhi weight, for a rupee. By refining it loses half its weight, but the thirty-two seers sell for five or six rupees. There is also a kind of smuggling trade carried on. The shepherds of these provinces receive a gratuity for pasturing the flocks of Kotch, Chamba, etc., on the borders of Lahoul (Lahul), but they sometimes take half the flocks with them to Bhot for borax, instead of leaving them to graze on the mountains, and are thus enable to sell the same at a lower price."[3]

Though Ladakh imported many manufactured articles such as silver vessels, silk, velvets, and brocades from these little yet, very was further imported to Keylong by Lahulies. The reason being their availability from the nearest *mundis* of Hindustan and Punjab. Therefore, they only purchased wheat for trade in excess quantity, the rest of the things were purchased according to their domestic requirements. When in Ladakh, they normally did not come to the Leh market preferring, to go to Rudok, Rupshu and Gartok; because their main purpose were to purchase pashmina and wool through or in cash.

REFERENCES

1. Gazetteer, Kashmir and Ladak; New Delhi, and Moorcroft, William; Trebeck, George; *Travels in Hindustan*, Sagar Pub., New Delhi, 1971, p. 348.
2. Sherring, Charles A., *Western Tibet and the Indian Borderland*, 1974, p. 146.
3. Moorcroft, William; *op. cit.*, p. 354.

12
INTER-REGIONAL TRADE

Ladakhis were confined to the manufacture of woollen cloth chiefly for home consumption in Ladakh. During summer season they were mostly engaged in either agriculture or trade activities. In winters they had enough time and hence in this period all the family members were busy in cottage industries of woollen cloth and manufactured them for their family members. For more details Alexander Cunningham made the following observations on home trade of Ladakh during 1846-47:

"The artificial production of Ladakh are confined to the manufacture of blanket and coarse woollens, chiefly for home consumption, and of black mohair tents, made form the hair of the yak or gaunting ox, which from the only habitations of the nomadic population. Both blanketing and sacking can be purchased in Le' (Leh), the former only in small quantities, the latter almost any quantity, as there is a constant demand for it for bag for the conveyance of goods. The blanketing is manufactured in pieces one foot wide and eleven to fifteen yards in length. The price varies from two to three rupees each, according to fineness. The quality of blanketing and of sacking annually expended in Ladakh on the carrying trade amounts to about 120,000 yards, in the manufacture of which 20,000 small maunds (or 640,000 lb.) of wool are consumed. The total value of the manufacture is only Rs. 7,500 or £750."[1]

However, to meet the wool and other basic demand, traders from the different regions of Ladakh came in caravans to Leh, Chang-Thang, etc. But, most of the trade was carried out under barter system.

Leh-based Merchants

They were comparatively wealthy traders than traders from the other parts of Ladakh and carried ration, viz., wheat, 'atta', etc., on mules, ponies and yaks. Sometimes they used donkeys, as donkeys in Ladakh are small but tougher than the Indian donkeys. The merchants carried their sleeping luggage with small tents to the Chang-Thang regions during summer season. They visited their contacts in Chang-Thang following different trade routes. Where they visited, was dependant on the location of the Chang pas like Chusul pas, Karzok pas, Kuyul pas, Rupshupas, etc.

Leh to Chushul

Traders started their journey in the month of August and via Tankse reached Chushul. Here follows the details:

Leh (11,500 ft.)

↓ 14 miles

Ranbirpur (11,000 ft.)

↓ 13 miles

Chimre (11,890 ft.)

↓ 10 miles

Zingral (15,780 ft.)

↓ 9 miles

Tsultak (15,950 ft.)

↓ 15 miles

Tankse (12,900 ft.)

↓ 14 miles

Chakar-ISO (13,950 ft.)

↓ 14.5 miles

Mang (13,900 ft.)

↓ 20.5 miles

Chushul (14,200 ft.)

Total distance 110.0 miles

cf. Arora. R.C.; *op. cit.,* pp. 164-65.

Traders, sometimes used this route during winter, when Pangong lake froze down to ice, they then track easily on iced lake.

Leh to Demchok Trade Route

This was the main trade route between Leh and Tibet. But in between Chushul and Demchok, herds people (*i.e.* Changpas) came down from the surrounding areas and negotiated with the Ladakhi traders, in case they reached some agreements, barter took place. Changpas got wheat, 'atta', gur, cheese (dry), etc., from the Leh based traders and gave them wool and pashmina. Thereafter according to the agreement this trade continued to the coming years. The trade route details given below:

Leh to Demchok Route

Sl. No.	*Stage*	*Inter Miles*	*Nature of Journey to Next Stage*
1	*2*	*3*	*4*
1.	Leh	—	—
2.	Ranhirpur	—	Sandy path
3.	Chimre (Chemrey)	—	Easy path
4.	Zingral	—	Ascend
5.	Tsultak	—	Steep Ascend to Chang-La
6.	Tankse	15	Descend to Durbuk then easy going
7.	Yokma (14,400 ft.)	15	Ascend along the Harong Luma banks
8.	Kungma (15,400 ft.)	14	Gradual ascending
9.	Chushul	15	—
10.	Dachaung	15	Gradual ascend, Chushul was the junction of Gartok and Rudok routes.
11.	Thangra	20	Ascend gradually to Tsaka (Thag-La), then descend
12.	Gangra La	17	Easy going
13.	Fuk-Cha	12	Easy going
14.	Lagankhal	18	Easy going
15.	Demchok	16	Easy going. Demchok was the Ladakh and Tibet boundary.

Leh and Demchok total distance 193 miles.

Leh to Skardu Route

Leh based Ladakhi traders brought wool and pashmina from Chang-Thang, Rudok and Gartok to Leh. After one month rest at Leh they carried Chang-Thang wool to Skardu for barter with dried fruits. They followed the following routes:

Winter Route

Sl. No.	*Stage*	*Inter Miles*	*Nature of Journey to Next Stage*
1	*2*	*3*	*4*
1.	Leh	—	Descend
2.	Nimu	18	Descend
3.	Saspoe	11	Gradually descend
4.	Nurlu	14	The road rought but level
5.	Khalatage	08	Gradually Ascend
6.	Skirbuchan	16	Track rough
7.	Nabi Brangsa (lower Hanu)	14	Track difficult
8.	Dah (Da)	13	Track unit for ponies
9.	Urdas	09	Track sandy
10.	Marol	19	Track sandy
11.	Kharmang	20	Cross rope bridge
12.	Tolti	12	Fair track
13.	Parkutta	18	Fair route
14.	Gol	14	Fair route
15.	Skardu (7,770 ft.)	21	—

Leh to Skardu total distance: 207 miles.

Source: Arora, R.C., *op. cit.*, p. 175.

Thus, during 1930-50 Leh based traders had good business with the herdsmen of Chang-Thang and Skardu people. In Chang-Thang the business was done both by barter, and cash transactions using Indian currency. The rates however, varied from year to year. Janet Rizviw had interviewed some Ladakhis who were engaged in this business and made following observations:

"Business was done both by barter, and by cash transactions using Indian currency. The rates varied from year to year, rising in those seasons when a hard winter might have led to a high mortality among the flocks and reduced the amount of *pashm* and wool available. Such rates are quoted differently by different informants, (that is) for one kilo of 'atta' he could get two kilos of wool, and that the rate for *pashm* was always double that of wool—that is, one kilo of 'atta' bought one kilo of pashm. Apricots were bartered for butter, at equal rate, weight for weight. In monetary terms, the price of a kilo of wool was in the region of one or two rupees; and of *pashm*, two to four rupees. The price of wool fluctuating around two to two and a half kilos to the rupee, and of *pashm* five to seven *pau* (for 'pau' to the kilo). Shahtoosh was in a different category altogether, even then Rs. 120-170 for two kilos.

"The bulk of the *pashm* trade seems to have been in the hands of the big merchants of the Leh area. Tashi Phunchok carried some 300-400 kilos a year to Leh, and Stobdan about 200 kilos. This they sold to Kashmiri merchants who had come from Srinagar for this purpose only. Considering the amount of effort they had made, their profits do not seem exorbitant. Pashm that had been bought for two to four rupees a kilo might sell for around six rupees, according to Stobdan; while Tashi Phuntsog reckoned on a 100 per cent profit, which he thought justified by his input of time and effort. Tsering Namgyal remembers selling *pashm* for anything from five to seven rupees a kilo. If the amount of wool and *pashm* purchased in Chang-Thang exceeded the carrying capacity of a trader's donkeys, a small flock of *huniya* sheep could be bought cheap and used to carry the excess, at the rate of 16 kilos per animal. After doing duty as pack animals, the sheep would then be disposed of in villages, or to the Leh butchers."[1]

In Chang-Thang, the Changpas keep black-faced huniya sheep which were chiefly used for carrying loads. Nearly all the traffic of Chang-Thang and Rupshu was transported on the huniya sheep. During 18-46-47 the average price was in the range of from Rs. 2.80 to Rs. 8.[2]

Captain Biddulph, one of the member's of Yarkand Mission, supplied the following note on the use of sheep carrying supplies:

"I left Tankse on the 18th September, taking with me thirty sheep, carrying loads of grain and flour. Wishing merely to test their marching capabilities, I looked upon the supplies they carried as extra, and their loads remained intact till within four marches of Shāhidūla, when I was forced to commence using them.

"The Tartars usually make their sheep carry a load of 32 lbs, and march 7 or 8 miles a day only, making frequent halts; as, however, I expected to be marching herd at times, I put only a load of 20 lbs., on each sheep. Beyond this I took no care of them, and simply let them take their chance.

"On fair ground, where they marched with a broad front, they marched at the rate of 1¾ miles an hour: a large number would no doubt travel slower, and much must depend upon the breadth on the road.

"The greatest difficulty they had to contend with was crossing the streams, and while marching in the Kárákash valley, they were sometimes obliged to cross the river three or four times a day. Not only were the loads liable to become damaged, but the weight of water hanging in their fleeces, and on several occasions freezing, greatly impeded progress.

"On the days on which they had no grass, they had literally nothing to eat, as they refused grain, not being accustomed to it. One man was sufficient to manage the lot, and two men, I should say, could easily drive and manage a hundred.

"On arrival in camp they were unloaded and turned out to shift for themselves till dark, when they were herded for the night.

"The fact that a flock of sheep carrying twenty lbs. loads should be able to march 330 miles in a month with only one casualty, through a country in which forage is always scanty and a very inclement season of the year, is remarkable. After the first march the elevation was never less than 11,000 feet, and the thermometer at night sank to 15° and 16° below zero. The sheep, however, did not apparently feel either cold or elevation.

"Future exploring parties on the Karakoram will, I fell certain, find a flock of sheep a most useful addition to their camp. Not only are they very easily looked after, but they can feed themselves as they go along among the rocks where horses would starve. Besides this, when their loads, are disposed off they can themselves be eaten"[3]

In Chang-Thang, Rudok and Gartok all the routes were sandy and the whole region is cold and arid, therefore, during summer season the day temperature increases up to 36°C but at night it falls to below zero degree under such circumstances local traders preferred to use sheep as carrier and could carry 20 lbs easily. On their way towards Chang-Thang when required they sluttered them and to eat with *sattu* and to make *thokpa*. Because of cold they could use meat for several days even in summers. On their return to Leh they disposed them after unloading.

The Leh based local traders on not getting Kashmiri dealers at Leh, carried the pashmina load to Srinagar to sell; sometimes they carried it to Skardu via Kargil and exchanged with dried fruits, receiving eight to ten times the wool's weight in apricots.[4]

Peasant Traders

They performed an important role to link pashmina trade with the shawl industry on one hand and with Skardu people from whom they purchased the dried fruits in exchange of wool, thus linking fruit industry of Skardu on the other hand. They used donkeys and sheep while carrying *atta*, *sattu* and dried fruits to Chang-Thang. Rizvi says:

"The Sham Ilaqa traders used to set off for Chang-Thang in May in groups of four to six, each trader having 10 to 15 donkeys, Tsering Namgyal made his first journeys, perhaps in the mid-30s, as a helper of Tashi Phuntsog, one of the richer of his group, who advanced him Rs. 100 to buy goods to load on his five animals. Later he increased his stock, and took some 15 animals. A donkey's load was in the region of 50 or 60 kilos; each merchant's consignment of 500-1000 kilos contains *atta*, *sattu* (parched barley flour, the staple food of most of Tibet and Ladakh), dried apricots and often small amounts of tea and textiles. Included in this were the supplies for the traders themselves and however many helpers they took for the tedious work of unloading at the end of each day's march and loading up again the next morning."[5]

The Sham Ilaqa traders while marching towards Chang-Thang, deposited supplies for the return, either with trading partners or simply concealed beneath a heap of stones at some camping ground. This system had the advantage of lightening the animals' loads, and also of making sure that there would be no shortfall of supplies on the way back. They carried basic supplies—*atta*, *sattu*, dried apricots, oil and spices for cooking. Milk, meat and butter could be bought from local people. A goat or sheep in 1930 costed not more than two rupees. They did not face any problem for sheep, donkeys, horses, etc., as Chang-Thang consisted plenty of grazing grounds. For details see the following Fig. 12.1.

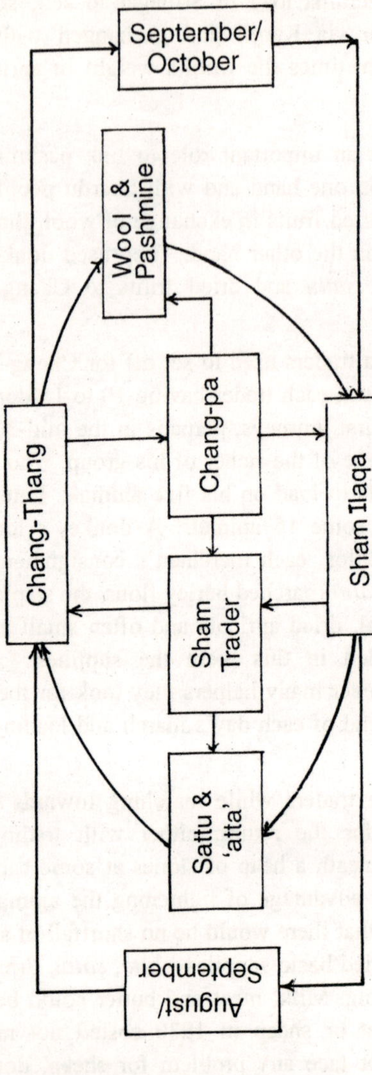

Fig. 12.1: Trade interaction between Sham traders and Changpas.

Fig. 12.2 shows that the Sham Ilaqa traders annually carried *sattu*, etc., to Chang-Thang and met Chang-pas at the assigned spots.

The Changpa also came down from Dok to the above spots and bartered their goods.

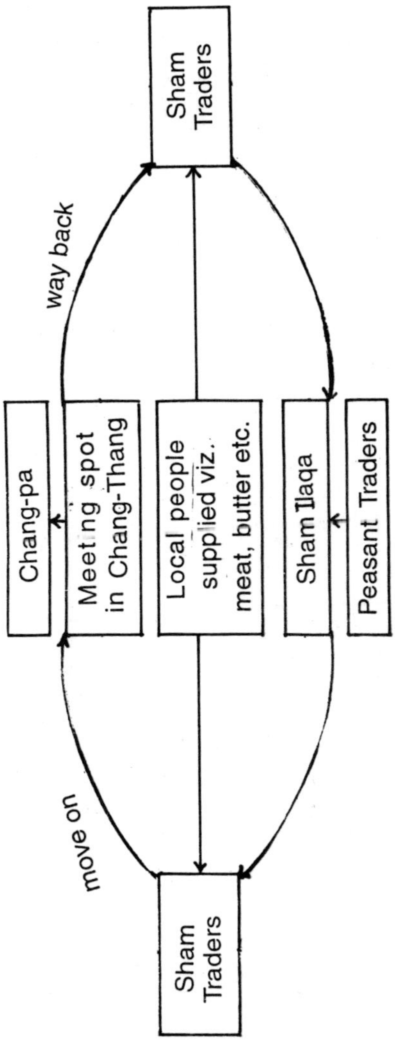

Fig. 12.2: Annual movement of peasant traders to Chang-Thang and back.

The peasant traders after returning from Chang-Thang used to go to Skardu. They spent winters in Skardu and after exchanging wool with dried apricots, returned the following summer or as the road opened for Kargil. Thus they spent two to three months in Skardu (Fig. 12.3).

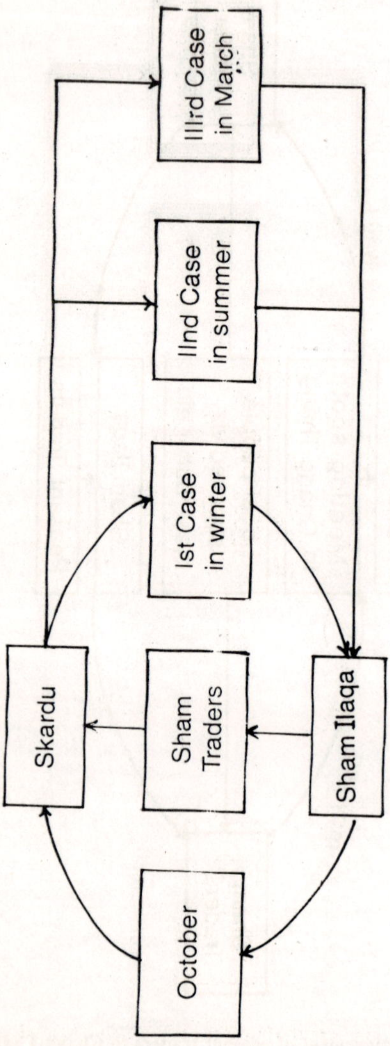

Fig. 12.3: Peasant traders movements from Sham Ilaqa to Skardu and back

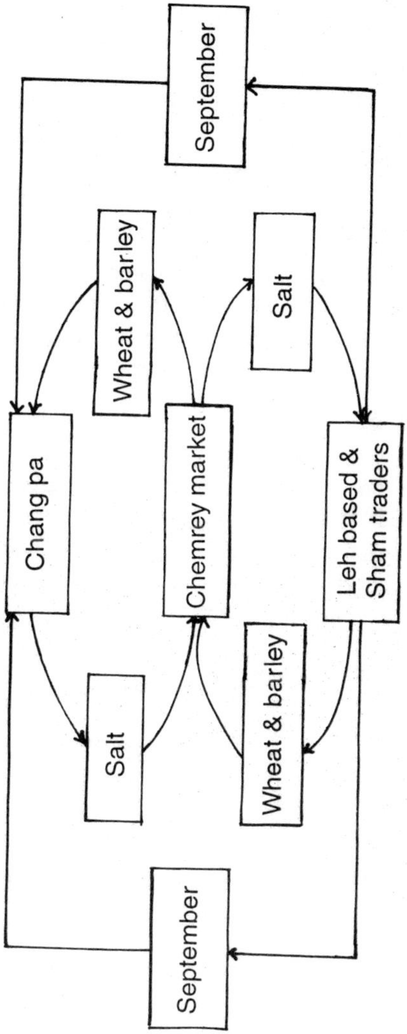

Fig. 12.4: Barter trade of salt and wheat/barley between Ladakhi and Changpa traders

Besides wool/shawl wool, Chang-Thang has innumerable salt lakes. The Sham Ilaqa traders while returning to Leh carried back only a few bags of salt, they got four or five measures for one of barley. But generally traders could get it after following a custom of offering a katak or khadak (the Tibetan ceremonial white scarf) and one rupee to the Changpas or the trading partners in Chang-Thang. Thereafter they were allowed to carry away as much salt as they wanted from the lakes. As it was difficult in any case, for any trader outside of Chang-Thang to reach up to lakes and extract salt from there. They only extract salt for their family use.[7]

In fact, the greater part of salt came to Chamrey market near Leh. The Changpas carried it on their sheep via Chang-La and exchanged with wheat and barley. The barter rate was always fixed at five measures of salt for four of wheat or four for four of barley (Fig. 12.4).[8]

Purig Traders

They were not involved directly in the pashmina trade with Chang-Thang, but to have patronised the Chemrey salt-market in a big way. The barter system was adopted in the market. They barter salt for grain. The measurement unit was by volume, not by weight and varied in the following ratio:

Salt	:	Grain
25	:	20
	or	
30	:	20
20	:	30
	or	
20	:	20

Sometimes barter was on the basis of weight at the ratio salt to grain 2: 1 also in practice (Fig. 12.5):

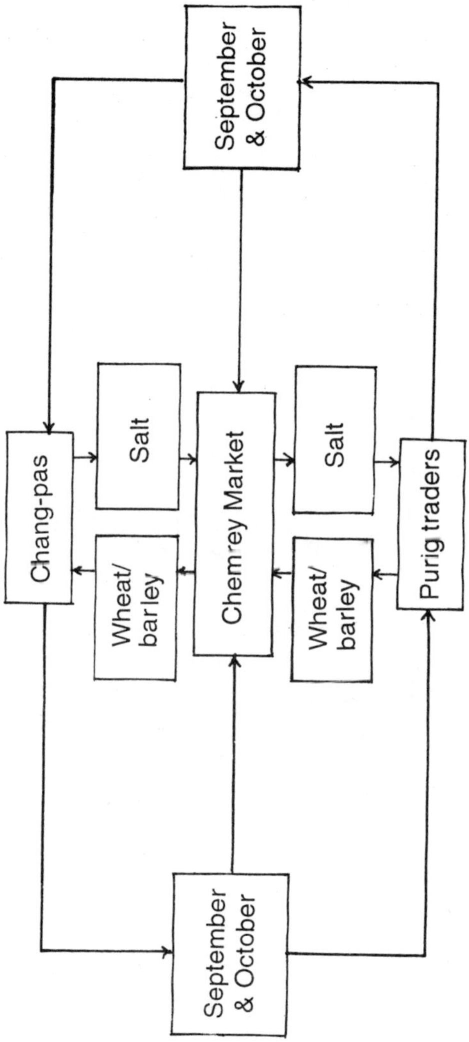

Fig. 12.5: Barter trade of salt and wheat/barley between Changpas and Purigpas.

After Chemrey market Purig-pa, carried salt to Skardu and exchanged it with butter-equal weight for weight. Some Purig-pas carried Yarkandi goods to Kashmir—for which they were paid ten rupees per head. They also carried dried fruits and butter and sold in the market to buy rice and 'atta' from Kashmir (Figs. 12.6 and 12.7).

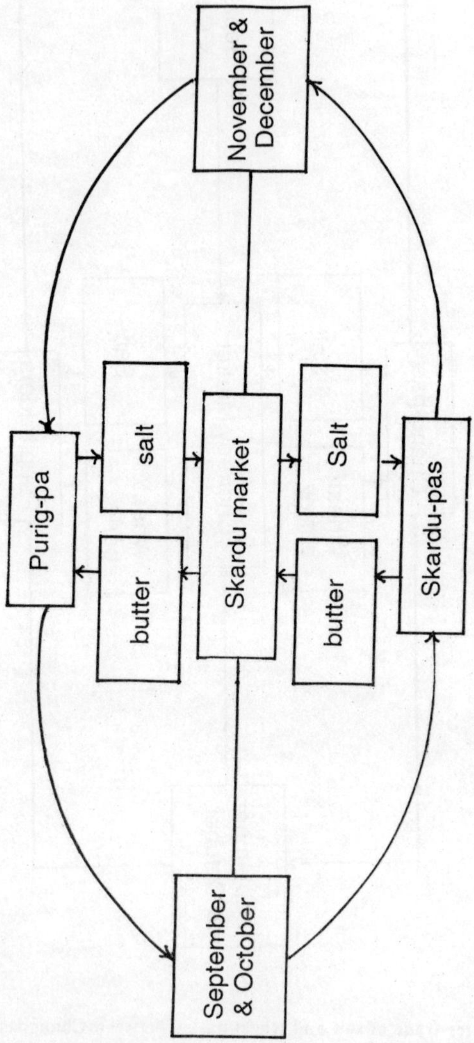

Fig. 12.6: Trade between Purig-pas and Skardu traders.

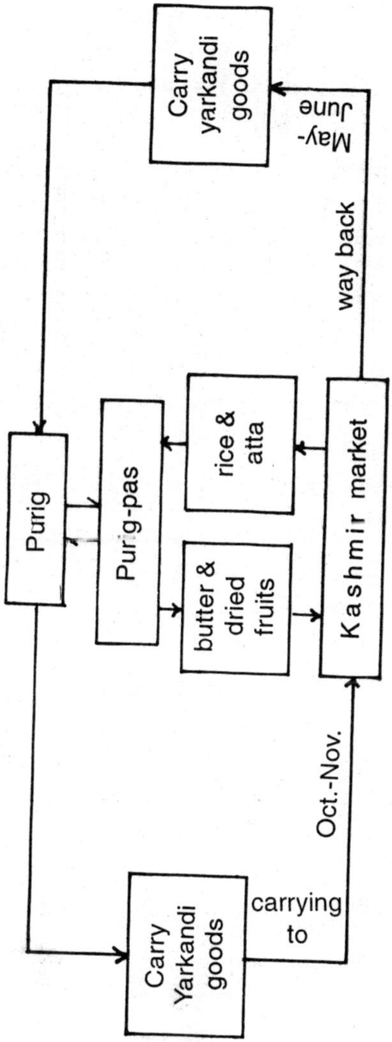

Fig. 12.7: Purig-pa carrying Yarkandi goods and trade with Kashmiri merchants at Kashmir market.

Nubra Traders

The Nubra traders were not directly involved in trade, however some traders carried phaps and yumbok to Leh market and returned with wool. However, they used to give their animals—yaks and double hump camel on rent to Yarkandi and traders from Hindustan side.

Zangskar Traders

They brought butter and dry cheese to Leh market but did not involve directly in trade. Zangskari butter had good demand in Leh. Besides, Zangskari horses were also popular among traders. They mostly used these horses while playing polo in Leh market.

Through the inter-regional trade was not very developed, yet, the traders of the different parts could get the same facilities at the different stages while marching towards Chang-Thang and Skardu or returning to Leh. Here follow the details:

Facilities along Leh to Chushul Route

Stage	*S*	*T*	*F*	*G*	*W*	*E*	*C*	*RH*	*Scanty*
1	*2*	*3*	*4*	*5*	*6*	*7*	*8*	*9*	*10*
Leh	✓	✓	✓	✓	✓	✓	✓	✓	—
Ranbirpur	✓	✓	✓	✓	✓	✓	✓	—	—
Chemrey (Chimre)	✓	✓	✓	✓	✓	✓	✓	—	—
Zingral	—	—	—	—	✓	✓	—	—	✓
Tsultak	—	—	✓	✓	✓	—	—	—	✓
Tankse	✓	✓	✓	✓	✓	✓	✓	—	✓
Chakar-Talao	—	—	✓	✓	✓	✓	—	—	✓
Mang	✓	✓	✓	✓	✓	✓	✓	—	—
Chushul	✓	✓	✓	✓	✓	✓	✓	✓	—

Facilities along Leh to Demchok Route

Stage	*S*	*T*	*F*	*G*	*W*	*E*	*C*	*RH*	*Scanty*
1	*2*	*3*	*4*	*5*	*6*	*7*	*8*	*9*	*10*
Leh to Tankse	✓	✓	✓	✓	✓	✓	✓	✓	—
	see above (*i.e.* Leh to Chushul route)								
Yokma	—	—	✓	✓	✓	✓	—	—	—
Kungma	—	—	✓	✓	✓	✓	—	—	—
Chushul	✓	✓	✓	✓	✓	✓	✓	✓	—
Dachaung	—	—	✓	✓	✓	✓	—	—	—

(Continued on next page)

(Table Continued)

1	*2*	*3*	*4*	*5*	*6*	*7*	*8*	*9*	*10*
Thangra	—	—	✓	✓	✓	✓	—	—	—
Gangra-la	—	—	✓	✓	✓	✓	—	—	—
Fuk-cha	—	—	✓	✓	✓	✓	—	—	—
Lagankhel	—	—	✓	✓	✓	✓	—	—	—
Demchok	—	—	✓	✓	✓	✓	—	—	—

Facilities along Leh to Skardu

Stage	*S*	*T*	*F*	*G*	*W*	*E*	*C*	*RH*	*Scanty*
1	*2*	*3*	*4*	*5*	*6*	*7*	*8*	*9*	*10*
Leh to Nurla		See the treaty High Road to Leh							
Khalatse	✓	✓	✓	✓	✓	✓	✓	✓	✓
Skirubuchan	—	—	✓	✓	✓	✓	—	—	—
Lower Hanu	—	—	✓	✓	✓	✓	—	—	—
Dah	✓	✓	✓	✓	✓	✓	—	—	—
Urdas	—	—	✓	—	—	✓	—	—	—
Marol	—	—	✓	—	✓	✓	—	—	—
Kharmang	✓	✓	✓	✓	✓	✓	—	—	—
Tolti	—	—	✓	✓	—	—	—	—	—
Parkutta	—	—	✓	—	✓	—	—	—	—
Gol	—	—	✓	—	✓	—	—	—	—
Skardu	✓	✓	✓	✓	✓	✓	✓	✓	—

Source. Arora, R.C.; *op. cit.*

C : Caravan Serai; E : Encamping ground; F : Fuel; G : Grass; RH : Rest House; S : Supplies; T : Transport

In conclusion, Leh based traders had their full control over inter-regional trade. However, Ladakhi peasants of Sham Ilaqa had good contribution in the acceleration of trade within Ladakh and Skardu (Fig. 12.8).

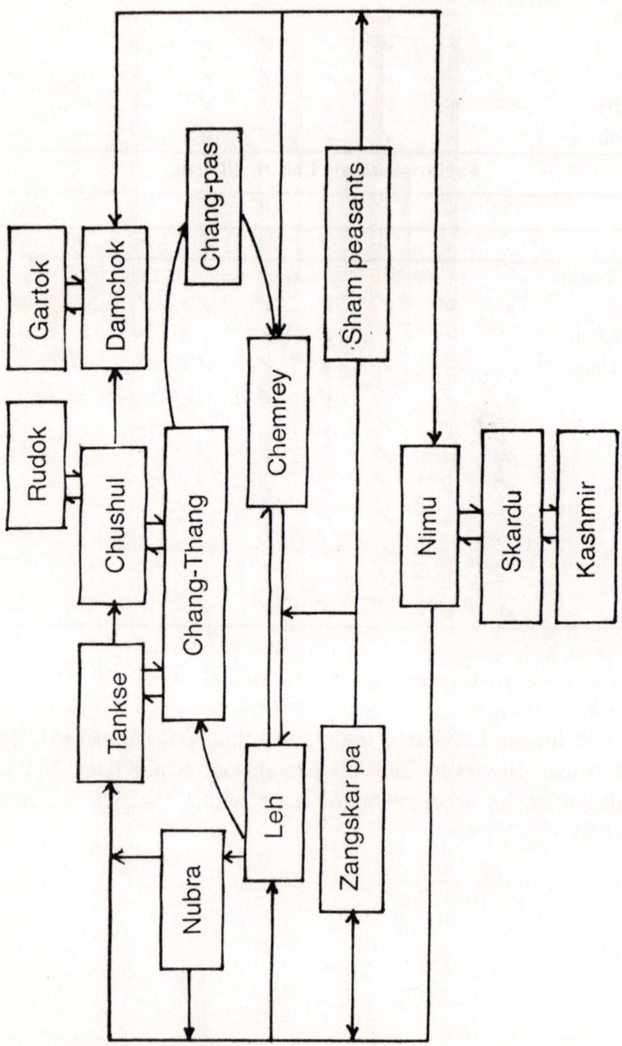

Fig. 12.8: Trade activities of local traders in Ladakh.

REFERENCES

1. Rizvi, Janet: 'Peasant, Traders of Ladakh: A Study in Oral History', *India International Centre Quarterly*, Vol. 12., No. 1, March 1985, pp. 19-21.
2. *Gazetteer of Kashmir and Ladakh* and Quoted from Cunningham; Vivek Pub., New Delhi, 1974, p. 86.
3. *Ibid.*, quoted from captain Biddulph's remarks on the use of sheep carrying supplies; *op. cit.*, pp. 86-87.
4. Rizvi, Janet; *op. cit.*, p. 21.
5. *Ibid.*, pp. 16-17.
6. *Ibid.*, p. 17.
7. *Ibid.*, p. 21.
8. *Ibid.*, p. 22.
9. *Ibid.*

13

COINS, WEIGHTS, MEASUREMENTS AND OTHER TERMINOLOGY USED IN TRADE

During nineteenth and twentieth centuries, traders were using some common terminology to make easy their trade activities such as—

Tshong: All the merchandises which were brought to or taken back to their countries were called Tshong.[1]

Tshong-pas: All kind of traders who come to Leh market and exchanged their goods with each other.[2]

Bal Tshongs: Those traders who were engaged in wool trade.[3]

Chhang-Tshong: The spirit or chang (local beer) called Chhang Tshong.[4]

Don-thun: The ware-gatherers.[5]

Tshong pon: The heads of the merchants.[6]

Tshong-dus: The regular gathering or annual meeting at 'Garo' or a meeting place was known as Tshông-dus.[7]

Tshong-chhang: Fair, festival; and the friendly glass, which was partaken togather after the completion of a bargain was known as Tshong-chhang.[8]

Aksaka: Elderly respectable officer. Aksaka is a Turki word which means white beard.[9]

Begar: The arrangement for the supply of ponies and coolies to travellers.[10]

Res: The supply of ponies and coolies to traders at the different stages along the Treaty High Road Leh.

Khang-chen: Main house of the family from which a man and a pony were arranged for travellers/traders at the allotted stage according to the chance.[11]

Kira-kash: The traders would usually send their goods from Leh to Srinagar direct with ponywallas known as Kira-kash. They belonged to people of Kargil and Dras.[12]

Bias: Top class traders were known as Bias. In English it can be translated as millionnaire.[10]

Caravan Bash: The head of the caravan or leader of the caravan.

Chakaras: The servants employed to look after ponies.[12]

Yarkandis: Traders who came from Sinkiang or Eastern Central Asia.[13]

Kohja: Traders who came from Sinkiang or Eastern Central Asia. Sometimes Ladakhis called those pilgrims who came from the above countries and passed through Ladakh for Haj.[14]

Sarai (Serai): Accommodation for traders.

Namdas: Small size carpets of Yarkand or Sinkiang.

Munshis: Clerks employed for making the trade—export and import statement at the Joint Commissioner's office.

Khuda Bardi: Restaurant owners who served Yarkandi food.[15]

Pichak: It is a Yarkand word meaning knife.[16]

Pichak Tungyu: The conch handled knife.[17]

Kosa-Masi: The long calf leather footwear, with separate pair of slippers, made of leather.[18]

Tungans: Chinese Muslims who came to Ladakh.[19]

Hor: People of Yarkand.

Tazaks: Turkis who plundered certain parts of Eastern Tibet around Kailas for more than two years before reaching Chang-Thang in 1941.[20]

Coins

Jod (or Jao): Ladakhi silver coin.[21]

Tila: It was the common gold coin of the Islamic countries, and was worth six rupees in Leh.[22]

Yambu: It was Tibetan plain bar of pure metal, costing Rs. 156.5. In 1847 it was valued at Rs. 166.[23]

Kuru: It was a Chinese silver ingot brought by Yarkandis.[24]

Ta'-Mikma: The lumps of bullion which were often bent in the middle into the shape of a horse-shoe. They called it Ta'-Mikma or horse hoofs.[25]

Nepali coins: Nepali coins were brought in Ladakh by Hindustani traders. These were of silver and each coin was worth half a rupee, or two jaos in Ladakh.[26]

Moghul rupee: The Moghul rupees had been superseded by the Nanak-sahi and company's rupee.[27]

Ser-jao: Golden coins of Ladakh, or simply Ser-ki-dong.[28]

Dong: All coins called Dong or Dong-tse.[29]

Nul-ki-dong: All local silver coins Nul-ki-dong or simply Nuk-dong.[30]

Zangi-dong: The coins made of copper called Zangi-dong or Zang-dong.[31]

Marba: The ready money or cash called Marba or Markyang.[32]

Aktanga: Chinese silver coin.[33]

Weights and Measure

Batti: One Batti = 2 kg

One Batti = 2 Indian seers

One Batti = 32 Chitaks

According to Cunningham the word Batti derived from Hindi word Battis (*i.e.* 32).[34]

Maund: It was also spelled as Man.

One maund = 40 kg

One maun = 8 battis

Eight battis = 16 seers

Khal: It was the universal measure for all kinds of heavy produce, but more especially for grain. Cunningham noticed two kinds of khal[35]:-

(1) The del-khal
(2) The shor-khal

The common 'khal', whether by weight or measure, was the well known quantity of a sheep's load (luk-khal), which was equal to 8 battis or a maund of sixteen seers. This was usually named khal, but when larger measures were to consider, the following prefixes were always used according to the kind of load, such as[36]:

Ta-khal (a horse-load) = 4 maunds, or 64 seers

Yak-khal (a yak-load) = 4 maunds, or 64 seers.

General Strachey made the following reports about the weight and measurements units in Ladakh—

"**Lineal measures:** The smallest is common use is the sor or sormo.

1 sor = a finger's breadth (The Indian angul).

5 sor = 1 lakpa, or hand's breadth.

2 lakpa = 1 bito, or short span with the fore and little finger.

12 sor = tokang, or full span with the thumb.

1.5 to = skangang, or short cubit from elbow to wrist.

2 to = 1 tugang, or long cubit with the hand extended (The long cubit, or tu, averages about 16 inches.).

4 tu = 1 domang, or fathom

500 dom = 1 gyangtak, or mile (1,000 yards?)

8 gyangtak = 1 paktsat, or league. (No actual computations are ever made by the mile and league, journeys being reckoned by the day).

Nyiama = a day's journey

Phet = 1/2 day's journey. It is also called tsal-lam. Smaller distances are reckoned thus:

Miktong = eyesight, or as far as one can see a man distinctly.

Dagang = bowshot.

Corn measures: For corn and salt Tibetans have a measure of capacity. Those generally used the bre (vulgo de), the bo, and the khal.

20 de always = 1 kal

From 2 to 5 de = 1 bo

There are several varieties of bre and ḵhal differing in size, name, and use. The principal are—

Pogbre = ration measure (the smallest).

Punbre = interest measure

Ongbre = harvest measure, the largest of all, and used for agricultural purposes."[37]

Approximate English equivalents: The approximate measurements of the above units was equal to[38]—

1 kha = about 2/5 of bushel

1 bre = about 1.5 pints

1 bo (na) = about 3 quarts

Weights, troy - A skarma (i.e., star) = the grain or minim.

2.5 skarma = 1 kagang

4 ka = 1 shogang

10 sho = 1 shogang

50 shang = 1 shilka or dotsat, or Chinese ingot (ṣilver)

The last of these, the shilka, was the standard, and weighs about 166⅔ Indian tolas.

English Equivalents[39]

1 skarma = 6 grains

1 ka = 15 grains

1 sho = 1 drachm

1 shang = 1¼ oz.

Avoirdupois[40]

4 shang or pore = 1 nyagang or nega (i.e. mark on steelyard)

20 nega = 1 kal

10 to 15 kal = a man's load

The nega = 1/12 of a Chinese ingot, or about 1/3 lb.

The kal = 7 lb avoirdupois.

The Tibetans measured the routes in the following ways:[41]

Every road is called - lam

Lam-chheu was a big road.

Gya-lam, a passable road.

Besides above measurement units, traders were very much involved in barter trade system and for the measurement of their goods they used Ñya-ga (Fig. 13.1).

Thus, maund, Khal and Batti were the popular measurement units among the traders of Yarkand, and Tibet or Chang-Thang; whereas seer and chitaks, popular among Kumauni, Nepali, Hindustani, Hoshiarpuri traders.

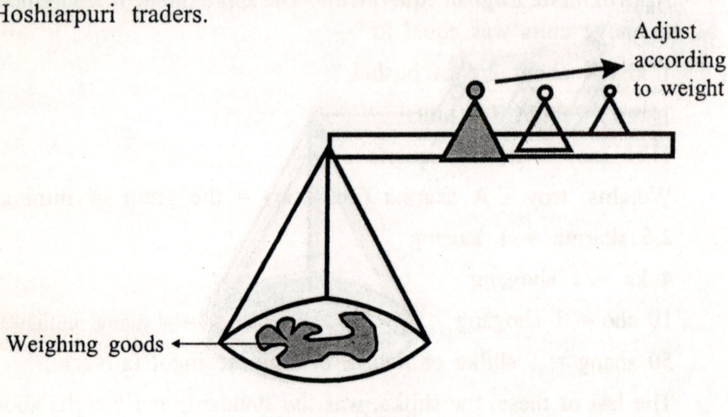

Fig. 13.1: Ñya-ga

REFERENCES

1. Cunningham, Alexander: *Ladak*; Sagar Pub., New Delhi, p. 253.
2. *Ibid.*
3. *Ibid.*
4. *Ibid.*
5. *Ibid.*
6. *Ibid.*
7. *Ibid.*
8. *Ibid.*
9. Joldan, E.: 'Harvest Festival of Buddhist Dards of Ladakh and other Essays', *op cit.*, p. 64.
10. *Ibid.*, p. 68.
11. *Ibid.*

12. *Ibid.*
13. *Ibid.*
14. *Ibid.*
15. *Ibid.*, p. 78.
16. *Ibid.*
17. *Ibid.*
18. *Ibid.*, p. 79.
19. *Ibid.*, p. 81.
20. *Ibid.*, p. 82.
21. Cunningham, Alexander; *op. cit.*, p. 253.
22. *Ibid.*
23. *Ibid.*
24. *Ibid.*
25. *Ibid.*
26. *Ibid.*
27. *Ibid.*
28. *Ibid.*
29. *Ibid.*
30. *Ibid.*
31. *Ibid.*
32. *Ibid.*
33. Joldan, E.; *op. cit.*, p. 70.
34. Cunningham, Alexander; p. 256.
35. *Ibid.*
36. *Ibid.*
37. *Gazetteer of Kashmir and Ladakh*; *op. cit.*, p. 548.
38. *Ibid.*, p. 549.
39. *Ibid.*
40. *Ibid.*
41. *Ibid.*, p. 550.

14

CENTRAL ASIAN TRADERS POSITION JUST AFTER THE BAN OF TRADE ROUTES

The central trade was almost closed in 1947. As a result many Yarkandi traders were either held up at Leh or in Srinagar. Besides, a few Yarkandi Haj pilgrims could not go back because their goods were lying in Leh or Srinagar. According to Joldan: "When the Central Asian trade closed in 1947, many Yarkandis were caught on this side of the Karakoram. Some were taken unaware, a few were on their way back from Haj pilgrimage, and quite a number of them could not go back because their goods were lying in Leh or Srinagar. Karim Haji Lakman, and Husain Haji and Tokhta-Niaz were some whom I knew. The former two were good businessmen, Hussain Haji was a short statured man several hundred bundles of his invoiced goods, remained stored in charas godown, for a number of years. Subsequently they were released to him and he opened a shop in Srinagar to sell these goods. Toktah Niaz Haji is settled in Kargil and Sadir Akhon in Leh. All the Yarkandis in Srinagar were housed in the Safa Kadal Serai (sarai) and they made a living by making caps, quilts, curing skins and furs and dealing in fur trade"[1]

There were many Yarkandis who had been involved in silk trade, among them Mian Abdul Rehman was a popular trader. In 1939 when Chinese Government closed the trade with India, Mian Abdul Rehman's some silk consignment was on the way via Ladakh to Srinagar. His 20 bundles of raw silk later reached Leh. Mian Abdul Rehman was then in Srinagar and was waiting for his consignments, so that when the raw silk bundles would reach Srinagar, he would sell them in the market. Like Mian, some Yarkandi settled down in Srinagar, e.g., the three sons of Khan Bahadur Noor Mohammad Khan who traded with Sinkiang before 1947.[2]

There were many Yarkandis who made correspondence with the Government of Turkey and finally succeeded in getting its consent to accept them as Turk citizens. The Government of Turkey sponsored their air travel in groups comprising about 300 men, women and children in all, in the course of about 10 years. Therefore, till 1983 all the Yarkandis who were willing to go to Turkey left Srinagar.[3]

Similarly some Indian traders were held up in Sinkiang before 1939, when the trade with China was completely closed. During the first world war the trade between Sinkiang and India in which Hoshiarpur traders were mainly involved in charas and silk trade got effected. However, after the war it got little momentum. But again during second world war imports of foreign goods such as dyes, cloth, etc., stopped, as England, Germany and Japan were involved in the war. The political conditions in Sinkiang were not stable, therefore, Punjabi Hindu traders stopped going there after 1939. Moreover, caravans continued coming upto 1946, and a few after this also. They sold or bartered their goods with Indian traders in Leh. The last caravan to cross the Karakoram into India was having members of Indian Consul, came in Ladakh in November 1953. Sethi Mehta, Aziz Din and Mohammad Khan were among them. As mentioned earlier Pt. Bihari Lal was the manager of Shadilal Dawarkanath firm in Sinkiang, he could not come with the last caravan in 1953 and remained in Yarkand to look after the business of Shadilal. He himself represented on behalf of Shadilal to the Chinese Government that either to give compensation of the goods supplied to the traders of their country or to make necessary arrangements for the supply of their own goods back to Hoshiarpur. In India Shadilal also sent his representations to the Prime Minister of India to give the compensation of the loss of the trade with Sinkiang. He continued his case for five to six years, but trade loss compensation was not given to him, however, Chinese Government sponsored Bihari Lal for Air travel to India.

Today India, China and Pakistan have huge expenses in imports. Sometimes these countries have to import things at a higher cost. In case the government of these countries try to establish their harmonious trade relations, open the Central Asian trade routes once again, the economy of these countries may be strengthened.

India and Pakistan Governments have often felt that both the countries should start trade. This would be a good step for establishing peace in South Asian countries. In the meanwhile both the governments should also think to open trade through Skardu via Dras to Kashmir and Ladakh via Chorbat la or via Charcha La. Similarly there is good scope of trade between Srinagar and Gilgit via Bandipur. Besides, there was direct trade route between Kashmir to Chilas. So, if the connecting routes will be opened between the countries, it would definitely accelerate the foreign as well as inter-regional trade, thus the economic development activities would be increased more faster than earlier.

REFERENCES

1. Joldan, E.; *op. cit.*, p. 79.
2. *Ibid.*, p. 80.
3. *Ibid.*
4. *Ibid.*, p. 71.

15
SUMMARY

In the preceding chapters I have made an attempt to review the trade activities between Ladakh and Central Asia during 1840 to 1947. While discussing the trade routes and other related activities of traders in Ladakh, some aspects about the journeys between Leh to Nubra and C.E. Tyndele Biscoe's journey between Srinagar to Leh have been touched. A brief introduction about the history, geography and religion has also been narrated in the first chapter.

The past history of Ladakh reveals that Ladakh was recognized as the centre of Central Asian trade. The trade route between Srinagar via Leh to Yarkand was the popular route among traders. However, for pashmina and wool, the route between Gartok, Rudok via Leh to Srinagar was also popular among Kashmiri and Ladakhi Leh based merchants. Thus, in Ladakh, traders came from Hoshiarpur, Srinagar, Yarkand, Turkey, Lahul, Kullu, Kumaun and Skardu and bartered their goods with the help of interpreters. From the Indian side, the traders were mostly Hindus from Hoshiarpur. There were a few Kashmiris such as Ahmad Shahdad and Qazi Brothers of Srinagar who mainly purchased small sized Namdas in Leh, got them dyed and embroidered in Srinagar, then exported them to foreign countries. Among Ladakhis, Najaf Shah Khan and Akhon Juma were the traders who dealt in the Central Asian trade. Besides Issa Ali of Chushod joined several times with Yarkandi caravans. He had considerable number of horses, which carried his goods while marching towards Yarkand or on the way back to Ladakh. Lala Dogar Mal Shadi Lal, Dina Nath, Bishembar Das, Bihari Lal, Rulia Ram, Het Ram, Bansi Lal, Rai Sahib and Gori Mal Gohal were some of the leading Punjabi traders.[1]

Hashish was the biggest single item of import from Sinkiang. Next were raw-silk, namdas, carpets, cured lamb skins, silk cloth, dust of gold, Russian velvets, long boots and silver bullion. Punjabi traders had their monopoly on Hashish trade. Ladakhis purchased rough cotton cloth, some silk cloth, readymade garments, long shoes called charoks, saddary items, warm sheep skin garments, big cotton bags, saddle bags, etc. Ladakhi purchased horses, sheep, donkeys from them. The rest of the items were either consumed in Srinagar and sent to Amritsar. Shadi Lal had a big firm in Ladakh. This firm purchased all items from Yarkand and sent them to Amritsar, Delhi and other big markets in India.[2]

During 1846-47, total imports to Ladakh from Yarkand and other Chinese territories were Rs. 2,67,650 and exports Rs. 2,38,000 to tune of from Ladakh. However, in the same period, goods worth Rs. 2,20,200 were imported to Ladakh from Indian territories. The imports consisted of opium, shawls, brocades, laki, spices, saffron and cloth. The exports from Ladakh, which mainly consisted of shawl wool, tea, charas, sulphur and borax were to the tune of 22,800. Thus the total imports were of Rs. 4,87,850 and exports of Rs. 4,54,000[3]. In 1886 imports from Central Asia were Rs. 16,52,413 and exports worth Rs. 12,32,229. Thus the total trade was of Rs. 28,84,642. During the First World War, the trade was slackened, but again picked up and in 1920 it reached Rs. 93 lakh.[4]

In sum, the commerce of Ladakh was of no great value or interest, because Ladakhis themselves were so poor to indulge in the trade. Their agricultural products too did not have much value except sometimes their horses, yaks and double humped camels were taken on hire by the Yarkandi and Kashmiri merchants. Besides these facts, Ladakh and Leh in particular gained importance due to their location as the great thoroughfare for an active commercial intercourse among Tibet, Turkistan, China and even Russia on one hand, and Kashmir, the Punjab, Lahul, Kulu, and the plains of Hindustan on the other.

REFERENCES

1. Joldan, E.; *op. cit.*, p. 69.
2. *Ibid.*, p. 70.
3. Cunningham, Alexander; *op. cit.*, p. 250.
4. Joldan, E.; *op. cit.*, pp. 70-71.

16

ETHNOBOTANY OF LADAKH HIMALAYA

OP Chaurasia, BB Bhatt** and Col DV Singh****

Ladakh, the northern most part of India, stretching over 360 km from north-west to east and widest distance 335 km from Karakoram pass to Rohtang pass is characterized by diverse flora and fauna, rare and threatened species of plants and animals, the genetic diversity and high degree of endemism.

The climate of the region is characteristically of cold desert type. During summer, days are usually very hot and dry while in winter, days are extremely cold and chilly. The temperature shows extreme variation –50°C to 39°C during different months of the year.

Physiographically the entire Ladakh can be divided into five valleys—Leh, Nubra, Changthang, Zanskar and Suru valley.

Leh Valley

It is the most populated and central valley of Ladakh and includes Lamayaru, Khalsi, Saspol, Nimmu, Likir, Phyang, Saboo, Thiksay, Leh, etc. The cultivated area lies between 9,500 ft and 13,000 ft. Wheat, barley, peas, beans, vegetables (potato, cabbage, cauliflower, radish, knol–khol etc.) lucerne, apricot and apple are grown on large scale.

Nubra Valley

It is the northern–most valley of Ladakh. Khardungla pass is the gateway of the valley and it includes Khardung, Khalsar, Diskit, Partapur, Thoise, Chalunka, Turtuk, Tegar, Panamic and Siachen area. The altitude of the valley is less in comparison to Leh valley.

* Scientist 'C', Field Research Laboratory, C/o 56 APO.
** JRF, Field Research Laboratory, C/o 56 APO.
*** Director, Field Research Laboratory, C/o 56 APO.

Changthang Valley

It is one of the most elevated valley of Ladakh and includes Chumathang, Mahe, Nyomma, Changla, Tangtse, Chushul, Pangong–tso, Tsomoriri, Rupsu and Usphi etc. The valley is famous for borax and sulphur mines as well as hot springs. The cultivated area is spread between 10,000 ft and 15,000 ft.

Zanskar Valley

It is one of the most backward valley of Ladakh bordering with Lahul and Spiti areas of Himachal. The cultivated area lies at an altitude between 10,000 ft. and 12,000 ft.

Suru Valley

The valley is situated on the Suru river and it includes Drass, Kargil, Batalic, Paskum, Bothkharbu, etc. The cultivated area is spread between 8,500 ft. and 10,500 ft. Most of the area is double cropped.

Botanical Curiosities

The flora of Ladakh Himalaya comes under alpine and high alpine zones. In western Himalaya alpine zone starts from 8500 ft where the trees are almost absent and the flora is dominated by wild annual and perennial herbs followed by dwarf bushes or shrubs. The alpine zone is mostly covered by beautiful meadows, vast pasture lands, colourful moraines, marshes and screeds. The alpine zone where the ground is almost covered permanently with snow for more than six months in a year and where scorching sun (more amount of ultra violet rays) powerfully stimulates the vegetation, the mountain slopes, meadows, moraines and pasture lands give a spectacular display of flowers to Ladakh's barren mountain during summer months. The principal vegetative growth starts at the commencement of summer when melting snow provides abundant moisture to the herbaceous vegetation to run its full course with great rapidity. The flora is in full bloom in the month of August but starts degenerating by the end of September or beginning of October.

The most significant feature of high altitude plants are adaptations on their habitats to withstand the adverse ecoclimatic conditions. The commonest adaptation observed is the cushion habit. Species of *Astragalus, Caragana* form spinescent cushions while the species of *Androsace, Arenaria, Draba, Rhodiola* form soft cushions with rosette arrangements of their leaves. The rigid mat farming plants are also frequent and represented by species of *Arenaria, Astragalus, Oxytropis* and *Stellaria.* The most curious of alpine taxa are species of *Saussurea* of which the development of profuse wool on the vegetative and floral parts is striking. Some species of *Anaphalis, Androsace, Arnebia, Leontopodium* and *Waldhemia* are also characterized by soft development of white hairs on the whole plant.

Another remarkable feature of this zone is vegetative propagation. Most of the taxa are perennial in nature and perennate by means of roots, root-stock, runners, bulbs, bulbils, rhizomes, tubers, etc. These herbs also exhibit a very interesting cycle of growth due to scanty rainfall, low temperature, snow storms, blizzards and extremely frigid conditions at this zone.

Ethnobotany

Ethnobotany deals with the direct traditional and natural relationship between human societies and plants. The term 'Ethnobotany' was coined by Harshberger in 1895 for the first time to indicate plants used by the tribals. It is obviously a very broad field including many aspects of botany and many other disciplines among botanists, anthropologists, pharmacognocists, phytochemists, pharmacologists, foresters, archeologists, palaeobotanists, linguists, folk-lorists, vaidyas, hakims, etc. The tribals belts are considered as the richest source of ethnobotany. The main objective of ethnobotany is to unearthern the hidden and secret multifarious uses of flora with specific names like ethnotaxonomy, ethnomedicine, ethnopharmacology, ethnonarcotics, ethnogynoecology, ethnoecology, ethnotoxicology, archaeo–ethnobotany, palaea–ethnobotany, etc. This field of botany plays an important role in preserving and conserving the floristic wealth and thereby environment throughout the ages due to the tribal's belief in not destroying the plant heritage.

Keeping in view the rich ethnobotany of Ladakh Himalaya, Field Research Laboratory, an establishment of Defence Research and Development Organisation has carried out detailed extensive survey of all the five valleys since 1993 and collected valuable ethnobotanical informations regarding their uses in the field of herbal medicine, edible, fodder, ornamental and others.

Ethnobotany of Ladakh can be studied under following sections:

Medicinal Plants

Medicinal value of plants was recognised as early as the Vedic ages (4500–1500 BC). The identity of several plants viz semal, pithoan and pipal referred to in the suktas of Rigveda can be fixed with reasonable certainty, while the Rigveda contains only little references about the medicinal plants the Atharveda contains more detailed informations on medicinal plants (approx. 2000) and their uses. After Vedic era the works of Charak and Susurta namely *Charak Samhita* and *Susrota Samhita* deal with about 700 drugs of daily and specific uses. The period of 16-17 century witnessed a great upheaval in the development of medical botany and most of world famous herbal drugs came into light during this period. For this reason the period is otherwise called "The Age of Herbal Medicine". It has been estimated that out of about 2000 drugs that have been used extensively in India, only 200 each are of animal and mineral origin while the rest are of plant origin.

The people of Ladakh Himalaya still prefer herbal prescriptions based on Tibetan system of medicine. The traditional medicine is practised by specialised local doctors called "Amchis". Herbal plants available in the region have been useful in the treatment of diarrhoea, cold and cough, stomach complaints, headache and skin diseases etc. Usually the specific parts or the entire plant are used by the Amchis. The useful medicinal plants have been collected from different areas during growing season (July – October) and are properly dried and packed to retain their potential. The important medicinal plants have been enumerated along with their botanical name, family, local name, brief character and ethnomedicinal uses (Table 1).

1. Achillea millefolium Linn (Asteraceae)

Locally called Pahal Kutch and a perennial herb up to 50 cm with white flower. Water extract of the plant is found effective against skin infections.

2. Aconitum heterophyllum Wallich ex Royle (Ranunculaceae)

Locally called 'Buma' and a perennial tuberous herb with greenish purple flowers. The root yields 'Aconite' which is used as aphrodisiac.

3. Aconitum violaceum Jacq ex Stapf (Ranuculaceae)

Locally called 'Buma' and perennial tuberous herb with blue flowers. Dried roots are used as a cure for cough.

4. Artemisa brevifolia Wall (Asteraceae)

Locally called 'Khamchu' and a much branched highly aromatic

TABLE 1

MEDICINAL PLANTS AND THEIR ETHNO–MEDICINAL USES

Sl. No.	*Botanical Name*	*Local Name*	*Family*	*Parts Used*	*Ethnomedicinal Uses*
1.	Achillea millefolium	Pahale katch	Asteraceae	Whole plant	Skin infection
2.	Aconitum heterophyllum	Buma	Ranunculaceae	Roots	Aphrodisiac
3.	Aconitum violaceum	Buma	-do-	Roots	Cough
4.	Artemisia brevifolia	Khampa	Asteraceae	Leaves	Anti–worm
5.	Berberis ulicina	Shingtingmona	Berberidaceae	----	As a tonic
6.	Bergenia stracheyi	Gotils	Saxifragaceae	Roots	Ulcers
7.	Biebersteinia odora	Khardung	Geraniaceae	Flowers	Opthalmic
8.	Dactylorhiza hatagirea	Angmolapo	Orchidaceae	Roots	Aphrodisiac
9.	Delphium brunonianum	Lunde–kaown	Ranunculaceae	Leaves	Neural pain
10.	Ephedra gerardiana	Chhapat	Ephedraceae	Stems	Asthma
11.	Euphrasia officinalis	Khankhung	Scrophulariaceae	----	Conjuctivitis
12.	Fritillaria roylei	Chikmo	Liliaceae	Bulbs	Asthma
13.	Gentiana aligida	Span–rgan–snon–po	Gentianaceae	Whole plant	As a tonic
14.	Herminium monorchis	Polisket	Orchidaceae	Bulbs	Kidney disease
15.	Hyoscyamus niger	Gyelamtag	Solanaceae	Leaves & seeds	Asthma
16.	Morina logifolia	Kim	Dispsacaceae	—	Anti–worm

(Continued)

(Table 1 Contd.)

Sl. No.	*Botanical Name*	*Local Name*	*Family*	*Parts Used*	*Ethnomedicinal Uses*
17.	Nepeta longibracteata	—	Lamiaceae	Whole plant	----
18.	Oxytropis tatarica	Shratkar	Fabaceae	Leaves	Diuretic
19.	Peganum harmala	Sepan	Zygophyllaceae	Whole plant	Aphrodisiac
20.	Physochlaina praealta	Langthang	Solanaceae	Leaves	Ulcers
21.	Podophyllum hexandrum	Demobkusu	Berberidaceae	Roots	Skin disease
22.	Potentilla anserina	Troma	Rosaceae	Roots	Fever
23.	Sausurea stolliczkai	Lupha	Asteraceae	Flowers	Fever
24.	Saxifraga flagellaris	Teetasarzing	Saxifragaceae	Leaves	Antiseptic
25.	Thymus serpyllum	Tumbrok	Lamiaceae	Whole plant	Gastro–intestinal
26.	Tribulus terrestris	Zemma	Zygophyllaceae	-do-	Kidney disease
27.	Verbascum thapsus	Dandashah	Scrophulariaceae	Leaves	Asthma
28.	Waldheimia tomentosa	Solokarpo	Asteraceae	Whole plant	Rheumatism

perennial plant. It yields a drug 'Santonin' which is useful against worms.

5. Berberis ulicina Hk. f. & T (Berberidaceae)

Locally called 'Shingtingnana' and a much branched shrub with organge–yellow flowers. It is used as a tonic.

6. Bergenia stracheyi Hk. (Saxifragaceae)

Locally called 'Gotils' and a perennial herb with thick rhizomatus rootstock. Roots are reported to cure ulcers.

7. Biebersteinia odora Stephan (Geraniaceae)

Locally called 'Khardung' and a strong aromatic herb with yellow flowers. It is used against opthalmic diseases.

8. Dactylorhiza hatagirea (D. Don) Soo (Orchidaceae)

Locally called 'Angmolapo' and a perennial herb with distinct palmatly lobed roots. The root is used as aphrodisiac.

9. Delphinium brunonianum Royle (Ranunculaceae)

Locally called 'Lunde–kaown' and a perennial herb with bluish purple flowers. It is used against neural pain.

10. Ephedra gererdiana Wall ex Stapf. (Ephedraceae)

Locally called 'Chhapat' and a perennial shrub with fleshy red fruit chiefly used for asthma.

11. Euphrasia officinalis Linn (Scrophulariaceae)

Locally called 'Khankhung' and an annual herb with 2–lipped flowers. It has soothing effect on eye in conjuctivitis.

12. Fritillaria roylei Hook (Liliaceae)

Locally called 'Chihmo' and a perennial herb with yellow–green flowers. Bulbs are effective against asthma.

13. Gentiana aligida Pallas

Locally called 'Spang–rgan–snon–po' and a small tufted perennial herb with dark blue flowers. It is found to be effective in fever.

14. Herminium monorchis R. Br. (Orchidaceae)

Locally called 'Polisket' and a tuberous slender herb with yellow–green flowers. The tuber is useful to cure kidney disease.

15. Hyoscyamus niger Linn (Solanaceae)

Locally called 'Gyelamtag' and a biennial herb with funnel shaped flowers. It is useful against asthma.

16. Morina longifolia Wall (Dipsacaceae)

Locally called 'Kim' and a perennial spiny herb with dull yellow flowers. It is used against worm infestation.

17. Nepeta longibracteata Benth

An annual prostrate herb with blue flowers. It is useful in stomach complaints.

18. Oxytropis tatarica Jacq (Fabaceae)

Locally called 'Shratkor' and a perennial aromatic herb with purple flowers. It is used as diuretic.

19. Peganum harmala Linn (Zygophyllaceae)

Locally called 'Sepan' and a perennial herb with greenish–white flowers. It is used as aphrodisiac.

20. Physochlaina praealta Miers (Solanceae)

Locally called 'Langthang' and a perennial herb with funnel shaped dull–yellow flowers. It is found effective against ulcers.

21. Podophyllum hexandrum Royle (Berberidaceae)

Locally called 'Demobkhusu' and a perennial scapigerous herb with reddish berry. Roots are used locally against skin diseases.

22. Potentilla anserina Linn (Rosaceae)

Locally called 'Troma' and a pernnial prostrate herb with yellow herb. It is used against fever, cold and cough.

23. Saussurea stolliczkai Clarke (Asteraceae)

Locally called 'Lupha' and a small tufted perennial herb with purple flower–heads. It is used to cure fever.

24. Saxifraga flagellaris Willd (Saxifragaceae)

Locally called 'Teetasarzing' and a small perennial herb with yellow flowers. The crushed leaves are used as an antiseptic.

25. Scorzonera virgata DC. (Asteraceae)

Locally called 'Tharnoo' and a slender much–branched perennial herb with yellow flower–heads. It is used against rheumatism.

26. Thymus serpyllum Linn (Lamiaceae)

Locally called 'Tumbrok' and an aromatic perennial herb with reddish flowers. It is used in gastro–intestinal disorders.

27. Tribulus terrestris Linn (Zygophyllaceae)

Locally called 'Zemma' and a perennial prostrate herb with spiny fruits. It is useful against Kidney diseases.

28. Verbascum thapsus Linn (Scrophulariaceae)

Locally called 'Dandashah' and a perennial tall shrub with yellow flowers. It is found effective against asthma.

29. Waldheimia tomentosa Regal (Asteraceae)

Locally called 'Solokarpo' and a perennial prostrate herb with light blue flowers. The whole plant is used against rheumatism.

Wild Edible Plants

A long spell of subzero temperature prevailing in Ladakh forced inhabitants to search for wild edible plants. At different elevations wild plants start growing as soon as snow melts and temperature is favourable for plant growth. Quite a good number of plants start growing during April–May. Over the years of experience perhaps by hit and trial method inhabitants of the area identified certain wild plants which are good to be used as vegetables. Since then tender shoots, leaves and stems of these plants are being used as green vegetables.

To have green vegetables during long winter the same is subjected to solar dehydration. Because of intense sunlight these leafy vegetables are dehydrated under shade having proper ventilation. Since humidity is low during August and September solar dehydration is quick and satisfactory. Dehydration and cooking as well as organoleptic properties of the products are quite satisfactory but require improvement by using solar dehydration technology mainly by deploying solar dehydrators/ driers. This will result in better products, free of dust and mixing of undesirable plants caused by unexpected strong winds.

The important wild edible taxa have been briefly enumerated along with botanical name, family, local name and brief characters (Table 2).

1. Allium przewalskianum Regal (Amaryllidaceae)

Locally called 'Skotche' and a perennial bulbous herb with lilac flowers in dense umbel. Young leaves are used to add flavour.

2. Capparis spinosa Linn (Capparidaceae)

Locally called 'Kabra' and diffuse prostrate shrub with large fleshy fruits. Tender leaves and fruits are used as vegetables.

3. Carum bulbocastanum Clarke (Apiaceae)

Locally called 'Kala zeera' and a perennial herb with white flowers. Fruits are used as a spice.

4. Carum carvi Linn. (Apiaceae)

Locally called 'Konyoet' and an annual herb with white pink flowers. Fruits are used a spices.

5. Chenopodium album Linn (Chenopodiaceae)

Locally called 'Elm' and an annual or biennial herb with small flowers in clusters. Tender leaves are cooked as potherb.

6. Fagopyrum esculentum Moench (Polygonaceae)

Locally called 'Dyat' and an annual herb with cordate leaves. Young leaves or tender shoots are used either as a fresh vegetable or dehydrated for winter use.

7. Hippophae rhamnoides Linn. ssp turkestainica Rousi (Elaeagnaceae)

Locally called 'Chhermang' and a dwarf much–branched shrub with small orange–red fruits. The fruits are rich source of Vit 'C' and used for making jam, sauce, jelly, etc.

8. Lactuca dolichophylla Kitam (Asteraceae)

Locally called 'Khala' and a tall perennial herb with blue to violet flower–heads. Tender leaves are used as vegetable.

9. Lepidium latifolium Linn. (Brassicaceae)

Locally called 'Sauson' and a perennial branched herb with tiny white flowers. The tender leaves are cooked as vegetable.

10. Mentha longifolia Hudson (Lamiaceae)

Locally called 'Pholoing' and an aromatic perennial herb with tiny purple flowers. The leaves and tender shoots are edible.

11. Oxyria digyna Hill (Polygonaceae)

Locally called 'Lamanchu' and a fleshy acid flavoured herb with pinkish flowers in branched inflorescence. The leaves are used both raw and cooked.

12. Rheum webbianum Royle (Polygonaceae)

Locally called 'Lachu' and a stout perennial herb with pale yellow flowers. Leaf stalk is used as raw or salad or added to custard.

13. Rhodiola imbricata Edgew (Crassulaceae)

Locally called 'Shrolo' and a succulent herb with rose scented massive rootstock. The young leaves and tender shoots are edible.

14. Rumex patientia Linn. spp tibeticus Rech. f. (Polygonaceae)

Locally called 'Shoma' and an erect perennial herb with tiny yellowish–green flowers in spike. The young leaves are used as vegetable.

15. Taraxacum officinale Wigg. Boiss (Asteraceae)

Locally called 'Han' and a scapigerous perennial herb with milky root and yellow flower–heads. Young leaves are cooked as vegetable.

16. Urtica hyperborea Jacq ex Wedd (Urticaceae)

Locally called 'Dzotsutt' and a densely tufted perennial shrub with stinging hairs. Young leaves are used as vegetable after proper solar dehydration.

Fodder Plants

Alfalfa locally called 'Ole' is the main and only cultivated legume fodder which also grows as wild. In addition, a number of wild plants abundant in alpine pasture are used as fodder for the livestock. Wild gram, an alpine pasture legume grows abundantly in certain areas of Ladakh at the height of 14,000–15,000 ft whose nutritive value is quite comparable with that of lucerne. Even the locals harvest certain wild plants and dry them properly for winter use. The fodder plants of the region is dominated by legumes and grasses. In addition to this, plant species of other families are also utilized as fodder. The legumes are riches in proteins than the ordinary grasses and therefore fodder is always nutritious if legumes are grown along with grasses. A brief of important fodder plants along with botanical name, family, local names and plant characters is as follows:

1. Aconogonum tortuosum Hara (Polygonaceae)

Locally called 'Itemeng' and a low dense perennial shrub with cream coloured flowers.

2. Agropyron repens Beauv (Poaceae)

Locally called 'Zamak' and a tufted perennial grass.

3. Astragalus frigidus Gray

Locally called 'Skarmalo' and a herbaceous erect perennial herb with yellow flowers.

4. Avena fatua Linn. (Poaceae)

An annual erect herb with pyramidal panicles and oblong caryopsis.

5. Cicer microphyllum Benth (Fabaceae)

Locally called 'Seri' and a spreading perennial legume with purple flowers.

6. Convolvulus arvensis Linn. (Convolvulaceae)

Locally called 'Tikticma' and a slender climbing perennial herb with pink purple flowers.

7. Heracleum pinnatum Clarke (Apiaceae)

Locally called 'Khros' and a tall perennial herb with white flower in umbel.

8. Lotus corniculatus

A prostrate perennial herb with yellow flowers in clusters.

9. Medicago falcata Linn. (Fabaceae)

Locally called 'Ole' and a semi–spreading perennial herb with yellow flowers in axillary clusters.

10. Medicago media (Fabaceae)

It is believed to be a product of natural hybridization between *M. Sativa* and *M. falcata* Flower colours are mixture of yellow and purple.

11. Medicago sativa Linn. (Fabaceae)

All the characters are same as in *M falcata* except flower colours which are mauve.

12. Melilotus officinalis Pallas (Fabaceae)

Locally called 'Ole' and are biennial or perennial herb with yellow flowers in spike.

13. Poa annua Linn. (Poaceae)

Locally called 'Wakung' and a perennial tufted grass with oblong spikelets.

14. Prangos pabularia Lindley (Apiaceae)

Locally called 'Prangos' and a robust perennial bushy herb with yellow flowers in compound umbels.

15. Stachys tibetica Vatke (Lamiaceae)

Locally called 'Yakjak' and a low much–branched perennial shrub with pinkish flowers.

Ornamental Plants

Flowers symbolize purity, beauty, love, passion and tranquility such as rose for love, pansy for thoughts, daffodil for regard, sweet pea for departure, lily for purity, etc. In Ladakh region only limited flowers such as sunflower, hollyhock, marigold, aster, poppy and cosmos are grown. In addition, several wild plants have also aesthetic importance. Some of them have got importance in the Gompas (religious places) and used for various purposes in special occasions. The potential wild ornamental plants are briefly described (Table 4):

1. **Aquilegia fragrans *Benth (Ranunculaceae)***

A sweet–scented perennial herb with cream–coloured flowers.

2. **Aster tibeticus *Hk. f. (Asteraceae)***

Locally called 'Skalzangmentok' and a herbaceous perennial plant with blue flower–heads.

3. **Cremanthodium ellisii *Kitam***

Locally called 'Lukumentok' and an erect perennial herb with solitary yellow flower–head.

4. Epilobium latifalium Linn.

An erect perennial herb with rose–purple flowers and borne in long raceme.

5. Geranium pratense Linn. (Geraniaceae)

Locally called 'Gugchuk' and an eract perennial herb with bluish–purple flowers in pairs.

6. Inula obtusifolia Kerner

Locally called 'Rupmak' and a much–branched perennial herb with yellow flower–heads.

7. Iris lactea Pallas (Iridaceae)

Locally called 'Tesmametok' and a perennial herb with stout rootstock and lilac flowers.

8. Lindelofia stylosa Brand (Boraginaceae)

Locally called 'Makpen' and an erect hairy perennial herb with claret–coloured flower.

9. Meconopsis aculeata Royle (Papaveraceae)

A slender rather delicate perennial herb with blue flowers in raceme.

10. Primala rosea Royle (Primulaceae)

Locally called 'Sulumentok' and a glabrous scapigerous perennial herb with rose–pink flowers in a lax umbel.

11. Rosa webbiana Wallich ex Royle

Locally called 'Siah' and a leaf shedding shrub with pink flowers.

12. Rosularia alpestris Boiss

Locally called 'Shrolo' and a perennial succulent herb with pink–purple flowers borne in terminal clusters.

17

RECENT ADVANCES IN HORTICULTURAL RESEARCH IN LADAKH

Sanjai K. Dwivedi and Col DV Singh** Field Research Laboratory (DRDO) Leh (Ladakh)*

Ladakh is characterized by uneven land at an altitude between 2900 and 5900 metres, mountains and arctic desert and extremely cold weather for long durations (7 months). Minimum winter temperature of –30°C (Leh) and –50°C (Dras) is not uncommon. The region gets snow clamped during winter and remains cut off from the rest of the country for about seven months in a year. Agricultural season is very short ranging from 5-6 months in summer only. The growing season starts with the melting of snow in April/May and ends with blowing chilly winds in September. Chilly winds damage the standing crops after mid of September. The annual precipitation is very scanty. Natural springs and perennial streams are the main sources of irrigation besides the rivers like Indus, Nubra, Shyok and Suru. In this paper, various aspects for improved horticultural practices for Ladakh have been discussed.

1. Summer Vegetable Production Technology

(a) Direct Sown. Local radish, turnip, swede and potato are the crops being grown since long back in the region. But now over 45 crops like carrot, radish, pea, broad bean, beetroot and various leafy vegetables like palak, methi, coriander, celery, parsely, etc. are being grown commercially by local farmers. The cultural practices of improved varieties, sowing time, seed rate, etc. have been standardized (Table 1).

* Scientist 'B', Field Research Laboratory, (DRDO) Leh (Ladakh).
** Director, Field Research Laboratory, (DRDO) Leh (Ladakh).

TABLE–1

Package of Vegetable Cultivation Practices in Ladakh

Vegetables	*Sowing Time*	*Seed Rate Kg/ha*	*Spacing Between* Rows	*Spacing Between* Plants	*Fertilisers (Kg/ha)* N	*Fertilisers (Kg/ha)* P^2O^5	*Fertilisers (Kg/ha)* K^2O	*Days to Harvesting*	*Av. Yield q/ha*
Beetroot	April–May	10	30	10	50	40	50	60-70	150-200
*Brinjal	April–May	0.5-0.6	60	45	80	40	50	90-100	80-100
Broccoli	April–May	0.5-0.6	60	45	100	50	50	100-110	200-250
Broad Bean	April–June	30-40	30	10	30	80	50	100-120	150-200
*Bottle gourd	May–June	5	180	60	60	40	40	90-100	100-150
Carrot	April–June	4-5	30	10	50	40	50	70-80	200-250
Cauliflower	March–June	0.4-0.5	60	45	100	50	50	90-100	250-300
Cabbage	March–June	0.5-0.6	60	45	100	50	50	90-100	300-350
*Cucumber	May–June	2.5-3	100	50	80	40	40	70-80	80-100
*Capsicum	April–May	0.7-0.8	60	45	80	40	50	100-120	50-60
Celery	March–May	0.125	75	20	100	40	80	70-80	60-70
Coriander	March–August	37-40	15	5	40	20	20	40-50	120-150
French Bean	April–June	50-75	30	3-5	30	80	50	70-80	100-150
Fenugreek	April–June	10-12	30	2-3	20	40	20	60-80	100-200
Knol–Khol	March–June	1-1.5	30	30	80	50	50	80-90	200-250

(Continued)

Vegetables	*Sowing Time*	*Seed Rate Kg/ha*	*Spacing Between*		*Fertilisers (Kg/ha)*			*Days to Harvesting*	*Av. Yield q/ha*
			Rows	*Plants*	*N*	*P^2O^5*	*K^2O*		
Karam Sag	March–June	0.7-0.8	30	20	80	50	50	70-80	80-100
*Lady's finger	May–June	8-10	30	15	60	40	40	80-90	70-80
*Longmelon	May–June	2.5-3	150	60	50	30	30	80-90	100-120
Lettuce	March–July	0.7-0.8	30	30	60	50	50	40-45	75-100
Onion	March–April	8-10	15	10	80	50	60	100-110	200-250
Potato	April–May	3000	45	30	120	60	80	120-130	300-400
Peas	April–June	75-100	30	2-3	30	60	50	90-100	120-150
*Pumpkin	May–June	7-8	180	75	80	30	30	80-90	200-250
Palak	March–August	10-15	30	5	60	30	30	30-40	50-60

* These crops to be grown in greenhouse or by mulching technology.

Introduction of potato variety Kufri Chandra Mukhi has revolutionized the potato production in the region.

(b) Transplanted Crop. Cole crops like cabbage, cauliflower, knol knol, broccoli, brussels sprout and other crops like tomato, onion can also be grown successfully in Ladakh during summer months. The seedlings are raised in April when fear of low temperature damage is over and transplanted in open field 40-45 days after sowing.

Frost susceptible tropical crops like cucurbits, capsicum, brinjal chilly, okra, etc. are rare for Ladakh since they cannot be grown by adopting normal cultural practices. The nursery for these crops can be raised in late April or early May. Greenhouses or polythene covering may be adopted for getting early nursery. Seedlings at 5-6 leaf stage should either be planted in greenhouse or in open field only by adopting the black polythene mulching technology to get early crop and high yield (Table–5) (Singh, 1992). Mulching also reduces the weed population and frequency of watering. Seeds of cucurbits are generally sown in the polytubes under greenhouse condition and 40-45 days after sowing they are transplanted to the fields. Recommended varieties and other tips are given in Table 1.

2. Winter Vegetable Production Technology

Ladakh remains cut off from rest of the nation from November–June every year due to blockage of roads. Subzero temperatures prevail from December to February throughout Ladakh whereas zero degree is experienced during rest of the winter period. Under such conditions, it is impossible to grow vegetables in open field and transportation of fresh vegetable is also a problem. This necessitates protected vegetable cultivation in the region (Singh, 1997).

Studies carried out at Field Research Laboratory (DRDO) Leh during 1996–98 indicate that for winter cultivation trench (underground greenhouse) is the best structure (Table 3) followed by local polyhouse (Singh *et al.* 1998) where the crops like mustard, lettuce, spinach, methi, coriander, etc. can be grown successfully in protected condition (Table 2).

Trench, an underground structure, may be of any variable convenient size but preferably of 30 x 12 x 3 ft. These structures are kept covered with UV stabilized transparent polythene (400 gauge). During night another covering of black polythene is given (Singh, 1995). Trench cultivation harnesses soil temperature to create congenial atmosphere inside for the growth of leafy vegetables when outside temperatures touch –30°C. Other greenhouse structures such as polyhouse, glasshouse etc are least effective and more expensive (Table 3).

3. Vegetable Seed Production

The long day length, high light intensity and low atmospheric humidity coupled with lack of diseases and pests throughout the growing season provides ideal conditions for production of quality seeds of temperate vegetables.

Field Research Laboratory has standardized the seed production technology for cabbage (Singh *et al.* 1997) beetroot (Singh *et al.* 1997) carrot, onion, knol khol, radish, spinach, true potato seeds without any modification. Quality of seeds and seed yield produced in the region are at par with international standards (Table–4).

It has been proved that the area has a vast potential for vegetable seed production and its scientific exploitation will not only improve the economic status of tribal farmers of Ladakh but also reduce the import of vegetable seeds like cabbage, beetroot etc.

4. Plastic Mulch

Covering of soil surface between plants using organic waste materials (plant straw, dry leaves, sawdust etc.) and synthetic materials (paper, polyethylene, wax–coated paper, aluminium foil, asphalt spray emulsion etc.) are known as mulching.

Mulching serves the following purposes:

1. It conserves soil moisture, though the type of mulch used affects the degree of conservation of moisture.
2. It raises soil temperature when atmospheric temperature is low. It maintains optimum soil temperature if atmospheric temperature is high.
3. Germination and nourishment of many weeds is reduced to physical barrier provided by mulching. Weed growth is totally checked by use of mulch like black polyethylene.
4. Mulching stimulate soil microorganism such as algae, mosses, actinomycetes, earthworm, etc. This results in rapid breakdown of soil organic matter and release of plant nutrients for better crop growth and yield.

Experiments were conducted at FRL using black polyethylene 150 gauge thick as mulch in transplanted vegetable crops such as cauliflower, cabbage, tomato, brinjal and capsicum. Favourable response was observed in cabbage, cauliflower and tomato pertaining to earliness and productivity. There was accelerated growth in mulched crop and no weeding was required. Crop yields under black polyethylene mulched crop and under unmulched crop recorded are given in Table–5.

5. Organic Farming

Dependence on synthetic chemical material like fertilizers, insecticides, pesticides, fungicides, weedicides and growth regulators are necessitated because of their quick response in overall crop production. In vegetable production these chemicals play important role. But besides damaging soil structure and the environment, these chemicals are potential health hazards in foods. Moreover, chemicals are costly both to the farmers and society. Organic farming makes positive contribution for the protection of soil, environment and human health. It is dependent upon maintaining ecological balance and developing biological processes to the optimum. Ladakh is following this traditional method of organic farming. In vegetable production use of fertilizers is mostly avoided. Use of pesticides and growth regulators is either nil or negligible. For enriching soil animal manure, night soil and kitchen waste etc. are used. At certain places legumes are included in crop rotations as well as mixed crops. Insects and disease though not many, but are left to natural factors for their control. These principles and practices resulted in the following:

1. Sustainable production of high quality vegetables in sufficient quantity.
2. Utilization of natural resources.
3. Encouragement and enhancement of biological cycles for maintenance of soil flora and fauna.
4. Maintenance of soil fertility.
5. Use of renewable resources.

Crops like palak, chinese cabbage, turnip, radish, knol khol, karam sag, bean, peas, summer squash and Jerusalem artichoke do not require inorganic manure if the soil is supplied with 15 tons of organic manure per hectare before taking the crops. Organically grown vegetables of Ladakh would fetch high price abroad if their export are promoted. Sustainability of organic vegetable production in cold desert regions has been proved successful.

6. Fruit Culture

Apricot (*Prunus armeniaca* L.) is one of the most important temperate fruits of India and the major fruit crop of Ladakh. The cultivation of apricot in Ladakh has been done since ages and it has taken deep root in the culture of local people. Besides using it for table purpose, it is also being used for dehydration, oil extraction (from bitter kernals) and sweet kernals are edible and used as dry fruits (Sharma, 1997).

Apples and other fruits like walnut, pear, peach, strawberry are also grown in the region but on a very limited scale. The performance and popularity of apricot is very high in the region because it can withstand very low temperature of –30°C during winter. It thrives well in marginal land and adverse climatic conditions. The incidence of pest and diseases is almost nil in apricot in the region. Thus, there is unlimited scope for further expansion of apricot cultivation in Ladakh. But non-availability of quality planting materials and technical knowhow regarding cultivation practices are the major hurdle in its expansion.

Keeping the above facts and problems in view, Field Research Laboratory, Leh initiated a programme on the standardization of propagational techniques and screening of local apricot germplasm during 1996. The salient findings are being discussed below:

(a) Standardization of propagational techniques. Non-availability of genuine planting material is the major hurdle in the expansion of apricot cultivation in Ladakh. It is surprising to note that not a single fruit nursery is operative in the region. Though the State Government Fruit Nursery, Saspol has a good germplasm of apricot and apple but poor management and lack of suitable propagation techniques has resulted in the fast decline of the quality germplasm.

The experiments conducted at FRL indicate that shield budding adopted during second fortnight of July results in 82 per cent success. Two year old seedling could be used as root stock. The efforts have also been made to standardized apricot propagation during winter month. Two-three years old seedling rootstocks can be uprooted by the end of January and the scion of the same thickness as stock can be grafted by cleft method in mid of February. The technique is called bench grafting which results over 90 per cent success. The technique has a vast potential in the region (Dwivedi *et al.*). Being operated in winter season, a large quantity of planting material could be made available as people find free time during winter. The growth of the plants are also much faster than those which have been budded. Adoption of bench grafting seems to be the most amicable solution to overcome the crisis of planting material in the region.

(b) Top Working of Apricot. Establishment and growth of plants is very poor in Ladakh because of poor soil, adverse climatic conditions and a very short growing period of 5-6 months. Besides apricot plantation in new areas, a number of wild seedlings are available in the region. These seedling trees have established their roots well in the rocky soil and hard terrain of Ladakh but they produce poor quality and small sized non-edible fruits. Such established trees can be converted to the productive ones by top working with promising cultivors after heading back the branches in March. The new shoots which arise from these trees, could be used for shield budding during mid June - early July where over 90 per cent success has been recorded (Dwivedi *et al*). Top working of apricot could be another way to boost the apricot cultivation in the region.

(c) Germplasm Evaluation. Ladakh has a large variation in apricot germplasm. Studies are being conducted to survey, analyse and evaluate the local germplasm of apricots and apple for proper conservation and exploitation. Over 15 types of local apricot and 06 types of local apples have been identified. Further studies on these crops are in the pipeline.

ANNEXURE—1

Promising Varieeties of Vegetables for Ladakh

Group	*Vegetable*	*Suitable Varieties*
Cole Crops	Cabbage	Golden Acre, Head, Early Drum Head, ARU-Glory, Pride of India.
	Cauliflower	Pusa Snowball, K-1, Pusa Snowball-1, Snowball-6, Silver King, Early Snowball.
	Knol-Khol	White Vienna, Purple Vienna
	Broccoli	Italian Green Sprouting
	Brussel's Sprouts	Hilds. Ideal.
	Kale	Kashmiri local
Root Crops	Radish	Pusa Himani, Scarlet Globe, Local
	Turnip	Purple Top White Globe, Golden Ball

(Continued)

(Table 1(A) *Contd.*)

Group	*Vegetable*	*Suitable Varieties*
	Carrot	Nantes, Local, Yamdagni
	Beetroot	Detroit Dark Red
	Swede	FRL Swede Sal-1
Leafy Vegetable	Beet leaf	K. Raya, FRL sel.
	Spinach	Prickly Seeded
	Palak	Mongol, All Green
	Mustard	ARU-Black, Zem, TM-4
	Fenugreek	Pusa Early Bunching, Kasuri
	Karam Sag	Kashmiri
	Orich (Ustakh)	Kashmiri
	Coriander	PD-1, Pant Haritima
Leguminous Crops	Pea	Bonnevillea, Arkel
	French Bean	Contender, VL-1
	Broad Bean	FRL Sel. Local
Bulb Crops	Onion	Local White, Pusa Red
Salad Crops	Celery	Early Zem
	Lettuce	Great Lake, Dum (Local)
Tuber Crops	Potato Kufri	Chandarmukhi, Kufri Jyoti
Solanaceous Fruit Crops	Tomato	Pusa Early Dwarf, Punjab Chhuhara, Rupali, Pusa Hybrid-1, Pusa Sheetal
	Brinjal	Pusa Purple Round, Pusa Purple Longe
	Capsicum	California Wonder, HC–202
	Chilli	Jawala
Cucurbits	Pumpkin	Pusa Vishwas
	Summer Squash	Australian Green
	Bottle gourd	Pusa Summer Prolific long, Pusa Naveen, Arka long, Pusa Sandesh
	Ridge gourd	Pusa Nasdar
	Spong gourd	Pusa Chikni
	Long melon	Tar Deshi, Green Long
	Cucumber	Poinsette, Pusa Sanyog
	Muskmelon	Hara Madhu, Punjab Sunehra
	Water melon	Sugar Baby, Arka manik
	Okra	Pusa Sawani, Parbhani Kranti, Varsna

ANNEXURE—2
Performance of Various Leafy Vegetables Grown Under Polyhouse During Peak Winter (Nov.–March)

Crop/Variety	*Av. Plant height (Cm)*	*Yield/m² (Kg)*
Beet leaf (All Green)	21.36	1.25
Beet leaf (Mangol)	34.44	2.50
Coriander (Local)	39.8	2.25
Lettuce (Great Lake)	23.84	4.50
Veg. Mustard (All Black)	46.56	4.50
Fenugreek (Kasuri)	39.92	2.50

ANNEXURE—3
Production Economics of Beet Leaf (Palak) In Protected Structure

Structure	*Cost of Structure Rs/M²/yr*	*Palak yield (Kg/m²)*	*Cost of produce @ Rs. 15/Kg*	*Profit (Rs./m²)*
Glasshouse	288	3.3	49.5	–238.5
Polyhouse	125	2.7	40.5	–84.5
Local Polyhouse	35	5.4	81.0	46.0
Unit Polyhouse	38	4.5	67.5	29.5
Trench	14	6.3	94.5	80.5
Tunnel 1	22	2.2	33.0	11.0

REFERENCES

1. Dwivedi, S.K. and Singh, B. (Communicated). Standardization of propagational techniques for apricot in Ladakh. 86th Indian Science Congress to be held at Chennai in January 1999.
2. Dwivedi, S.K, Paljor, E. and Singh, B. (Communicated). Top working of apricot in Ladakh, *Indian Horticulture.*
3. Singh, B. (1992). Vegetable production in Ladakh. Field Research Laboratory (DRDO)–Leh.
4. Singh, B. (1995). Greenhouse development in Leh. Paper presented in National workshop on commercialization of tissue culture and greenhouse Technology, 5-6 May 1995, Bangalore, India.
5. Singh, B., Jadhav, K.L. and Paljor, Eli (1997). In high altitude cold desert of Ladakh.... protected vegetable farming potentials. *Indian Horticulture.* 42 (3), pp. 16-17.

6. Singh, B., Jadhav, K.L. and Paljor, Eli (1997). Potentials of cabbage seed production in Leh valley. *Indian Horticultre.* 41(4), pp. 36-37.
7. Singh, N., Singh, B. and Sareen, S.K. (1997). High altitude cold desert beet seed production. *Indian Horticulture.* 41(4) : 57-58.
8. Singh, B., Dwivedi, S.K. and Paljor Eli (1998). Studies on suitability of various structures for winter vegetable production at subzero temperatures, Paper presented in 25th IHC -Belgium, August 1998. Abstract. pp. 290.
9. Sharma, J.L. (1997). Fruit industry status in Ladakh. Office of the Chief Horticulture Officer, Leh (Ladakh).

BIBLIOGRAPHY

Ali, Aamir: *'Environmental Protection of Himalaya—A Mountaineers View*; New Delhi: Indus Pub. Co.

Arora, R.C.: *In the Land of Kashmir, Ladakh and Gilgit*, Jay Kay Book House, Jammu, 1940.

Band, George: 'The Green Expedition of Bhutan; In : *Environmental Protection of Himalaya–A Mountaineers' View*; Indus Pub. Co.

Beek, Martijin and Bertelsen, Kristoffer Brix: 1995. 'Ladakh: Independence is not Enough,' *Himali* Vol. 8. No. 2. March/April.

Chopra, Pran: *On an Indian Border*, Asia Pub. House, 1964.

Cook, W.: 1973. *Races of Northen India;* Delhi: Cosmo Pub., Reprint.

Datta, C.L.: *Ladakh and Western Himalayan Politics: 1819-1848*, Munshiram Manoharlal Pub., New Delhi, 1973.

Drew, Frederic: *Jammu and Kashmir Territories*; New Delhi: Cosmo Pub.

Edelman, D.I.: 1983. *Dardic and Nuristani Languages,* Moscow.

Francke, A.H.: 1977. *History of Western Tibet*, Delhi; Reprint.

Ganju, O.N.: 1989. Lessons from Ladakh; *Frontline*, July 28-Aug. 4.

Gazetteer of Kashmir and Ladakh: Vivek Pub., Delhi, 1974.

Grimshaw, Anna: 1983. 'Celibacy, Religion and Economy, activity in a monastic Community of Ladakh', In *Recent Research on Ladakh;* Band I., Germany.

Jamyang Gyaltsan: 1885. 'Sabd Vidhya' In" 'Ladakh Prabha (3); Tashi *paljor* (ed.); C.I.B.S. Leh.

Jina, Prem Singh: Ladakh Aur Paryatan (Tourism in Ladakh), In: Ist National Conference, CIBS, Leh (Ladakh), 1981.

————: Foreign Tourists and their Impact on Ladakh, In: IIIrd National Conference, Ladakh Prabha (3), 1985 paper read in the conference in 1983, CIBS, Leh.

Jina, Prem Singh: *The Foreign Tourist Traffic in Ladakh Himalaya Research and Development (Problem Oriented Studies),* Vol. 3 (1), Nainital, 1984.

———: Boudh Bikskus of Ladakh, In : Proceed. of All India Conference on Buddhist and Jaina Monasticism, Deptt. of Buddhist Studies, Delhi University, Delhi, 1983-84.

———: Buddhism in Ladakh and World Peace, In: 10th International Buddhist Conference on 'Buddhism and World Peace,' Japanese Temple, Bodh Gaya, Vol. X, 1984.

———: A Brief Introduction of Ladakhi Gonpas, In : All India Conference Kashmir University, Srinagar, Deptt. of Centre for Central Asian Studies; Proceed, Ladakh Life and Culture, 1986.

———: Socio-Economic and Cultural Relations between Ladakh and Lahul and Spiti, In: All India Conf. at Boudh Darshan Mahavidayalaya, Keylong (Himachal Pradesh), 1986.

———: A Survey of Buddhist Community in Ladakh Himalaya. In: 12th International Buddhist Conference on Buddhism and Social Harmony, Japanese Temple, Bodh Gaya, India, Vol. XII, 1986.

———: Pastureland of Zangskar and its effects on Ecology. In: Ist National Conference on Desert Development Agency, Leh, Ladakh, 1986.

———: Monasteries in the Economy of Leh-Ladakh. In: All India Conference on Buddhist Monasteries of Himalayan Region, Various Aspects, 9-13 Aug., CIBS., Leh, 1988.

———: Eco-Environmental Study of Tourist Industry in Ladakh Himalaya. In: All India Conference, Kashmir University, Srinagar, Deptt. of Centre for Central Asian Studies, 1989.

———: Buddhism and 'Human Values in the History of Ladakh Himalaya, In: International Buddhist Conference, Japanese Temple, Bodh Gaya, India, 1990.

———: Pasture Ecology of Leh, Ladakh, In: Wisenschafts Gegschichte and Gegenivartige Forschungen in Nordwest Indian Staaliches Museum Fur Volkerkunde, Dresden Forschungsstelle, Germany, 1990.

Jina, Prem Singh: Impact of Tourism on Ladakh Society and Culture, paper presented in the All India Conference; J.N.U., New Delhi, 1993.

———: Impact of Tourism on Ecological set-up of Ladakh Himalaya, In: International Conference on Ladakh Studies (Sixth Colloquium), Aug. 16-20, Leh, 1993.

———: Poultry Industry in Ladakh, *Himalaya Today*, Sept. 92. Feb. 1993, Vol. IX, Nos. 2 and 3, p. 7.

———: Dasvi Shatabadi Purva Lahul me Bodh Dharm Evam Sanskriti, *Janjati Mela Samarika*, pp. 60-62.

———: Buddhism in Ladakh and its Approach to Material World, In: International Buddhist Conference, Japanese Temple, Bodh Goya, 8-10 Dec., India, 1993.

———: Tourist Industry in Ladakh, *Himalaya Today*, Jan-March, 1994, Vol. V, No. 2, p. 20.

———: Tourism in Ladakh Himalaya, Indus Publishing Company, New Delhi, 1994.

———: Bhikshunis in Ladakh (Nuns in Ladakh) National Conference, 14-15 July 1994, Keylong (H.P.).

———: *High Pasturelands of Ladakh Himalaya*, Indus Pub. Company, New Delhi, 1995.

———: Famous Western Explorers to Ladakh, Indus Publishing Company, 1995.

———: Kesar: A Great Epic (Hindi), *Seeraja*, Vol. 2 (June-July), 1994, pp. 17-20.

———: *Ladakh: The land and the people*, Indus Publishing Company, New Delhi, 1996.

———**(ed):** Recent Researchers on the Himalaya, Indus Publishing Company, New Delhi, 1997.

———: Travel Accounts of the Chinese Pilgrims in the Himalaya. In: *Recent Researchers on the Himalaya*, 1997, pp. 35-42.

———: A.H. Francke's contribution in the Cultural History of Ladakh. In: *Recent Researches on the Himalaya*, 1997, pp. 43-52.

Jina, Prem Singh: Nawang Tsering: A Brilliant Sculptor of Ladakh. In: *Recent Researches on the Himalaya;* 1997, pp. 61-64.

———: Botias of Nepal: A Socio-Economic and Cultural Study. In: Recent Researches on the Himalaya; 1997, pp. 74-77.

———: Lamayuru Monastery of Ladakh. In: *Recent Researches on the Himalaya;* 1997, pp. 82-86.

———: Modernisation and Buddhism in Ladakh. In: *Recent Researches on the Himalaya*; 1997, pp. 106-13.

———: Impact of Tourism on the Ecological setup of Ladakh Himalaya. In: *Recent Researches on the Himalaya,* 1997, pp. 122-25.

———: Susma Mehra and Jina, Manju: Utility of Nemo-Padam Road for the Economic Development of Zangskar. In: *Recent Researches on the Himalaya*, 1997, pp. 126-28.

———: Turmoil and Success in Ladakhi Politics. In: *Recent Researches on the Himalaya,* 1997, pp. 160-204.

———: Poultry Industry in Nainital District, Kumaun Himalaya. In: *Recent Researches on the Himalaya,* 1997, pp. 216-19.

———: Ladakhi Bodh Vivah Geet (Marriage Folk Songs of Ladakhi Buddhists), *Seeraja*, Feb-March 1998, Vol. 6, pp. 21-26.

———: Tibetan Manuscripts and Inscriptions on Ladakh Himalaya, Sriguru Pub., Delhi, 1998.

———: *Some Monasteries of Drigung pa order in Central Ladakh* (in press); Sriguru Pub., Delhi.

———: *Lamayuru Monastery of Ladakh Himalaya* (in press); Om Pub., Delhi.

———: *Changing Face of Ladakh Himalaya,* (in press); Om Pub., Delhi.

———: *Ladakh ki Kala Avam Sanskriti* (in press), Indira Gandhi National Centre for Arts, New Delhi.

———: 1983-84. 'Boudh Bikshus of Ladakh', In: Proceed of All India Conference on Buddhist and Jain Monasticism, Deptt. of Buddhist Studies, Delhi University.

Jina, Prem Singh: 'Buddhism in Ladakh and World Peace', In : 10th International Buddhist Conference on Buddhism and World Peace, Japanese Temple, Bodh Gaya, Vol. X. , 1984.

————: 'A Brief Introduction of Ladakhi Gonpas', In: All India Conference Kashmir University, Srinagar, Deptt. of Centre for Central Asian Studies, Proceed. Ladakh Life and Culture, 1986.

————: 'A Survey of Buddhist Community in Ladakh Himalaya', In: 12th International Buddhist Conference on Buddhism and Social Harmony, Japanese Temple, Bodh Gaya, Vol. XII, 1986.

————: 'Monasteries in the Economy of Leh-Ladakh' In: All India Conference on Buddhist Monasteries of Himalayan Region: Various Aspects, 9-13 August, C.I.B.S., Leh, 1988.

————: 'Buddhism and Human Values in the History of Ladakh Himalaya', In: International Buddhist Conference, Japanese Temple, Bodh Gaya, India, 1990.

————: Dasvi Shatabadi Purva Lahul me Bodh Dharm Evam Sanskriti (Hindi), *Janjati Mela Samarika*, 1993, pp. 60-62.

————: 1994. *Tourism in Ladakh Himalaya;* New Delhi: Indus Pub. Co.

————: 1995. *High Pasturelands of Ladakh Himalaya,* New Delhi: Indus Pub. Co.

————: *Changing Face of Ladakh Himalaya;* New Delhi: Om Pub., (in press).

Jina, Prem Singh and Lamayuru Monastery: *Lamayuru Monastery in Ladakh Himalaya;* New Delhi: Om Pub., (in press)

Jina, Prem Singh and Mir A.A.: 'Pastureland of Leh and its Effects on Ecology. In: Ist National Conference Organised by Indian Army, Trishul Nature Conservation, 1986.

Jina, Prem Singh and Namgyal, Konchok: *Phyang Monastery of Ladakh,* New Delhi : Indus Pub. Co.

————: 1995. Famous Western Explorers to Ladakh, New Delh: Indus Pub. Co.

————: 1996. Ladakh: *The Land & the People;* New Delhi: Indus Pub. Co.

———— **(ed.):** 1997. *Recent Researchers of the Himalaya,* New Delhi: Indus Pub. Co.

————: 1998. *Tibetan Manuscripts and Inscriptions of Ladakh Himalaya,* New Delhi: Sri Satguru Pub.

Jina, Prem Singh and Namgyal, Konchok: *Ladakh Ki Kala Avam Sanskriti;* New Delhi: I.N.C.A., (in press).

————: *Spiti ka Sanskritik Itihas,* Janjati Mela Samarika, 1994.

————: Phyang Monastery of Ladakh, Indus Pub. Company, New Delhi, 1995.

Joldan, E.: *Harvest Festival of Buddhist Dards of Ladakh and other Essays;* Kapoor Brothers, Srinagar, 1985.

————: 1985. *Harvest Festival of Buddhist Dards of Ladakh and other Essays,* Srinagar.

Kak, B.L.: *Chasing Shadows in Ladakh,* Light and Life Pub., New Delhi, 1978.

Kapoor, M.L.: *History of Jammu and Kashmir State*, Jammu.

Khoo, Mick: 1995. *'Himalayan Ecotourism'*, Ladags Melong, 1995.

Leitner, G.W.V.: 1877. *The Languages and Races of Dardistan, Lahore.*

Menon, Appan: 1989. 'The Political Overtones', *Frontline*, July 22-Aug. 4.

Mohammed Yusuf Teng (ed.): Rassul Galwan-Arz-e-Kashmir Ka ed namwar sapoot; *Daily Aftab*, Srinagar.

Moorcroft, W and G. Trebeck: Travels in the Himalayan Provinces of Hindustan and Punjab, in Ladakh and Kashmir, in Peshawar, Kabul, Kunduz and Bokhara (1819-1825), Two volumes, London, 1841.

Morgen Stierne, George: 1926. Report on Linguistic Mission to Afghanistan, Oslo.

————: 1932. Report on Linguistic Mission to North-Western India, Oslo.

Paul, K. Benedic: 1972. *Sino-Tibetan: A Conspectus,* Cambridge University Press.

Peter, Hopkirk: *The Great Game.*

Rassul Galwan: *Servant of Sahibs.*

Rigzin, Tsewang: 1979. Shey palace: In: *Rigpe Dudachi,* C.I.B.S., Leh.

Robert Shafer: 1974. *Introduction to Sino-Tibetan,* Wiebbadan, Otto Harrasowitz.

Sir Walter Lawrance (ed.): *The Pamirs.*

Sharma, D.D.: 1977. *Tribal Languages of Ladakh,* Part I & II, Delhi.

Sharma, D.D.: 1997. *A Comparative Grammar of Tibeto-Himalayan Languages,* Delhi.

————: 1998. Himalaya Ki Vismayabum: *Lahul* (Hindi), Solan.

Sheik, Abdul Ghani: Rassul Galwan (Mashaheer Number) in *Urdu Hamara Adab,* J & K Cultural Academy, 1977-78.

Sheik, Abdul Ghani: 1997. Some Well-Known Adventurers to Ladakh, Recent Research on Ladakh, 6.

Sumi, D. Tokan; Oki Masato and Hassnain, M. Fida: 1975. *Ladakh: The Moonland*; New Delhi: Light and Life Pub.

Tsewang, Lobzang: 1985. Problem of Ladakhi language and its solution, In: *Ladakh Prabha* (3); Tashi Paljor (ed.), C.I.B.S.

Tullah, Hashmat: 1939. *Tarik Jammu.*

Younghusband: *The Heart of the Continent.*

————: *The Northern Frontier of Kashmir.*

Warikoo, K.: Gateway to Central Asia the Transhimalayan Trade of Ladakh, 1846-1947. In: *Recent Research on Ladakh 4 and 5,* Motilal Banarsidas Pub., Delhi, 1995.

Index